Communities of Work

This series of publications on Africa, Latin America, Southeast Asia, and Global and Comparative Studies is designed to present significant research, translation, and opinion to area specialists and to a wide community of persons interested in world affairs. The editor seeks manuscripts of quality on any subject and can usually make a decision regarding publication within three months of receipt of the original work. Production methods generally permit a work to appear within one year of acceptance. The editor works closely with authors to produce a high quality book. The series appears in a paperback format and is distributed worldwide. For more information, contact the executive editor at Ohio University Press, Scott Quadrangle, University Terrace, Athens, Ohio 45701.

Executive editor: Gillian Berchowitz
AREA CONSULTANTS
Africa: Diane M. Ciekawy
Latin America: Thomas Walker
Southeast Asia: William H. Frederick
Global and Comparative Studies: Ann R. Tickamyer

The Ohio University Research in International Studies series is published for the Center for International Studies by Ohio University Press. The views expressed in individual volumes are those of the authors and should not be considered to represent the policies or beliefs of the Center for International Studies, Ohio University Press, or Ohio University.

Communities of Work

RURAL RESTRUCTURING IN LOCAL AND GLOBAL CONTEXTS

Edited by
WILLIAM W. FALK,
MICHAEL D. SCHULMAN,
and ANN R. TICKAMYER

Ohio University Research in International Studies
Global and Comparative Studies Series No. 2

Ohio University Press
Athens

The books in the Ohio University Research in International Studies Series
are printed on acid-free paper ⊗™

12 11 10 09 08 07 06 05 04 03   5 4 3 2 1

Cover art: "Full Production and Full Employment
under Our Democratic System of Private Enterprise"
by Michael Lenson, crayon and ink, ca. 1940.

Library of Congress Cataloging-in-Publication Data

Communities of work : rural restructuring in local and global contexts/
edited by William W. Falk, Michael D. Schulman, and Ann R. Tickamyer.
    p. cm. — (Research in international studies. Global and comparative
studies series; no. 2)
    Includes bibliographical references and index.
    ISBN 0-89680-234-5 (pa : alk paper)
    1. United States—Rural conditions.   2. United States—Rural
conditions—Case studies.   3. Sociology, Rural—United States.
I. Falk, William W.   II. Schulman, Michael D.   III. Tickamyer, Ann R.
IV. Series

HN59.2C64   2003
307.72'0973—dc22   2003058093

Contents

Acknowledgments

All books, whether edited or authored, represent the work of far more people than simply those whose names appear on the cover. This book is no exception. First, we would like to thank all of the authors whose work is found here. In all cases, authors responded to our critical assessments and worked with us as well as the Ohio University Press editorial staff to make this the best book they could. Second, we want to thank all of our colleagues on U.S. Department of Agriculture regional project S-296. This was a project on which many of the authors worked for five years or more. The project did—and in its current manifestation still does—focus on labor market dynamics and especially inequalities. The interdisciplinary although heavily sociological mix of scholars provided a wonderful intellectual environment to nurture a book such as this one. Third, we were helped greatly by reviews on an earlier version of the book from Professors Bo Beaulieu and Charles Tolbert. Our sincere thanks to them both. Fourth, we want to thank our respective staffs—Wanda Towles at Maryland; Jeanne Gurthrie, Penny Lewter, and July Cline at North Carolina State; and Rebecca Collins, Caroline Spurlock, and Cheryl Cotterill at Ohio University—who helped with the endless chores associated with assembling an edited book. Fourth, thanks, also, to the students who have assisted us with this project in recent years—Gwyn Weathers and Tony Hatch at Maryland, Kevin Stainback, Marlee Gurrera, and Linda Treiber at North Carolina State, and Theo de Jager and Eric Neuhart at Ohio University. Fifth, to our respective spouses/partners—Geraldine Falk, Pat Garrett, and Cecil Tickamyer—we can finally say, "Yes, it's finished!" Sixth, but by no means least, a huge thanks to the Ohio University editorial staff: Gillian Berchowitz for believing in the book's importance from the outset, Nancy Basmajian for assisting with all stages of production, and Sharon Arnold for helping to promote it.

Communities of Work

Rural Restructuring in Local and Global Contexts

William W. Falk, Michael D. Schulman,
and Ann R. Tickamyer

THE TWENTIETH CENTURY was the first in which the industrial revolution was a dominant force for social change. With it came urbanization, suburbanization, and the radical transformation of the countryside. While these social forces were felt in all industrialized countries, the results were most dramatically apparent in America. As urban as the country became, rural areas nonetheless continued to fight for their survival. Their struggle was all the more striking in that the rural proportion of the total U.S. population was only about half of what it had been a hundred years earlier. Indeed, it would be fair to say that by the end of the twentieth century many rural areas had weathered multiple waves of out-migration as millions left farms and small towns in search of urban jobs. Today, rural areas in the United States are subject to a new set of forces—in particular the development of capital-intensive industrial agriculture and meat processing, the rise of the service sector, the development of new patterns of amenity consumption, the increase in women's off-farm employment, and the expansion of commuting to suburban or urban jobs.

Change in America's rural industries and communities is, in part, a story about the effects of a global economy, something often overlooked in treatments that depict rural America as a bastion of tradition and backwater folksiness. One of the most significant aspects of the industrial revolution was that rural areas provided many of the original workers. Not only was America transformed from mostly rural to mostly urban in the process of industrialization, the entire twentieth century was one of huge changes for rural America—from residents migrating out to seek a better life in industrialized, urban places to the more recent phenomenon of former residents moving back to rural areas for retirement; from the mechanization of agriculture that pushed people off the land to a series of farm crises related to the American way of financing agriculture; from large-scale vertical integration and consolidation within some agricultural sectors and the role of multinational firms in these various industrial shifts to the rise of flexible, niche manufacturing and production, especially near urban markets. Recent economic restructuring has altered inner-city life and in the process affected rural areas, since many U.S. manufacturing industries fled urban areas in favor of rural ones, first within the United States and eventually moving again, this time overseas. Work in the formal sector has been supplanted by work in the informal sector in both urban and rural communities. Rural America, no matter how bucolic and remote it might seem to many urban residents, has seen the effects of a global economy both in its markets and in those who work in them.

But as with all social forces, the effects of these various processes have not been felt evenly: some rural areas and residents have fared much better than others. The most advantaged areas seem to be those close to large urban areas. The most disadvantaged, however, are not only those more remote from urban areas, but those that have also been affected adversely by race and ethnicity. Parts of white, rural New England and Appalachia, historically black counties in the South, areas with large Hispanic populations in the Southwest, and reservations housing Native Americans, are all places with disproportionate and persistent poverty. None is likely to see significant new investment from either private or public sources. The very forces that coalesce to produce a global economy also work to perpetuate the lack of opportunity in persistently poor areas. Furthermore, their effects are found in all aspects of local life, not just the economic ones. In sum, the story about major shifts in the economy and how they play out varies considerably across the country (indeed, across the world), and rural areas are not immune. Regrettably, however, this story has mostly gone untold and these areas remain largely ignored by planners, politicians, and the public.

In this book we document part of this "story," focusing especially on how industrial and occupational changes have had ripple effects in local communities. We provide results from a series of case studies, most of which grew out of an interdisciplinary regional research project conducted during the 1990s to document the effects of industrial restructuring on local communities, families, and individual livelihood practices. While most of the project participants were sociologists, not all were, and we present a diversity of perspectives with chapter authors that include sociologists, economists, political scientists, and anthropologists. The studies included areas with considerable ethnic and social differentiation—historically black areas of the rural South and virtually all white areas of the Northeast and Appalachia, as well as areas from the Midwest, the Northwest, and Puerto Rico. We report on towns and communities in these places, in some cases focusing on individual families, in others focusing on entire communities or even entire regions. We report on nonfarm extractive industries as well as value-added industries and jobs within them—in textiles, fishing, mining, oil and gas, timber, and meat packing. We conclude the volume with our own sense of lessons learned from the diversity of studies that we offer.

Community of Work

The key concept of this volume, community of work, brings together two fundamental concepts in the study of human society. The concept of community is one of the oldest in sociology. German sociologist Ferdinand Toennies was among the first to discuss its importance, noting especially its contrast with the larger urbanized society (gemeinschaft vs. gesellschaft). What Toennies analytically understood was that the industrial revolution revolutionized not only where and how we worked but also where and how we lived. Thus, culture, work, and community are necessarily intertwined. Writing a century after Toennies, and in the tradition of other classical sociologists such as Marx, Weber, Durkheim, and Martineau, we too argue for the importance of understanding this relationship. Indeed, the relationship between work and community is a fundamental dynamic of social organization in any society, whether traditional or modern, rural or urban, and regardless of whether one's focus is local or global.

Community, then, is a concept of paramount interest in all the case studies in this book. For the contributors, the community is the setting for social action. It is the place to search for better understanding of how economic forces, many of them external to local communities, create and re-create the relationships and practices of daily life in both social and spatial contexts. Work, the second key component of our central concept, takes place in a local community and is part of the process that forms that community. It is something individuals do for a wage or in some way contributing to economic production and exchange. Thus *communities of work* has both micro and macro elements and a dialectic operating between them.

At the micro level, people both work to live and live to work, a stance that essentially reflects the Marxist notion that work equals life, that only through work is life meaningful and possible, and only through work are human institutions constructed. Control over one's work was, for Marx, essential to shaping one's identity and attaining full human potential. The reality of work rarely provides this level of attainment, however. The need to work for others, to sell one's labor power, creates exploitative relationships that deny the development of full human capacity. At the macro level, different modes of production create class structures that deny workers control over the products and processes of work. In the context of capitalism, where labor power itself becomes a commodity, working for others and selling one's labor alienates the worker from his or her very existence, or "species being" in Marx's term. In more current parlance, the exploitation of labor can also be described as a type of embeddedness whereby relationships of domination and exploitation are interwoven with existing class, race, gender, and spatial power relationships in local communities.

The communities of work concept allows us to integrate micro and macro approaches to work and community using ideas from disparate fields of study. Our basic assumptions are that communities are formed and sustained by work and that the social and spatial relations of communities shape work and economic activities. Thus, to understand how communities and their residents languish or thrive and how both are transformed by large-scale historical processes, it is important to examine the formal, informal, and reproductive activities that provide livelihoods for residents of different locales. It is equally important to scrutinize the ways these locations are structured by forms of work and employment. To understand work as the focus of human action and social organization, scholars need to contextualize it in particular settings and locales. Work is embedded in relationships and structures that transcend formal economic processes, as it is set in communities with their own histories, geographies, and social relations. The literature of social science reflects this articulation, especially in typifying communities as agricultural or mining or fishing, cotton counties or welfare counties, and so on. All these appellations also reflect, by implication at least, the ways in which descriptive terms about work are suggestive about the nature of community life.

A central theme of this collection is the importance of space and place for social theory and for the analysis of social phenomena. Space is not just another variable to be added to race, gender, class, or age. Instead, we use the words *embedded* and *contextualized* to refer to the idea that space is part and parcel of structural, cultural, and social psychological processes. Such a focus heightens the probability of interdisciplinary dialog among scholars within the discipline of sociology and its sister social sciences.

In adopting this approach, we simultaneously challenge a long tradition of isolating fields of study and we embrace recent efforts to construct sociological models that recognize the contextual and embedded nature of human and social relations. Thus, old analytic categories that form the basis of empirical social science—work, family, household, community, labor market, occupation, industry, as well as bipolar oppositions that characterize twentieth-century transformations such as rural-urban, local-global, gemeinschaft-gesellschaft, traditional-modern, mechanical-organic solidarity, Fordist/post-Fordist—are made part of a larger view that emphasizes embeddedness and linkages among overlapping processes. We do not discard previously useful concepts; instead we seek to contextualize them in time, space, and social relations.

Embedded Case Studies

We collected a series of case studies that are place specific and that use varying methods to tell the story of the community-work connection. One part of this story is that work experiences, in both their material and ideological forms, define social networks and organizations. Another part of the community-work story is that work is not just production, but also informal activities, reproduction, and consumption. The case studies demonstrate, too, that work, community, production, and reproduction intersect with social structure, population, environment, and culture in historically specific and distinct regional locations that constrain and enable human action.

We focus on rural places and practices. Despite their often heralded demise, rural places remain an important part of American society. They are too often neglected in current accounts of social change, even those that are mindful of space and place. To ignore rural locales is to ignore a substantial portion of the population, industry, resource base, and territory. In addition, the uneven social and economic transformations of the last century created serious but often unaddressed disadvantage for rural places. Rural America remains a prime site for disproportionate and persistent poverty, a situation that is unlikely to change appreciably in a time of accelerating globalization guided by free market politics and policies. Despite global social and economic transformations, politics remains local, requiring scrutiny of the particular forces that shape globalization as well as the impacts of the global economy on local places. Focusing on rural communities of work remedies a major gap in the research and highlights the places where livelihoods are pursued and policies implemented. Finally, rural places provide an exemplary laboratory for documenting and dissecting the complex intersections between work and community.

In advocating embedded models of community-work interaction, we do not privilege one methodology over another, nor any single analytic approach. Quite the contrary, in this collection we feature diverse methods, including both qualitative and quantitative data and analysis. Similarly, the studies focus variously on individuals, families, occupations, industries, or communities. We asked all the authors to use a case study approach to document the unique features of both industry and place in order to create an informative analysis of how work and community shape each other. We also asked that each chapter be written to tell a story, to provide a coherent narrative account that captures the richness and meaning of the social and spatial relations analyzed, regardless of methods and data employed.

In sum, communities of work are places in which individuals and industries meet; where existing social relations empower some and disenfranchise others; where most local people act in response to economic forces, having little direct control over them; where habitualized behaviors and social networks developed over a lifetime lead to varying forms of social capital and the gains (or losses) that come with them; where meaning is grounded heavily in local opportunities that by and large have little to do with human capital and individual motivation; where family relations are powerful in shaping one's sense of a life's meaning; where place has significance for everyone, and none more so than the indigenous population, who have the greatest stake in it; where community is understood largely on the basis of work that has historically been done there; and where work is a necessary but hardly sufficient element for understanding what a community ontologically *is*.

Overview

This book is organized into three broad sections based on methodological approaches, central themes, and the stories that are told about the processes and impacts of restructuring on contemporary rural communities. It concludes with a discussion of lessons learned from all the case studies and a return visit to the power of communities of work as a conceptual frame of reference.

A substantial body of research attempts to identify and describe macro-level changes and their impacts on rural regions. While much of this research is descriptive, a core focus of the chapters in the first section, "Region, Work, and Restructuring: Structural Processes and Trends," is the investigation of whether or not global or national-level structural processes and changes are actually happening at the regional level. In other words, do certain regions (e.g., Appalachia, the rural South) have unique characteristics that modify or interact with the global to produce unique local outcomes? This focus is important for countering the urban industrial bias in much of sociology that assumes that the urban regions of advanced industrial nations are the engines of social change and that rural is an empty category of people and places.

The chapters in this section examine broad trends and changes at regional or county levels. They describe structural and economic changes in work and economic activities and identify regionally specific factors that modify the processes and consequences of restructuring. The authors of the chapters link these transformations and impacts to theories about global or national-level changes (or both) in social and economic relations in the late twentieth century. In addition, the chapters in this section use ecological-level data to describe geographical and social contexts and to analyze key processes and trends. They emphasize structural processes and the embeddedness of regions in contexts that constrain change and development.

In this section, chapters cover regions from the rural South to the Mountain West. In "Old Industrial Regions and the Political Economy of Development," Linda Lobao, Lawrence Brown, and Jon Moore test the utility of the region concept and post-Fordist theories of restructuring by examining the Ohio River Valley. Their findings suggest that local places must increasingly use their own funds to supplement private sector development; thus one by-product of globalization may be shifts in political power in local places when economic demands must be met for businesses to remain. In "Place, Race, and State," Cynthia Anderson, Michael Schulman, and Philip Wood focus on Southern textile development. The authors argue that the industry is rooted in a "security zone" of race, class, and place and that theories of de-industrialization that predict the inevitable decline of rural manufacturing tend to be one-dimensional. Another key regional rural industry is the subject of "Meat Processing in Rural America" by Mark Henry, Mark Drabenstott, and Kristin Mitchell. The authors address the question, Is smaller better? by examining an industry that moved from urban to rural areas and, in the process, became increasingly low-wage, ethnic, and spatially concentrated. The mining industry is the focus of "Socioeconomic Trends in Mining-Dependent Counties in Appalachia." Melissa Latimer and Carson Mencken find stability and stagnation over time in the area's political domination and demography of the workforce. In "From Extraction to Amenities: Restructuring and (In)Conspicuous Consumption in Missoula, Montana," Richard Goe, Sean Noonan, and Sherry Laman shift our attention to a Western, mountainous place in an area that has become increasingly urbanized. The authors explore what happens when an area becomes a "place of consumption" with an increasing emphasis on services of all types.

Another important research tradition in rural studies involves detailed study of local communities. While many classic sociological studies are community based (Lynd and Lynd 1929; Pope 1942), community case studies fell out of favor when national-level data, both ecological and individual, become readily available for statistical analysis. The second section of the book, "Work and Community: Ethnic, Racial, and Regional Embeddedness," consists of community-based studies that recognize the importance of context and of the embeddedness of social phenomenon in local social and economic relationships. Despite global and national-level structural changes, work remains embedded in local social relations, including occupational communities, family ties, and organizational networks. The chapters in this section focus on the embeddedness of work, family, and local networks in time and place. Special attention is given to racial, ethnic, and regional-identity relations and their interaction with work and community networks at the local level. While the case studies employ a variety of data collection techniques, they share a common methodological approach. The authors used existing data to define the context and then collected original data, mainly through various intensive interview techniques, to document the intersectionality of class, race, ethnicity, region, and locality. Their strong emphasis on the embeddedness of ethnicity, race, and regional identity with work and community is an important counter to structural perspectives that neglect the local.

This section opens with a case study from southwest Louisiana, "Troubled Waters or Business as Usual?" Forrest Deseran and Carl Riden focus on a Louisiana oyster fishing community where Croatian immigrants have become major participants. The study finds that in this community, work and ethnicity are often blurred and major values and worldviews center around the occupation and its culture. "Identity of Self and Others through Work" by Ralph Brown is a study of an older, white, commercial fisherman in the context of black-white relations in the Mississippi Delta. The emphasis is on the notion of an occupational community and how it grounds the individual in the larger sociocultural structures where he lives and also results in social isolation. In "Sense of Place and Rural Restructuring," William Falk relates one family's experience in a historically black county. In this case, the family-place relationship is shown to be sufficiently strong to offset virtually all other forces and pressures, especially ones based on the intersection of race, politics, and economics. The rural Midwest is the site of "Housing Labor's Unrest" by Jeff Crump. This chapter explores "glocalization" whereby some communities have emerging ties to broader economic-sociospatial processes (including the diminishing role of organized labor and the rise of ethnic immigrant populations) whereas other communities are increasingly isolated from these phenomena. In "Hogs and Citizens," MaryBe McMillan and Michael Schulman examine race and opposition to large-scale industrial agriculture among rural residents reacting to the industrialization of hog production in North Carolina. The authors suggest that as industries have profited, rural residents have lost, especially in terms of quality of life. "Does Welfare to Work Work?" by Julie White, Ann Tickamyer, Debra Henderson, and Barry Tadlock analyzes welfare to work in Appalachia, paying particular attention to rural employers. These employers support, in general, welfare reform but believe that problems in rural areas are related to regional issues of structure, culture, and regional identity.

Social relations are not just embedded in a local context: people within a locality actively react, resist, and adapt to the global and local structural constraints they encounter. The third section of the volume, "Reaction and Resistance: Survival Strategies of Rural People," offers case studies that document ways in which rural residents have demonstrated that they are not just passive victims of global forces, national policy, or the power relations embedded in the local context. Rather, rural residents have been able, albeit sometimes with great difficulty, to develop livelihood practices and survival strategies despite the lack of organizational capacity and inequality in resources.

The chapters in this section emphasize survival strategies and reactions to structural trends in work and employment, especially with regard to livelihood and income generation issues and problems in the traditional rural industries of agriculture and manufacturing. These studies show the importance of age, race, gender, and region in terms of adaptation to changing social and economic contexts. The informal economy, service employment, and gender-based survival practices are central themes. While the studies focus on individual action, they document how individuals become active negotiators of their situations.

In "The Bus from Hell Hole Swamp," Susan Webb focuses on African American women from a coastal community who commute up to 150 miles to work in low-skilled, low-paying jobs in hospitality services in a resort area. Their work is analyzed as a survival strategy that allows them to continue to live in their historically black communities. "Stretched to Their Limits" by Cynthia Struthers and Janet Bokemeier reports on how rural, nonfarm mothers in the Midwest balance family demands with those of a changing local economy. The authors show how farm-based values remain in place long after the decline of production agriculture as a major source of employment. Another Midwestern site is the setting for "Earning a Living and Building a Life." Ann Ziebarth and Leanne Tigges explore the linkages and strategies used in income-generating, income-saving, and sustaining families; self-provisioning and social networks prove to be crucial. In "Livelihood Strategies of Farmers in Puerto Rico's Central Region" Viviana Carro-Figueroa and Gwyndolyn Weathers explain that Puerto Rican farmers, to remain financially solvent, must combine earnings from agriculture with transfer payments and other nonfarm income sources. They must do so in an environment that is increasingly tied to global considerations and to the island's relationship to the United States. "Older Workers and Retirement in Rural Contexts" by Nina Glasgow and Alan Barton explores the ways in which residence inhibits or enhances the likelihood for different kinds of work opportunities and adaptations for older workers. In "The Social and Economic Context of Informal Work," Ann Tickamyer and Teresa Wood explore the extent of participation in informal livelihood practices in Kentucky, finding extensive participation across all social and economic groups.

A Background Note

The research project that stimulated the work presented in this book has itself been a kind of community of work, or at least a community of workers. The project is nearly twenty-five years old and has produced an enormous volume of scholarship, especially about work in rural America. Besides a huge number of refereed journal articles, book chapters, masters theses, and doctoral dissertations, it has produced a sizeable number of books from the scholarly press (including those listed below). The present volume merely concludes one part of the project's history. We are confident that others will follow and we are indebted to all project scholars, including those whose work does not appear in this book.

References

Anderson, C. 2000. *The Social Consequences of Economic Restructuring in the Textile Industry: Change in a Southern Mill Village.* New York: Garland.

Colclough, G., and C. Tolbert. 1992. *Work in the Fast Lane: Flexibility, Divisions of Labor, and Inequality in High-Tech Industries.* Albany: SUNY Press.

Falk, W. W., and T. A. Lyson. 1988. *High Tech, Low Tech, No Tech: Recent Industrial and Occupational Change in the South.* Albany: SUNY Press.

———, eds. 1989. *Research in Rural Sociology and Development.* Vol. 4. London: JAI Press.

Horan, P., and C. Tolbert. 1984. *The Organization of Work in Rural and Urban Labor Markets.* Boulder: Westview.

Lobao, L. 1990. *Locality and Inequality: Farm and Industry Structure and Socioeconomic Conditions.* Albany: SUNY Press.

Lynd, R. S., and H. M. Lynd. 1929. *Middletown, A Study in Contemporary American Culture.* New York: Harcourt, Brace.

Lyson, T., and W. W. Falk, eds. 1992. *Forgotten Places: Uneven Development and the Loss of Opportunity in Rural America.* Lawrence: University Press of Kansas.

Pope, L. 1942. *Millhands and Preachers, A Study of Gastonia.* New Haven: Yale University Press.

Singelmann, J., and F. A. Deseran, eds. 1993. *Inequalities in Labor Market Areas.* Boulder: Westview.

Communities of Work

Part I

Region, Work, and Restructuring

Structural Processes and Trends

1

Old Industrial Regions and the Political Economy of Development

Linda Lobao, Lawrence A. Brown, and Jon Moore

IN THE PAST two decades, there has been increased interest in society and space across the social sciences. A central reason for pursuing this research direction is to question whether social science generalizations are modified under different territorial settings. The use of spatial context to assess the claims of social science frameworks takes various analytic forms. Community case studies, macro and micro labor market analyses, and comparative, cross-national research are long-standing strategies. Another, less-recognized approach is the recent resurrection of region as an object of study. By region, we refer to real or imagined places where social structure, population, environment, and culture are attached to distinct territorial formations that span multiple communities. This recent interest in region comes mainly but not exclusively out of political economy theory. Much research centers on regions presumed representative of a new, post-Fordist economy, such as southern California and Boston's Route 128, whose sociospatial order illustrates what is to come for other places.

This paper builds on recent literature by employing region as an analytical strategy for assessing political economy claims. We cast a broad discussion, illustrated with a specific empirical example. In contrast to most research, we focus on an old industrial region, the Ohio River Valley, which spans six states and extends from Pittsburgh to Cairo, Illinois. As part of the Midwestern manufacturing belt, the Ohio River Valley was the engine of national growth, an agro-industrial and energy heartland that paved the way for Fordism (Page and Walker 1991). In the first section, we briefly describe past regional research traditions and recent political economy views of development and its regional expression. The second section discusses methodology. The third section uses the Ohio River Valley to elaborate and challenge political economy generalizations. We examine three periods, early manufacturing belt development, the 1970s, and the contemporary era, but give primary attention to the last period and to issues involving de-industrialization, growth enclaves, and globalization.

Regions, the Political Economy of Development, and the American Manufacturing Belt

Interest in the spatial aspects of social life has varied by social science discipline over time (Soja 1988). Insofar as *region* refers to any territorial setting, from local to global, empirical research on regions has ebbed and flowed with general social science interest in space. Our concern, however, is with the conceptualization of regions for analytic purposes, as in schools of regional research. Here the concept is treated more narrowly, usually referring to a place within a nation, encompassing multiple communities, and possessing a distinct identity inclusive of factors of theoretical significance (Markusen 1987). Traditional schools of regional research characterized geography and sociology until the 1970s. These schools shared principles of human ecology, intrinsic interest in the region itself, and offered a gestalt-view of regional attributes. Through the 1960s, human geography followed an idiographic tradition concerned with cataloging regional characteristics. Then, as today, regions studied were historical, nominal, functionally linked (such as labor markets), or homogeneous (or a combination of these), sharing elements in common such as urban areas and manufacturing and farm belts. In sociology, regional research emphasized regions defined historically, such as the South and Appalachia, and by settlement patterns. Sociology as a whole took a regional bent with the prominence of the Southern Regionalists in the 1930s and 1940s (Odum and Moore 1938). Urban and rural sociology also reflect the institutionalization of a regional studies approach.

Social science treatment of space shifted in the 1980s. Marxian theory gained a foothold in geography, and in urban and rural sociology, largely replacing human ecology. Research emerged on a new topic, the regional expression of capitalist development, directed to stages of capitalist development and their accompanying social-territorial formations (Kratke 1999).

THE POLITICAL ECONOMY METANARRATIVE OF DEVELOPMENT

Contemporary political economy theory is a rich family that includes regulation theory (Aglietta 1979; Lipietz 1987) and the Social Structures of Accumulation approach (Gordon, Edwards, and Reich 1982, 1994).[1] While each is a distinct school, they share common assumptions to warrant joint consideration (Kotz 1994). Both see labor, the state, and capital as principle actors, periodize capitalism, and recognize uneven development. They also share limitations. Both were developed to explain macro-level, national relationships but implied and incompletely theorized, relationships for lower spatial units (Lobao, Rulli, and Brown 1999). To understand macro-level relationships, analysts often infer upward from local or regional findings. Attention to regions thus is necessary to clarify political economy theory and extend it territorially (Peck 1996).

Political economy perspectives define broad stages of development, taking as their conceptual touchstone the Fordist period, to which prior and subsequent stages are compared. The Fordist period is considered to begin in the early 1900s with the development of mass production technologies, as exemplified in Henry Ford's auto plants. Mass production technologies created mass consumer markets, which spurred national growth and an institutional environment of Keynesian demand management and labor union power. Political economy perspectives give most attention to the period after

World War II through the 1970s Fordist era, with descriptions of this period resting heavily on the manufacturing belt. As we note below, analysts debate the extent to which the Fordist development stage has eroded since the 1970s and whether a fundamentally new, post-Fordist stage has emerged.

The late nineteenth century is treated mainly as an incubator for Fordism. Manufacturing and large urban centers are the motors of change. The modern economy gets its start as the manufacturing sector subsumes farmers and farming (Gordon, Edwards, and Reich 1982, 57). In regulation theory, manufacturing technologies are key to explaining development. Production processes are seen as relatively primitive, limiting output and consumer markets, problems whose solution is found in the semiautomatic assembly line and other new technologies.

The period from after World War II to the 1970s represents the era of Fordist stability. High-wage durable manufacturing firms in the oligopoly sector drive development. Capital accumulation expands because of stability in the institutional environment made possible by collective bargaining arrangements, state support for citizen welfare, and Keynesian demand policies. The leading industries and institutions of Fordism coalesce in the Northern manufacturing belt.

The post-1970s period is interpreted in light of movement away from Fordism. Pressures arise from global competition, union power, and crises of state legitimation. Manufacturing declines and lower-wage services expand. The Fordist institutional structure of capital-labor and state-citizen relationships breaks down. These changes are expressed regionally, in the decline of manufacturing-belt cities, rise of the sun belt, and heightened capital mobility.

Beyond 1970s restructuring, the political economy metanarrative becomes increasingly tentative. First, a point of contention is the extent of the break in industrial and institutional structure. Some analysts see the present period as a protracted restructuring phase (Gordon, Edwards, and Reich 1994), while others see the dawn of a new stage of capitalist development. Second, though accounts of Fordism emphasized production, they also attended to institutional arrangements and consumption outcomes, topics given shorter shrift in the contemporary era. Third, the geographic expression of current development is not well explicated (Storper 1997). Focus is on exceptional places seen as harbingers of a new economy, such as Los Angeles, global headquarters cities, and the relatively few identifiable new industrial spaces. The fate of older regions—in some sense, the ordinary contexts where most people live and work—are neglected. This, in part, contributes to the overemphasis of globalization. Cox (1997) argues that localization is a similarly powerful trend. Many firms are embedded in territorial settings and cannot easily replicate conditions of accumulation elsewhere.

REGIONAL EXPRESSIONS OF CAPITALIST DEVELOPMENT: THE U.S. MANUFACTURING BELT

Three literatures directly address parts of the political economy meta-narrative by examining the manufacturing belt. The first seeks to extend political economy theory spatially by examining how the post-1970s crisis unfolds regionally, as reflected in the large research on de-industrialization. Focus is on industrial de-agglomeration, weakening of past comparative advantages, and barriers for firms competing globally. The crisis in Fordism is expressed through de-territorialization: the manufacturing belt progressively loses its unique identity through the uprooting of industries, firms, jobs, people, and social institutional traditions.

The second literature also seeks to extend the political economy account spatially, but addresses the postrestructuring or post-Fordist period. It focuses on how the new economy is expressed territorially, seen in distinct growth enclaves in the manufacturing belt. Flexible specialization in machine tools, electronics, automobiles, and steel revitalize some traditional industries and produce new industrial spaces, such as the Midwestern automobile supplier-assembler networks (Piore and Sabel 1984; Scott 1988). New agglomerations are created as firms avoid core Fordist labor forces, with their fixed skills and union traditions. Certain metropolitan areas regenerate. Financial and producer services that facilitate the ascendant economy expand selectively in Chicago, New York, and Minneapolis, but also in cities like Pittsburgh that experienced severe de-industrialization (Deitrick and Beauregard 1995). This literature thus sees a spatial reorganization based on newly realized or reconfigured industrial, labor force, and other regional endowments. The manufacturing belt becomes reterritorialized as specific places are privileged as regional-growth enclaves.

The third literature uses old industrial regions less to extend political economy theory spatially and more to point out needed revisions. Unlike the two previous approaches, which treat regions as relatively isomorphic reflectors of changes in capitalism, this literature stresses the unique qualities of regions, the cumulative nature of development, and how regional social forces mediate global changes. Examples include regional and community case studies that reject homogenous portrayals of the manufacturing belt (Crump and Merrett 1998; Horan and Jonas 1998; Hudson 1989; Page and Walker 1991). These studies speak to missing links in theory: greater attention is given to institutional exigencies, to localizing over homogenizing globalizing forces, and to continuity in social processes. This literature indicates that political economy theory has produced an overgeneralized account of the stages of development.

Our analysis draws from all three literatures. We are especially sympathetic to the last literature, which cautions against overgeneralizing about regional paths of development. However, from a theory-building standpoint, it is also important to question if political economy generalizations hold across different regional contexts, thus allowing for spatial extensions of theory. To assess the correspondence between political economy claims and Ohio River Valley development, we limit our focus to claims about two key social forces, industrial structure and institutional arrangements, and give most attention to the contemporary period.

Methods

The Ohio River Valley (ORV) was the nation's first frontier, recognizable as a distinct region since the late eighteenth century (Reid 1991). With fertile soil, a large timber supply, and a navigable watershed system, it was an important corridor for expansion into our national interior. Coal, natural gas, oil, and other materials for new industrial activities were discovered early in its Pennsylvania, West Virginia, southeastern Ohio, Indiana, and Illinois portion. Throughout U.S. history, the Ohio River Valley was a primary source of raw materials for the entire Northern manufacturing belt. Today regional coherence lies in ecological, economic, and policy attributes. The ORV remains a dense network of small urban places and rural towns interrelated through river transportation and watershed development, the valley's function as a national power grid and source of coal, and continued specialization in manufacturing and mining. The region's distinct ecology, energy dependence, and microclimate made it the target of the 1990 Clean Air Act. Policy initiatives such as the Appalachian Regional Commission and various Ohio Basin programs continue to link states and communities in the region. We operationalized the ORV study area as counties three deep on each side of the Ohio River, and for counties that are part of a metropolitan statistical area (MSA), we included the additional MSA counties (e.g., counties surrounding Canton, Columbus, Dayton-Springfield, Lexington). This results in 222 counties and the study area shown in figure 1.1.

Research that informs this study is from multiple sources. Our brief historical account draws from archival and census data and Page and Walker's study of the Midwestern manufacturing belt (1991), an area they explicitly define as including the border communities of the six-state Ohio River Valley. Discussion of the contemporary period is based on secondary data and findings from our previously published work using these data. General community fieldwork techniques were also employed. We made site visits to firms and communities. Two communities, Jackson and Nelsonville, both in Ohio, were selected for more in-depth study. Interviews with key informants in government, business, and community organizations were conducted in 1998–99 and are discussed further below. It should be noted that while a number of recent studies exist on large ORV cities such as Pittsburgh and some on smaller industrial cities, few consider the region as a whole, particularly its rural communities. Two-thirds of ORV counties and about 70 percent of the total population are nonmetropolitan. Our

Fig. 1.1. Ohio River Valley region, cities and boundaries

discussion is weighted toward the region as a whole and the smaller, rural places within it.

The use of region to assess generalizations about capitalist development is most clearly articulated as a research approach by geographers (Brown 1999; Kratke 1999; Peck 1996). Considerable attention has been given to critical realism, analytical strategies that seek to assess how general tendencies outlined by theory work out in "real" situations, with the territorial unit representing the real, or concrete, situation. Interest in a particular region is theoretically driven, because abstract forces are "reconciled on the ground" in regionally concrete situations (Peck 1996, 93). As in our study, interest is often in time-space linkages, whereby analysts question how stages of capitalism are related to regional development patterns. There is a dialectical quality to critical realist analysis, in that observed regional patterns are seen as simultaneously produced by present and past processes, giving them a contingent quality. Conceptually, regions represent a bundle of contingent conditions that modify relationships outlined by theory. Our analysis draws from these critical realist insights. We first examine the rise of Fordism in the ORV and the emergence of a distinct industrial, institutional, and spatial structure that varied from conventional portrayals of the manufacturing belt. We then describe how rounds of restructuring in more recent periods wash over, interact with, and are modified by social forces in place. Contemporary development is only understandable through tracing its threads from the past.

Constructing the Fordist Manufacturing Belt: The Case of the Ohio River Valley

Page and Walker (1991) evaluate the political economy account of the rise of Fordism using the case of the Midwestern manufacturing belt. We summarize and extend their findings, which provide an important window on the contemporary Ohio River Valley. Page and Walker's historical account, from early settlement to the beginning of the twentieth century, challenges several assumptions about the rise of Fordism, those involving the subsumption of manufacturing over farming, the nature of key manufacturing industries, the importance of large urban areas, and the extent of the break between the pre-Fordist period and Fordism itself.

First, Page and Walker challenge portrayals of manufacturing as the single driver in regional development. Rather, they argue that nineteenth-century growth needs to be understood as agro-industrialization. Manufacturing did not subsume farming but both evolved symbiotically, propelling growth. The large regional family farm population was early integrated into manufacturing as suppliers of products for food processing and as consumers of farm implements and machinery. Second, in contrast to the importance placed on durable metal manufacturing, nondurable manufacturing industries, particularly food processing and lumber, were lead sectors for most of the century. Iron, machine tools, and machine making took off as growth sectors later, at the end of the nineteenth century. Third, large cities were not the only regional growth machines. The Midwestern manufacturing belt was characterized by many small cities engaged in industrial production, not merely service center functions. Its network of small cities, farm hinterland, as well as large urban areas facilitated growth. In sum, Page and Walker (1991) show that the manufacturing belt was far more diverse in its industrial and urban structure than political economy theory has assumed. They argue that the regime of accumulation was not an "extensive" regime with a backward farm sector, low levels of consumption, and few advances in industrial productivity, as argued by regulation theorists. Mass production technologies and high levels of consumption characterized the nineteenth century and farmers formed one of the first mass markets for the Model T. Thus, the political economy view of a sharp break between Fordism and the earlier period is incorrect.

Page and Walker provide a compelling challenge to conceptualizations of the pre-Fordist period, in turn calling into question the nature of Fordism itself. However, they focus on providing essentially a growth model of the manufacturing belt, based on its distinct industries and urban-regional structure. We note two missing pieces. First, Page and Walker give little attention to the regulatory institutions involving the state and capital-labor relationships that fostered growth. An important state policy is the 1787 Northwest Ordinance, which assured that territory north of the Ohio River would be free from slavery. The Ordinance also established bases for local government and educational infrastructure. With slavery outlawed, large-scale plantation agriculture was difficult to sustain, making possible the system of small family farms that underwrote agro-industrialization. The importance of small communities in building the Midwestern manufacturing belt also affected capital-labor relations. Small communities often were characterized by low labor-force bargaining power and paternalistic relationships, as opposed to the widespread labor militancy of the urban cores. Although mining-company towns may have been an exception in their lack of quiescence, Varano (1999, 42) notes that in the early 1900s, small Ohio River Valley towns, isolated from the growing labor movement and offering greater social control over workers were locations sought after by large firms in steel and other manufacturing. In small towns, community fortunes hinged on labor quiescence, maintained by local state control and community ideologies boosting local firms and products (Contosta 1999).

The second point, is that Page and Walker's focus on growth (1991) neglects community decline, which also characterized the manufacturing belt. Social scientists tend to treat the 1970s as ushering in dramatic economic restructuring that deviated from past epochs. Historically, however, rapid restructuring frequently buffeted the manufacturing belt. In the Ohio River Valley there was rapid growth of towns along the canals of the Ohio River and its tributaries during the early 1800s and subsequent dramatic decline of the same places as railroads replaced the canal transportation in the latter three decades of that century. Even as the U.S. population streamed westward, average annual rates of population change between 1850 and 1890 were negative for at least ten Ohio River Valley counties while the Valley itself on average grew about 2.7 percent annually. The canal system connected much of the ORV to global markets via New York and New Orleans, bringing not only the vagaries of international trade but also epidemics such as cholera from locations as far as India (Contosta 1999). Cities rose and fell in the regional hierarchy. By 1900, Pittsburgh, better linked to eastern markets through railroads, replaced Wheeling as the region's manufacturing center, the latter having early advantages due to its location on the National Road as well as the Ohio River. Mechanization of farming brought waves of community decline in the 1940s and 1950s, particularly in the Appalachian portion of the ORV, where farms were smaller and less competitive.

The present-day landscape also tells the story of past restructuring. Abandoned farmhouses, churches, schools, and industrial buildings dot the ORV. Vestiges of once thriving communities are seen in large (often three or more stories high) industrial plants and service buildings abandoned early in the twentieth century, some standing in the center of locales that today possess no more than a convenience store. Some places in the region have become the equivalent of ghost towns. The landscape suggests that throughout the twentieth century industries, firms, communities, and individuals' lives underwent dramatic changes.

Population shifts show the rise and fall of ORV communities. From 1850 to 1950 the area from Wheeling northward grew most rapidly, increasing its share of the ORV's population from 27 to 41 percent. Both the Appalachian area, from Charleston to Wheeling, and the western ORV, from Louisville to Evansville, declined relatively—each contained about 30 percent of the ORV population in 1850 but only 21 percent in 1950—while the Cincinnati–Miami Valley area experienced little change in population share. In 1990, 67 of the 222 ORV counties had smaller populations than they did at the turn of the century and 12 counties were less populated than in 1850.

This brief historical discussion highlights a different set of industries, urban-regional structures, and capital-labor relations than those studied in most political economy accounts of the rise of Fordism. We have also noted that economic restructuring and community decline are not unique to the post-1970s but have historically punctuated the manufacturing belt.

THE CONTEMPORARY PERIOD: THE OHIO RIVER VALLEY IN LATE FORDISM AND BEYOND

This section examines political economy portrayals of the contemporary manufacturing belt. We discuss the extent to which industrial decline and de-territorialization occurred and the types of growth enclaves that exist. We also extend the political economy account to examine contemporary institutional arrangements and issues related to globalization.

The 1970s to the 1990s: De-industrialization and De-territorialization?

To examine industrial restructuring and its aftermath, we compare the ORV to other U.S. regions. A description of how the Fordist and the post-Fordist transition periods are manifest is shown in table 1.1. Data are means for ORV counties and other contiguous U.S. counties on various industrial, institutional, and population attributes for 1970 and 1990.[2] Comparing ORV with other counties for the 1970 Fordist, pre-restructuring period shows that the region fits descriptions of an industrial and energy heartland. Relative to other counties, ORV counties have on average nearly double the proportion of employment

Table 1.1
Industrial, Institutional, and Other Characteristics,
Ohio River Valley and U.S. Counties, 1970 and 1990[a]

	1970		1990	
	U.S.	ORV	U.S.	ORV
Industrial structure				
Percent employed in:				
core manufacturing	.097	.188*	.097	.144*
peripheral manufacturing	.113	.099*	.086	.073*
mining	.019	.035*	.016	.031*
agriculture	.159	.088*	.090	.046*
consumer services	.222	.202*	.213	.200*
distributive services	.066	.068	.083	.087*
producer services	.050	.045*	.080	.075*
social services	.140	.134	.196	.198
public administration	.047	.045	.049	.043*
Occupational structure				
Percent:				
managers	.081	.067*	.086	.081*
professional/technical	.112	.102*	.221	.186*
crafts/operators	.323	.398*	.273	.313*
general laborers	.054	.060*	.048	.057*
farm owners/workers	.122	.074*	.082	.046*
services	.132	.122*	.141	.140
sales	.054	.053	.098	.095
clerical	.122	.124	.131	.132
Institutional context				
% unionized (state average)	.223	.340*	.186	.320*
% unemployed	.045	.052*	.061	.076*
% high school graduates	.449	.409*	.700	.663*
women's labor force share	.354	.334*	.405	.398
AFDC per recipient (1982 dollars)	$118.88	$108.92*	$80.24	$74.67
Transfer payments per capita (1982 dollars)	$1,008.56	$1,004.53	$2,079.32	$2,164.62

Table 1.1 (continued)

	1970		1990	
	U.S.	ORV	U.S.	ORV
Sociodemographic characteristics				
% white population	.891	.964*	.868	.961*
% over age 65	.119	.119	.150	.143*
% mother-only headed households	.090	.090	.132	.132
% urban	.347	.331	.369	.330*
Socioeconomic well-being				
median family income (1982 dollars)	$20,240.98	$20,522.96	$22,897.19	$22,016.95*
% families in poverty	.173	.167	.130	.143*
income inequality, gini	.385	.371*	.378	.381

[a]Means for the ORV counties ($N = 222$) and other U.S. counties ($N = 2888$) and results of differences of means tests ($*p < .05$) are reported.

in mining and core manufacturing, defined here as higher-wage, mainly durable manufacturing in metal, machinery, equipment, transportation, and nondurable printing, publishing, chemical and allied products. There is also a smaller proportion of manufacturing in lower-wage peripheral sectors, which include all remaining nondurable manufacturing as well as furniture, lumber, and wood. While we noted the importance of nondurable sectors in the rise of Fordism, much of this region's industry declined before the 1970s. Services, described using Singelmann's categorization (1978), make up a smaller share of ORV employment. In 1970, ORV counties had significantly smaller shares of employment in higher-wage services such as producer or advanced corporate services but also in lower-wage consumer services. Not surprisingly, the occupational structure shows a relatively blue-collar, male labor force, employed as craftspeople, machine operators, and general laborers, and a smaller proportion of managers, professionals, and service occupations. The institutional context of the ORV is shown through characteristics reflecting the bargaining power of labor with capital and state intervention on behalf of citizens. Although ORV counties are more highly unionized than others, higher unemployment and lower education indicate that labor's ability to bargain for better jobs is relatively weak. Welfare benefits, indicated by Aid to Families with Dependent Children (AFDC) payments, are also somewhat low. These attributes contrast with portrayals of manufacturing belt institutional arrangements as more favorable to citizens and labor. However, income inequality is significantly lower and family incomes slightly higher in the ORV. With the exception of a larger white population, ORV population attributes are similar to those nationally.

The post-restructuring period is characterized by data for 1990. First, contrasts between the ORV and other counties show that the ORV continues to maintain territorial coherence, despite de-industrialization. In 1990, ORV counties continue to have significantly higher employment in core manufacturing and mining and in blue-collar craft, operative, and general labor occupations, and lower employment in consumer and distributive services, and managerial and professional positions. Institutional characteristics indicate higher unemployment, lower education, higher unionization, and lower AFDC benefits, although somewhat higher total per capita income transfers. Population characteristics remain similar over time, with the exception of women's labor force participation, which increases.

Second, contrasts between 1970 and 1990 highlight the effects of de-industrialization. On average, ORV counties lost about 23 percent of their core manufacturing employment between 1970 and 1990, while shares of core manufacturing in other counties remained stable. Distributive and producer services experienced notable growth, and peripheral manufacturing experienced notable declines both nationally and in the ORV. Relative to the past, however, a more bifurcated occupational structure has emerged in the ORV. On average, the proportion of craft and machine operator positions declined by 21 percent in ORV counties compared to about 15 percent nationally, while the proportion of managers increased in the ORV by more than 20 percent, compared to about 6 percent nationally. Professional and technical occupations almost doubled in employment share in other counties, an increase far exceeding that in the ORV. These contrasts show that the contemporary ORV is characterized by relative declines in higher-wage manufacturing, growing inequality in occupational structure, and weak bargaining power for higher-skilled professional and technical jobs, in part due to chronically low educational attainments. That the ORV counties have lost ground is shown in their lower median family income, higher poverty rates, and higher income inequality relative to the past.

The political economy account comes closest to working out empirically for the ORV with regard to claims about de-industrialization. The Fordist period in the ORV was characterized by high-wage manufacturing, mining, a predominantly male labor force, and high unionization, all of which declined in the post-1970 period. As would be expected, the fortunes of the ORV also declined as the region experienced higher poverty and income inequality. However, in contrast to political economy views, with the exception of unionization, institutional arrangements in the ORV did not provide strong support for labor or citizen well-being, even during Fordism. Further, in the presumed post-Fordist period, we do not see strong evidence of de-territorialization or loss of regional distinctiveness, which was expected from the de-industrialization literature: despite declines in high-wage manufacturing, the ORV, relative to the nation, maintains much of its past character.

Growth Enclaves and New Regional Responses to Change

The second set of literature on the contemporary manufacturing belt deals with intraregional development and the extent to which growth enclaves have appeared. We address this issue by summarizing findings from previous quantitative analyses of changes in employment and net migration in the ORV counties, and we draw from site visits to selected firms. We mapped both intraregional employment changes, using County Business Patterns data files for 1980 to 1990 (Brown, Lobao, and Verheyen 1996), and county-to-county migration streams from a special run of the U.S. Census of Population data, which tabulates place of residence in 1985 and 1990 (Brown, Lobao, and Digiacinto 1999). Between 1980 and 1990 a corridor of high employment growth is found in the west-central ORV, from Evansville through Louisville-Lexington, Cincinnati-Dayton, and on to Columbus. With the exception of Columbus, growth is around, not within the core metro counties in which these cities are located. This west-central section saw relative increases in both durable and nondurable manufacturing, and distributive, producer, and social services. During this period, retail services and outlet malls particularly expanded along Interstate 71 between Cincinnati and Columbus. Marked net in-migration occurs in this area. Similarly, there was low or negative employment growth and net out-migration in most of West Virginia, southeastern Ohio, southwestern Pennsylvania, southern Illinois, and western Kentucky. These areas, at the western and eastern extremities of the Ohio River, were traditional centers of steel, manufacturing, and extractive industry. Patterns of intraregional employment and migration change suggest, in accordance with political economy views, that growth enclaves in the manufacturing belt are more likely to emerge outside former Fordist centers of industrial activity. However, as typical nationally, most employment growth in the ORV does not appear to be from new, incoming firms but from existing ones. For example, a 1993 study found that the share of new jobs from existing businesses in ORV counties ranged from 5 to 100 percent, with most at the upper tail of this continuum (Kraybill 1995).

The rise of new industrial spaces is seen by some political economists as heralding a post-Fordist economy (Scott 1988). The global economy is seen to create new or revitalized industries that take on distinct territorial organization due to learning and production-based firm networks. In this view of the new economy, industries and firms create regions. A common Midwestern example of new industrial spaces is the Japanese supplier–assembly plant complex, a portion of which extends into the west-central ORV growth corridor noted above (Mair, Florida, and Kenney 1988; Storper and Walker 1989).

We found, however, another type of growth enclave in the ORV. In contrast to the "territorial production complexes" noted in the literature, these enclaves are better described as territorial consumption complexes. Here, the firm could not exist without its regional embeddedness. The region itself serves as a marketing tool, legitimizing the firms' products in the context of a presumed historical past and, less critically, serves the production needs of raw materials and supplier inputs. We provide several examples of these firms. Most are indigenous, locally owned, in traditional industries that have remained at or near the same business site for decades, and located in small communities at some distance from metro areas.

Two examples of firms producing territorial consumption complexes are Longaberger Baskets, established in Dresden, Ohio, and Rocky Shoe and Boot Corporation, in Nelsonville, Ohio, both which grew out of Depression-era businesses. Longaberger, the far more territorially expansive and successful example, produces expensive, hand-woven maple baskets, considered collector's items. It has seven thousand employees and more than fifty thousand independent sales associates (Wolf 1999, 2H). Rocky Shoes was one of the few shoe manufacturers left in the U.S. It shifted production from moderately priced dress shoes to specialty boots to compete with international manufacturers in the late 1980s. Until November 2001 it employed over three hundred manufacturing workers. The family owners of Longaberger Basket and Rocky Shoes are considered hometown heroes, responsible for saving their towns during economic downturn, when other firms relocated. Much like traditional paternalistic capitalists, the owners of both firms have invested in local infrastructure, schools, labor force training, and community organizations. A near cult following for Longaberger baskets has turned Dresden into a national tourist destination, while Rocky Shoes has cultivated a more regional following. In the late 1990s Longaberger expanded along about twenty miles of state highway through Newark, altering the landscape with its signature white picket fences and construction of a new $30 million headquarters building in the shape of its main product—a wooden basket, complete with handles. The building stands several stories tall and is visible for miles across a flat landscape, impressing upon viewers that the company has progressed beyond establishing a company town and is creating a company region. A massive, Disney-like shopping and entertainment complex, Longaberger Homestead opened in 1999. As Dave Longaberger, the company's chairman, notes in a *Wall Street Journal* interview, "This kind of marketing, you can't buy this" (Quintanilla 1997, B18). Nelsonville officials indicate they would like to emulate the Longaberger model, with a marketing theme geared to the outdoor, sportsperson image connoted by Rocky Shoes. In the mid-1990s, Rocky opened a new corporate headquarters and outlet store in downtown Nelsonville. To complement Rocky, hunting clothing and accessory manufacturers were recruited and retail shops established in the town center. For Longaberger Baskets and Rocky Shoes, firm and community are intertwined and part of an extralocal marketing strategy.

The glass industry in southeastern Ohio and western West Virginia provides another example where corporate tourism embeds firms in the region. Here, however, coherent consumption complexes, such as those as surrounding Longaberger or even Rocky, have not emerged. Much of the region's glass industry, which grew up in the early 1900s, entered into decline in the 1960s due to global competition. Large firms, such as Anchor Hocking, ceased regional operations in the 1980s (Contosta 1999). Existing firms are generally locally owned, small to moderate size, serve national and international markets, and produce traditional products, often collector's items. For example, Fenton Glass in Williamstown, West Virginia, is a major destination for collectors of carnival and other decorative glass. Blenko Glass, in Milton, West Virginia, is also known nationally for its art glass. Marble King, in Paden City, West Virginia, is one of a handful of remaining glass marble companies that thrived regionally from the 1920s to the 1960s, when the industry moved to Asia and Mexico. Marble King's old, lower-price glass marbles are collector's items. It has recently shifted to high-quality decorative marbles for European markets and to producing marble games for children, with national competitions sponsored by the company throughout the United States. Glass items discarded by Fenton are purchased by Marble King for use in marble production. Booming interest in Victorian-era glass gazing globes have made tourist destinations out of Marietta Silver Globe Manufacturing and other smaller producers along the Ohio–West Virginia border (Aeppel 1996).[3]

Roots of corporate tourism undoubtedly extend from traditional community boosterism of local industries and products. Even today communities across the ORV hold annual festivals for indigenous manufactured products, crowning pottery, glass, and other product "queens"—and sometimes "kings." Present-day corporate tourism, however, is different from the traditional celebration of local products. Corporate branding is much more important, particularly as old companies decline and products become irreplaceable antiques. The buoyant economy of the late 1990s has created a consumer segment with discretionary income to support these small, niche-market firms. Similarly, nostalgia for products once owned by ancestors or remembered from childhood adds a life-cycle dimension, in which baby boomers and the elderly appear the most avid collectors. For many of these products, what was once kitsch has become classic.

In sum, recent rounds of restructuring build on earlier regional endowments. Firms are embedded in regional production, consumption, and institutional contexts often difficult to reproduce elsewhere. Employers become accustomed to dealing with particular labor forces and invest in the communities that reproduce them. The examples above reflect the importance of localizing tendencies in the face of macro-level changes identified by theory.

Industries, Institutional Arrangements, and Communities in the Global Economy

The contemporary ORV maintains its historical legacy of manufacturing and an institutional context not strongly supportive of labor or citizens. Educational attainments also remain low and socioeconomic conditions have become poorer. While we described localizing tendencies in this distinct regional context, a converse issue is how globalization is manifest. We note observations from two ORV communities in Ohio which have been the subject of more in-depth case study. We chose these communities because they represent different contemporary linkages with external firms and capital, while being similar in population size, rurality, and past dependence on traditional ORV industries. Jackson (population 6,500) and Nelsonville (population 4,500), are both located about an hour and a half drive from the largest metropolitan center, Columbus. Historically, both communities were similarly engaged in metal manufacturing and farming, while Nelsonville also had a relatively large mining sector. Jackson today is dependent on nonlocal capital, large or multinational corporations. None of the six major firms in Jackson are locally owned; two, Campbell's and Pillsbury, are multinational food-processing firms. In contrast, Nelsonville is dependent on government employment in a local junior college and three correctional facilities and on locally owned Rocky Shoes. Rocky's CEO noted that to maintain Rocky Shoes in Nelsonville without laying off workers, two sewing plants were set up in the Dominican Republic in the 1980s to reduce labor costs, particularly for training new workers. However, in November 2001 the company moved the remainder of its manufacturing jobs to Puerto Rico, where labor costs are $6.00 an hour, compared to approximately $11.00 in the Nelsonville area (Price 2002). Rocky still retains its headquarters and large retail outlet in Nelsonville. Company officials maintain that their commitment to the community has not changed. Newspaper accounts indicate the move has not been contentious among the workforce, in part because the company remains a large local employer (Price 2002). Interviews with eighteen key informants were conducted in 1998–99, nine in each community, and of these, three each representing community organizations, business, and local government. This information was further updated for changes from 2000 to 2002.

Despite different linkages with global and local firms and reliance on state sources of development, key informants described quite similar conditions in their communities. First, the power of employers to set the terms and conditions of local development appears to have increased relative to the past and to other community decision makers such as citizens groups, labor unions, and local government. In both Jackson and Nelsonville, the Chambers of Commerce are the local entities reported as most involved in local economic development. Political party lines in local government are blurred, as informants noted. Officials from both the Democratic and Republican Parties expose similar growth-machine policies. Tax abatements are typically used to retain or attract business. In the late 1990s Rocky Shoes received an abatement for improvements that was to guarantee an additional seventy jobs but also placed some burden on Nelsonville's finances. The city government was declared in fiscal emergency in 1992, recovering only in 1999. While the United Mineworkers is still regarded as one of the region's most militant unions, there are few members in either community, and other unions operating in local firms, principally in Jackson, are viewed as quiescent.

Second, informants recognize that local-area firms generate mainly low-skilled manufacturing and service jobs. Community and government informants report concerns about upgrading job quality but note two problems in doing so: the labor force lacks education and technical skills, and highway infrastructure remains poor.

Third, local citizens, as opposed to the state or business, seem to absorb the costs of social change. Informants noted that in the past several years, residents were commuting much longer distances to jobs in metro areas outside their counties. There are also large segments of the poor and unemployed. In 1997 poverty rates were about 21 percent in both communities and unemployment stood at 7.7 percent in Jackson and 5.8 percent in Nelsonville. Both communities are faced with dealing with the effects of welfare reform, as time limits expired for Ohio recipients in the fall of 2000.

Finally, for both communities the precise source of capital, whether domestic or local, appears to have marginal impact on day-to-day life. Effects of global competition in these communities are little evident in recent firm closings or downsizing and more through implicit threats that ever increasing public subsidization of private business is necessary. Relying on the state as a major employer also offers no development panacea. Though specialization in corrections and education offers Nelsonville growth industries insulated from private-sector woes, respondents are concerned that corrections facilities are deterring recruitment of higher-skill firms and the budding tourist complex around Rocky Shoes.

While most attention to globalizing processes at the local level is directed to production, effects on institutional arrangements have been neglected. The cases of Nelsonville and Jackson suggest that institutional arrangements between capital, citizens, and the state are becoming further disadvantageous for the latter two actors. Citizens are increasingly subject to market discipline and the severing of nonmarket state supports, while local government is increasingly called on to use its own source funds to underwrite private-sector development.

Studying change through a regional lens entails a holistic approach that goes beyond the conventional focus on production activities. In addition, regions embody the past and present history of institutional arrangements between labor, the state, and capital, as well as the position of the region itself in the national and global economy. The social forces involved are thus complex and easily missed in macro-level political economy theory. Focusing on the old manufacturing belt allows political economy claims about the stages of capitalism to be assessed, claims involving the rise and consolidation of Fordism in these regions, post-1970s restructuring, and discourse about their post-Fordist trajectory. The fact that these issues intersect in a single region, makes the manufacturing belt a fertile empirical location for assessing how theory works out territorially. Studying old industrial regions such as the Ohio River Valley also extends research beyond studies of exceptional locales, to incorporate the typical places where most Americans live and work.

Our research informs theory in the following ways. First, we extend Page and Walker's insights (1991) that early Fordism in the Midwestern manufacturing belt entailed a different industrial and spatial structure than assumed in political economy accounts. Capital-labor relations also varied from portrayals of an independent, educated, highly skilled, and militant proletariat in a strong bargaining position with capital. Community ideologies boosting local firms and products fostered a workforce that identified with and saw their fortunes tied to local employers.

Second, researchers also have tended to treat the post-1970s as ushering in dramatic economic change. However, restructuring brought on by external national, and even global, events often buffeted the Ohio River Valley. Past institutional arrangements and restructuring experiences laid the foundation for subsequent development. Community identification with local firms and industrial products, corporate tourism as a development strategy, fear of firm flight, and chronically low educational attainments are today's remnants of past bargaining with capital.

Political economy perspectives see global and national changes as washing over the manufacturing belt, increasing firm mobility, severing previous employer-worker-community relationships, and creating new industrial sites. The ORV has experienced overall deindustrialization and differential intraregional growth much in accordance with political economy perspectives. The region, however, is not a blank slate reflecting global change. As we noted, the ORV today has retained much of its historical industrial and institutional character. Recent rounds of restructuring can only be understood insofar as they build on earlier regional endowments. The case of the ORV also shows that firm and labor-force mobility is sticky. Firms are embedded in regional production as well as consumption networks that are often difficult to reproduce elsewhere. Important localizing tendencies in the face of macro-level changes therefore remain. Globalizing tendencies also need to be understood in light of previous rounds of development, which historically undercut the bargaining power of local labor and citizens vis-à-vis employers. The contemporary global economy and its accompanying neoliberalism, reinforce previous regional relationships but in new ways, as citizens and labor underwrite the costs of private-sector development through long-distance commuting and direct subsidization with public funds.

The case of the Ohio River Valley highlights the complexity by which economic changes unfold across regions and the difficulty of capturing them in the conceptual frameworks that we have at hand. It suggests the need for revising political economy theory to produce a more nuanced account of development and to reassess claims about institutional arrangements in the manufacturing belt. Finally, the case of the ORV suggests no clear break in development that heralds the arrival of post-Fordism or profoundly different linkages with the global economy. Rather, there appears to be continual layering of the economic structure, social relationships, and built environment of past periods with the present. Inertia as well as change and a complex rather than clear trajectory constitute the broader pattern of the region's development.

Notes

1. One way to classify these schools is point of origin, with regulation theory representing the French school (Lipietz 1987) and Social Structures of Accumulation, the U.S. school (Gordon, Edwards, and Reich 1994).

2. With the exception of government income transfers, data for variables in table 1.1 are from the Census of Population (U.S. Bureau of the Census 1970; 1980; 1990). Income transfer variables are from the Regional Economic Information System (REIS) (U.S. Department of Commerce 1999) and Area Resource File (U.S. Department of Health and Human Services 1993).

3. Pottery is another indigenous industry spawning corporate tourism. Large companies, such as Homer Laughlin, the maker of Fiestaware in Newell, West Virginia, have thriving domestic and international markets, but many small companies throughout eastern Ohio also have loyal collector followings.

References

Aeppel, Timothy. 1996. "Neither Lawn Jockey nor Pink Flamingo Compares to Orb." *Wall Street Journal,* November 21, 1.

Aglietta, Michael. 1979. *A Theory of Capitalist Regulation: The U.S. Experience.* London: Verso.

Brown, Lawrence A. 1999. "Change, Continuity, and the Pursuit of Geographic Understanding." *Annals of the Association of American Geographers* 89 (1): 1–25.

Brown, Lawrence A., Linda Lobao, and Scott Digiacinto. 1999. "Economic Restructuring and Migration in an Old Industrial Region: The Ohio River Valley." In *Migration and Restructuring in the United States: A Geographic Perspective,* ed. Kavita Pandit and Suzanne Withers, 37–57. Lanham, Md.: Rowman and Littlefield.

Brown, Lawrence A., Linda Lobao, and Anthony Verheyen. 1996. "Continuity and Change in an Old Industrial Region" *Growth and Change* 27 (Spring): 175–205.

Contosta, David R. 1999. *Lancaster, Ohio, 1800–2000.* Columbus: Ohio State University Press.

Cox, Kevin R. 1997. "Introduction: Globalization and Its Politics in Question." In *Spaces of Globalization: Reasserting the Power of the Local*, ed. Kevin R. Cox, 1–18. New York: Guilford Press.

Crump, Jeffrey, and Christopher D. Merrett. 1998. "Scales of Struggle: Economic Restructuring in the U.S. Midwest." *Annals of the Association of American Geographers* 88 (3): 496–515.

Deitrick, Sabina, and Robert A. Beauregard. 1995. "From Front-Runner to Also Ran: The Transformation of a Once Dominant Industrial Region: Pennsylvania, USA." In *The Rise of the Rustbelt*, ed. Philip Cooke, 52–71. New York: St. Martin's.

Dicken, Peter, Jamie Peck, and Adam Tickell. 1997. "Unpacking the Global." In *Geographies of Economies*, ed. Roger Lee and Jane Wills, 158–66. London: Arnold.

Gordon, David. M., Richard Edwards, and Michael Reich. 1982. *Segmented Work, Divided Workers: The Historical Transformation of Labor in the United States*. Cambridge: Cambridge University Press.

———. 1994. "Long Swings and Stages of Capitalism." In *Social Structures of Accumulation: The Political Economy of Growth and Crisis*, ed. David. M. Kotz, Terry McDonough, and Michael Reich, 11–28. Cambridge: Cambridge University Press.

Horan, Cynthia, and Andrew Jonas. 1998. *Governing Massachusetts: Uneven Development and Politics in Metropolitan Boston. Economic Geography AAG* 74 (special issue): 83–95.

Hudson, R. 1989. "Labour-Market Changes and New Forms of Work in Old Industrial Regions." *Environment and Planning D: Society and Space* 7:5–30.

Kotz, David. M. 1994. "Interpreting the Social Structure of Accumulation Theory." In *Social Structures of Accumulation: The Political Economy of Growth and Crisis*, ed. David. M. Kotz, Terry McDonough, and Michael Reich, 50–71. Cambridge: Cambridge University Press.

Kratke, S. 1999. "A Regulationist Approach to Regional Studies." *Environment and Planning A* 31:683–704.

Kraybill, David S. 1995. "Facts on Job Creation in Ohio." *Ohio's Challenge* 8 (2): 4–7.

Krugman, Paul. 1991. *Geography and Trade*. Cambridge, Mass.: MIT Press.

Lipietz, Alain. 1987. *Mirages and Miracles*. London: Verso.

Lobao, Linda, Jamie Rulli, and Lawrence A. Brown. 1999. "Macro-Level Theory and Local-Level Inequality: Industrial Structure, Institutional Arrangements, and the Political Economy of Redistribution, 1970 and 1990." *Annals of the Association of American Geographers* 89 (4): 571–601.

Mair, Andrew, Richard Florida, and Martin Kenney. 1988. "The New Geography of Automobile Production: Japanese Transplants in North America." *Economic Geography* 64:352–73.

Markusen, Ann. 1985. *Profit Cycles, Oligopoly, and Regional Development.* Cambridge, Mass.: MIT Press.

———. 1987. *Regions: The Economics and Politics of Territory.* Totowa, N.J.: Rowman and Littlefield.

Miller, D. W. 2000. "The New Urban Studies: Los Angeles Scholars Use Their Region and Their Ideas to End the Dominance of the Chicago School." *Chronicle of Higher Education* 56 (50): A15–16.

Odum, Howard W., and Harry Estill Moore. 1938. *American Regionalism: A Cultural-Historical Approach to National Integration.* New York: Holt.

Page, Brian, and Richard Walker. 1991. "From Settlement to Fordism: The Agro-Industrial Revolution in the American Midwest." *Economic Geography* 67 (4): 281–315.

Peck, Jamie. 1996. *Work-Place: The Social Regulation of Labor Markets.* New York: Guilford Press.

Piore, Michael, and Charles Sable. 1984. *The Second Industrial Divide.* New York: Basic Books.

Price, Rita. 2002. "Rocky Clocks Out." *Columbus Dispatch,* April 28, A1.

Quintanilla, Carl. "A Seven-Story Basket Goes Up in the Fields of Ohio." *Wall Street Journal,* November 15, B1–B18.

Reid, Robert L. 1991. Introduction to *Always a River: The Ohio River and the American Experience,* ed. Robert Reid, xi–xvi. Bloomington: Indiana University Press.

Rigby, David L., and Jurgen Essletzbichler. 1997. "Evolution, Process Variety, and Regional Trajectories of Technological Change in U.S. Manufacturing." *Economic Geography* 73 (July): 269–84.

Scott, Allan. 1988. *New Industrial Spaces: Flexible Production Organization and Regional Development in North America and Western Europe.* London: Pion.

Singelmann, Joachim. 1978. *From Agriculture to Services: The Transformation of Industrial Employment.* Beverly Hills: Sage.

Soja, Edward. 1988. *Post-Modern Geographies: The Reassertion of Space in Critical Social Theory.* London: Verso.

Storper, Michael. 1997. *The Regional World: Territorial Development in a Global Economy.* New York: Guilford Press.

Storper, Michael, and Richard Walker. 1989. *The Capitalist Imperative: Territory, Technology, and Industrial Growth.* Oxford: Basil Blackwell.

U.S. Bureau of the Census. 1970. *Census of Population and Housing,* Summary Tape Files 3 and 4.

———. 1980. *Census of Population and Housing,* Summary Tape Files 3 and 4.

———. 1990. *Census of Population and Housing,* Summary Tape Files 3 and 4.

U.S. Department of Commerce. 1999. *Regional Economic Information System 1969–1996* (CD-ROM).

U.S. Department of Health and Human Services. 1993. *Area Resource File* CD-ROM.

Varano, Charles S. 1999. *Forced Choices: Class, Community and Worker Ownership.* Albany: SUNY Press.

Wolf, Barnet. 1999. "Amid Changes, Longaberger Continues to Weave a Tale of Success." *Columbus Dispatch,* August 8, 1H–2H.

2

Place, Race, and State

Sustaining the Textile Security Zone
in a Changing Southern Labor Market

Cynthia D. Anderson, Michael D. Schulman,
and Philip Wood

IT IS NOW more or less conventional wisdom that global restructuring will result in the loss of manufacturing jobs in the United States and in other advanced industrial economies (Tonelson 2000). While no sector is immune from the effects of this process, labor-intensive mass-production industries are thought to be especially vulnerable given the relentless "race to the bottom" that is required of firms in the new global marketplace (Brecher and Costello 1998). The textile industry is often cited as an exemplar of this globalizing logic. Contemporary observers of Southern textiles tend to accept the logic of the new industrial division of labor (NIDL) literature: employment in the U.S. textile industry will decline because of global restructuring (Gaventa and Smith 1991; Glasmeier and Leichenko 1996, 613; Lyson 1989, 109).[1]

According to arguments about textile globalization, whether neoclassical or neo-Marxist in origin, factors of production, especially labor, are cheaper in the Third World, and there is a clear global hierarchy of capitalist platforms. Corporations are forced to adjust to the new reality by relocating production to low-cost sites or face extinction. It is not difficult to find examples of offshore manufacturing by American textile firms, since the process began more than fifty years ago (Callahan 1997; Millman 1998; Obermayer 1996; Wood 1986, 195–98). The important question is not whether there exist cases that exemplify the process in question, but whether they define it. In general, we think that these accounts are too often mechanical, linear, abstract, and economistic.

Some of the facts may be correct, but this global version of the neoclassical competitive model analyzes investment decisions without much reference to the embeddedness of industrial structures in local political, cultural, and geographic "security zones."[2] The construction of such zones is not a simple matter, but rather a product of long-term engagement in power politics (Boyer and Drache 1996; Easterbrook 1990, 5, 7). Also, the differences between apparel (e.g., needles and scissors) and textiles (e.g., looms and spindles) are often ignored in the NIDL accounts. While apparel provides the classic example of an industry that has become highly internationalized by relying on foreign production sites, the domestic textile industry (the focus of this chapter) remains relatively unscathed by increasing imports because of its amenability to technological innovations (Mittelhauser 1996) and, as we argue, its location in a Southern spatial security zone.

In short, abstract models of globalization pay insufficient attention to the concrete structure and organization of Southern textile capital and the context within which it operates. To explain the pattern of Southern textile development, we need to pay attention to the unique ways textile accumulation is embedded in Southern society and politics, particularly the complex interactions associated with class, race, and spatial organization. First, we describe the Southern textile security zone. Next, using county-level data on textile employment, we model changes in regional employment using variables that address demographic, labor market, industrial structure, racial composition, and state policy characteristics. We find that employment change in the Southern textile industry is embedded in a historically rooted yet evolving security zone of race, class, and place.

The Southern Textile Security Zone

Southern textile industrialization in the long term has been structured by a variety of factors, including capital shortage, power sources, and transportation needs. One of the most crucial was political and racial: the class alliance of planters, industrialists, and small-town merchants and lawyers who turned to textile industrialization after the Civil War as a source of personal and regional salvation (Key 1949). To preserve this alliance, the mobilization of a textile labor force had to avoid destabilizing the plantation economy and the system of racial segregation. Industrialization thus took place in the predominantly rural and small-town Piedmont region of the South, where white farm families, facing declining world prices and increasing debt, were driven to the mills, where they were reconstituted as a textile proletariat (Billings 1979; Hall et al. 1987). A downward spiral of wages converging to those paid to black farm workers (Wright 1986, 1987) led to the relocation of textile capital from other parts of the United States (Wood 1986). By 1911 virtually all the nation's coarse cotton goods were produced in the South by nonunionized white men and women living in mill villages.

Industrialists not only had to mobilize a textile labor force, they also had to control and exploit workers. Company towns and social services were important parts of a strategy of exploitation that denied workers autonomy (Cash 1941; Pope 1942; Wood 1991). Racial politics maintained the illusion that white workers and owners were united in a "white family" and reinforced occupational and residential segregation that kept black workers from mill production jobs and the formation of class alliances with white workers (Frederickson 1982; Hall et al. 1987). The result was dependence, the development of a culture and politics of paternalism, and the manipulation of gender and race in relatively isolated small-town and rural textile communities (Jackman 1994).

Textile relocation, motivated by the Northern industry's need for a "spatial fix" (Harvey 1982), reinforced the Southern accumulation strategy. A spatial fix resolves crises of accumulation by means of geographic relocation to areas where rates of exploitation, costs of materials, or infrastructure favor capital over labor. The logic of this spatial fix (and of similar strategies in apparel, furniture, and other low-wage sectors that began to concentrate in the South) was not to dissolve Southern production and race relations, but to stabilize them as far as possible and use them to the industry's advantage. This was accomplished in part by Southern governments taking the conditions created by textile capital—low wages, low taxes, deferential, nonunionized white workers—and making them the centerpiece of their industrial recruitment campaigns. The use of public power to guarantee the political and social conditions for low-wage, high-exploitation capital accumulation thus lies at the core of the Southern pattern of industrialization and uneven development.

Textile profitability began to be squeezed in the 1960s, by rising wages, sluggish growth, and increased foreign competition. The industry's adaptation to these conditions has been multifaceted, involving both innovations and historical continuities. After the Civil Rights Act of 1964, blacks entered textile production jobs in significant numbers (Frederickson 1982; Heckman and Payne 1989). In the 1980s a wave of mergers combined with investment in new technologies, market rationalization (e.g., quick-response systems), and labor process rationalization resulted in increasing production and falling employment (Dicken 1998; Morrissett and Dawson 1998; Zingraff 1991). Many other aspects of the Southern accumulation strategy—the search for low-wage, union-free, racially divided locations, along with the merging of public and private power to create industrial zones—continue to set the context for Southern economic development and provide for the risks and uncertainly associated with the textile industry's increasing fixed-capital investment. Despite metropolitan growth, tight urban labor markets, and the desegregation of employment, this security zone remains feasible because the pattern of Southern development continues to conserve it. The South still acts as a magnet for firms seeking affordable land, low labor costs in a largely nonunion environment, and generous packages of tax incentives (Carney 2002).

In the second half of the twentieth century, the South was the poorest region in the United States, with a third of the nation's population, but about 40 percent of its poor. Census figures from 1990 show that 58 percent of all the African American poor and 35 percent of all the white poor lived in the South (U.S. Census Bureau 1990). The rural South, in turn, contained 44 percent of the rural population of the United States, but 55 percent of all rural poor and 96 percent of all black rural poor. In the late 1980s a fifth of all Southern full-time jobs were low wage, and the share increased to 40 percent if part-time and seasonal workers were included. Most of these jobs were held by white women and African Americans (Tomaskovic-Devey 1991, 2–3, 28, 31), who therefore constituted a large component of the region's pool of cheap labor-power. African Americans and women have been the main targets of textile recruitment since the mid-1960s, permitting the industry to cope with an increasingly tight Southern labor market in the region as a whole (Toyne et al. 1984, 106–7; Wood 1986, 194–97). Recently, new immigrants are taking the place of African Americans at the bottom of many Southern labor markets. Hispanic workers are moving out of agriculture into service and manufacturing employment, where they dominate the growing animal-processing sector (Johnson-Webb 1999). For them, textile employment represents a move up the occupational and income ladder, adding to the low-wage labor pool and creating additional complexity to social relations in the community and mill (Anderson 2000).

Historically, the industry created a security zone by exploiting agrarian white families. Racial segregation and disenfranchisement segmented the labor force while allowing white workers to believe that their interests were congruent with the interests of mill owners. In the 1960s branch plant industrialization provided Southern white workers with new job opportunities and civil rights legislation permitted black workers to move into mill employment. Over the next decades, the textile industry expanded its nonunion workforce to include female, black, and Hispanic workers while technological innovation decreased the total number employed. Local politics and race relations continued to be used to the industry's advantage as it rebuilt its Southern security zone.

Data and Method: The Restructuring
of Southern Textiles, 1972–1992

Despite technological change and restructuring, the Southern textile industry remains dependent on low-wage, highly exploited labor. The South's uneven development continues to provide the conditions in which these needs can be met. The industry's traditional ability to pursue a "spatial fix" to deal with competitive crises has become more difficult in recent decades, but is not yet exhausted. In this section, we use county-level data for 1971 and 1992 to investigate the extent to which this spatial strategy has been typical of the Southern textile industry as a whole. Then we try to identify key social and political determinants of the pattern of textile employment restructuring. The 1970s data correspond to what some have called the starting point for the decay of the Fordist period of industrial organization (Harrison and Bluestone 1988) and the 1990s data correspond to the period when globalization, restructuring, and the NIDL were in full swing (Harrison 1994).

We created a database on textile employment and county-level socioeconomic conditions by merging county-level (and in Virginia, independent city-level) Southern textile employment and establishment data from the Census of Manufacturing and from County Business Patterns. Textile employment data are based on Census Standard Industrial Code (SIC) 22. The South is operationally defined as the eleven former Confederate states. There are two data-related limitations to this exercise. First, confidentiality rules in some cases prohibit releasing data that would reveal the operation of individual firms. In these cases, county employment data are given in ranges rather than actual numbers. Where this is the case, we have used the range midpoints. Second, unlike the 1992 data, the 1972 census shows employment levels only to the nearest hundred employees. Hence, some counties with minor or small amounts of textile employment in 1972 may have been eliminated by rounding from the 1972 data. Where possible, when drawing empirical conclusions from the data, we have tried to take these limitations into account. Despite these limitations, we think the data provide a useful and relatively accurate picture of geographic shifts in Southern textile employment between 1972 and 1992.

Table 2.1 summarizes the pattern of geographical shifts in Southern textile employment between 1972 and 1992 and confirms the continuing importance of spatial reorganization. In 1972 there were at least 343 counties with textile employment. Mean county employment was 1,884, with a maximum of 29,200. The average textile county had about nine establishments. In 1992, 469 counties could be identified as textile counties. The average county had 1,073 employees (with a maximum of 17,300) and an average of six establishments.

The overall pattern is one of regional employment decline. From 1972 to 1992 there was a net loss of about 140,000 Southern textile jobs in the eleven former Confederate states, representing about 22 percent of the 1972 total. The Carolinas account for the bulk (about 138,000) of these.[3]

On the other hand, within this pattern of employment decline, there is also evidence of growth in some states and counties. The number of textile establishments in the region as a whole shows an increase of twelve, despite the net loss of nearly four hundred operations in the Carolinas. At the state level, Arkansas, Florida, Louisiana, Mississippi, Texas, and Virginia produced net employment gains, while all states but North Carolina, South Carolina, and Virginia showed increases in the number of establishments. At the regional level, the industry in 1992 was spread wider and thinner than it was at its employment peak in the 1970s. Textile employment has shifted away from the Carolinas and spread more evenly across the Southern region with the Deep South states of Alabama and Georgia the main targets of restructuring.

We may conclude from this brief review that the tendency toward declining employment in the textile sector is the product of a complex process of restructuring and accumulation. What we are dealing with is not solely decline but a more multifaceted process of spatial reorganization of the Southern textile sector. According to the Bureau of Labor Statistics, since 1969, despite the loss of almost a quarter of its employment, the Southeastern textile industry has continued to account for about 70 percent of all U.S. textile jobs. These jobs are no longer concentrated in the Carolinas, however, as the core of textile establishments is being transferred to other areas in the South. This

Table 2.1

Pattern of Restructuring in Southern Textiles, 1972–1992

State	1) Net Change in Emp.	2) Net Change in # Estabs	3) # of Textile Cnties 1972	4) Mean Cnty Est. Size 1972	5) # of Textile Cnties 1992	6) Mean Cnty Est. Size 1992	7) Job Growth Cnties	8) % of All Counties	9) Mean Job Growth in Growth Cnties
AL	−4,246	+138	36	315	36	194	15	22	630
AR	+2,785	+9	8	246	13	235	12	16	369
FL	+1,143	+96	2	77	19	25	17	25	80
GA	−10,328	+62	77	276	89	226	46	29	529
LA	+4,405	+12	3	253	13	402	12	18	433
MS	+3,177	+16	14	296	22	243	17	12	296
NC	−79,211	−286	75	228	86	205	31	31	430
SC	−58,543	−104	38	312	44	224	13	28	284
TN	−7,065	+2	35	260	49	166	27	28	188
TX	+2,616	+84	11	182	47	59	41	16	115
VA	+4,226	−17	44	269	51	359	33	24	495
SOUTH	−141,040	+12	343	267	469	209	264	23	352

Calculated from Data in: U.S. Department of Commerce, Bureau of the Census, *1972 Census of Manufacturing*. Vols. 4 and 5: Geographic Area Series. Washington: USGPO, 1975; U.S. Department of Commerce, Bureau of the Census, *County Business Patterns 1972*. Washington, USGPO, 1973; U.S. Department of Commerce, Bureau of the Census, *1992 Economic Census CD-ROM*. Report Series, Disk 1H: Manufacturers: Geographic Area Series. Data Users Services Division 1996; 1992 County Business Patterns data obtained from the North Carolina State University Textile/Apparel Business Information System (TABIS)] structural stability reflects both "the continuing importance of the Southeast in the textile industry" (U.S. Department of Labor 1994) and the continuing ability of Southern textile capital to meet competitive challenges by means of spatial reorganization.

In the following analysis, we use regression models of county-level changes in textile employment between 1972 and 1992 to shed light on this restructuring process.

The dependent variable, numerical county-level change in textile industry employment, 1972–1992, was calculated from the same data used to construct table 2.1. It is, in effect, a merging of data on textile employment (SIC 22) from the Census of Manufacturing and County Business Patterns (CBP). The CBP reports textile employment for counties that the Census of Manufacturing does not, due to differences in reporting thresholds. Accordingly, we supplemented the census data with additional counties reported by the CBP and corrected the census estimates where the CBP found more textile workers than the census. This resulted in two composite variables, textile employment for 1972 and 1992. The dependent variable is the difference between the two in thousands. For all Southern counties (including counties with no textile workers), the variable has 994 cases with a mean of −0.142 and a standard deviation of 1.070.

We selected independent variables to represent demographic, labor market, agricultural structure, racial composition, and state fiscal policy determinants of textile industrialization (Cobb 1993; Wood 1996). Measurements of the majority of the independent variables in the regression analyses (see table 2.2) are from County and City Data Book Consolidated File, County Data 1947–1977 (U.S. Census Bureau 1978). The only exceptions to this are: the African American voter registration variable, which was calculated from county-level data used in Matthews and Prothro 1996, U.S. Commission on Civil Rights 1968, and the 1970 Beale Rural-Urban Continuum Codes, which were obtained electronically <http://www.ers.usda.gov/briefing/rurality/ruralurbcon/code93.txt> from the U.S. Department of Agriculture. The Beale Rural-Urban Index ranges from 0 (central metro counties of 1 million or more) to 9 (rural or under 2.5K population and not metro adjacent). The dependent variable (numerical county-level change in Southern textile industry employment, 1972–92, in thousands) has 535 cases, a mean of -0.2565 and a standard deviation of 1.37.[4]

Results: County-Level Textile Employment Shifts, 1972–92

The regression models, summarized in table 2.2, were designed to test hypotheses suggested by the previous discussion of sociopolitical context, focusing on uneven development within the Southern spatial security zone. First, we examine the extent to which the "spatial fix" of Southern textile restructuring is shaped by the distribution of minority workers and is directed at the more rural parts of the region (equation 1). Second, we explore the degree to which the racial composition of Southern counties moderates the relationships involved in the "spatial fix" (equation 2).

We include the Beale Rural-Urban Index in order to test the hypothesis that hard-pressed labor-intensive industries respond to tight labor markets and rising costs of agglomeration in metropolitan settings, where possible, by moving to greenfield sites in smaller towns and rural counties (Storper and Walker 1989). Research on Southern textiles in an earlier period provided evidence of textile expansion along these lines (Wood 1986, 195–96). The data used here confirm this tendency toward decentralization since 1972. Equation 1 suggests that each step along the Beale continuum from metropolitan counties to those that are least urbanized and most distant from metropolitan areas is associated with a gain of about one hundred textile jobs. Textile job creation is highest in the South's most rural counties, which remain, despite sunbelt growth in metropolitan areas, reservoirs of relatively cheap labor power (Lyson 1989).

Historically, the textile accumulation strategy has been most successful when the industry has gained control of locations where political and social conditions were conducive to the imposition of a low-wage, high-exploitation accumulation strategy. Conversely, the industry has experienced difficulties when competition from more advanced sectors has impeded that control. The industry's historical

Table 2.2
Explanation of County-Level Change
in Southern Textile Employment, 1972–1992

Independent Variable	Equation 1	Equation 2
Beale Urban-Rural Index, 1970	.095***	.069**
County civilian labor force, 1970	−.0002***	−.00001***
% County labor force in manufacturing, 1970	−.033***	−.032***
% Farms less than 10 acres 1974	.085***	.081***
% County population black, 1970	−.008**	−.022***
Black mobilization, 1958–67	.0001***	.0004***
Per capita property tax, 1971–72	−.006***	−.012***
% Local govt expenditures for highways 1971	.037***	.037***
Civilian labor force * % black	−.0000009***	
Black mobilization * % black	−.000005***	
Per capita prop tax * % black		.0003***
Constant	.155	.597
Adjusted R-square	.250	.291
Standard error	1.190	1.157
Number of counties	535	535
Incremental F-test		9.79***

* $p \leq 0.1$; ** $p \leq .05$; *** $p \leq .01$

transformation from a predominantly Northeastern to a predominantly Southern one between the first decade of the twentieth century and the eve of World War II exemplifies this logic (Storper and Walker 1989; Wood 1986). The second and third independent variables (labor force participation and percentage employed in manufacturing) are designed to test this proposition in the context of the contemporary restructuring of the industry, and the data suggest that the logic still holds. The larger the local labor market pool, the poorer the record of job creation. Similarly, the stronger the competition for labor from a large manufacturing sector, the greater the job loss. Here, every increase of one percent in the manufacturing share of the county labor force reduces textile employment by about thirty-three jobs.

The relationship between agricultural vulnerability and textile accumulation has been central to the industry's expansion in the South since the late nineteenth and early twentieth centuries, when impoverished farm families provided the labor power on which the early stages of industrial expansion were built (Hall et al. 1987; Wood 1986). We use the percentage of farms of less than ten acres as an index of marginal agriculture in order to test for the continuing importance of this link. Again, the results confirm the persistence of the traditional relationship. The larger the percentage of farms less than ten acres, the better the record of textile job creation. Between 1972 and 1992 each increase of one percent in the share of small farms is associated with an increase of eighty-five textile jobs.

Two variables are used to investigate the racial dimension of textile employment change. Following V. O. Key's analysis in *Southern Politics* (1949) of the effects of black county population concentrations on Southern social relations, we included a black concentration variable (percentage of county population black) in order to investigate its role in industrial restructuring. Since the 1960s, the Southern textile industry has been forced by a combination of tight metropolitan labor markets, the civil rights movement, and equal employment opportunity legislation to employ more African American workers. Yet in the context of spatial restructuring from 1972 to 1992, the data used here suggest a negative relationship between textile employment change and the concentration of black population in a county. Each one-percent increase in county black population concentration is associated with a loss of eight textile jobs. This appears to support the position advanced in an earlier survey of Southern manufacturing data by Glenna Colclough, who argued that "manufacturing gains are more likely in predominantly rural, white counties, and deindustrialization is more likely in predominantly black counties" (1988, 83). On the other hand, equation 1 also registers a positive relationship between job creation and the number of African Americans registered to vote between 1958 and 1967. This suggests, perhaps, that the politics of race are more important than the demographics. In an analysis of race and politics in eastern North Carolina, Vincent Roscigno and Donald Tomaskovic-Devey (1994) argue that social and economic outcomes are structured by the combined effects of race and class. Poverty rates, for instance, are highest in counties that combine both large African American populations and political domination by a traditional landed plantation elite. The latter shape local policy so as to perpetuate poor educational facilities and inadequate public services generally and to maintain relatively low levels of black political mobilization in order to keep African American workers tied to agriculture and related activities. Similarly, Paul Luebke (1998) has argued that the textile industry, though technologically modernizing, remains in the same "traditional" camp as agriculture and other low-wage sectors when it comes to political and social development. If these arguments are correct and can be generalized to the rural South beyond North Carolina, they may help to contextualize the findings reported here. The pools of surplus, low-wage African American labor power that exist in the South's rural areas can only become targets for textile industry relocation if the traditional social and political structures that formerly constrained them are weakened or destroyed.

Finally, as a variety of commentators on Southern politics have stressed, state activities and policy have always played an important role in the textile industry's low-wage, high-exploitation Southern accumulation strategy (Cobb 1993; Key 1949; Wood 1986). Tax regimes have traditionally been regressive, relying heavily on consumption taxes while limiting the burden of businesses and property generally. Similarly, patterns of public expenditure have been designed to reinforce an environment of low wages and minimal social services on the one hand and to provide for industrial relocation incentive packages on the other. The last two independent variables in our equation are intended to test for the effects of state policy on the pattern of recent textile employment change. We use the per capita property tax rate to test the relationship between tax regimes and textile employment change, while the share of county public expenditures for highway construction provides an indicator of a pattern of expenditure tilted toward physical rather than social infrastructure. As we might predict on the basis of the literature, equation 1 suggests that every dollar increase in per capita property taxes is associated with a reduction of six textile jobs. Similarly, counties that direct a relatively large percentage of their expenditures to the construction of highways do relatively well, gaining thirty-seven textile jobs for every percentage point increase. It appears that textile job expansion gravitates to counties that keep property taxes low and emphasize the development of physical rather than the human infrastructure.

Equation 1 cannot be claimed as a full analysis of the determinants of Southern county-level textile employment change. A large proportion of the variation in employment change remains unexplained and several factors (such as state and local relocation incentives; transportation and communications networks) could be added. Nevertheless, the data analyzed here suggest that, despite (or because of) rapid technological change and the uncertainties that result from capitalist globalization, the pattern of textile employment restructuring from 1972 to 1992 retains many of the characteristics of earlier periods of textile development.

One of these characteristics is race, which has played a variety of important historical roles in textile accumulation. Traditionally, textile jobs were reserved for whites, while racism and the threat of black replacement workers were used to maintain labor discipline and work intensity. Since the mid-1960s, tight labor markets in metropolitan areas and civil rights legislation have forced textile corporations to integrate their labor forces, and black workers have come to play an important role as textile workers. Since the results reported above suggest a negative relationship between textile employment change and county racial concentrations, however, we need to try to shed more light on the topic.[5]

Recent research has established the important contextual effect of race and the existence of strong race-class interactions (Alt 1994; Roscigno and Kimble 1995; Roscigno and Tomaskovic-Devey 1994; Wood 1996). Equation 2 follows the lead of this research by investigating the moderating effect of county racial concentration. The three statistically significant interaction terms in equation 2 indicate that levels of African American population concentration condition the size and direction of some of the effects discussed above.[6]

Two patterns are present in these conditional effects. One is evident in the interaction between county racial concentration and the size of the county labor force. Here, black concentration exacerbates the tendency of counties with large labor forces to lose textile jobs. Counties with larger civilian labor forces in 1970 lost more textile employment in the ensuing two decades than counties with smaller labor forces and they did so at a rate that increased with higher black population concentrations. In an all-white county, an increase of one thousand persons in the civilian labor force in 1970 is associated with a net loss of ten textile jobs from 1972 to 1992. At "low" African American population concentrations, the size of the loss associated with a one-thousand increase in the labor force increases to $(-0.00001 - (.0000009*13.09))*1,000 =$ a net loss of 22 jobs. In "medium" and "high" black concentration counties, the associated job losses are 38 and 53 respectively.

In the two other interaction variables, the interaction coefficients moderate, rather than reinforce, the direction of the main effects of the independent variables at higher levels of black concentration. If we take black voter mobilization as an example, in a county with a low black concentration, an increase of a thousand black voters is associated with an increase of 335 textile jobs between 1972 and 1992. At a medium black concentration, the rate of increase falls to $0.0004 - (0.000005 * 30.65)$, which is 0.000247, or 247 jobs. At high concentrations, the equivalent figure is a gain of 159 jobs. In the handful of counties with black concentrations above 70 percent, the positive impact of black mobilization on textile employment begins to disappear. In other words, the rate at which the weakening of elite domination of traditional social and political structures increases textile employment is highest in counties where African Americans are in the minority. As black concentration increases, the rate at which textile employment grows is gradually reduced, tapering off in the context of large black majorities. For textile capital perhaps, resistance to elite domination is one thing; the possibility of local black political power is another.

Finally, while the main effect of property taxes on county change in textile employment is negative (which can be interpreted as the effect when the value of the moderator variable is zero), the conditional effect shows that the negative effect of property tax on employment change diminishes as the percentage of a county's black population increases. At low and medium levels of black concentration, higher property tax levels reduce textile employment. But beyond about a 35 percent black population share, increases in average property taxes are associated with net textile job creation after 1972.

Equation 2 of table 2.2 therefore allows us to refine our image of the political economy of textile employment change by adding the moderating effects of race and illuminating the complex interactions of race, class, and state that facilitate (or not) black employment. To summarize the findings of our two-stage analysis, counties that have been most successful at retaining or expanding textile employment in a period of general contraction are:

- rural counties or counties with relatively small civilian labor forces, with only limited competition from other industrial employers, and with predominantly white populations. The combination of large labor force and high black concentration accelerates textile job loss;
- counties with relatively large numbers of small-scale, economically marginal farms;
- counties in which political mobilization in the period around the Voting Rights Act had been sufficient to weaken traditional social and political structures and allow the penetration of external capital, but not counties in which large politically mobilized African American populations threatened existing white political power;
- counties in which tax and public expenditure regimes are skewed in favor of capital and the propertied in general, and against workers and the poor (i.e., where private inequalities are reinforced by the state). Higher average property taxes are associated with net textile job loss, except in counties whose populations are more than about a third African American. Here, higher property taxes are associated with net textile job creation.

The traditional relationship between the textile industry and African Americans has been altered substantially in recent decades as the industry has been forced to employ greater numbers of black workers. Nevertheless, the results reported here suggest that there is still an important conditionality to black textile employment as the industry continues to pursue a spatial fix by gradually decamping from its Carolina home to greenfield sites in the deeper South. In general, textile employment growth occurs within limits set by county black population concentrations and the way they interact with other social and political forces. Since African Americans remain a major source of cheap surplus labor in the region, it appears that the racial logic of textile employment change may be partially at odds with the economic logic of an industry undergoing restructuring while trying to maintain traditional social and spatial security zones. Our data suggest that counties with relatively large black concentrations can attract textile jobs, but only if they are prepared to pay a premium. To be successful, they must raise taxes to above-average levels, presumably in order to provide the necessary physical infrastructure and underwrite corporate risk to a greater extent than that expected in white counties. However, caution should be used with this interpretation, as it does not adequately reflect possible forms of "new racism" resulting from the recent influx of Hispanic workers into Southern labor markets. Such analysis requires more contextualized data currently obtainable only from case study and is beyond the scope of this paper.

Southern historian David Carlton has commented that in view of the great human cost of a century of textile accumulation, it is "arguable that the traditional textile industry, at least, is an incubus of which the South may be well rid" (1992, 1146). Though it is in some sense difficult to disagree with the spirit of Carlton's comment, this paper suggests that the obituary may be premature. Our empirical results are consistent with Doreen Massey's (1984) emphasis on the embeddedness of local industrial employment structures in contexts that reflect previous rounds of capital-labor and state-citizen relations and with Lobao, Rulli, and Brown's (1999) conclusion that relationships between local level inequality and manufacturing employment remained similar in 1970 and 1990. For the Southern textile industry, textile employment continues to develop unevenly, simultaneously reflecting and reproducing the spatial fix within which the industry has historically been embedded.

Arguments about the decline of the textile industry and its regional accumulation strategy rest on a partial view of globalization and on insufficient attention to the contemporary specifics of industrial strategy, to the dynamics of the industry's Southern security zone, and to the embeddedness of the industry in a local context where race relations are especially important. The textile industry is currently in a long period of modernization, dominated by the introduction of new technologies and organizational forms. Yet these modern elements are integrated into an overall spatial and industrial restructuring package that is reminiscent of the traditional textile accumulation strategy in two significant ways. First, it retains commitments to low wages, to a union-free business climate, and to small-town, rural settings with racially structured labor markets. Second, it continues to rely on sympathetic state and local governments and a skewed pattern of public policy in its attempts to manage the lock-in effects of fixed capital investment and past practices and the new uncertainties produced by global economic restructuring.

Recently, North Carolina firms, such as Cone and Guilford Mills, are building plants in Mexico to produce basic fabrics (e.g., denim) for the Mexican and Caribbean apparel industry (Millman 2000). The firms are attracted by low wages, state-financed road improvements, and cheap power and water. Previously, the firms produced fabric in the United States and then sent it to Mexico for sewing into clothes that were imported back into the United States. Anticipating China's entry into the WTO, the firms are now establishing integrated production lines in Mexico. While this may appear to counter our analysis of spatial security zones, we argue that this recent development reinforces our position that regimes of accumulation and modes of regulation are embedded in history and a local geographical context. Mexico becomes a textile production security zone only if the complex set of social relations that enforce capital's power over labor can be constructed across geographical space. It is not a question of running away from North Carolina but of reproducing the accumulation strategy in Mexico.

Globalization is not a free-market free-for-all, but a structured process in which the instability and contradictions inherent in the expansion process necessitate strategies of uncertainty reduction around the world that are similar to the one we describe in the South. Only those places that can provide both the production conditions that textile industry needs and the associated political and economic guarantees can serve as textile platforms. While it is premature to tell what the long-term impact of the Mexican expansion will have on Southern textiles, the formation of a regional textile division of labor within North America that is designed to perpetuate the Southern security zone is a distinct possibility. In this regard, we can regard NAFTA and other free-trade agreements as part of a campaign of regional uncertainty reduction and geographic expansion of spatial security zones.

Notes

1. *Textile industry* refers to the mills that manufacture yarn, thread, and fabric for clothing by spinning, weaving, and knitting in highly automated mills. In 1995 the textile industry employed approximately 650,000 workers in the United States. *Apparel industry* refers to the firms that cut and assemble finished goods for the retail market. Most of the 915,000 workers in 1995 are sewing machine operators (Murray 1995).

2. Easterbrook (1990) argues that macro-uncertainty—"the continuous pattern of stressful uncertainties, political, social, economic and ideational, in which investment decisions involving time must proceed"—and the politics of uncertainty reduction are the central concepts in the political economy of long-term development. From this perspective, the structure of the world economy at any point in time is not simply a reflection of the distribution of factors of production, it is also the product of past strategies of uncertainty reduction that involve a potentially wide array of "security devices" (e.g., diversification). Corporate decisions about restructuring thus involve not only considerations of profit, but also the need for political, cultural, and geographic security zones whose construction is not a simple matter, but rather a product of long-term engagement in "power politics" (Easterbrook 1990, 5–7).

3. Employment in textiles in the United States peaked at 1.3 million workers in 1948 and has dropped by almost 50 percent, to approximately 624,000 workers in 1996. Three states—Georgia, North Carolina, and South Carolina—account for the majority of employment (Mittelhauser 1997).

4. All counties are potentially included, even those with no textile employees

in either year, but the availability of data for the independent variables reduced the N to 535. In addition, we initially included a measure of population size as an independent variable, but there was strong multicollinearity with other independent variables in the model and therefore we dropped the population size variable. Subsequent tests for multicollinearity revealed no major problems. A correlation table is available from the authors.

5. Starting in the late 1980s Hispanics moved into many of the labor-intensive jobs in the construction, meatpacking, and hospitality industries. Estimates of the 1997 Hispanic population of North Carolina range from 149,390 to 229,902 (Johnson-Webb 1999). Evidence from case studies shows that they are moving into low-wage manufacturing, but this is after the 1992 data used in the current study (Schulman and Anderson 1999).

6. The relationships discussed here are derived from the bilinear interaction model ($y = a + b_1 x_1 + b_2 x_2 + b_3 x_1 x_2 + e$) and calculated from the coefficients in table 2.2, equation 2. Following Jaccard, Turrisi, and Wan 1990, b_3 is interpreted as the number of units that the slope of y on x_1 changes, given a one-unit change in x_2. The slope coefficient of x_1 at some value of x_2 is $b_1 + b_3 x_2$. Where b_3 reverses the sign of b_1—that is, the value of x_2 at which the slope changes direction is b_1/b_3. In the discussion, the values that define low, medium, and high black counties are, respectively, one standard deviation below the mean black county population concentration for 1970, the mean, and one standard deviation above the mean. Their numerical equivalents for 535 Southern counties in 1970 are as follows: 13.09%; 30.65%; and 48.21%.

References

Alt, James E. 1994. "The Impact of the Voting Rights Act on Black and White Voter Registration in the South." In *Quiet Revolution in the South,* ed. Chandler Davidson and Bernard Grofman, 351–77. Princeton: Princeton University Press.

Anderson, Cynthia D. 2000. *The Social Consequences of Economic Restructuring in the Textile Industry: Change in a Southern Mill Village.* New York: Garland.

Billings, Dwight B. 1979. *Planters and The Making of a "New South": Class, Politics, and Development in North Carolina, 1865–1900.* Chapel Hill: University of North Carolina Press.

Boyer, Robert, and Daniel Drache. 1996. Introduction to *States against Markets,* ed. Robert Boyer and Daniel Drache, 1–30. London: Routledge.

Brecher, J., and T. Costello. 1998. *Global Village or Global Pillage: Economic Reconstruction from the Bottom Up.* Cambridge, Mass.: South End Press.

Callahan, Marion. 1997. "Rocky Times." *Raleigh News and Observer,* October 5.

Carlton, David L. 1992. Review of *Hanging by a Thread: Social Change in Southern Textiles,* ed. Jeffrey Leiter, Michael D. Schulman, and Rhonda Zingraff. *Social Forces* 70:1145–46.

Carney, Susan. 2002. "Alabama Strong with Autos." *Autos Insider,* April 3, <http://detnews.com/2002/autosinsider/0204/06/b01–455636.htm.

Cash, Wilbur J. 1941. *The Mind of the South.* New York: Knopf.

Cobb, James C. 1993. *The Selling of the South.* 2d ed. Urbana: University of Illinois Press.

Colclough, Glenna. 1988. "Uneven Development and Racial Composition in the Deep South, 1970–1980." *Rural Sociology* 53:73–86.

Dicken, Peter. 1998. *Global Shift: Transforming the World Economy.* New York: Guilford Press.

Easterbrook, W. T. 1990. *North American Patterns of Growth and Development.* Toronto: University of Toronto Press.

Frederickson, Mary. 1982. "Four Decades of Change: Black Workers in Southern Textiles." *Radical America* 16:27–44.

Gaventa, John, and Barbara E. Smith. 1991. "The Deindustrialization of the Textile South: A Case Study." In *Hanging by a Thread,* ed. by Jeffrey Leiter, Michael Schulman, and Rhonda Zingraff, 181–96. Ithaca: ILR Press.

Glasmeier, Amy K., and Robin M. Leichenko. 1996. "From Free Market Rhetoric to Free Market Reality: The Future of the U.S. South in an Era of Globalization." *International Journal of Urban and Regional Research* 20:601–15.

Hall, Jacquelyn Dowd, James Leloudis, Robert Korstad, Mary Murphy, Lu Ann Jones, and Christopher B. Daly. 1987. *Like a Family.* Chapel Hill: University of North Carolina Press.

Harrison, Bennett. 1994. *Lean and Mean.* New York: Basic Books.

Harrison, Bennett, and Barry Bluestone. 1988. *The Great U-Turn.* New York: Basic Books.

Harvey, David. 1982. *The Limits to Capital.* Chicago: University of Chicago Press.

Heckman, James J., and Brook S. Payne. 1989. "Determining the Impact of Federal Antidiscrimination Policy on the Economic Status of Blacks: A Study of South Carolina." *American Economic Review* 79:136–77.

Jaccard, James, Robert Turrisi, and Choi Wan. 1990. *Interaction Effects in Multiple Regression.* Beverly Hills: Sage.

Jackman, Mary. 1994. *The Velvet Glove: Paternalism and Conflict in Gender, Class, and Race Relations.* Berkeley: University of California Press.

Johnson-Webb, K. D. 1999. "Hispanics are Changing North Carolina." *Journal of Common Sense* 5 (1): 8–13.

Key, V. O., Jr. 1949. *Southern Politics in State and Nation.* New York: Knopf.

Lobao, Linda, J. Rulli, and L. A. Brown, 1999. "Macrolevel Theory and Local-Level Inequality: Industrial Structure, Institutional Arrangements, and the Political Economy of Redistribution, 1970 and 1990." *Annals of the Association of American Geographers* 89:571–601.

Luebke, Paul. 1998. *Tar Heel Politics 2000.* Chapel Hill: University of North Carolina Press.

Lyson, Thomas A. 1989. *Two Sides to the Sunbelt.* New York: Praeger.

Massey, Doreen. 1984. *Spatial Divisions of Labour: Social Structures and the Geography of Production.* Basingstoke, England: Macmillan.

Matthews, Donald R., and James W. Prothro. 1996. *Negroes and the New Southern Politics.* New York: Harcourt, Brace.

Millman, Joel. 1998. "Mexican Textile Makers Find a Protector in NAFTA." *Wall Street Journal,* July 21.

———. 2000. "Mexico Weaves More Ties—No. 1 in Garments, It Might Soon Be Top Textile Source." *Wall Street Journal,* August 21.

Mittelhauser, Mark. 1996. "Job Loss and Survival Strategies in the Textile and Apparel Industries." *Occupational Outlook Quarterly* 40 (3): 18–28.

———. 1997. "Employment Trends in Textiles and Apparel, 1972–2005." *Monthly Labor Review* 120 (9): 24–35.

Morrissett, Bill, and Coco Dawson. 1998. "Pace of Mill Mergers Is Quickening." Textile World 148 (5): 50–54.

Murray, Lauren A. 1995. "Unraveling Employment Trends in Textiles and Apparel." *Monthly Labor Review* 118 (8): 62–72.

Obermayer, Joel. 1996. "Wake Forest Plant Closing Will Idle 730." *Raleigh News and Observer,* June 6. <http://www.news-observer.com/newsroom/nao/biz/060696/bizt_1105.html>.

Pope, Liston. 1942. *Millhands and Preachers: A Study of Gastonia.* New Haven: Yale University Press.

Roscigno, Vincent J., and M. Keith Kimble. 1995. "Elite Power, Race, and the

Persistence of Low Unionization in the South." *Work and Occupations* 22:271–300.

Roscigno, Vincent J., and Donald Tomaskovic-Devey. 1994. "Racial Politics in the Contemporary South: Toward a More Critical Understanding." *Social Problems* 41:585–607.

Schulman, Michael D., and Cynthia D. Anderson. 1999. "The Dark Side of the Force: A Case Study of Restructuring and Social Capital." *Rural Sociology* 64:351–72.

Storper, Michael, and Richard Walker. 1989. *The Capitalist Imperative: Territory, Technology, and Industrial Growth.* Oxford: Basil Blackwell.

Tomaskovic-Devey, Donald. 1991. *Sundown on the Sunbelt.* Raleigh, N.C.: Ford Foundation/Aspen Institute.

Tonelson, Alan. 2000. *The Race to the Bottom: Why a Worldwide Worker Surplus and Uncontrolled Free Trade are Sinking American Living Standards.* Boulder: Westview.

Toyne, Brian, J. S. Arpan, A. H. Barnett, D. A. Ricks, and T. A. Shimp. 1984. *The Global Textile Industry.* London: Allen and Unwin.

United States. Bureau of the Census. 1978. County and City Data Book Consolidated File, County Data 1947–1977 (machine-readable data file). Washington, DC: Department of Commerce, Data Users Services Division.

———. 1990. *Statistical Abstract of the United States.* 110th ed. Washington, D.C.: GPO.

———. 1998. *Statistical Abstract of the United States.* 118th ed. Washington, D.C.: GPO.

United States. Commission on Civil Rights. 1968. *Political Participation.* Washington, D.C.: GPO.

United States. Department of Labor. 1994. *Textile Plant Employment in the Southeast: 1993.* Southeast Division, Bureau of Labor Statistics, Atlanta.

Wood, Phillip J. 1986. *Southern Capitalism.* Durham, N.C.: Duke University Press.

———. 1991. "Determinants of Industrialization on the North American 'Periphery.'" In *Hanging By a Thread,* ed. Jeffrey Leiter, Michael Schulman, and Rhonda Zingraff, 58–78. Ithaca: ILR Press.

———. 1996. "The Political Economy of Discrimination: Industrialization, Race, and Voter Registration in the South." *American Review of Politics* 17 (Summer): 89–112.

Wright, Gavin. 1986. *Old South, New South.* New York: Basic Books.

————. 1987. "Postbellum Southern Labor Markets." In *Quantity and Quiddity,* ed. Peter Kilby, 98–134. Middletown, Conn.: Wesleyan University Press.

Zingraff, Rhonda. 1991. "Facing Extinction?" In *Hanging By a Thread,* ed. Jeffrey Leiter, Michael Schulman, and Rhonda Zingraff, 199–216. Ithaca: ILR Press.

3

Meat Processing in Rural America

Economic Powerhouse or Problem?

Mark S. Henry, Mark R. Drabenstott, and Kristin Mitchell

INDUSTRIAL ORGANIZATION ISSUES in both meat and poultry processing—market power, efficiency, risk shifting—have been examined by Connor (1996), Connor and Schick (1996), Knoeber and Thurman (1995), MacDonald and Ollinger (2000), and Melton and Huffman (1995). However, rural development implications of the evolving spatial distribution of meat and poultry processing are largely unexplored.[1] Some case studies describe the social consequences for rural counties with new large-scale meat-processing plants (e.g., Stull, Broadway, and Griffith 1995), but surprisingly little attention has been paid to documenting the rural development dimensions of the dramatic changes in the industrial organization of the poultry-processing industry since the 1960s and more recent changes in beef and hog processing.[2] Given that rural development policy should, in part, focus on manufacturing industries for which rural areas can compete effectively with metropolitan areas, it is important to understand the economic forces shaping the geography of production in industries that are promoted as rural oriented—like food processing.

Recent manufacturing employment trends give credibility to a focus on food-processing employment opportunities in rural America for

several reasons. First, the Economic Research Service (ERS 1998) identified food processing as the most important manufacturing sector (two-
digit Standard Industrial Code aggregation) in rural America. At the
two-digit SIC level, about 14 percent of all nonmetropolitan manufacturing jobs are in food processing (SIC 20). The next largest industries, industrial machinery and chemicals, each provide between 8
and 9 percent of all rural manufacturing jobs (ERS 1998).[3] From 1989
to 1994, while all rural manufacturing jobs grew by 1.2 percent, food-
processing jobs expanded by 8.5 percent (ERS 1998). With about one-
half of all rural food-processing jobs, the meat products sector (SICs
2011, 2013, 2015) is particularly important in shaping trends in rural
food processing. Moreover, rural counties contain 52 percent of all
meat products jobs, while in every other food-processing industry the
vast majority of jobs are still in metropolitan counties (ERS 1998).

Recent growth in food-processing employment in rural counties
has been dominated by meat packing—the only Food and Kindred
Products industry projected to add jobs from 1998 to 2008 and at a
healthy 1.4 percent annual growth rate (Gale and Kilkenny 2000).
While most food-processing industries were shedding jobs between
1989 and 1994, employment in plants processing meat products grew
by 17 percent, to about 420,000 by 1994—a growth rate more than
three times that of the next-fastest-growing food-processing industry,
food grains (ERS 1998, 13).

A second reason for focusing on meat packing as a possible source
of new rural jobs is suggested by research on the spatial distribution of
rural manufacturing. For example, Kim, Barkley, and Henry (2000) find
strong tendencies toward spatial agglomeration of manufacturing
establishments in industries that are characterized by large plant size,
low-skill labor requirements, and where localities offer natural advantages in the procurement of raw material inputs. Meat packing has
dramatically changed its industrial organization since the 1960s and
now strongly matches the industry characteristics that promote increased spatial concentration. This raises concerns for rural development
focused on meat packing since many rural communities are likely to
see small meat-packing establishments close down while a few rural
communities experience expansions of large meat-packing plants.

Two rural development issues underscore the importance of the changes in scale and geography of production in meat and poultry processing. First, there is the smaller-is-better thesis that an array of smaller manufacturing establishments in a rural county will yield a robust local economy while the domination of rural counties by a few large plants results in lower levels of community well-being (Lyson and Tolbert 1996; Tolbert, Lyson, and Irwin 1998).

Second, other analysts suggest a link between the size distribution of rural manufacturing plants and rural employment growth—that networks of small-scale, flexible, and specialized production units are more efficient than large-scale units (e.g., Storper and Walker 1989). A smaller-is-better rural development strategy implies that programs to promote rural industrial districts should be pursued.

However, since the 1960s, the organization of production in meat products has shifted toward large-scale processing plants that are integrated with feedlot operations or contracts with "growers" of animals (or both). Thus, the economics of production suggests that firms charting the future course of industrial organization in meat and poultry processing envision a few large plants, while some rural development analysts seek ways to promote industrial districts and flexible networks of smaller establishments. Of course, it may be that the two concepts of how industry should be organized are complements, not substitutes. For example, rural industrial districts with networked groups of small establishments in industries linked to meat processing (food-processing machinery and equipment, repair and business services, etc.) may be able to provide the array of products and services needed by large plants collectively that individual companies cannot.

In this chapter, we document the changing geography of meat and poultry processing and examine the smaller-is-better issue by analysis of job creation and destruction rates by size of meat- and poultry-processing plants across counties. In the next section, basic trends in the geography of production in meat and poultry processing are depicted. This is followed in the third section by empirical analyses to identify plant and geographical characteristics that are important determinants of the changing spatial distribution of these industries across counties in the United States. In the concluding section, the effects on rural development from the changing geography of meat and poultry processing are examined.

The New Geography of Production in Meat and Poultry Processing

Analysis of establishment data from the Longitudinal Research Database, Center for Economic Studies, U.S. Bureau of the Census (table 3.1), reveals fundamental changes in the geography of the meat and poultry processing industries since the early 1960s.

CHANGING EMPLOYMENT SHARES

The most striking change in the spatial distribution of employment in meat packing (SIC 2011) is the loss of employment share, from 36 percent in 1963 to 11 percent in 1992, in core urban counties of the largest metropolitan areas (Beale code 0). Most of the reduction occurred from 1982 to 1992. At the same time, rural counties gained meat-packing employment share—from 39 percent in 1963 to 52 percent by 1992. Among urban counties, the smallest (Beale code 3) gained share, from 13 percent in 1963 to 21 percent in 1992, while medium-size urban counties (Beale code 2) lost share, from 21 percent to 13 percent over the same period. Since the Beale codes are 1989 characterizations of the rural-urban continuum, it is likely that many of these small MSA counties in 1989 were nonmetro counties in 1963 and 1972. So the small metro gain may simply reflect activity in formerly rural counties. By 1992 the largest share of meat-packing employment (31 percent) was found in the most remote rural counties—those not adjacent to a metropolitan area. In effect, by 1992 most meat-packing employment had moved from the urban core, where it was concentrated in 1963, to smaller urban centers and to the most rural areas of the country.

While other meat processing (SIC 2013) remains mostly urban despite recent rural gains, poultry processing is primarily rural (63 percent of employment was in rural counties by 1992). Unlike meat packing and other meat processing, poultry processing (SIC 2015) has been mostly rural since 1963. Meat packing is following two spatial patterns evident in the poultry industry for decades—movement to the rural hinterland and spatial concentration. From 1963 to 1992 there was almost a ninefold increase in spatial concentration of meat-packing plants in fewer states and counties using an Ellison-Glaeser (1997) index.

The second striking result in table 3.1 is the dramatic decline in real wages per production worker in meat packing from 1963 to 1992 and especially the sharp drop across both rural and urban counties since 1982. Reductions in real-wage rates of 20 percent to 30 percent are typical across most county types from 1982 to 1992. While wages for meat-packing production workers were generally double those in poultry processing from 1963 to 1982, by 1992 there was little difference in average wages paid across the meat products industry.

Surprisingly, rural counties have not been low-wage enclaves in the meat-packing industry. Over the thirty-year period, on average in each county type, most urban and rural county plants had similar levels of production worker wages. In 1992 smaller urban county types (Beale codes 2 and 3) had wages similar to the most remote rural (nonadjacent) counties. The results in table 3.1 present a mixed view of the role of wage costs and productivity (proxied by value added per production worker) in explaining changes in meat-packing employment across rural and urban counties over the thirty years. This suggests that a broader array of economic forces is shaping the geography of meat packing across the nation.

Why Do Meat Plants Expand Where They Do?

What explains the dramatic shift of meat packing to rural counties while processed meats remain urban oriented and poultry processing,

Table 3.1
Rural-Urban Changes in the Location of Meat Products Plants, 1963–1992

Meat Packing (SIC 2011)—Characteristics across the Beale Continuum

Beale Code	Employment Shares (percent)				Value Added/Worker (1,000)*				Hourly Wage*			
	1963	1972	1982	1992	1963	1972	1982	1992	1963	1972	1982	1992
Metro												
0	36.0	23.6	16.6	10.8	44.00	69.28	65.68	54.08	12.82	14.58	13.22	9.76
1	1.6	2.5	2.9	3.0	39.09	43.33	58.72	48.83	7.97	9.72	8.95	8.04
2	23.7	23.2	20.6	13.2	42.83	54.90	53.87	42.72	11.94	14.47	13.8	8.08
3	17.6	20.8	19.8	21.2	47.15	51.48	59.04	66.79	12.61	14.76	13.92	8.37
Nonmetro												
4,6,8	10.5	14.2	17.0	20.9	43.60	57.89	74.17	74.87	12.08	14.39	13.28	9.15
5,7,9	10.6	15.7	23.0	30.8	44.00	58.07	64.83	47.50	11.19	13.06	13.42	8.19

Other Meat Processing (SIC 2013)—Characteristics across the Beale Continuum

Beale Code	Employment Shares (percent)				Value Added/Worker (1,000)*				Hourly Wage*			
	1963	1972	1982	1992	1963	1972	1982	1992	1963	1972	1982	1992
Metro												
0	77.6	68.4	51.5	40.7	48.74	58.36	68.98	67.49	11.05	14.30	13.81	10.13
1	0.7	1.3	2.1	2.7	38.05	39.89	55.68	40.43	6.66	8.63	9.24	8.30
2	13.2	15.2	20.8	22.9	47.49	58.69	50.52	69.54	9.74	11.22	12.11	10.65
3	2.7	5.3	8.4	11.7	40.76	49.76	62.33	62.63	8.81	11.40	12.00	8.51
Nonmetro												
4,6,8	2.1	5.5	10.8	11.4	39.91	49.51	68.43	56.11	7.89	11.92	11.63	8.61
5,7,9	3.7	4.3	6.5	10.7	37.83	64.8	68.75	56.97	8.39	9.14	11.73	8.96

Poultry Processing (SIC 2015)—Characteristics across the Beale Continuum

Beale Code	Employment Shares (percent)				Value Added/Worker (1,000)*				Hourly Wage*			
	1963	1972	1982	1992	1963	1972	1982	1992	1963	1972	1982	1992
Metro												
0	13.1	9.2	6.6	4.8	30.58	38.90	31.92	47.35	6.23	7.87	8.68	8.46
1	4.0	3.6	4.5	3.7	22.74	28.42	26.33	34.64	5.37	7.46	7.10	7.08
2	16.6	14.7	14.4	13.3	25.23	28.33	30.59	37.82	6.09	7.99	8.20	8.12
3	10.2	11.1	13.4	15.7	24.93	24.53	26.03	35.91	5.75	7.25	7.01	7.33
Nonmetro												
4,6,8	30.3	29.3	28.6	30.6	23.16	27.67	28.04	31.08	5.92	7.43	7.42	7.23
5,7,9	25.9	32.1	32.6	31.9	23.27	29.57	28.30	33.56	5.66	7.34	7.26	7.19

*1992 dollars

Beale codes (4, 6, 8 are adjacent to an MSA; 5, 7, 9 are nonadjacent to an MSA)

0. Core: central counties of an MSA; population > 1 million.

1. Fringe: other counties of core MSA.

2. Medium: counties in MSA: population 250,000–1,000,000.

3. Small: counties in MSA: population < 250,000.

4. Adjacent to an MSA: urbanized: largest place has population > 20,000.

5. Nonadjacent to an MSA: urbanized: largest place has population > 20,000.

6. Adjacent to an MSA: less urbanized: largest place has population > 2,500–19,999.

7. Nonadjacent to an MSA: less urbanized: largest place has population > 2,500–19,999.

8. Adjacent to an MSA: completely rural: largest place has population < 2,500.

9. Nonadjacent to an MSA: completely rural: largest place has population < 2,500.

a mostly rural activity? Analysts point to three explanations: traditional location analysis focused on labor costs and changes in transportation economics; a strengthening of agglomeration economies; and changes in the scale of plant production.

LABOR COSTS AND PRODUCTIVITY

The few empirical studies that have attempted to identify the causes of the shifts provide mixed messages. Martin, McHugh, and Johnson (1991) found that total factory productivity varies across rural and urban counties in meat products manufacturing (SIC 201). Between 1972 and 1982, they show that meat products plants in metropolitan counties (Beale codes 0–3), all else being equal, produce 5.2 percent more output than plants in small urban counties (Beale codes 4–5) or in rural counties (Beale codes 6–9) (1991, 15). However, after adjusting for the effects of plant scale on productivity, the location advantage for metropolitan counties disappears except for the smallest plants (26). The findings of Martin, McHugh, and Johnson (1991) demonstrate that rural counties can compete effectively with metro areas for meat products employment in all but the smallest plants (perhaps those that produce specialty meats requiring a proximate and large metropolitan market).

Gale (1997) finds that both labor productivity and wage rates are generally lower in rural manufacturing plants than in metropolitan plants—putting them at risk of competing with very low wage areas of the world. Melton and Huffman (1995, 484) hypothesize that firms in meat processing seek low-cost labor regions. However, Goetz (1997b) finds no wage rate effect on establishment growth in the meat products industry from 1987 to 1993 using either state or county observations.

TRANSPORTATION ECONOMICS

One shortcoming of the Goetz and Martin, McHugh, and Johnson studies is the aggregation to a three-digit SIC code (201) that mixes plants that slaughter livestock and poultry (SICs 2011 and 2015) with plants that process meat into products like sausages (SIC 2013). One might expect that SIC 2011 and 2015 would prefer rural locations near sources of livestock and poultry while meat processors would look to market access via more densely developed transportation hubs.

Since firms choose locations for new plants to maximize profits, they must evaluate trade-offs between transporting raw materials to the processing plant and the finished product to consumers. In general, processing operations that result in large weight losses in important inputs (like cattle or hogs) before the final product is shipped to users tend to locate near the source of the raw material to avoid transportation of the materials that will not be part of the finished product. When meat packers located near Midwest urban centers in the early part of the twentieth century, there were cost advantages to locating near consumers: stockyards and processors located near urban rail and river transportation nodes. Perishable animal carcasses were warehoused and distributed to nearby wholesalers and retailers who made the final cuts for consumers.

In the 1970s meat-packing plants began to extend their processing activities, for example, to boxed beef products like frozen ground-beef patties. With truck transport the most efficient mode of transporting meat products from processor to final user, transportation cost advantages turned in favor of locating processing plants near the source of the animals in selected regions of rural America. This is not a new story (see Ward 1998a and 1998b, for example). However, it is an excellent example of the natural advantage some industries have that favor increasing spatial concentration.

AGGLOMERATION ECONOMIES

Ellison and Glaeser (1997) attribute the spatial agglomeration of an industry's establishments (industry clustering) to two principal forces: industry-specific spillovers and natural advantages.[4] Industry-specific spillovers are economies external to the establishments but internal to the regional industry cluster. These external economies are referred to as static localization economies if they are attributable to the current scale of the industry cluster (e.g., employment or number of establishments).[5]

Alternatively, Marshall-Arrow-Romer externalities are derived from the accumulation of knowledge and knowledge spillovers among local firms in the same industry (Glaeser et al. 1992; Henderson, Kuncoro, and Turner 1995). The build-up and sharing of knowledge among area firms in the industry are enhanced by a local legacy of and specialization in a particular industry. Both static and dynamic externalities encourage the clustering of industry establishments in a limited number of locations. Yet Ellison and Glaeser suggest that "some of the most extreme cases of concentration are likely due to natural advantages" (1997, 921).[6]

If these agglomerative forces are strengthening over time in meat products, we should observe increasing spatial concentration of employment in these industries at both the state and county levels. Moreover, future growth in these industries would be expected to continue to concentrate in regions where there is already a strong presence. To test for changes in spatial concentration over time, we construct the Ellison-Glaeser (EG) index for SICs 2011, 2013, and 2015 for each of the five years of the Census of Manufacturers from 1963 to 1992 (1997 data were not available at the time of this analysis).[7] If the EG index is increasing over time, then geographic concentration has increased. If the EG is higher for SIC 2015 than 2011, then poultry processing is more geographically concentrated than meat processing.

THE EG INDEX

Significant geographical concentration in an industry exists if the actual clustering of plants across regions exceeds what is expected from a random distribution of plants across space. If plants are located as a dartboard throw by firms (with regions like counties as the targets on the board), then the industry is not spatially concentrated. In practice almost all industries exhibit some degree of geographical concentration (Ellison and Glaeser 1997). The EG index controls for changes over time and across industries in the number of plants of different employment sizes in the industry. In effect, it allows comparisons of geographical concentration between industries and over time even as the size and number of plants changes.

To find the EG index of geographical concentration, each region's share of SICs 2011, 2013, and 2015 employment is divided by the region's share of total manufacturing employment. Differences are squared and summed to arrive at a G statistic. The G statistic is adjusted for the size distribution of plants in the industry to reflect varying degrees of plant concentration in the industry. This step recognizes that plants are discrete observations—some with thousands of employees and some with a handful. These adjustments are made using indices that measure plant shares of total industry activity (see the appendix for computational procedures). The EG indices in table 3.2 are based on individual plant observations from 1963 to 1992.

In 1963 the poultry processing industry was about ten times more geographically concentrated than meat processing at both the state and county level (see table 3.2). An EG index of 0.05 or greater at the state level for four-digit industries is about double the median industry EG value (in 1987) and about equal to the mean EG for these industries (Ellison and Glaeser 1997, 908). Using this rough guideline, it is reasonable to conclude that poultry processing had a fairly high degree of geographical concentration as early as 1963, while meat processing was very widely dispersed throughout the United States compared to other four-digit industries.

Table 3.2
The Ellison-Glaser Index of Spatial Concentration

Year	Meat-Packing Plants SIC 2011		Prepared Meats SIC 2013		Poultry-Processing Plants SIC 2015	
	State	County	State	County	State	County
1963	.00587	.00088	.00392	.00999	.05853	.00741
1967	.01178	.00018	.00307	.00977	.05433	.00607
1972	.01232	.00175	.00725	.01305	.04957	.00592
1977	.00697	.00039	.00607	.00633	.04477	.00445
1982	.00978	.0004	.00614	.00473	.03953	.00489
1987	.04268	.0026	.00995	.00291	.05901	.00592
1992	.0567	.00226	.01049	.00134	.06118	.00461

Since 1963 there have been dramatic increases in the degree of geographic concentration of the meat-packing industry. At the state level, the EG index for meat packing increased ninefold from 1963 to 1992. Over the same period, spatial concentration of prepared meats increased by a factor of two to three while poultry showed little change— a 4.5 percent increase in geographical concentration. By 1992 the meat packing index was about the same as poultry. By this measure, meat packing has become much like the poultry-processing industry three decades earlier—concentrated in a short list of states.

Using counties as the target regions, the absolute degree of concentration is smaller but the same trends are evident—meat packing approaching the levels of geographic concentration of the poultry industry. Across counties, poultry processing has become about 38 percent less geographically concentrated than in 1963—it is spreading out to more counties. At the same time, meat packing has tended to concentrate its production in smaller numbers of counties. Only in prepared meats has there been a substantial decline in geographic concentration across counties.

SCALE OF PRODUCTION

MacDonald and Ollinger (2000) examine the striking shift to large-scale meat-packing plants (1 million or more hogs per year or 500,000 or more cattle per year) over the past twenty years. In 1980 large-scale plants slaughtered less than 25 percent of the cattle. By 1995 this share had increased to 75 percent. Large-plant hog slaughter increased from 63 percent in 1980 to 88 percent of all hog slaughter by 1997 (MacDonald and Ollinger 2000, 23). Why?

Two reasons stand out. First, scale economies have become more important since 1980. The relative cost advantage of large hog processing plants compared to small plants in 1992 was twice as large as the 1982 advantage. For cattle, the relative cost advantage of large plants increased by 50 percent from 1982 to 1992 (MacDonald and Ollinger 2000, 24). These scale economies are the result of using inputs more intensively—fewer inputs per pound of meat slaughtered. Large scale plants that run twenty-four hours a day allow capital inputs to be used more intensively but they also require a steady flow of animals that meet the physical constraints for the slaughter lines. Improved genetics and contracting arrangements with growers of animals to ensure that animal attributes meet plant requirements have provided large plants with the steady supply of animals needed to keep the lines in operation.

The second source of reduced costs for larger plants has been a dramatic reduction in wage costs in all sizes of plants since 1982, associated with the move from the Midwest urban core to the rural Southeast and Great Plains. Associated with these moves has been a reduction in the share of labor that is unionized—in 1987 it fell to about 20 percent, where it remains (MacDonald and Ollinger 2000, 25). By 1997, according to preliminary analysis by MacDonald and Ollinger, wage differentials across regions and plant sizes had become very small. Interestingly, small plants had lower wage costs before the 1980s than large plants, allowing them to offset scale economies and remain competitive with the larger plants. With the disappearance of the wage advantage in smaller plants, they now have difficulty in competing with large plants, which reap even small advantages in scale economies. MacDonald and Ollinger (2000, 24) find that a 4 million–head hog plant has about a 25 percent advantage in slaughter costs alone over a 1 million–head plant. However, the large plant's advantage in total costs per animal slaughtered is much smaller since the cost of the hog input represents about 80 percent of all input costs. This emphasizes the cost savings that large-scale packers can obtain from contracting with hog growers rather than buying on the open market, adding substantially to their cost advantages over smaller plants.

Changes in regional employment share should follow scale and unit labor costs change across regions—given ample time to write down capital investments, build and expand plants, and recognize the regional variation in unit labor costs.[8] If agglomeration economies are important, regions that gain initial clusters of plants will expand at the expense of other areas. There has been a dramatic increase in employment creation in large plants over the past three decades. Job creation (new plants and expansions) and destruction (plant deaths and contractions) rates, by size of plant,[9] are tabulated in table 3.3. In

Table 3.3
Creation and Destruction Rates, Industries 2011, 2013, and 2015

Creation and Destruction Rates, 1963–1972

Size	Metro			Nonmetro		
	Job Change Rate per Year (percent)	Number of Plants	Share of Employment (percent)	Job Change Rate per Year (percent)	Number of Plants	Share of Employment (percent)
1–99						
Creation	15.5	1,784	9.5	6.2	888	3.6
Destruction	−18.9	2,145	8.4	−7.6	1,095	3.3
100–449						
Creation	11.6	271	15.6	9.5	193	11.5
Destruction	-10.2	223	10.1	−4.0	83	3.8
450+						
Creation	4.5	28	8.5	5.6	28	4.8
Destruction	−16.5	55	16.2	−2.6	13	4.5

Creation and Destruction Rates, 1972–1982

Size	Metro			Nonmetro		
	Job Change Rate per Year (percent)	Number of Plants	Share of Employment (percent)	Job Change Rate per Year (percent)	Number of Plants	Share of Employment (percent)
1–99						
Creation	15.2	1,444	6.9	7.2	881	3.0
Destruction	−19.6	1,760	7.9	−7.7	897	2.7
100–449						
Creation	11.9	251	13.4	7.3	171	11.1
Destruction	-10.7	228	11.1	−4.7	106	5.8
450+						
Creation	8.3	43	10.5	11.8	66	13.8
Destruction	-8.2	40	10.40	-2.8	15	3.3

Creation and Destruction Rates, 1982–1992

Size	Metro			Nonmetro		
	Job Change Rate per Year (percent)	Number of Plants	Share of Employment (percent)	Job Change Rate per Year (percent)	Number of Plants	Share of Employment (percent)
1–99						
Creation	14.9	1,155	4.9	6.1	700	2.1
Destruction	−19.4	1,393	5.2	−7.8	791	2.0
100–449						
Creation	12.5	232	11.0	9.6	153	8.9
Destruction	−12.4	221	8.5	−5.9	108	4.6
450+						
Creation	8.9	74	15.8	13.9	115	24.8
Destruction	−4.0	32	7.2	−2.1	26	5.1

each period, the small plants (fewer than 100 employees) greatly out-number the middle-size (100–449) and large plants (450 or more)—in both rural and metro counties. However, in metro counties there are about twice as many small plants, despite the fact that rural counties outnumber metro counties about four to one.

Most important, the metro turbulence, or rate at which plants create jobs or destroy jobs, is about twice the rural rate. This added metro turbulence means that metro counties are more likely to see small plants come and go and thus have a nonzero observation in meat products employment during a ten-year period. On the other hand, more than 50 percent of the jobs in 1992 were in the largest plants, up from about 35 percent in the 1963–72 period.

Net job creation rates (creation less destruction) are much higher in rural medium-size and large plants than they are in their metro counterparts. Large and medium-size meat plants in rural areas create many more jobs than they destroy. In urban counties, the net job creation rate is about zero for mid-size plants and 4.9 percent for large plants. In contrast, rural plants are adding (net) jobs at about a 3.7 percent rate per year in mid-size plants and 11.8 percent rate for the large plants. Rural areas now have more large plants and are generating net job growth at over twice the rate of their urban counterparts, leading to the increased rural shares of employment observed in table 3.1.

The geographical distribution of plants in meat processing has changed in several important ways over the past three decades, most dramatically between 1982 and 1992. Plants are bigger and expanding in rural counties and away from old metro core areas in meat packing and to a lesser extent in other meat processing. Poultry processing has been predominately rural over the entire thirty years. Spatial concentration of production has also dramatically increased in the meat-packing industry.

These meat-packing trends are associated with changes in the organization of the industry linking production of livestock to the needs of processing plants, changing transportation and scale economies, spatial agglomeration economies, and biological innovations. The well-known move to integrate production of hogs on contract with large-scale growers with large-scale (more than 4 million head per year) slaughter facilities has been driven by increasing scale economies in slaughter since the 1980s and biological innovations to produce animals to specifications by the processing plant. Beef processors locate near sources of cattle to economize on transport costs of boxed beef products and also have seen scale economies increase since the 1980s.

The trends toward large plant size were also shaped by dramatic decreases in real wages, especially since 1982. While a lower wage bill was obtained at one time by a move from the unionized urban core to the rural Midwest and Southeast, these regional wage differentials have largely disappeared. Smaller plants now find that their low-wage advantage in the 1960s and 1970s no longer offsets the scale economies from large plants (MacDonald and Ollinger 2000).

Spatial concentration has grown ninefold in meat packing since the 1960s, with rural areas grabbing the largest share of new jobs. While wage differentials across regions have largely disappeared (MacDonald and Ollinger 2000), meat packing now resembles the levels of spatial concentration in the poultry-processing industry.[10] Over the next decade, spatial agglomeration economies may reinforce geographical concentration in meat packing in regions that have established large-scale plants.

An important implication of our findings for proponents of value-added food processing as a rural development strategy is that meat products processing appears to offer good opportunities, but only for rural communities situated in places that can draw a large and stable supply of livestock from proximate producers. Since, in general, food processing is quite stable over the business cycle (ERS, 1998, 9) and large plants seem to be more persistent net job creators, large-scale meat packing should provide a steady source of employment even during recessions. In contrast to suggestions (Lyson and Tolbert 1996; Tolbert, Lyson, and Irwin 1998) that small manufacturing plants are beneficial to rural economies, small plants reduce the rate of net job creation and seem unlikely to be able to sustain employment growth in rural areas.

Meat products plants have the added benefit of strong economic linkages to the local economy and should provide larger local multiplier effects than other food processing manufacturing plants. In terms of economic impacts on the local economy, both meat processing and poultry processing stand out as key sectors. Meat-processing plants purchase more material inputs per plant (about $32.5 million in 1995) from local sources (within a one-hour drive of the plant) than any of the twenty-five industries in value-added manufacturing (VAM) of food and forestry products (ERS 1998, 25). Poultry processing generates more jobs, on average, at each processing plant (467 per plant) than any other kind of VAM plant. Meat processing is second in jobs generated per plant (370). While average pay in these plants tends to be lower than the average pay in manufacturing, local processing plant payrolls are $7.6 and $7.0 million per plant for meat processing and poultry processing. Each of these characteristics— large number of employees and payroll per plant, and large volumes of purchases of local inputs—means that meat and poultry processing plants will have more significant impacts on the local economy than other VAM plants. By these measures, meat and poultry processing are among the top four "high local economic impact" VAM industries (ERS 1998, 25).

These local multiplier effects suggest that communities that have large-scale plants are likely to promote growth associated with static localization economies. Increased plant size often leads to a greater availability of specialized intermediate input suppliers, local business services, a larger pool of specialized workers, and reduced search costs for firms looking for workers with specific skills. However, this kind of economic growth in rural communities has and is likely to continue to raise both environmental and social problems that will be difficult to solve (for some case studies, see Stull, Broadway, and Griffith 1995). Water pollution from lagoon spills and odor spillovers to residential areas proximate to larger processing plants and large growers of animals are the kinds of problems that can be serious enough to get the attention of state legislatures and the EPA.

In-migration of labor to rural areas to work in meat and poultry processing plants is often substantial. By shifting the local labor supply function to the right, in-migration may be associated with lower real wages in these industries. The dramatic decline in real wages in both rural and urban counties in meat packing and other meat processing since 1980 suggests that these jobs will not generate large increases in rural per capita incomes. However, in-migrants to rural areas should help sustain local trade and service establishments in rural counties of states that have experienced population losses over the last decade.

If environmental and social concerns associated with large-scale processors can be adequately addressed, large-scale meat-packing plants seem to offer an excellent opportunity for sustained employment growth—albeit in fewer and fewer rural communities. EPA guidelines on Confined Animal Feed Operations, the Clean Water Act, and state regulation of large-scale grower operations and proximate processing plants address some of the environmental concerns. Effective enforcement remains a challenge. In-migration of Hispanic and Asian workers to remote rural areas has state and local agencies scrambling to provide educational and other public services to the new residents. Nevertheless, anecdotal evidence of active recruiting of these workers to rural areas by processors suggests that these communities are willing to provide services to the new residents. However, as Lyson and Tolbert (1996) imply, if social and environmental costs with large meat-processing plants in rural communities are great and persistent, then smaller may be better. The problem is that it is unlikely that most small processing plants can survive in today's economic environment.

Appendix

The EG index is thus computed for counties, and states as follows:

$$G \equiv \sum_i (s_i - x_i)^2$$

where s_i is the share of the industry's employment in area i and x_i is the share of aggregate manufacturing employment in area i.

$$s_i = \sum_k z_k u_{ki}$$

where z_k is the kth plant's (exogenously fixed) share of the industry's employment and u_{ki} is an indicator variable equal to 1 if plant k chooses to locate in region i.

$$\gamma \equiv \frac{\dfrac{G}{1-\sum_i x_i^2}}{1-H}$$

where $H = \sum_{j=1}^{n} z_j^2$

Notes

1. Drabenstott 1998; ERS 1998; and Ward 1998a, 1998b, 1998c are good overviews of industry trends.

2. Boehlje (1999) identifies differential community economic impacts as one key consequence of the evolving agricultural industry in the United States.

3. See ERS 1998 for an excellent review of value added manufacturing of agricultural and forestry products. Note that *rural* is defined as the set of non-metropolitan counties.

4. This section, in part, is from Kim, Barkley, and Henry (2000, 233–34).

5. According to Henderson (1986) and Kim, Barkley, and Henry (2000), static localization economies have the following characteristics: economies of intra-industry specialization where increased industry size permits greater specialization among industry firms in addition to a greater availability of specialized intermediate input suppliers, business services, and financial markets; labor market economies resulting from a larger pool of trained, specialized workers and reduced search costs for firms looking for workers with specific skills; scale for networking or communication among firms to take advantage of complementarities, exploit new markets, integrate activities, and adopt new innovations; and scale in providing public goods and services tailored to the needs of a specific industry.

6. McCann (1995) divides natural advantages into distance-transactions cost advantages and location-specific factor efficiency cost advantages. Distance-transactions costs are the expenses associated with transporting inputs and outputs. If such costs are relatively significant, industry concentrations will result as firms select locations that minimize proximate transportation costs. Location-specific factor efficiency costs refer to the costs associated with local

capital, land, labor, and climate. Industry concentrations will result if numerous firms select the same location in order to economize on a specific input or set of inputs.

7. Data from 1963 to 1992 at the plant level in SIC 2011, 2013, and 2015 were obtained from the Longitudinal Research Database (LRD), Center for Economic Studies, Census Bureau, U.S. Dept. of Commerce.

8. Census value added is the difference between gross receipts and value of material purchased. As Gale (1997, 7) notes, some analysts argue that establishments in urban places have upwardly biased estimates because the value of purchased services is included in the estimate of value added and urban firms are expected to use more of these services (Ciccone and Hall 1996). Others (e.g., Israilevich and Testa 1989) suggest there is an urban understatement of value added since it is assigned to the production location (plant) while auxiliary urban-oriented units are assigned no value. In his analysis of rural and urban employment change, Gale finds that these sources of bias may offset each other.

9. Following Davis, Haltiwanger, and Schuh (1996, 60–63), we use average plant size over the period in calculations of the job creation and destruction rates by size of plant. This avoids the size distribution fallacy, which often gives misleading information on the contribution of small plants to net job creation. (For a discussion, see Davis, Haltiwanger, and Schuh 1997, 63.)

10. Important differences in pork, beef, and poultry processing remain. Major centers for feeding and packing pork did not change during the 1970s and 1980s. However, beef feeding moved from small-scale corn belt feedlots and Midwest processors in the early 1970s to the Southern plains with large scale feedlots integrated with processing plants (Melton and Huffman 1995, 480). More recent evidence suggests that pork processing is following the lead of beef packers as new large-scale operations open in the Southeast. Melton and Huffman (1995) also suggest that meat packing firms have closed older plants and moved to locations where unions have less influence.

References

Butler, M., and C. Beale. 1994. *Rural-Urban Continuum Codes for Metro and Non-Metropolitan Counties.* Agriculture and Rural Economy Division, ERS Staff Report no. AGES 9425. Washington, D.C.: U.S. Department of Agriculture.

Boehlje, M. 1999. "Structural Change in the Agricultural Industries: How Do We Measure, Analyze, and Understand Them?" Waugh Lecture, Annual

Meetings of the American Agricultural Economics Association, Nashville, August 11.

Ciccone, A., and R. E. Hall. 1996. "Productivity and the Density of Economic Activity." *American Economic Review* 86:54–70.

Connor, John M. 1996. "Did the Competitive Regime Switch in the 1980s?" *American Journal of Agricultural Economics* 78:1192–97.

Connor, John M., and W. A. Schick. 1996. *Food Processing: An Industrial Powerhouse in Transition.* 2d ed. New York: Wiley.

Davis, Steven J., John C. Haltiwanger, and Scott Schuh. 1997. *Job Creation and Destruction.* Cambridge, Mass.: MIT Press.

Drabenstott, Mark. 1998. "This Little Piggy Went to Market: Will the New Pork Industry Call the Heartland Home?" *Economic Review* 83 (3): 79–97.

Dumais, Guy, Glenn Ellison, and Edward L. Glaeser. 1997. "Geographic Concentration as a Dynamic Process." NBER Working Paper 6270.

ERS (Economic Research Service). 1998. *Rural Conditions and Trends* 8 (3).

Ellison, Glenn, and Edward L. Glaeser. 1994. "Geographic Concentration in U.S. Manufacturing Industries: A Dartboard Approach." NBER Working Paper 4840.

———. 1997. "Geographic Concentration in U.S. Manufacturing Industries: A Dartboard Approach." *Journal of Political Economy* 105:889–927.

Gale, Fred. 1997. "The Rural-Urban Gap in Manufacturing Productivity and Wages: Effects of Industry Mix and Region." Center for Economic Studies Discussion paper, CES 97-6, U.S. Bureau of the Census, U.S. Department of Commerce.

Gale, Fred, and Maureen Kilkenny. 2000. "Agriculture's Role Shrinks as the Service Economy Expands." *Rural Conditions and Trends* 10 (2): 26–32. Economic Research Service, U.S. Department of Agriculture.

Gibbs, R., and G. A. Bernat, Jr. 1997. "The Wage Effects of Local Industry Clusters: An Analysis of Multi-County Labor Market Areas." Paper presented at the Southern Regional Science Association Meetings, Memphis, April 18.

Glaeser, Edward L., Hedi D. Kallal, José A. Scheinkman, and Andrei Schleifer. 1992. "Growth in Cities," *Journal of Political Economy* 100:1126–52.

Goetz, Stephan. 1997a "Location Decisions of Energy-Intensive Manufacturing Firms: Estimating the Potential Impact of Electric Utilities

Deregulation." Contractor Paper 98-3. TVA Rural Studies Program, Lexington, Ky.

———. 1997b. "State and County-Level Determinants of Food Manufacturing Establishment Growth: 1987–93." *American Journal of Agricultural Economics* 79:838–850.

Henderson, J. Vernon. 1986. "Efficiency of Resource Usage and City Size." *Journal of Urban Economics* 19:47–70.

Henderson, J. Vernon, Ari Kuncoro, and Matt Turner. 1995. "Industrial Development in Cities." *Journal of Political Economy* 103:1067–90.

Israilevich, P. R., and W. A. Testa. 1989. "The Geography of Value Added." *Economic Perspectives* (Federal Reserve Bank of Chicago), September–October, 2–12.

Kim, Yunsoo, D. L. Barkley, and M. S. Henry. 2000. "Industry Characteristics Linked to Establishment Concentrations in Non-Metropolitan Areas." *Journal of Regional Science* 40 (2): 231–59.

Knoeber, Charles, and Walter Thurman. 1995. "Don't Count Your Chickens Before They Hatch: Risk and Risk Shifting in the Broiler Industry." *American Journal of Agricultural Economics* 77:486–96.

Longitudinal Research Database. Center for Economic Studies, U.S. Bureau of the Census, Washington D.C.

Lyson, T., and C. Tolbert 1996. "Small Manufacturing and Non-Metropolitan Socioeconomic Well-Being." *Environmental and Planning* A28:1779–94.

MacDonald, James M., and Michael E. Ollinger. 2000. "Consolidation in Meat Packing: Causes and Consequences." *Agricultural Outlook,* June–July, 23–26. Economic Research Service, U.S. Department of Agriculture.

"Manufacturing Industries: A Dartboard Approach." *Journal of Political Economy* 105:889–927.

Martin, S. A., Richard McHugh, and S. R. Johnson. 1991. "The Influence of Location on Productivity: Manufacturing Technology in Rural and Urban Areas." Center for Economic Studies Discussion paper, CES 91-1, U.S. Bureau of the Census.

McCann, Philip. 1995. "Rethinking the Economies of Locations and Agglomerations." *Urban Studies* 32:563–77.

Melton, B., and W. Huffman. 1995. "Beef and Pork Packing Costs and Input Demands: Effects of Unionization and Technology." *American Journal of Agricultural Economics* 77:471–85.

Storper, M., and R. Walker. 1989. *The Capitalist Imperative.* New York: Basil Blackwell.

Stull, D., M. Broadway, and D. Griffith. 1995. *Any Way You Cut It: Meat Processing and Small-Town America.* Lawrence: University of Kansas Press.

Tolbert, C., T. A. Lyson, and M. Irwin. 1998. "Local Capitalism, Civic Engagement, and Socioeconomic Well-Being." *Social Forces* 77:401–28.

Ward, Clement E. 1998a. "Packer Concentration and Its Impacts." *OSU Extension Facts.* WF-554, Oklahoma Cooperative Extension Service, Oklahoma State University, Stillwater.

Ward, Clement E. 1998b. "Structural Changes in Cattle Feeding and Meat Packing." *OSU Extension Facts.* WF-553, Oklahoma Cooperative Extension Service. Oklahoma State University, Stillwater.

Ward, Clement E. 1998c. "Vertical Integration Comparison: Beef, Pork, Poultry." *OSU Extension Facts.* WF-552, Oklahoma Cooperative Extension Service, Oklahoma State University, Stillwater.

4

Socioeconomic Trends in Mining-Dependent Counties in Appalachia

Melissa Latimer and F. Carson Mencken

THERE IS A SIGNIFICANT body of literature that documents the important socioeconomic implications of extractive industry dependency (e.g., Jensen et al. 1999; Lobao 1996; Nord and Luloff 1993; RSS 1993a). Since 1980 places with a higher concentration of employment in extractive industries have higher levels of poverty (Lichter and McLaughlin 1995), greater racial and gender inequality (Tickamyer and Latimer 1993; Tickamyer and Tickamyer 1991), and higher levels of under- and unemployment (Couto 1994; Jensen et al. 1999; Maggard 1994) than areas with low extractive employment. While all extractive industries have faced severe economic problems over the last few decades (Gramling 1996; Lobao 1990; Nord and Luloff 1993), the effects of industrial restructuring have been very tough on the coal-mining industry. This is particularly true in the rural regions of Appalachia, where nearly 75 percent of all coal miners have historically been employed and where coal-mining dependency led to record levels of unemployment, poverty, and significantly lower incomes in the 1980s (Billings and Tickamyer 1993; Couto 1994; Isserman 1995; Maggard 1994; Mencken 1997).[1]

While a volume of research has focused on the impact of industrial restructuring in coal communities during the 1980s, less work has been done on these communities during the 1990s. In this analysis we examine trends since 1970, with an eye toward post-1980s trends in the most coal intensive counties in Appalachia.

Industrial Restructuring in the Coal Industry

Coal mining, along with steel, textiles, and apparel, formed the basic foundation for the industrial revolution in the United States (Couto 1994). The initial coal mines in Appalachia provided fuel for the foundries, factories, and steel mills of the early industrial revolution. Coal mining had an important presence in Appalachia during the 1900s. Many Appalachian boomtowns, such as Clinchco, Virginia, were created during the first half of the century. From World War II through the early 1960s, the demand for Appalachian coal was strong and consistent. In the late 1960s coal companies began replacing labor with capital as some workers were phased out by new production processes (particularly long-wall mining). However, the energy crisis of the 1970s created a greater demand for alternative energy sources including electrical power generated by coal. The increase in demand for coal created more job opportunities in the industry, and thus the 1970s was a period of expansion in the coal industry, with coal-mining earnings growing 214 percent in inflation-adjusted dollars, and employment in mining growing by 50 percent (Couto 1994).

Dilger and Witt (1994) identify three trends that transformed the industry during the 1980s. First, the economic restructuring from manufacturing to services lessened the demand for coal to produce direct energy for factories. In fact, coal consumption by coke plants declined by 59 percent between 1980 and 1998 (*Energy Statistics Sourcebook* 1999). Second, new environmental laws decreased the demand for high-sulfur Appalachian coal. Extracting this type of coal was a labor-intensive process. Cleaner burning low-sulfur coal is located near the surface, and mechanized capital intensive surface or strip mining is used to extract it.

The third, and perhaps most important, trend is the further mechanization of the coal extraction process. Foreign competition accelerated the mechanization of many manufacturing processes in the United States. However, since 1980, 95 percent of all coal produced in the United States was consumed domestically, and only 0.8 percent of the coal consumed here was imported (*Energy Statistics Sourcebook* 1999). Unlike in manufacturing, where restructuring was a product of global competition, in the coal-mining industry competition came among domestic producers. Keen competition further accelerated cuts in production costs through mechanization. Mechanization increased the productivity of coal extraction, thus lowering the price per ton. Falling prices created even greater competition among suppliers of coal. Competition shut down many of the less competitive mines, which could not survive on small profit margins, particularly the underground mines that employed more workers. Over sixteen hundred mines were closed in West Virginia from the late 1970s through the mid-1980s, and the number of coal miners in that state decreased from 55,627 in 1980 to 28,876 in 1990 (Couto 1994; Dilger and Witt 1994; C. Hawley 1994; Maggard 1994).

However, the demand for Appalachian coal remained strong during this period. Clifford Hawley (1994) shows that 40 percent more West Virginia coal was produced in 1990 than in 1980, despite a 47 percent decrease in the number of coal industry workers. Moreover, during the 1980s over 50 percent of all electricity produced in the United States was generated from coal. And in 1998 a record 187 million tons of coal were produced in West Virginia (*Energy Statistics Sourcebook* 1999). Furthermore, employment downturns in the industry were not the product of lessened demand, but of a number of interrelated market factors that conjoined to displace workers in the industry.

The Sociology of Regional Processes

Sociological theories of regional processes generate a set of expectations about the socioeconomic conditions in coal-dependent counties for periods following the coal bust of the early 1980s. Overdependence on natural-resource-based industries is problematic for regional development. First, many extractive-industry communities are geographically isolated from urban centers (RSS 1993b). As a result, they are not integrated into agglomeration economies and therefore lack access to those labor markets and community resources during contractions in that industry (Lobao 1996).

Natural-resource-based economies are less likely to keep up in the rapidly changing high-technology economy because natural-resource-extractive industries are primarily labor intensive, and firms in these industries do not invest in human capital (RSS 1993b). As a result workers are not developing human capital on the job, and coal miners did not develop job skills that are useful in a postindustrial economy. Furthermore, many jobs in these industries have not required a high school diploma, which explains the higher high school dropout rates in natural-resource-dependent counties (Isserman 1995). Billings and Tickamyer (1993) imply that when employment in the mining industry declined significantly in the early 1980s, what was left behind were communities with large pools of unemployed workers not prepared for the postindustrial job market, and such communities lacked the skilled workers that are necessary to attract private capital (Gottdiener 1994).

Second, based on an analysis of Clay County, Kentucky, Billings and Blee (2000) argue that development in central Appalachia is limited by historical patterns of economic and political domination by absentee owners and local elites. This pattern, set before the Civil War, established an institutionalized framework of local social and economic arrangements such that market-driven capitalism "resulted in the production of wealth for only a privileged few in Clay County, not prosperity for the majority" (320). Decisions are made in corporate headquarters located in major metropolitan areas, with little incentive to reinvest in the extractive-industry communities (Matvey 1987; RSS 1993). In addition, natural-resource communities tend to be dominated by one absentee firm, which gives the firm tight control over the local community. Lack of competition essentially creates monopsonistic labor markets, giving firms greater control over workers and workers, significantly less power and choice.

Not only does this system work to exploit labor (Haynes 1997), it also works to dominate local governance in Appalachia. Often these firms will purchase surrounding lands in order to control land use. Being the major employer in town means that they have exceptional political power and influence and exert significant control over local taxation and expenditures (RSS 1993). Billings and Blee (2000) reveal a corrupt system of clientelism in Clay County, Kentucky, in which rival local elites patronize clients to further their own (elite) interests. The system limits the ability of local governments to foster and manage economic development policies and actions that could bring positive change. Economic and political domination by absentee owners in conjunction with local elites creates an environment whereby local tax revenues and social and public infrastructure expenditures are limited to the interests of local and absentee elites.

Third, the consequences of absentee ownership are also consistent with the expectations of the systems approach of human ecology. System growth in size and complexity is partly a function of new resources (A. Hawley 1986). Profits from coal represent resources that local social systems need for development. If resources are exported elsewhere then the local system will not increase in complexity, and the system will only vary in size with fluctuations in the niche (the national and global coal market). Furthermore, the mechanization of the industry, and the resultant standardization and routinization of sustenance procurement functions, creates a state of equilibrium, or stasis, between the local system and its environment. Coal production can be adjusted to fluctuations in the market without significantly affecting the number of workers needed.

The geographical isolation of these counties, the lack of community investments that accompany absentee ownership, and the lack of human capital investments in coal production workers, have combined to create communities ill equipped to participate in the postindustrial economy of the 1990s (Billings and Blee 2000). Like the inner-city communities in William Julius Wilson's *The Truly Disadvantaged* (1987), coal counties in Appalachia are not going to attract the private capital necessary to generate economic growth. The goal of this analysis is to learn as much as possible about the socioeconomic conditions in the coal counties in Appalachia after the employment downturn of the 1980s. The sociological ideas reviewed above suggest that we will find little change in the socioeconomic conditions in these counties since the coal bust. In the analysis that follows we explore this expectation for coal dependent communities in Appalachia.

Data and Analysis

We identify eighteen historically coal-dependent counties in Appalachia (see map 4.1). In our analysis we utilize Couto's definition of a coal dependent county (1994): one in which at least 10 percent of total earnings were in the Standard Industrial Code (SIC) two-digit coal-mining code in 1970. All the coal-dependent counties are in Kentucky (Clay, Floyd, Harlan, Letcher, Martin, Perry, Pike), Virginia (Buchanan, Dickenson, Tazewell, Wise), and West Virginia (Boone, Fayette, McDowell, Mingo, Nicholas, Raleigh, Wyoming). The task of documenting changes in the region during the 1990s is made more difficult because of our reliance on decennial census information. Where possible, we have supplemented our analysis with measures from other data sources to provide a description of the socioeconomic conditions in the region since 1990.

We analyze these counties on key socioeconomic indicators. Our preliminary analysis showed that these eighteen counties are homogenous on most indicators. We have aggregated indicators for these

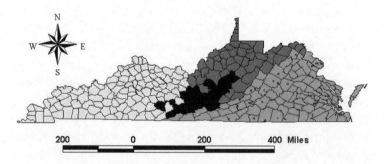

Map 4.1. Mining-dependent counties in Appalachia

counties to construct measures for the entire coal-mining region. The analysis is conducted for the four broadly defined categories of socio-economic indicators: earnings and income; employment and population; local government; and general welfare. Each of these categories represents key sets of issues to be explored in socioeconomic impact assessment (Burdge 1998). We examine a number of empirical indicators within each of these categories.

EARNINGS AND INCOME

Earnings and income are standard indicators used to analyze economic growth trends. Figure 4.1 presents the trend in two-digit SIC coal-mining earnings for this eighteen-county region (REIS 2000). Comparing earnings across time requires that they be standardized into constant dollars in order to adjust for inflation. We standardized these yearly earnings using the Consumer Price Index. Between 1970 and 1979 coal-mining earnings for the region grew by 121 percent in inflation-adjusted dollars. However, between 1979 and 1990 coal-mining earnings decreased by 52 percent, and between 1990 and 1999 the rate of decline was 45 percent. In fact, in inflation-adjusted dollars, coal-mining earnings in 1999 were 71 percent of their value in 1969. This decline in coal-mining earnings reflects the further mechanization of the production process, using fewer workers to produce more coal, because data on coal production suggest little downturn in production during the same period (*Energy Statistics Sourcebook* 1999).

Figure 4.2 shows the trends in coal-mining earnings as a percentage of total nonfarm earnings for 1969 through 1999. These data show the dominance of the coal industry in this region. During parts of the 1970s, over half of all earnings in this region were from coal mining. Even after 1983, these percentages are well above 20 percent, or more than twice the percentage needed for a county to be considered coal dependent. The simultaneous decline and continued dominance of coal in the late 1980s and 1990s indicates a lack of development of new and alternative industry in this region. Coal is still king following the bust of the early 1980s, there are just fewer subjects on the king's payroll.

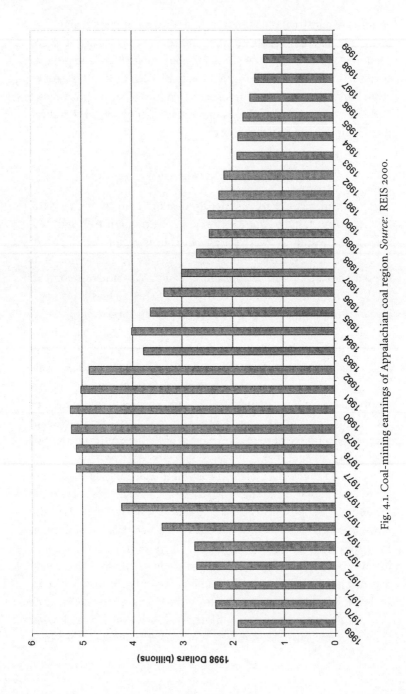

Fig. 4.1. Coal-mining earnings of Appalachian coal region. *Source:* REIS 2000.

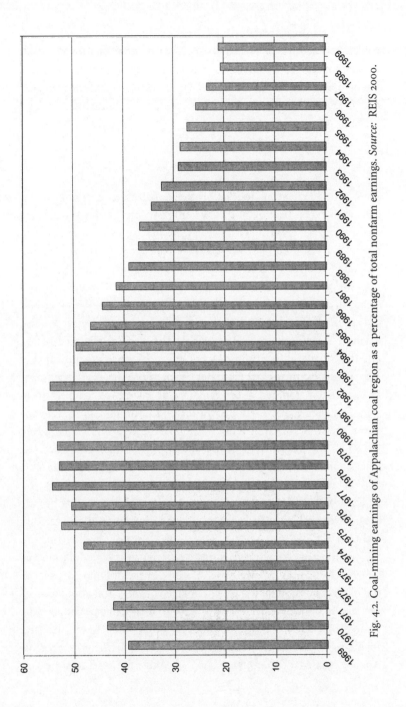

Fig. 4.2. Coal-mining earnings of Appalachian coal region as a percentage of total nonfarm earnings. *Source:* REIS 2000.

Figure 4.3 presents data on per capita income as a percent of U.S. per capita income. In 1980 the per capita income rate for the coal-dependent region of Appalachia reached its zenith, 80 percent of U.S. per capita income. By 1988, the per capita income rate for this region had fallen to 65 percent of the U.S. rate and remained at this level through 1999.

EMPLOYMENT AND POPULATION

In 1975 the civilian labor force in the Appalachian coal region was 221,790 workers. The size of the civilian labor force in the Appalachian coal region peaked in 1983 at 275,421. By 1989 the size of the civilian labor force returned to its pre-1980s level—224,240 workers—and has remained relatively stable since then.[2] Figure 4.4 presents the trends in mining employment from 1969 through 1999. The data show a steady decline in employment since 1982. Moreover, between 1990 and 1999 mining employment declined by 42 percent in this region. We also examine unemployment rates for both the Appalachian coal region and the United States from 1975 through 1996. These data show that in the early 1980s unemployment rates began to rise sharply in the Appalachian coal region, reaching a region-wide rate of over 20 percent in 1983. The unemployment rate in the region fell throughout the remainder of the 1980s, reaching a low point of 10 percent in 1990. However, since 1990 the unemployment rate for the Appalachian coal region has consistently remained above 10 percent and has been at least twice the national unemployment rate for each year following 1990.

Data on population change in the Appalachian coal counties are presented in table 4.2 (below). In 1980 the population of the region's eighteen counties was 756,214. By 1990 that number had declined to 657,510. Each of the eighteen counties experienced net population loss between 1980 and 1990. McDowell County, West Virginia, experienced the highest net population loss (42 percent), while the population of the region as a whole decreased 15 percent during this period. For the nation as a whole, the population growth rate between 1980 and 1990 was 9.8 percent. The decline in the unemployment rate for the Appalachian coal region in the late 1980s most likely reflects the out-

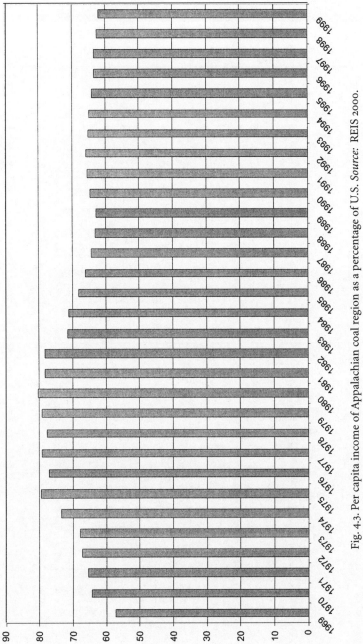

Fig. 4.3: Per capita income of Appalachian coal region as a percentage of U.S. *Source:* REIS 2000.

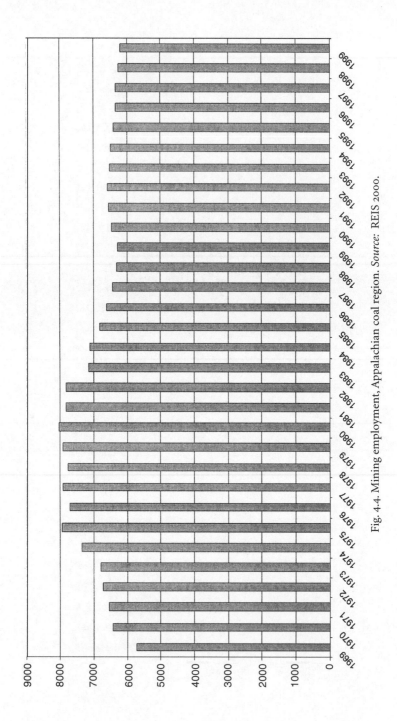

Fig. 4.4. Mining employment, Appalachian coal region. *Source:* REIS 2000.

migration of unemployed workers, as opposed to the reemployment of the unemployed. Population projection data for the region provided by the REIS of the Bureau of Economic Analysis suggest a 0.1 percent decrease in population between 1990 and 1999 in the Appalachian coal region.

We do not have data on out-migration from 1990 to the present. However, we did examine a proxy measure: trends in the annual birth rate (U.S. Census Bureau 1998). From 1980 to 1994 the U.S. birth rate has remained relatively constant at approximately sixteen per thousand. The rate in the Appalachian coal region declined from sixteen per thousand in 1982 to approximately twelve per thousand in 1989. Since then it has remained relatively constant. We propose that the decline in the birth rate between 1982 and 1989 represents, in part, out-migration of child-bearing-age population. The lack of a continuing downward trend since 1990 suggests that out-migration, particularly of the child-bearing-age population, has decreased significantly. When new census data are released, we will be better able to test this idea.

LOCAL GOVERNMENT

Another area where the impact of overdependence and boom-and-bust cycles can be felt is through its impact on local institutions, particularly local governments and their ability to raise revenue and provide local services (Gramling 1996; Johnson et al. 1995). Local governments rely mostly on locally generated revenues to provide key infrastructure and social services. Using Census of Governments data, we examine trends in local government finances from the 1970s through the early 1990s. We compare Appalachian coal region rates to the U.S. rate for the years available. Table 4.1 presents a variety of local government finance data from 1972 to 1992. These data show that the per capita revenue rate for the Appalachian coal region is about 50 percent of the per capita rate for all local governments in the United States. Moreover, the general expenditure data show the same trend. Local governments in this region spend significantly less per capita than the national rate. However, this gap has remained consistent from the early 1970s through the early 1990s. There was no significant drop-off between 1982 and 1987 in the Appalachian coal region, which we might have expected, given the downturn in the coal industry during the early 1980s.

We also examine several specific measures of local government spending: per capita spending on health services, police protection, and highways (table 4.1). These comparisons reveal remarkable differences in the per capita spending rates between the counties in the Appalachian coal region and the U.S. rate. For each measure, the Appalachian coal region rate lags far behind. However, these trends have remained consistent over time. A significant gap in the late 1970s has remained relatively constant through the early 1990s. Surprisingly, the

Table 4.1
Government Finances of the Appalachian Coal Region, 1972–1992

	Per Capita Revenues				
	1972	1977	1982	1987	1992
U.S.	$1,956.67	$2.184.02	$2,048.76	$2,436.36	$2,659.85
Coal region	$882.71	$1,039.01	$1,116.84	$1,384.35	$1,571.41

	Per Capita Expenditures				
	1972	1977	1982	1987	1992
U.S.	$1,980.01	$2,085.04	$1,927.15	$2,320.21	$2,580.91
Coal region	$865.11	$1,046.68	$1,049.71	$1,365.01	$1,505.63

	Per Capita Health Services Spending			
	1977	1982	1987	1992
U.S.	$144.85	$156.11	$176.90	$213.63
Coal region	$18.38	$21.48	$41.03	$63.69

	Per Capita Education Spending			
	1977	1982	1987	1992
U.S.	$927.00	$816.32	$976.54	$1,084.14
Coal region	$760.92	$725.28	$926.31	$1,028.97

Per Capita Highway Spending				
	1977	1982	1987	1992
U.S.	$144.85	$156.11	$176.90	$213.63
Coal region	$18.84	$39.90	$48.17	$57.21

Per Capita Police Service Spending				
	1977	1982	1987	1992
U.S.	$108.68	$102.89	$124.94	$139.04
Coal region	$35.75	$32.47	$36.28	$40.01

Per Capita General Debt			
	1982	1987	1992
U.S.	$1,874.27	$2,732.31	$2,746.28
Coal region	$755.34	$1,158.55	$928.21

Per Capita Long-Term Debt			
	1982	1987	1992
U.S.	$456.46	$642.96	$614.96
Coal region	$89.24	$120.58	$111.47

Source: Census of Governments, USA Counties 1998 CD.

data for local government spending on education shows little difference in the local government per capita spending rate in the Appalachian coal region and the national per capita rate for local governments around the country. However, due to the geographic isolation of many of the Appalachian coal counties, a substantial proportion of this spending is on transportation.

The analysis of local government spending and revenues shows dramatic differences in per capita rates between the counties of the Appalachian coal region and the local government rates for the nation as a whole. However, these trends did not emerge after the coal bust of the 1980s but were present during the 1970s. Local government finances are similar in the late 1980s and 1990s in the Appalachian coal region, as they were before the bust of the 1980s. What these data suggest is that local government spending in the Appalachian coal region faces tighter prioritizing than what is typical for a local government in the United States. Local government spending on education is on par with the national per capita average in most years. But all other spending categories are significantly lower.

Overdependence and boom-and-bust cycles can also create problems for local government finances, particularly if shortfalls in revenue create debts for local governments. Table 4.1 also presents data on general and long-term debt for the Appalachian coal county rates and the U.S. local government rate. For both general and long-term per capita debt, the Appalachian coal region had rates significantly lower than the U.S. rate for all years available. On the positive side, local governments in this region were not saddled with huge debts following the coal bust of the early 1980s. However, the lack of general and long-term debt may also reflect the inability of local governments to pass bonds for capital and school improvement projects.

GENERAL WELFARE

We examine trends in levels of education, poverty, disability rates, and SSI rates. Table 4.2 shows the situation for education and poverty in the Appalachian coal region at the end of the 1990s. These data show that the counties in the Appalachian coal region were far behind the nation in educational attainment at the end of the 1980s. Some counties have non–high school completion rates at least twice the national rate of 24 percent, and all Appalachian coal counties in 1990 had percentages of adults not graduating from high school higher than the U.S. rate. This is one of the legacies of natural-resource dependency. These industries employ larger proportions of non–high school graduates. As with Chicago's inner city in Wilson's work (1987), when the jobs leave and the people move away, those with the fewest skills (i.e., those that did not graduate from high school) are often left behind. The data from table 4.1 on poverty rates are almost a direct replication of the high school completion data. All Appalachian coal counties

Table 4.2

General Welfare Indicators in Appalachian Mining Counties

County	Not H.S. Graduates 1990	Percent in Poverty 1989	Pop. Change 1980–90	Disability Recipients Percent Change 1990–96	SSI Recipients Percent Change 1990–96
Clay, Ky.	61.13	40.18	−4.91	67.74	48.26
Floyd, Ky.	49.17	31.23	−12.03	42.98	64.61
Harlan, Ky.	50.53	33.08	−14.9	72.91	70.72
Letcher, Ky.	54.5	31.77	−13.7	87.2	77.19
Martin, Ky.	55.62	35.38	−11.5	64.29	73.7
Perry, Ky.	52.42	32.14	−11.12	90.29	85.09
Pike, Ky.	49.85	25.41	−11.9	47.67	74.23
Buchanan, Va.	57.5	21.85	−21.5	60.69	58.69
Dickenson, Va.	52.95	25.88	−12.8	48.3	53.4
Tazewell, Va.	42.69	19.02	−9.7	17.68	56.45
Wise, Va.	47.86	21.61	−10.9	37.76	55.29
Boone, W.V.	45.91	26.99	−18.03	32.47	59.75
Fayette, W.V.	42.93	24.36	−20.7	38.17	57.17
McDowell, W.V.	57.67	37.72	−42.1	23.71	75.36
Mingo, W.V.	49.63	30.93	−11.1	31.68	73.18
Nicholas, W.V.	38.82	24.38	−5.3	59.12	46.84
Raleigh, W.V.	36.82	19.88	−13.1	25.29	53.29
Wyoming, W.V.	47.01	27.68	−23.9	39.18	77.26
Nation	24.76	13.1	9.8	26.1	37

Source: U.S. Census of Population Housing 1990; Social Security Administration 1998.

had poverty rates higher than the national rate. The counties where the poverty rates are the highest (e.g., Clay, Kentucky, and McDowell, West Virginia) are also the counties where the high school completion rates are the lowest.

The data on Supplemental Security Income show that the rate of SSI cases in the Appalachian coal region has grown at a rate much greater than the national rate between 1990 and 1996.[3] One of the most interesting findings in this study is the significant growth in the number of people on disability in the Appalachian coal region, particularly after 1989. From 1990 to 1996 the national growth in the number of persons receiving disability payments grew by 26 percent; in the Appalachian coal region it grew by 37.5 percent. Coal mining is dangerous work and the industry has a high rate of worker injury. However, these data show a marked increase in disability rates during a period in which mining employment continued to decrease rapidly, and these post-1990 disability growth rates are much higher than they were during the 1980s. In figure 4.5, we contrast the decline of mining employment with the growth of disability benefits between 1992 and 1996. There is a remarkable similarity in these traits. We believe that disability has become a de facto strategy for income maintenance in depressed regions of Appalachia, as unemployed workers are placed on disability. There are some suggestions of this trend in existing research (Dorsey 1991), but this conclusion needs further empirical investigation.

Much of the research on coal-mining dependence produced over the last ten years has focused on the trends during the 1980s (Billings and Tickamyer 1993; Couto 1994; Maggard 1994; Mencken 1997). However, it has been seventeen years since the mining-dependent counties in Appalachia started experiencing significant, permanent downturns. What is absent from the current body of literature is an examination of trends since this period. We have attempted to fill this gap with a descriptive analysis of socioeconomic conditions in Appalachian coal-mining counties since 1970, with an emphasis on trends during the late 1980s and 1990s.

Sociological theory and research on regional processes generated expectations about the socioeconomic conditions of coal-dependent

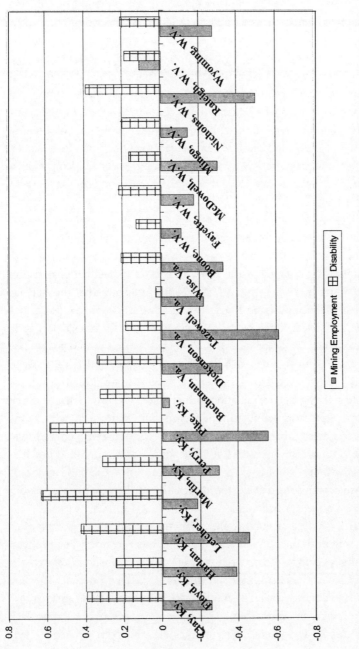
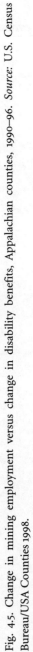

Fig. 4.5. Change in mining employment versus change in disability benefits, Appalachian counties, 1990–96. *Source:* U.S. Census Bureau/USA Counties 1998.

counties following the employment downturn in the industry during the 1980s. Due to the geographical isolation of these counties, the system of political and economic exploitation that accompanies absentee ownership, and the lack of human capital investment in coal production workers, we expected to find economically stagnant communities that were ill equipped to participate in the postindustrial economy of the 1990s. The task of documenting socioeconomic conditions in the region during the 1990s is made more difficult because much of the socioeconomic analysis relies on decennial census data. However, using a variety of other data we have been able to present a picture of a region after 1990 that meets with the expectations we presented above.

First, the data from the end of the 1980s show a region with low education levels and high rates of unemployment and poverty. What data we do have from the 1990s show that there has been some relative stability—compared to the 1980s—in the Appalachian coal region since 1990. Trends in per capita income data show that the Appalachian coal region is no longer losing ground to the U.S. per capita rate, after 1990. However, the coal region percentage of U.S. per capita income has remained steady at 65 percent since the mid-1980s. The regional birth rate had stabilized since 1990, after a decline between 1985 and 1989, suggesting a slower rate of out-migration of women of child-bearing age. Population projection data also indicate much more population stability in the region than before 1990, with a projected decrease in population of 0.1 percent between 1990 and 1999 (REIS 2000). However, the finding of more stability in the region during the 1990s is not a good sign. It indicates that the poor socioeconomic conditions that existed at the end of the 1980s, documented in table 4.2, have not changed.

This finding of stability and stagnation is consistent with expectations in both the human ecology and political economy perspectives. Human ecology theory predicts a state of equilibrium between the Appalachian coal counties and their external environments after the coal bust of the 1980s. The conditions of the Appalachian coal region's biophysical and ecumenical environments (geographic isolation, lack of access to agglomeration economies, etc.), coupled with overdependence on one market niche (coal production) for sustenance, created a situation such that when shrinkage in the niche occurred, there was a corresponding contraction in the ecosystem. Furthermore, the system will remain in a state of equilibrium until other forms of sustenance are introduced. The lack of well-educated workers, and the lack of access to agglomeration economies, however, makes it unlikely that new forms of sustenance will be found.

Critical political economy perspectives predict that stability arises from a system of domination and exploitation as well as surplus extraction. Historically the coal industry has created a system of exploitation and dependence in Appalachia by purchasing surrounding lands so that other competitors and industries cannot compete for labor. This gave coal companies total control over their workers' lives, and that control was reflected in the old company stores and scrip systems (Haynes 1997). The harsh socioeconomic conditions in the Appalachian coal region during the 1980s were created by the imperative of capitalism. Intense competition among coal producers during a period of falling prices accelerated the process of revolutionizing the means of production through mechanization of the extraction process. Many of the mines closed and thousands of workers lost their jobs (Dilger and Witt 1994). Those mines that remained opened were employing fewer and fewer workers. The aftermath of this transformation was a region of geographically isolated, very poor people unprepared to participate in the high-skill economy of the 1990s.

We presented the argument above that the system of economic and political domination (extended to local governance in Appalachia such that economic and political domination by absentee owners in conjunction with local elites) creates an environment whereby local tax revenues and social and public infrastructure expenditures are controlled by the interests of local and absentee elites. Our analysis on local government finances revealed some very interesting trends. The data show that both general revenues and expenditures are significantly lower in the Appalachian coal region than the average local government rates for the United States. This is not surprising. However, this trend remained constant over time, from 1972 through 1992. The 1970s were a period of expansion in coal-mining employment, while the 1980s were a period of contraction. Yet there were no discernable patterns regarding local government finances among the Appalachian coal counties across this period. And the only notable trend was that the per capita rate for both revenues and expenditures in the Appalachian coal region was about half the national rate for local governments in each year.

This analysis is consistent with the arguments concerning elite domination of local governance. Extending back in time before the downturn in coal-mining employment of the 1980s, we see significantly lower local government spending rates for local services and infrastructure. Therefore, the low levels of spending that we see for the later 1980s and 1990s are not necessarily a reflection of changing economic conditions but the continuation of a pattern of spending that began before the downturn in the coal industry. This finding is consistent with a pattern of historical, political, and economic domination of the local community by absentee owners and local elites. A system of low taxation and low expenditures has been in place in this part of Appalachia for as far back as these data allow us to measure.

Finally, over the last fifteen years employment levels in the Appalachian coal industry have remained static, while the production and consumption of Appalachian coal has steadily increased (*Energy Statistics Sourcebook* 1999). We foresee no change in this situation. Furthermore, it appears that a large percentage of displaced workers were moved to the disability income maintenance program. This is not a long-term solution to the current problem. Beginning in the 1980s, the Appalachian Regional Commission has spent considerable money on its distressed counties program (Wood and Bishack 2000). However, our data indicate that there is very little progress to show for it. The federal government must find more effective ways of managing distressed areas. The federal government must produce a better response.

Our analysis indicates that the coal industry will not be a new source of employment growth in Appalachia. Meanwhile, the coal counties in Appalachia have slipped farther behind all nonmetropolitan counties on key socioeconomic indicators. The average nonmetropolitan poverty rate in 1989 was 18.3 percent. Every county in the Appalachian coal region had a higher poverty rate, and half the coal region counties had a poverty rate at least 1.5 times greater than the average rate for all nonmetropolitan counties. The 1990 average percentage of adults who did not graduate from high school was 32.4 percent. Over 60 percent of Appalachian coal region counties have rates at least 1.5 times greater. The future holds more of the same. Like the truly disadvantaged trapped in inner-city poverty by industrial restructuring in the manufacturing sector, structural changes in the coal industry have created a region of truly disadvantaged people in rural America, with little prospect for change.

Notes

1. For example, coal-dependent McDowell County, West Virginia, experienced a 42 percent loss in population between 1980 and 1990 and during that same period experienced a 34 percent increase in the number of recipients of Supplemental Security Income. In 1987 per capita income in McDowell County reached only 50 percent of that for the entire United States, and in 1990 the county had an official poverty rate of 38 percent, almost three times the national rate (13 percent).

2. Supplemental Security Income (SSI) is a federal income supplement program to provide monthly payments for people who have limited income and resources if they are blind, are sixty-five and older, or have another disability. <http://www/ssa/gov/pubs/11001.html>.

References

Billings, Dwight B., and Kathleen M. Blee. 2000. *The Road to Poverty: The Making of Wealth and Hardship in Appalachia.* New York: Cambridge University Press.

Billings, Dwight, and Ann Tickamyer. 1993. "Uneven Development in Appalachia." In *Forgotten Places: Uneven Development in Rural America,* ed. Thomas A. Lyson and William W. Falk, 7–29. Lawrence: University Press of Kansas.

Burdge, Rabel J. 1998. *A Conceptual Approach to Social Impact Assessment.* Middleton, Wis.: Social Ecology Press.

Couto, Richard A. 1994. *An American Challenge: A Report on Economic Trends and Social Issues in Appalachia.* Dubuque: Kendall/Hunt Publishing.

Dilger, Robert Jay, and Tom Stuart Witt. 1994. "West Virginia's Economic Future." In *West Virginia in the 1990s: Opportunities for Economic Progress,* ed. Robert Dilger and Tom Witt, 3–16. Morgantown: West Virginia University Press.

Dorsey, Stuart. "The Strange Case of the Missing West Virginia Labor Force." *Growth and Change* 22:49–65.

Energy Statistics Sourcebook. 1999. 14th ed. PennWell, Oil and Gas Energy Database, August.

Gottdiener, Mark. 1994. *The New Urban Sociology.* New York: McGraw-Hill.

Gramling, Robert. 1996. *Oil on the Edge.* Albany: SUNY Press.

Hawley, Amos. 1986. *Human Ecology: A Theoretical Essay.* Chicago: University of Chicago Press.

Hawley, Clifford B. 1994. "Demographic Change and Economic Opportunity." In *West Virginia in the 1990s: Opportunities for Economic Progress,* ed. Robert Dilger and Tom Witt, 47–72. Morgantown: West Virginia University Press.

Haynes, Ada F. 1997. *Poverty in Central Appalachia.* New York: Garland Publishing.

Isserman, Andrew. 1995. "Then and Now: An Update of 'The Realities of Deprivation' Reported to the President in 1964." Working paper 9505, Regional Research Institute, West Virginia University, Morgantown.

Jensen, Leif, Jill L. Findeis, Wan-Ling Hsu, and Jason P. Schachter. 1999. "Slipping Into and Out of Underemployment: Another Disadvantage for Nonmetropolitan Workers." *Rural Sociology* 64 (3): 417–38.

Johnson, Kenneth M., John P. Pelissero, David B. Holian, and Michael T. Maly. 1995. "Local Government Fiscal Burden in Nonmetropolitan America." *Rural Sociology* 60:381–98.

Lichter, Daniel, and Diane K. McLaughlin. 1995. "Changing Economic Opportunities, Family Structure, and Poverty in Rural Areas." *Rural Sociology* 60 (4): 688–706.

Lobao, Linda. 1990. *Locality and Inequality: Farm and Industry Structure and Socioeconomic Conditions.* Albany: SUNY Press.

———. 1996. "A Sociology of the Periphery vs. a Peripheral Sociology." *Rural Sociology* 61:77–102.

Maggard, Sally W. 1994. "From Farm to Coal Camp to Back Office and Mc-Donald's: Living in the Midst of Appalachia's Latest Transformation." *Journal of Appalachian Studies Association* 6:14–38.

Matvey, Joseph J. 1987. "Central Appalachia: Distortions in Development, 1750–1986." Ph.D. dissertation, University of Pittsburgh.

Mencken, F. Carson. 1997. "Regional Differences in Socioeconomic Well-Being in Appalachia during the 1980s." *Sociological Focus* 30:79–97.

Nord, Mark, and A. Luloff. 1993. "Socioeconomic Heterogeneity of Mining-Dependent Counties." *Rural Sociology* 58:492–500.

REIS (Regional Economic Information Systems). 2000. U.S. Department of Commerce, Economics and Statistics Administration, Bureau of Economic Analysis. Washington, D.C.

RSS (Rural Sociological Society). Task Force on Persistent Rural Poverty. 1993a. Introduction to *Persistent Poverty in Rural America*, 1–19. Boulder: Westview.

———. 1993b. "Theories in the Study of Natural Resource-Dependent Communities and Persistent Rural Poverty in the United States." In *Persistent Poverty in Rural America*, 136–72. Boulder: Westview.

Tickamyer, Ann R., and Melissa Latimer. 1993. "A Multi-Level Analysis of Income Sources of the Poor and Near Poor." In *Inequalities in Labor Market Areas*, ed. Joachim Singelmann and Forrest Deseran, 49–68. Boulder: Westview.

Tickamyer, Ann R., and Cecil Tickamyer. 1991. "Gender, Family Structure, and Poverty in Central Appalachia." In *Appalachia: Social Context Past and Present*, ed. Bruce Ergood and Bruce E. Kuhre, 307–14. Dubuque: Kendall/Hunt Publishing.

United States. Bureau of the Census. 1991. *Census of Population and Housing, 1990.* Summary Tape File 3. Washington, D.C.: U.S. Bureau of the Census [producer and distributor]. Computer file.

———. 1998. *USA Counties 1998 on CD-ROM.* Washington, D.C.: U.S. Bureau of the Census [producer and distributor]. Machine-readable data files.

Wilson, William Julius. 1987. *The Truly Disadvantaged: The Inner City, the Underclass, and Public Policy.* Chicago: University of Chicago Press.

Wood, Lawrence E., and Gregory A. Bishack. 2000. "Progress and Challenges in Reducing Economic Distress in Appalachia: An Analysis of National and Regional Trends since 1960." Appalachian Regional Commission, Washington, D.C.

5

From Extraction to Amenities

Restructuring and (In)Conspicuous Consumption in Missoula, Montana

W. Richard Goe, Sean A. Noonan, and Sherry Thurston

OVER THE LAST several decades, the institutional practices by which firms conduct business activity in the U.S. economy, and the broader global economic system, have undergone substantial change. Corporate expansion, mergers, and acquisitions have furthered the development of multinational corporations. Labor processes have been transformed as the result of information technology, new labor policies, and innovative ways of organizing work. Markets for many goods and services have become global or regional in scale. Competition among firms in many industries has intensified, and the geographic location of business activity has undergone substantial change. These are but a few of the dimensions of change that have become collectively labeled as the process of economic restructuring.

In academic research on rural development in the United States, much discourse has focused on how economic restructuring has produced poor economic prospects for nonmetropolitan communities. Dependence on agriculture and natural-resource-based industries has resulted in diminishing employment opportunities for workers and residents in nonmetropolitan communities. This is attributable to the ongoing decline and consolidation of farm enterprises and firms in mining and other natural-resource-based industries, and to the further automation of these industries. In turn, the loss of employment opportunities for nonmetropolitan workers promotes outmigration to metropolitan centers, population loss, and increased poverty. For many nonmetropolitan communities, economic restructuring has led to a downward economic spiral of stagnation and decline, as such communities become peripheral or disarticulated from the broader economic system.

However, restructuring can also provide opportunities for nonmetropolitan communities to become further articulated, or reintegrated, with the broader economic system, perhaps resulting in growth and development. Recent academic discourse on rural development has given less attention to how economic restructuring may produce growth and development for nonmetropolitan communities. This chapter will examine this process through a case study of a former nonmetropolitan community that has experienced growth and development over the past two decades—Missoula, Montana. The city of Missoula, and its surrounding area, experienced sufficient growth after 1980 that it became reclassified over the course of the 1990s as a small metropolitan area. Our primary objective will be to use the data drawn from this case study to inductively construct elements of a theoretical model of community economic development that represents one path by which nonmetropolitan communities may achieve growth and development in the context of the post-1980 period of economic restructuring.

Research Methods

Both primary and secondary data were collected for the study. Primary data were collected through personal observation, focus groups, and personal interviews with members of selected groups of community residents from the city of Missoula in Missoula County, the city of Hamilton in nearby Ravalli County, and their surrounding areas. These two cities represented the two largest settlements in the Missoula commuting zone as delineated by Tolbert and Sizer (1996) to include Missoula, Ravalli, and Mineral Counties. The city of Missoula is the largest community within the commuter zone and the center of the local labor market. During the 1980s the spatial dimensions of the Missoula commuter zone experienced little change. Commuting workers from Granite County had been strongly tied to the three-county area (see Tolbert and Killian 1987). However, by 1990 these workers were tied to a different commuting zone, centered around Butte, Montana. Using the commuter zone as the unit of analysis for the case study permitted an examination of the ways in which the growth of the central community of Missoula affected the broader labor market area encompassing it.

The groups of community residents targeted in the focus groups and personal interviews included community leaders from the public and private sectors and workers employed within the local labor market. These groups were selected because of their knowledge of local development processes and conditions facing local workers. Members from each of these groups were administered an interview schedule designed to elicit their perceptions of local socioeconomic conditions and the social change that had occurred as a result of the growth of the local area. The focus groups and personal interviews primarily yielded qualitative data. These data were supplemented by secondary data drawn from public, statistical databases, including the Census of Population and Housing, County Business Patterns, and the Regional Economic Information System. In addition, relevant historical documents were examined, articles from the largest local newspaper, the *Missoulian,* were collected, and supplemental statistical information was collected from local government agencies during the fieldwork.

Local Growth and the Restructuring of the Missoula Economy after 1980

Before 1980 the development of the Missoula regional economy was primarily based on natural-resources extraction, education, and government services. The private sector of the local economy was dominated by the lumber and wood products industry. Over the course of the twentieth century, large, nationally based firms established and expanded operations in the Missoula commuting zone. Unionized jobs allowed large numbers of unskilled and nonprofessional workers to earn a living wage working in local sawmills. The public sector was dominated by the University of Montana, which grew steadily over the course of this period. Also, with a substantial number of national forests located in the vicinity, Missoula became the regional headquarters for the Northern Region of the USDA Forestry Service. With the ongoing development of retail trade and other support services, Missoula evolved into a trade center serving other communities in the surrounding area.

At the beginning of the 1980s, the Missoula commuting zone was in the nascent stages of an extended period of growth in population, jobs, and real income. The population within the three-county area increased from 102,433 persons in 1980 to 129,022 in 1999, for a net increase of 26,589 persons (U.S. Bureau of Economic Analysis 2001). Total employment increased from 48,666 jobs in 1980 to 84,568 jobs in 1999, for a net gain of 35,902 jobs (ibid.). Finally, the real aggregate income of the population (in 1980 dollars) increased from approximately $895.7 million in 1980 to $1.432 billion in 1999, for a real net increase in aggregate income of $536.1 million (ibid.). A breakdown of these trends indicates that the majority of this growth occurred during the 1990s compared to the 1980s. A substantial component of the new population settled within the city of Missoula. The population of the city increased from 33,388 persons in 1980 to 42,918 in 1990 to 52,239 in 1998 (Missoula Chamber of Commerce 1998).

This growth has both contributed to and been influenced by an extensive restructuring of the local economy. Among the historically important sectors of the local economy, employment in the lumber and wood products sector declined drastically from 3,468 jobs in 1980 to 1,899 in 1997, for a net loss of 1,569 jobs (U.S. Census Bureau 1980, 1997). This loss reflects the broader restructuring of the timber industry in the United States. As a result of corporate consolidation, the local lumber and wood products industry became dominated by a few large corporations, including Plum Creek Timber Corporation, Louisiana Pacific Corporation, and Smurfit-Stone Container

Corporation (Montana Department of Labor and Industry 1998). This resulted in fewer, but larger, sawmills operating within the area. Lumber production underwent further automation, which reduced the number of workers required to staff the production lines of the smaller number of mills that remain in operation. The end result of both these dimensions of change has been a substantial reduction in the number of local jobs available in the lumber and wood products industry.

The globalization of markets for timber and wood products has created new opportunities for local producers, while at the same time introducing new sources of instability that have had implications for local employment. The need for lumber to fuel construction in Southeast Asia provided an important source of demand for Missoula-based establishments in the lumber industry. However, the financial crisis in Asia in the latter half of the 1990s reduced this demand, creating instability for local timber firms. For example, during our fieldwork in Missoula, in September 1998, a smaller timber firm, Darby Lumber, was forced to lay off half its workers as a result of the Asian crisis (Rider 1998a). With the easing of the Asian crisis, global demand for local timber products began to pick up again (Keegan 1999).

The decline in timber harvesting and lumber production within the Missoula region has been somewhat offset by a shift toward the manufacturing of wood products with higher value added. One product that has become especially important to the local economy is the production of custom log homes, which command high prices in the housing market. With these homes, a design is created and dry logs are carefully selected to ensure the best fit as the home is test-assembled on the company's site. Next, all the pieces are numbered and inventoried and the house frame is disassembled. The pieces are then shipped to the construction site for reassembly. The market for custom log homes has also become globalized, as demand for the products of local firms was also affected by the Asian financial crisis. As will be detailed below, custom log homes are perceived to be a part of the Montana lifestyle that has attracted in-migrants into the local area. In sum, although the timber and wood products sector continues to provide a major source of employment within the Missoula region, it provides far fewer jobs than it did at the onset of the 1980s.

The drastic loss of jobs in the timber and wood products industry has been more than offset by the extensive growth of new jobs in the service sector of the economy. Employment growth has been primarily undergirded by the creation of new jobs in health services, retail trade, business services, and selected consumer services, such as eating and drinking places and amusement and recreation services.

Between 1980 and 1997 an estimated 3,241 new jobs were created in health services within the Missoula commuting zone (U.S. Census Bureau 1980, 1997). This growth was primarily accounted for by the development and expansion of local hospitals as well as the formation of the International Heart Institute of Montana as a joint venture between the local St. Patrick Hospital and the University of Montana. The institute is comprised of an internationally recognized team of cardiologists, heart surgeons, and researchers that perform the most advanced cardiac procedures and conduct research on new and improved ways to treat heart disease. An important factor that influenced this growth was the in-migration of doctors to the Missoula region because of its environmental (i.e., natural-resource) amenities. One local business leader stated,

> There are a variety of factors [why health care services are developing in Missoula] and part of it is environmental. . . . look at the . . . new heart center . . . he [the chief surgeon] moved up here because he wanted to be here. He liked the environment. . . . if somebody doesn't want to live in an urban center, Missoula is the place to be. In fact, they [doctors] don't even typically live in Missoula; a lot of them live in the Bitterroot [Valley] on a ranch . . . and commute to town.

Between 1980 and 1997, an estimated 3,100 new jobs were created in retail trade within the Missoula commuting zone (excluding eating and drinking places) (U.S. Census Bureau 1980, 1997). Over the last several decades, retail trade within the city of Missoula has undergone several distinct phases of development. In the late 1970s the region's first shopping mall (Southgate Mall) was constructed on a site several miles southwest of downtown Missoula. This had the short-term impact of depleting the composition of retail stores in the downtown area and prompted further retail development in this area of the community (rather than downtown). Both K-Mart and Walmart eventually built stores in this area.

In the 1990s another wave of investment in the area's retail infrastructure occurred. On a site northwest of downtown Missoula that is close to Interstate 90 (known as the Reserve Street corridor), strip development and the construction of retail space has occurred at a rapid pace. Major corporate retail chains, including Costco, Target, Barnes and Noble, and restaurant chains such as Fudruckers, have all invested in the construction of stores at this site. At the time the field research was conducted in 1998, new construction was still underway at this site and the road system was being expanded to accommodate higher volumes of traffic. Local business leaders stated that the investment by large retail chains was forthcoming after certain threshold levels in commuter traffic were reached. According to a local business leader,

> I think Missoula also got discovered . . . by the national market; we've gone from a lot of independent, locally owned businesses, to having every major national retailer known to man come to town. . . . But I think it is still a question mark about whether this town will support all those businesses which could have negative repercussions in the future. And small businesses are already feeling the repercussions. . . . all the retail shopping is going out to that Reserve Street corridor. I think that what a lot of it is based on is that the Reserve Street corridor finally reached a daily traffic count that met their marketing feasibility studies. . . . So they have reached eighteen thousand cars going by a day and they figured it means automatic success. So somehow we reached that level and all of the sudden there was a huge influx of national businesses.

In response to the development of new retail spaces within the community, Missoula's downtown now primarily consists of office space, restaurants, and specialized boutique and retail shops (e.g., branch offices of stock brokers, coffee bars, and outlets for mountain-climbing and outdoor sporting gear).

Employment in business services also increased substantially in the Missoula commuting zone over the 1980–97 period as a net 2,054 new jobs were created (U.S. Census Bureau 1980, 1997). The business services industrial group (as defined by the Standard Industrial Classification code) encompasses a diversity of services. Reflecting national trends, important components of this growth in Missoula included computer and data-processing services and personnel supply services (i.e., temporary employment agencies). Other two-digit industrial groups that provided over one thousand new jobs during the 1980–97 period included eating and drinking places and trucking and warehousing services (U.S. Census Bureau 1980, 1997). Sectors that provided less than a thousand but more than five hundred new jobs included social services (i.e., day care, elderly care) and amusement and recreation services (U.S. Census Bureau 1980, 1997).

The growth of retail trade and amusement and recreation services reflects, in part, the importance of tourism as a source of external income for the local economy. The expansion of Missoula's retail capacity enhanced the role of the community as a regional trade center, drawing in consumers from the surrounding region. The cultural events provided by the University of Montana (e.g., sporting events, concerts, theater) also provide an important source of tourist income. Additionally, public awareness of the natural resource and outdoor recreational amenities available in Montana has been heightened by numerous movies shot in the state, including *A River Runs Through It,* which was shot near Missoula. Missoula is located approximately 270 miles from Yellowstone National Park and 140 miles from Glacier National Park. As a result, it has become a destination for tourists seeking to consume the environmental amenities, recreational opportunities, and experiences provided by the Rocky Mountains.

In summary, with the post-1980 economic restructuring, Missoula not only is characterized by its traditional economic bases in educational services, timber and wood products, and government, but also serves as a large regional center for health services, retail and wholesale trade, consumer services, and to a limited extent, producer services. The severe structural decline of employment in timber harvesting and lumber production has been offset by the growth of new jobs in the service sector of the local economy. The local population has expanded as new migrants have moved into Missoula and the surrounding area. Moreover, the real aggregate income held by the local population has increased. As will be detailed below, this growth has created problems, as well as opportunities, for the community.

One effect of the growth experienced in the Missoula region after 1980 has been increased socioeconomic inequality among the expanding population. For example, despite the growth in real aggregate income discussed above, the average income per household declined from $31,498.26 in 1980 to $28,870.65 in 1990 when expressed in 1990 dollars (U.S. Census Bureau 1983, 1993). The percentage of households earning less than half the average household income increased from 28.4 percent in 1980 to 31.7 percent in 1990 while the percentage of households with incomes below the poverty threshold increased from 13.6 percent in 1980 to 17.3 percent in 1990 (U.S. Census Bureau 1983, 1993). Simultaneously, the percentage of households with twice the average household income increased from 6.5 percent in 1980 to 9.1 percent in 1990 (U.S. Census Bureau 1983, 1993). These data indicate substantial increases in the proportions of wealthy households and of lower-income or impoverished households between 1980 and 1990. While data from the 2000 census are not yet available, qualitative data from the field research suggests that the growth of inequality became further exacerbated over the course of the 1990s.

Key factors promoting the growth of inequality within the Missoula region include the growth of low-wage jobs in the regional labor market and the in-migration of new residents as reflected in the population and employment growth figures noted above. The growth of the number of households in the lower tail of the regional income distribution is a result of the growth of low-wage jobs. As noted above, the Missoula region experienced substantial job growth after 1980 in medical services, retail trade, and other services. However, a substantial proportion of the new jobs—in such occupations as clerical workers, administrative assistants, retail sales clerks, and cashiers— required low skill levels (U.S. Census Bureau 1983, 1993). The vast majority of these jobs paid at, or slightly above the minimum wage. As one worker stated,

Target comes in, and Costco comes in. . . . They come in and they do their research. They know what the level of pay is in this area and they are not going to pay anything far above that. They are going to make more of a profit margin just because their payroll is one of their largest items. If they can move into an area like this where they have a ready supply of kids that are willing to take minimum wage, they are going to pay minimum wage. What about the noneducated employee? The nonunionized, noneducated employee? They're also going to have to take $5.15 an hour.

Also, following national trends, some of the new jobs, particularly those in retail trade, have been part-time or temporary (or both). Another worker offered,

We are being crushed by huge corporations coming in. . . . Gart Sport moves in. It's a [nonlocal] corporation. Their funds move out of the area and go back to wherever they go. Yes, they employ thirty-five students at $5.15 an hour. I don't believe that minimum-wage service jobs benefit anyone other than the students who can barely survive. They work part-time shifts. They are not working in a full-time situation.

While job growth has been extensive over the past two decades and the unemployment rate is low, fierce competition exists in the regional labor market for scarce employment opportunities that pay well above the minimum wage, or are middle- and high-income salaried positions. In-migrants and recent college graduates searching for employment in the local labor market typically face considerable difficulty in landing such positions. As noted by an administrator at a local employment agency,

You've got a very competitive job market here and if you're not competitive . . . you are going to have trouble getting a job. We have people come into the agency from Minneapolis or someplace else and they'll go . . . "I can get a job in three or four days in Minneapolis or Seattle. I've been looking for four weeks here and I still haven't found anything." When we talk to people about it, we sort of say . . . this is an environmental desert in terms of jobs. If you've got a job skill, in a week you can go through every place in Missoula and determine where there is work. So we say, if you are going to look for a job . . . you've got to do it absolutely right. You've got to make sure you got your resume, interviewing skills, and so forth, because you only get one or two chances. And then a lot of times the good jobs at the middle-income level, you are essentially waiting for someone to die.

One result of this is that many highly educated or qualified in-migrants and University of Montana graduates that opt to remain in Missoula are forced to apply for and accept jobs for which they are overqualified or underpaid. In turn, this increases competition for low-end jobs and helps suppress local wages.

There is the perception among local workers and employers that people do not choose to work and reside in the Missoula area because of the limited opportunity for high-wage employment. Rather, they accept low-wage employment in order to take advantage of the local environmental and recreational amenities, lifestyle, and quality of life. As put by another administrator of a local employment agency,

> I think everybody who lives here is living here by choice. And they are living here because of the lifestyle.... even those that are unemployed or underemployed, I think, for the most part, say they would rather be unemployed here than to move to Seattle and live in a big city and raise their children there. There's a lot of those kinds of choices being made.

There is also the perception among local workers that the low-wage nature of the Missoula labor market is not just restricted to the contingent jobs and low-level service sector jobs that have been created. This problem also exists in many professional and other higher-level occupations as well. Personal interviews with college professors, lawyers, and other professionals revealed that they fully realized they could be earning much higher wages in other parts of the country. However, they chose to accept this situation in order to be able to enjoy the amenities and quality of life the Missoula region offers. As put by a loan fund administrator at a local financial services organization,

> I know if I moved to a big city I could make one and a half to two times what I make here. It's known if you live in Missoula, it's for qual-ity of life, not for making big bucks. But it's beautiful here. I love the rivers and rafting, so there is no better place in the world as far as I'm concerned.

And an educational administrator stated,

> Missoula and Montana are less populated. There are many sports available in this state. There is clean air for the most part. There's scenery. There's a more relaxed pace. People that are very educated are willing to earn much, much less. . . . for example, a Harvard professor moved here and took a $28,000 cut in pay, but was willing to trade that because he was a sportsman.

Outdoor recreational activities include fishing, hunting, whitewater rafting, kayaking, mountain biking, climbing, and hiking in the warmer months, and skiing, snowboarding, sledding, and snowmobiling in the winter. The ability to consume local environmental amenities and participate in outdoor recreational activities was found to be a major pull factor influencing the in-migration of new residents and the rapid population growth that has occurred within the Missoula region after 1980.

According to local community leaders and residents, the in-migrant stream has included not only lower-income persons seeking employment in the local labor market, but also a substantial stream of wealthy persons with high incomes. It is this part of the in-migrant stream that has contributed to the growth of the high-income segment of the income distribution. Among the high-income segment, four different types of in-migrant groups are perceived as having important effects on the local economy: celebrities; elderly retirees; early retirees; and telecommuting workers. Montana has become a choice location for the purchase or construction of leisure homes by celebrities. As noted by one local business leader:

> It's real hip to own property in Montana for the wealthy. . . . just to have that in your portfolio as something you might boast about. . . . Ranches in the Bitterroot Valley have been purchased whole and turned into preserves. . . . the value of those things has grown rapidly.

Celebrities such as David Letterman and Ted Turner have purchased ranches in Montana, not far from the Missoula commuting zone. Other public figures, such as Intel CEO Andrew Grove, own homes near the city of Hamilton in the Bitterroot Valley, as did the late Hoyt Axton. At the time this field research was being conducted, financier Charles Schwab was a partner in the construction of Stock Farm LLC, a 2,600-acre, upscale, gated community for the wealthy, also near Hamilton. Stock Farm includes such amenities as a golf course designed by Tom Fazio, a health club, equestrian center, and thirty miles of bridle trails. It was planned that 1,289 acres would be left undeveloped so that elk herds, which traditionally have used the area as a winter range, could remain. Prices for lots started at $250,000, while prices for finished, custom log homes ranged from $500,000 to $550,000 (Rider 1998c).

The Missoula region has also become an important retirement destination. As with the celebrities, this is due to the environmental and recreational amenities and the "Montana lifestyle." In one sense, the distinction between retirees and early retirees is superficial, as it is based solely on the age at which a person is able to retire from his or her job. However, early retirees were found to be more likely to invest their savings in the start-up of local businesses. According to one local business leader, there is a lot of volatility in the number of small business start-ups formed by retirees:

> We have a lot of people . . . who come here and retire, and are retiring early. . . . What they do is open their own retail business, or something like that . . . and decide that they can't make it; the competition is too heavy; it's too small for this economy to support, and they go out of business. We have a lot of those small businesses in and out on a regular basis. They close up and either move or they just can't make it.

It has long been contended that information technology has the capacity to free businesses and workers from the necessity of a centralized location. Evidence collected from the Missoula area suggests that the development of the Internet has had an effect on the in-migration of high-income residents. This has occurred through the creation of home-based, Internet-related businesses by recent in-migrants and the increasing prevalence of telecommuting by workers and business owners who have migrated to the Missoula region as a residential location. An official at the local Chamber of Commerce said:

> We're pretty lucky that they [businesses] come here for the location, and for the area, and they can now do business out of their home via

the Internet. We're seeing a lot of small starts that are growing into larger businesses in the community because of the recreational opportunities of rural Montana. . . . This is prevalent enough that we had at one time tried to start a home-based business committee on the chamber because there is a need for those people that are out there to network at some point with the business community . . . because of the nature of what they are doing. And sitting at home, they don't get out and meet everybody. . . . What we found is that they have a group that they work with already. I think in time . . . they'll probably grow into the business world with us in the chamber, but there are enough of them. We had quite a few in the mailing that we sent out. We were pretty amazed at how much that has grown.

A local housing expert said:

One of the things that builders will tell you is that a lot of the houses they are building, particularly for folks coming in, are very heavily computer-modem-oriented; and some of the folks coming in are those footloose folks who could locate anywhere; and they have high incomes. But they aren't hiring people. . . . They contribute insofar as they consume, but they are not employers.

The in-migration of persons running Internet-based businesses and telecommuting workers into the Missoula region has occurred predominantly for the same reasons the celebrities and retirees come. Given adequate telecommunications links, these workers are able to run their businesses or telecommute from their homes during the day, and then, for example, go rafting or mountain biking after work. They are then able to fly out of Missoula periodically to their place of employment for meetings. A real estate agent in the Bitterroot Valley stated:

A friend of mine owns a golf course in San Francisco and the biggest industrial building-cleaning and janitorial service in California and Hawaii. He can run his operation out of his office way up in the woods with a fax machine, and of course, his computers and modems . . . taking two or three trips down a year just to check on things. . . . He's got his machines in place and now he is free to escape.

An important effect of the growth in the upper tail of the income distribution via the in-migration of celebrities, retirees, and telecommuting business owners and workers is that it has served to stimulate a wave of inflation in the local economy. As a result, the cost of living in the region has increased substantially, particularly housing and real estate prices. Data from the Missoula Housing Authority (1998) indicate that the average cost of a home in the city of Missoula increased from $70,448 in 1990 to $145,859 in 1998. While this has a positive economic effect for long-term homeowners and the segment of community residents who have reaped the windfall from selling their homes at inflated prices, the downside is that wages in the local labor market have not kept pace.

Estimates from the Missoula Housing Authority (1998) also indicate that the annual income based on the average wage in the Missoula urban area was $18,790 in 1990, while the income needed to pay the mortgage, taxes, and insurance to purchase the averaged-priced home was $28,086. Thus, the income needed for a mortgage was approximately 149 percent of the annual average wage income. In 1996 the annual average wage income had risen to $21,814, but the income needed to pay mortgage, taxes, and insurance had risen to $41,852. The income needed for a mortgage had thus increased to approximately 192 percent of the annual average wage income.

As the cost-of-living has escalated in the Missoula region and wages have not kept pace, lower- and middle-income families and residents have had trouble making ends meet. Local workers described numerous cases of persons having to work two jobs in order to get by financially. This included not only female heads of families, but also members of married-couple families. One worker said:

> People are working two jobs to survive in Montana. So yes, we have an increase in jobs, but many people have two. . . . Thirty-five to forty percent of the state employees . . . on our campus work a second job so they can make choices besides just [paying] the rent, which is as much as a large metropolitan area here. . . . For instance, $600 is a normal rent. Our minimum wage is $5.15. So they may make over $8 an hour in one position, but that doesn't give them any money to spend on . . . what perhaps you would call luxuries, such as buying clothing for their job. So they work a second job at $5.50 an hour in . . . a service industry . . . so they will have enough money to pay for what their children

need for sports programs. Clothing for their kids, extras like trips, vacations, things like that, would be impossible, given the income of most of the middle class in Missoula.

One result is that an increasing proportion of employed residents in the lower tail of the income distribution can no longer afford to purchase a home in the city of Missoula and housing development has shifted outward from the city of Missoula to the outlying areas of Missoula County and into Ravalli and Mineral Counties. The city of Hamilton and the Bitterroot Valley in Ravalli County, in particular, have undergone rapid growth in the 1990s (see Rider, 1998b). In addition to ranches and housing developments for the wealthy, housing subdivisions for middle- and low-income families have been constructed at a rapid pace, particularly during the extended economic boom of the 1990s. Low- and middle-income families have moved outward into these housing developments because they can more readily afford to rent or purchase a home. Property values, taxes, and rents are lower compared to the city of Missoula. One worker in Missoula stated,

> I have a lot of friends that go to the university that live out in Florence now because the rent's cheaper. . . . Native Montanans are finding it harder and harder to live because they're usually in lower-income jobs . . . and so a lot of people, I hear, have a hard time making the rent and they start moving farther and farther out. They move east, west, and south just to get cheaper living conditions.

A business owner in Missoula said:

> I think that one of the effects of the population influx on employees has been the cost of housing. I think it has obviously exceeded the rate of any kind of income growth. And it has made it more difficult. We are in danger of reaching the thing that happened in Sun Valley [Idaho], where the people that worked in Sun Valley couldn't afford to live in Sun Valley. They kept moving further and further out and commuting into Sun Valley. I think we are starting to see that here.

The outward shift in housing development has had several effects on the structure of the local economy and the quality of life within the region. First, this has led to a further decline in the small agricultural base in the region as farmers have found it lucrative to sell land to developers. At the time the field research was being conducted, Highway 93, which connects Missoula and Hamilton, was being expanded to four lanes near Missoula in order to accommodate the greatly increased commuter traffic into the city on work days. Traffic congestion has emerged as a significant problem in the 1990s. This is a serious problem for the city of Missoula because the surrounding valleys tend to experience thermal inversions during the winter. As a result, smog from auto exhaust poses a health threat. Finally, the movement of young families outward in search of affordable housing has led to a decline in the elementary school enrollments within Missoula County, despite the net population growth that has occurred (*Missoulian* 1998).

In summary, the increase in income inequality within the Missoula commuting zone is attributable to: (1) the in-migration of wealthy families and individuals into the region, many of whom do not depend on the local labor market for their high incomes; (2) the extensive growth of low-wage, service-sector jobs; (3) the loss of high-wage jobs in the timber and wood products sector; and (4) the depression of wages in the labor market as a whole. The growth of inflation in the local cost-of-living as a result of the influx of wealth has heightened the economic pressure on low- and middle-income households and made it more difficult for them to make ends meet. Within the city of Missoula, the cost of home ownership has been pushed out of reach for many low-income families and young families, unless they opt to move outward and reside in the more remote areas of the commuter zone. Land in these remote areas of the commuter zone is also being purchased for the ranches and housing developments for the wealthy. In the future, this may threaten the capacity to develop affordable housing in these areas for low- and middle-income families.

The case study of Missoula, Montana, suggests several elements of a new model of development for nonmetropolitan communities in the United States in the context of the post-1980 restructuring. The findings allow for the inductive construction of several testable propositions, including the following:

- Change in the structure of the social stratification system in the United States over the past several decades has promoted the growth and development of nonmetropolitan communities.

The character of the in-migration and population growth in Missoula suggests that over the past several decades, the expansion of the U.S. economy, the extensive growth of the stock market, and the development of new institutionalized forms of work compensation (e.g., 401K plans, stock options) has expanded the upper-middle and upper-income strata, consisting of business owners, and professional, managerial, and highly skilled technical workers. Second, many members of these strata have locational freedom to migrate, reside, and work where they choose (either full-time or seasonally) and have opted to relocate to nonmetropolitan communities. Third, this has been facilitated by the rapid development of the Internet and other information technology, which has permitted new forms of on-line business and work, including telecommuting. According to the case study of Missoula, an important factor inducing members of this strata to migrate to nonmetropolitan communities is the presence of amenities and the lifestyles that such amenities permit.

- The amenities possessed by nonmetropolitan communities have become an important factor influencing where growth and development takes place.

The stock of amenities present in a nonmetropolitan community—such as natural resources, desirable climate, outdoor recreational opportunities, and cultural attractions—can influence growth and development by inducing in-migration, business investment, local spending, and new employment opportunities. In the case of Missoula, growth and development has been influenced by the presence of scenic natural resources (mountains, rivers, forests), outdoor recreational opportunities, and the lifestyles that such amenities permit. The desire to consume and experience these amenities and lifestyles has stimulated the in-migration of wealthy or high-income celebrities, retirees, and telecommuting workers, and increased the inflow of income from tourism. The growth of the local population expanded the inflow of wealth into the region and stimulated business investment in industries targeted toward meeting the consumption needs of local residents and tourists.

The importance of amenities has increased the complexity of the role of natural resources in influencing the growth and development of nonmetropolitan communities. In earlier historical periods, the primary role of natural resources was to serve as a raw material, or factor of production, that was to be extracted, or harvested, and exported outside the community as an input to be used in a broader "commodity chain" (Gereffi 1994).

With the restructuring processes, the key role of the local stock of natural resources is to serve as part of the landscape that promotes various forms of commodification within the locality of the community and its labor market. The landscape induces investment in goods and infrastructure that can be used to provide commercial recreational services (e.g., white-water rafting outfits, fishing camps, ski resorts). Note that the consumption of these services does not involve the destruction and export of pieces of the landscape but rather interaction with it. In turn, this interaction can bring about a different form of degradation (e.g., litter, overcrowding). Additionally, the landscape serves as a backdrop that induces and enhances other forms of commodification within the community, such as investment in housing developments, shopping areas, and commercial buildings and infrastructure. These forms of commodification are oriented primarily toward consumption rather than production.

- Economic growth in expanding nonmetropolitan communities is being undergirded primarily by investment in industries that support the consumption needs of the local population.

Employment growth in Missoula has occurred predominantly in industries that support the consumption needs of the expanding population, including health care, elderly care, retail trade and shopping, and various types of consumer services (e.g., eating and drinking places, recreational services). Part of the investment to expand these sectors of the economy has come from multinational retail chains seeking new markets, which represents one way in which the community has become more strongly integrated into the global economy. Another part has come from local entrepreneurs or in-migrants who have invested in the creation of small business such as local retail boutiques or home-based Internet businesses (see, for example, Rider 1999).

This implies that economic growth in expanding nonmetropolitan communities that follows this model does not result from investment and expansion in traditional extractive industries (agriculture, mining, forestry) or manufacturing. While such industries may continue to provide an important foundation for the local economy, they do not represent an important source of new jobs or business investment. Moreover, the extensiveness of their role as a source of income for local workers has diminished. In the case of Missoula, timber harvesting and wood products continue to be important in the local economy, but employ far fewer workers than during earlier periods.

- Most of the income and financial capital needed to stimulate growth in expanding nonmetropolitan communities is derived from external sources rather than local production and export of agricultural commodities, natural resources, or manufactured goods.

Traditional models of economic development, such as the economic base model (Thompson 1965), posit that communities grow and develop through extracting natural resources or producing goods that are exported outside the community. Export income then flows back into the community, where it is used to support the growth and development of other sectors of the economy. The case of Missoula suggests an alternative process in which nonmetropolitan communities may be integrated into the broader global economy and circuits of capital.

First, the income brought in to the region by celebrities, retirees, early retirees, telecommuting workers, and tourists was, or is, earned in regional economies and labor markets outside the Missoula commuting zone. This income is then drawn into the Missoula region, where it is used primarily to support the consumption of amenities, particular lifestyles, living needs, and leisure or recreational activities of these groups. Second, as noted above, the development of Missoula has attracted outside investment from multinational retail chains in search of expanding markets. In effect, the development of a consumption-oriented service economy is the driving force in increasing the external inflow of income and wealth into the region.

It is important to emphasize that the traditional-economic-base model may still provide an important foundation in the income flow required to sustain nonmetropolitan communities conforming to this model of development. Indeed, in the case of the Missoula, the export of goods produced by local firms such as timber, custom log homes, medical and dental supplies, sporting goods, and educational services was drawing in external income from national and global markets. However, this income is not primary in sustaining the expansion of the community.

The findings from this case study suggest that in the period of economic restructuring after 1980, some nonmetropolitan communities in the United States achieved growth and development through the transformation of their role in the circuits of capital of the global economy. In earlier historical regimes of accumulation, the primary role of Missoula and its surrounding region was to serve as a location for the education of workers and the production of timber and wood products. These products were then exported to be used as inputs in broader commodity chains, which in turn, sustained the growth and development of the community. With the recent period of economic restructuring, Missoula, as well as other nonmetropolitan communities that are following this path of development, have become places of consumption, where the circulation of commodities for final consumption has become of paramount importance in supporting economic growth and the employment of local workers.

As a place of consumption, Missoula is an appealing locality, in part because it is unlike so many other places. The natural beauty of the mountains, forests, and streams, as well as the relatively less urbanized character of the city of Missoula itself, combine to make the Missoula region desirable as a place of consumption in which to reside, meet living needs, and engage in leisure activities (Rojek and Urry 1997; Urry 1995). As in-migration has proceeded and the local economy has grown, Missoula has increasingly come to exhibit consumption patterns that closely parallel the "cathedrals of consumption" that dominate so much of the U.S. economic and cultural landscape (Ritzer 1999). Specialized boutiques and services that cater to the high-income in-migrants and national-brand retail stores and restaurants have flocked to Missoula, producing a significant expansion in the local means of consumption.

An important contradiction to this path of development is that these cathedrals of consumption, which involve the mix of entertainment and enchantment that characterize the contemporary shopping mall, have begun to transform the Missoula region into the very places many in-migrants left in the first place (Kowinski 1985).

In the case of Missoula, the transformation into a place of consumption has resulted in increased inequality. The growth of the community has stimulated high inflation in the local cost of living, but increases in local wages have not kept pace. Workers dependent on the local labor market for their incomes have faced increased difficulty in making ends meet, with many being forced to reside in more affordable, peripheral areas of the commuting zone. At the time the field research was being conducted in Missoula, the community was experiencing many of the disruptions associated with rapid growth, including increased crime, traffic congestion, road rage, smog, and population congestion (see, for example, England and Albrecht 1984; Freudenberg and Jones 1991; Hunter, Krannich, and Smith 2002). It remains to be seen how these problems will affect the future course of development in the community.

References

England, J. Lynn, and S. L. Albrecht. 1984. "Boomtowns and Social Disruption." *Rural Sociology* 49:230–46.

Freudenberg, William L., and R. E. Jones. 1991. "Criminal Behavior and Rapid Community Growth: Examining the Evidence." *Rural Sociology* 56:619–45.

Gereffi, Gary. 1994. "The International Economy and Economic Development." In *The Handbook of Economic Sociology,* ed. Neil J. Smelser and Richard Swedberg, 206–33. Princeton: Princeton University Press.

Hunter, Lori M., Richard S. Krannich, and Michael D. Smith. 2002. "Rural Migration, Rapid Growth, and Fear of Crime." *Rural Sociology* 67:71–89.

Keegan, Charles. 1999. "Rising Lumber Prices Drive Up Production, Wages." News Releases, University of Montana, Missoula, June 21, <http://www.umt.edu/urelations/releases>.

Kowinski, William. 1985. *The Malling of America: An Inside Look at the Great Consumer Paradise.* New York. Morrow.

Missoula Area Chamber of Commerce. 1998. *Demographics: Missoula Community Profile.* September, <http://www.missoulachamber.com/fcmain.asp>.

Missoula Housing Authority. 1998. "Data on Housing Costs and Income for the Missoula Area." Memo.

Missoulian. 1998. "Where Have All the Children Gone?" Editorial, *Missoulian,* September 27, A8.

Montana Department of Labor and Industry. 1998. "Labor Market Information for Missoula, Ravalli, and Mineral Counties." Memorandum.

Rider, Jane. 1998a. "Darby Lumber Lays Off Forty Workers." *Missoulian,* September 29, A1.

———. 1998b. "Ravalli County Development Slows as Room to Grow Narrows." *Missoulian,* October 3, A1.

———. 1999c. "Up on the Farm: Golf Memberships for $35,000, Lots for $250,000, Cabins for $500,000." *Missoulian Online,* September 1, <http://www.missoulian.com/archives/>.

———. 1999. "Bitterroot Main Street Circling the www.globe" *Missoulian Online,* January 29, <http://www.missoulian.com/archives/>.

Ritzer, George. 1999. *Enchanting a Disenchanted World: Revolutionizing the Means of Consumption.* Thousand Oaks, Calif.: Pine Forge Press.

Rojek, Chris, and Urry, John, eds. 1997. *Touring Cultures.* London: Routledge.

Thompson, Wilbur R. 1965. Preface to *Urban Economics.* Baltimore: Johns Hopkins University Press.

Tolbert, Charles M., and Molly Sizer Killian. 1987. *Labor Market Areas for the United States.* Staff Report no. AGES-870721. Washington, D.C.: Economic Research Service, U.S. Department of Agriculture.

Tolbert, Charles M., and Molly Sizer. 1996. *U.S. Commuting Zones and Labor Market Areas: A 1990 Update.* Staff Paper no. AGES-9614. Washington, D.C.: Rural Economy Division, Economic Research Service, U.S. Department of Agriculture.

United States. Department of Commerce. Bureau of the Census. 1980. *County Business Patterns.* Washington, D.C.: Bureau of the Census, Unites States Department of Commerce.

———. 1983. *Census of Population and Housing, 1980.* Summary Tape File 4c. Washington, D.C.: Bureau of the Census, Unites States Department of Commerce. Machine-readable data files.

———. 1993. *Census of Population and Housing, 1990.* Summary Tape File 4. Washington, D.C.: Bureau of the Census, United States Department of Commerce. Machine-readable data files.

———. 1997. *County Business Patterns.* Washington, D.C.: Bureau of the Census, United States Department of Commerce.

United States. Department of Commerce. Bureau of Economic Analysis. 2001. *Regional Economic Information System, 1969–99.* Washington, D.C.: Bureau of Economic Analysis, United States Department of Commerce. Machine-readable data files.

Urry, John. 1995. *Consuming Places.* London: Routledge.

Part II

Work and Community

Ethnic, Racial, and Regional Embeddedness

6

Troubled Waters or Business as Usual?

Ethnicity, Social Capital, and Community in the Louisiana Oyster Fishery

Forrest A. Deseran and Carl M. Riden

THE OYSTER HAS long been an integral part of Louisiana culture. From its humble beginnings as an accessible staple for native peoples and early colonists, the oyster has been transformed, through intensive mariculture, into a plump, juicy cultural icon. In fact, Dixie Beer and oysters on the half shell are to the New Orleans French Quarter what a hot dog with mustard is to Coney Island. Despite its cultural and culinary importance, however, the plight of Louisiana's extensive oyster cultivation and harvesting industry has received little attention. In this chapter we examine the Louisiana oyster industry as an occupational community that is struggling to survive in the face of changing economic and social conditions. Our primary objective is to empirically analyze the effects of social and human capital and ethnic identity on the viability of this long-established but threatened occupational community. We begin with a brief overview of the history and character of this fishery, followed by a discussion of how Louisiana oystermen comprise a type of ethnic occupational community that gives rise to social capital.

An Overview of the Louisiana Oyster Industry

THE EARLY DAYS

Oyster harvesting is the oldest of Louisiana's state-managed seafood industries. In the early nineteenth century oysters were harvested from natural reefs for local use. Although beds were set aside for private culture as early as the 1840s, it was not until after the Civil War that large-scale bedding and transplanting of oysters began. With the development of the oyster canning process in the 1880s and the immigration of Croatians skilled in oyster cultivation, the oyster industry entered a period of rapid expansion (Padgett 1960). It was at this time that the practice of transplanting oysters from natural reefs east of the Mississippi delta to the more saline waters west of the river began. In this brackish-water environment, maximum growth and development of adult oysters could be achieved (Van Sicle et al. 1976). By the beginning of the twentieth century cultivating oysters had become the mainstay of Louisiana's seafood industry and the remaining natural reefs were put under state control. Comprehensive oyster management legislation, first passed in 1902, further encouraged the practice of oyster mariculture and established the basic structure of the industry we see today, including public management of reefs for seed oyster production and private leasing of water bottom from the state.

ETHNIC ROOTS

The history of the Louisiana oyster industry is closely intertwined with the contributions of a variety of ethnic groups, including English, French, Italian, and Irish (Wicker 1979). Each of these groups settled in geographically distinct areas, where their impact can still be noted today. Those of French descent comprise the largest percentage of harvesters, while the Croatians (alternatively referred to as Yugoslavs, Slavonians, or Dalmatians) make up the next largest presence in the industry. The Croats were the pioneers who developed oystering from a "haphazard, part-time, extractive industry to a highly organized and year-round occupation" (Padgett 1960). Arriving in New

Orleans from the Dalmatian coast of Eastern Europe in the mid- to late 1800s, many Croatian immigrants eventually moved south to Plaquemines Parish to take up fishing when they were unable to find work in New Orleans. Some of these early settlers had immigrated from areas along the Adriatic Sea where oysters had been cultivated for centuries, so it was natural for them to take up this activity in Louisiana waters (Vujnovich 1974). Croatian harvesters were also responsible for the development of gear that improved the efficiency of harvesting operations, including dredges (1905) and power winches for lifting dredges (1913) (Padgett 1960; Van Sicle et al. 1976).

A FIXED-BOTTOM ENTERPRISE

To appreciate the nature of the Louisiana oyster fishery, it is important to understand that oyster fishing is a fixed-bottom enterprise. Oyster mariculture is much closer to farming than to other fisheries. Oysters develop while attached to reefs. Their propagation thus involves the private leasing of water bottoms on which reefs can develop, the transfer and bedding of seed oysters to those reefs, and the eventual harvest of oysters as they reach marketable size. This complex and labor-intensive system continues to be the mainstay of the state's oyster industry. Roberts and Keithly (1993) estimate that of the approximately three hundred thousand acres of Louisiana water bottom in oyster production, over 80 percent were leased privately.[1] One consequence of the fixed-bottom character of the fishery is that it makes the oyster harvester very vulnerable to adverse effects of both nature and human activity on oyster populations. This is quite different from the open-access nature of the shrimp and fin-fish fisheries, in which fishermen can move their operations when problems arise. Oyster harvesting is particularly sensitive to problems like pollution and changes in water salinity.

The Louisiana Oyster Industry Today

Louisiana is the largest producer of oysters in the United States today. Data from the National Marine Fisheries Service (1999) indicate that

Gulf of Mexico waters accounted for 58 percent of all U.S. production and Louisiana claimed nearly 60 percent of all Gulf landings. These statistics leave little doubt about the importance of the fishery to both Louisiana and to the nation.

Yet, despite Louisiana's leadership in oyster production, local harvesters are facing an array of biological, environmental, and management problems that threaten the industry. Like other commercial fishermen operating out of Louisiana, oyster harvesters have been adversely affected by pressures from environmental disturbances associated with the deterioration of wetlands and the increase in effluents from land-based industries. These environmental disturbances increase predation, parasite infestation, and pathogenic problems. Predation from southern oyster drills ("conches"), blue and stone crab, and black drum fish is an ongoing hazard for oysters. In addition, the costs of equipment and operations have grown substantially while imported seafood products have taken an increasing share of the U.S. market. Finally, regulatory restrictions on harvesting locations and seasons have reduced the industry's productive capacity.

Perhaps the most highly publicized problem facing the industry is a series of deaths and illnesses attributed to a bacterium (*Vibrio vunificus*) that can develop in oysters, especially during the summer. Due to this virus, in the summer of 1994 the U.S. Food and Drug Administration proposed an annual April through October ban on the sale of raw oysters. Should such a ban have been implemented, it was estimated that up to half the Louisianans involved in the oyster industry could lose their jobs (McKinney 1994). Although such a far-reaching closure has not been implemented, the possibility continues to be a major threat to the future of the industry.

SOCIAL CAPITAL, OCCUPATIONAL COMMUNITY,
AND RECRUITMENT

Faced with this array of economic and environmental obstacles is a geographically concentrated oyster harvesting community comprised mainly of owner-operated enterprises and centered around families with extensive histories in oyster production. How are these oystermen reacting to the pressures and what are the prospects for the future of their occupational community? We do know that, despite the bleak outlook, almost none of the currently active oystermen have plans to exit the fishery in the near future (Deseran and Riden 2000). But what about the next generation of oystermen? Are oystermen encouraging their children to carry on the occupational traditions of their fathers and grandfathers? The recruitment of future generations into the occupation is at the heart of the persistence of this occupational community and the focus of the research we report here.

In general, fishing groups within complex stratified societies can be described as occupational communities (Davis 1986; Lummis 1977; Nadel 1984; Nadel-Klein and Davis 1988). Fishermen tend to have strong kinship and community ties. The nature of their occupation tends to isolate them, both temporally and geographically (Nadel-Klein and Davis, 1988). They often share a strong sense of occupational identity and their work and family lives are heavily interwoven (Margavio and Forsyth 1996). As both Blauner (1960) and Salaman (1971) state, an occupational community is characterized by a high degree of convergence between work and nonwork life. Members share a "common life" that is distinct from others in society and their values and worldviews tend to center on the occupation and its culture. This strong group solidarity leads to a shared identity and a distinct self-image. Many fishermen, for example, continue to identify themselves as such whether they are currently fishing or not (Ellis 1984; Garrity-Blake 1996; Margavio and Forsyth 1996). Affiliation with an occupational community can provide both powerful incentives for members to hang on during difficult periods and the necessary support for them to do so.

The close-knit social networks that arise in communities like these can be viewed as social capital on which individual members can rely. Social capital is rooted in networks of kin, neighbors, and friends operating in ways that influence local economy and lifestyle (Richling 1985). It consists of "obligations and expectations, information channels, and a set of norms and effective sanctions that constrain and/or encourage certain kinds of behavior" (Wall, Ferrazzi, and Schryer 1998, 308). The networks of relationships, norms, and trust, so integral to the concept of social capital, are most often viewed as resources that facilitate coordination and cooperation and enhance the benefits of investment in physical and human capital (Putnam 1993). Social capital can thus be used by individuals to enhance features such as "learning, social mobility, economic growth, political prominence, or community vitality" (Wall, Ferrazzi, and Schryer 1998, 304). Social capital may also contribute to children's development of human capital (education, skills) and affect their goals and life chances (Coleman 1988).

The relationships that, at least partially, comprise social capital can be both formal ties, such as membership in voluntary organizations, and informal ones based in friendship, kinship, and proximity in space or exchange (Paxton 1999; Wasserman and Faust 1994). The location of these relationships in both social and geographic space has been used to distinguish between dimensions of social capital that may offer different possibilities for those who utilize them. Woolcock (1998) argues that there are two key dimensions of social capital at the micro level: integration and linkage. Integration consists of intracommunity ties, which are an important source of social capital that allows members to provide one another with services and resources such as job referrals or child care. Linkage refers to extracommunity networks. Linkage ties can provide an individual with both greater freedom and the opportunities to participate in a wider range of activities. The presence or absence of these two components greatly impacts the role social capital plays. Portes and Sensenbrenner (1993) support this argument when they describe the role of intra- and extracommunity ties in immigrant communities. They found that individuals who can draw on a variety of social resources, including social approval and business opportunities, from outside their ethnic community, were less constrained by the norms and expectations of that community. At the same time, individuals often chose to maintain ties to their ethnic community because of the opportunities such networks provide.

While much of the research into the development and function of social capital's various forms has focused on entrepreneurship in urban ethnic and minority enclaves (see Light 1972; Portes and Sensenbrenner 1993; Portes and Stepick 1993), there is no reason to assume that these dimensions of social capital cannot arise in other similarly close-knit communities. We believe that Louisiana oystermen, with their deep historical roots and distinctive ethnic composition (Cajun French and Croatians have dominated the industry for the last century), represent a type of ethnic enclave and occupational community within which social capital should be of particular importance. Even when faced by environmental, regulatory, and market circumstances that cast a shadow over the future of the fishery, it is an occupation and community few wish to leave. In the face of this uncertain future, questions arise not only about the work-related decisions of the current oystermen, but also about their children's decision to take up the occupation of their forebears.

Methods

TARGET POPULATION AND SAMPLING

In 1998 we conducted a telephone survey of Louisiana commercial oystermen. The target population was all Louisiana residents who held a commercial oyster-harvesting license at least once between 1994 and 1997. The Louisiana Department of Wildlife and Fisheries has records for 1,794 holders of commercial oyster licenses for this four-year period. From this pool we contacted 618 randomly selected subjects, of which 76 percent (469) completed the interview, 21 percent declined to participate, and 3 percent did not fully complete the instrument. Of those who completed the survey, only 316 (67.4 percent) were currently active in the industry. The data for our analyses are from interviews with the currently active harvesters.

MODEL AND VARIABLES

Dependent Variable

Our analysis examines the influence of human and social capital to determine whether oystermen encourage their children to enter the oyster-harvesting business. Our dependent variable is based on a simple question: Have you encouraged, or would you encourage, your children to enter oyster harvesting? (Yes = 1; No = 0).[2]

The Model

Our model consists of three major categories of independent variables. To disentangle the effects of social and human capital, we distinguish between forms of capital that are uniquely linked to commercial fishing (our first category of independent variables) and those forms we consider to be more applicable to the broader labor market (our second category). Additionally, although the line between indicators of social capital and of community attachment is fuzzy, we treat separately those community-based factors that are not explicitly linked to the fishing industry or to the more general labor market.

SOCIAL CAPITAL ASSOCIATED WITH OYSTER HARVESTING

We include four indicators of social capital that are linked to commercial fishing. The first is ethnic identity. As we mentioned above, ethnic composition is a definitive characteristic of the oyster-harvesting industry in Louisiana. In particular, Cajun French and Croatian identities define distinct sectors of this occupational community. Although these sectors may not attain the ethnic density of some urban ethnic enclaves as discussed in other studies (e.g., Portes and Sensenbrenner 1993), we do feel that sharing traditions, customs, and language in small rural communities fosters social networks similar to those found in urban ethnic enclaves. Membership in these ethnic groups, and the occupational community of which they are a part, should thus indicate access to strong social capital. We would anticipate that members of these ethnic groups will be more motivated to encourage their children to maintain family occupational traditions than those without ethnic ties. In addition, because Croatians historically have played the most central role in the development of the industry (through the development of extensive mariculture techniques and introduction of successful marketing practices), we would expect this group to be the most likely to encourage their children. Our second indicator of social capital in this category is family history in the industry, measured as one of three possibilities: (1) both father and a grandfather were commercial fishermen, (2) either father or a grandfather was a commercial fisherman, or (3) neither father nor a grandfather was in the business. Third, we distinguish those who claim to have inherited the family business from those who did not. Finally, we treat having a family member or close relative as a crew member as an indicator of social capital. These final three indicators represent a harvester's embeddedness in the industry and his or her access to social ties that are often necessary for the maintenance of an oyster operation.

HUMAN CAPITAL ASSOCIATED WITH OYSTER HARVESTING

Turning to human capital, we include two indicators of investment in the industry: number of years in the business and cross-species fishing. Number of years in the business, as an indicator of work experience,[3] is categorized as less than 10 years, 10 to 19 years, and 20 or more years. Cross-species fishing is an economic strategy used by many commercial fishermen. We consider this to be a form of human capital investment in the oyster fishery in that this extra effort involves investments and commitments that are transferrable to oyster-harvesting efforts (maintaining and operating a vessel, keeping contacts with wholesalers, etc.). We expect that fishing-specific human capital factors, excluding all other effects, will increase the odds that children will be encouraged to enter the industry.

SOCIAL CAPITAL ASSOCIATED WITH THE GENERAL LABOR MARKET

Our data provided us with three measures of family-based social capital that appear to be relevant to the broader labor market. The first involves the educational attainment in oyster harvesters' families of origin. Although educational attainment is generally considered to be a human capital measure, we consider the educational levels of oyster harvesters' families to be a potential resource available to harvesters by virtue of their family membership. The possible benefit (or lack of benefit) from family educational attainment is a property of family affiliation, not individual attainment. We distinguish between families where neither parent completed high school and those where at least one parent did.[4] We also consider the educational attainment of an oysterman's spouse to be a type of social capital at the household level.[5] Finally, the paid employment of a spouse in a job other than commercial fishing is included as a form of social capital that links the household to the more general labor market. We suspect that oyster harvesters families' investment in education and in the broader labor market would diminish the propensity of oystermen to encourage their children to enter the profession.

HUMAN CAPITAL ASSOCIATED WITH THE GENERAL LABOR MARKET

Our models contain three types of human capital that we consider to be oriented to the more general labor market–educational attainment, prior work experience (other than commercial fishing), and holding a second job outside of commercial fishing. Educational attainment is dichotomized between those with and those without a high school diploma. Prior and current work experiences are each dichotomized in the same manner. As with our indicators of social capital, we expect to find that human capital investments that are relevant to the broader labor market would have a dampening effect on encouraging children to take up oyster harvesting.

COMMUNITY ATTACHMENT, ORGANIZATIONAL MEMBERSHIP, AND COMMUNITY PARTICIPATION

In our third category of variables we examine the effects of several factors grounded in community of residence. First, we create a measure of community attachment based on three aspects of community life–satisfaction with community as a place to live, how pleased one would be to move to another location, and having enough people to talk to. For our models we aggregate scores into three categories of community attachment: high, intermediate, and low.[6] We also include organizational membership as an indicator of civic involvement. Here we record if respondents are a member of more than one type of organization, a member of only one type, or a member of no organization. Next, to measure community involvement, we asked our subjects if they had ever personally spoken or written to some member of local government or some other person of influence in the community about some needs or problems (yes = 1, no = 0). We anticipate that each of these three measures of community will have a positive effect on our dependent variable.

CONTROL VARIABLES

We include three control variables in our analysis. First, to control for biases that may be introduced by the parental status of respondents, we assigned a value of one to those with children and a value of zero to those without children. Second, we control for the effects of oystermen's unhappiness with regulatory demands. Our survey found strong feelings about what oystermen perceive to be overbearing governmental rules and regulations (Deseran and Riden 2000). These sentiments were particularly volatile at the time of the survey because of recent threats of closing the fishery due to food safety concerns. We asked subjects if they felt overburdened by government rules and regulations—a lot of the time, some of the time, only once in a while, or never. We dichotomize responses into "a lot of the time" versus other responses. Finally, we add community size as a control, dichotomizing between those above and those below a population of five thousand.

Findings

Tables 6.1 and 6.2 offer a descriptive summary of our model variables. We present our findings by ethnic category to allow a comparative overview across ethnic groups.

The pattern of responses to our question of whether or not oyster-men encourage their children to take up oyster harvesting is of interest for a couple of reasons (table 6.1). First, nearly two-thirds of the oystermen we interviewed claimed they did not or would not encourage their children. This was somewhat surprising in that commercial fishing tends to be passed down through generations of a family. Indeed, almost 70 percent of the oystermen in our sample reported that at a minimum either their father or a grandfather was in the business. Second, a substantially higher proportion of Croatian oystermen, especially compared to Cajun oystermen, responded that they would not encourage their children. This is particularly interesting because, as noted earlier (and reflected in the findings below), compared to others in the fishery, Croatians represent a disproportionate share of the industry both in terms of historical background and invested resources. Why are Croations so much less likely than others in the industry to encourage their children to stay in the family business? This is the question we will address in our analysis.

Social Capital Associated with Oyster Harvesting

Table 6.1 displays the percentages for four social capital indicators—ethnic identity, family background in commercial fishing, inheritance of the family business, and family as crew members. Our findings for these harvesting-linked dimensions of social capital underscore the embeddedness of the Croatians in the industry. Although a distinct minority in numbers (14.2 percent), members of this ethnic group are much more likely to be preceded in the business by a father and grandfather (53.3 percent) and to have inherited the family business (66.7 percent). Interestingly, Croatians are less likely to have family members on their crews than are Cajuns or others.

Human Capital Associated with Oyster Harvesting

Our findings for the human capital resources relevant to oyster harvesting reveal even more about the extent to which Croatians are entrenched in this Louisiana fishery (table 6.1). As indicated by the number of years in the business, Croatians clearly represent the most experienced segment of the fishery. In addition, we find that cross-species fishing is a strategy used by nearly a third of non-Croatian harvesters, but by less than 7 percent of the Croatians.[7]

Community

The indicators of local community attachment reveal some noteworthy differences, especially between Croatian and Cajun respondents. Our community satisfaction results show that, compared to Cajun and other oystermen, Croatian oystermen express far less satisfaction with their communities, while at the same time reporting much higher rates of participation in local organizations. Although the differences are not as extensive, our indicator of community influence reveals the Croatians are more likely than their counterparts to have ever personally spoken or written to some member of local government or some other person of influence in the community about needs or problems.

SOCIAL AND HUMAN CAPITAL ASSOCIATED WITH THE GENERAL LABOR MARKET

Turning to capital resources oriented toward the general labor market (table 6.2), we continue to find marked differences between the Croatians and others. The educational attainment levels of Croatian oystermen's parents and of spouses are substantially higher than those of the parents and spouses of other oystermen. It appears, however, that this higher educational attainment level is not related to wives' participation in the labor force, where we find essentially no ethnic differences for the percent of spouses participating in the nonfishing labor force. As with parental educational attainment, Croatian oystermen

Table 6.1
Dependent Variable, Human and Social Capital Resources Relevant to Commercial Fishing, and Community Attachment by Ethnic Identity (percent)

	All Oystermen (N = 316)	Ethnic Identity		
		Cajun (N = 116)	Croat (N = 45)	Other (N = 155)
Dependent Variable				
Encourage child to harvest oysters (1 = yes)	35.8	46.6	24.4	31.0%
Independent Variables				
Capital Resources (Commercial Fishing)				
Social Capital				
Ethnic identity				
Cajun	36.7	—	—	—
Croatian	14.2	—	—	—
Other	49.1	—	—	—
Father/grandfather a commercial fisherman?				
Both fished	32.9	31.9	53.3	27.7
One fished	37.0	36.2	26.7	40.6
Neither fished	30.1	31.9	20.0	31.6
Inherited the family business (1 = yes)	41.1	39.7	66.7	34.8
Family serve as crew members (1 = yes)	43.3	49.1	33.3	41.9

Table 6.1 (continued)

	All Oystermen (N = 316)	Ethnic Identity		
		Cajun (N = 116)	Croat (N = 45)	Other (N = 155)
Human Capital				
Years harvesting oysters				
Less than 10 years	19.6	20.7	02.2	23.9
10–19 years	39.2	36.2	35.6	42.6
20 or more years	40.8	43.1	62.2	32.9
Other species fishing (1 = yes)	29.4	34.5	06.7	32.3
Community Attachment				
Community Satisfaction				
Highest	38.0	52.6	13.3	34.2
Intermediate	31.6	24.1	35.6	36.1
Lowest	30.4	23.3	51.1	29.7
Organizational Membership				
Member of more than one type of organization	21.8	18.1	48.9	16.8
Member of one type of organization	34.5	35.3	31.1	34.8
Member of no organizations	43.7	46.6	20.0	48.4
Community Influence (1 = personally used influence)	57.0	60.3	66.7	51.6

Table 6.2
Human and Social Capital Resources Relevant to the General Labor Market and Control Variables by Ethnic Identity (percent)

	All Oystermen (N = 316)	Ethnic Identity		
		Cajun (N = 116)	Croat (N = 45)	Other (N = 155)
General Labor Market Factors				
Social Capital				
Family educational attainment				
Parents (1 = one completed high school)	40.5	32.8	53.3	42.6
Spouse (1 = completed high school)	54.7	54.3	64.4	52.3
Spouse in labor force (1 = yes)[a]	32.6	31.0	31.1	34.2
Human Capital				
Educational attainment (1 = High School)	50.3	45.7	68.9	48.4
Work experience (not commercial fishing) (1 = yes)	42.1	51.7	17.8	41.9
Current other job (not commercial fishing) (1 = yes)	27.5	32.8	04.4	30.3
Control Variables				
Burdened by govt. rules and regs. (1 = all the time)	64.9	72.4	53.3	62.6
Parental status (1 = has children)	82.9	87.1	77.8	81.3
Community size (1 = 5,000 or more residents)	28.5	25.0	42.2	27.1

[a] Because our major interest here is with the extent to which households are attached to the paid labor force and not with family structure, both married and unmarried oystermen are included in the creation of this variable.

have the highest educational attainment level of the three groups. Although this would appear to be an advantage in the nonfishing labor market, these oystermen are much less likely than their counterparts to have reported prior or current work experience outside of the oyster fishery.

Logistic regression analysis is used to estimate the relative effects of our independent variables on the odds that oystermen would encourage their children to take up the profession. We conducted four separate analyses—one for each of the three major categories of factors we are considering and one for all the variables combined (table 6.3).

Our first model examines social and human capital resources that are linked to commercial fishing. Three of the social capital variables yielded significant differences in the odds that oystermen would encourage their children to take up the business—ethnicity, family history, and a family member serving on the crew. With respect to ethnic identity, our results show that the odds that Cajun oystermen will encourage their children are significantly greater than for Croatians or others ($p < .01$). As mentioned earlier, we expected to find ethnicity to be positively related to our dependent variable, but we did not anticipate the negative direction of the Croatian response. Results for family history in oyster harvesting and of family involvement are as expected. Being a third generation fisherman (both father and grandfather were commercial fishermen) and having family members serving on crews increase the odds that children will be encouraged.

Of the fishing-related human capital variables, only number of years harvesting oysters has a significant effect. This effect is curvilinear where those who have been in the business from 10 to 19 years are much less likely to encourage children than are those who have harvested oysters for less than 10 years or those who have harvested for 20 or more years. The two younger age categories are negative relative to the omitted reference category (20 or more years), so our expectation that the more years in harvesting the greater the encouragement given to children to become involved in the industry is somewhat supported.

Table 6.3

Logistic Regression Coefficients for Encouraging Children (N = 366)

	Model			
	I	II	III	Full
I. Capital Resources (Commercial Fishing)				
Social Capital				
Ethnic identity				
Cajun	.700**			.655*
Croatian	-.630			-.603
Other	—			—
Father/grandfather a commercial fisherman?				
Both fished	.739*			.595
One fished	.533			.454
Neither fished	—			—
Inherited the family business (1 = yes)	-.241			-.316
Family serve as crew members (1 = yes)	.606*			.582*
Human Capital				
Years harvesting oysters				
Less than 10 years	-.196			.010
10–19 years	-.617*			-.503
20 or more years	—			—
Other species fishing (1 = yes)	-.487			-.612

II. Community Attachment				
Community Satisfaction				
Highest		—		—
Intermediate		-.411		-.308
Lowest		-.963**		-.726*
Organizational Membership				
Member of more than one type of organization		.174		.240
Member of one type of organization		.431		.484
Member of no organizations		—		—
Community Influence (1 = personally used influence)		.237		.210
III. Capital Resources (General Labor Market)				
Social Capital				
Family educational attainment				
Parents (1 = at least one completed high school)			-.365	-.204
Spouse (1 = completed high school)			.547*	.474
Spouse in labor force (1 = spouse has paying job)			-.009	.003
Human Capital				
Educational attainment (1= high school)			-.414	-.204
Prior work experience (1 = yes)			.165	-.029
Current other nonfishing work (1 = yes)			.211	-.245
Control Variables				
Community size (1 = 5,000 or more residents)	.252	.004	.194	.210
Burdened by govt. rules and regs. (1 = all the time)	-.623*	-.605*	-.444	-.763**
Parental status (1 = has children)	.184	.181	.010	-.051

$p < .05$; ** $p < .01$; *** $p < .001$

Our second model includes our measures of community attachment. We argued that within an occupational community, local attachment may be related to parents' occupational desires for their children. In this regard, we expect that the higher the attachment to oyster harvesting, the greater the likelihood of encouraging children to take it up. As can be seen by the results shown in table 6.3, our community satisfaction measure is the only significant predictor and it supports our argument. Specifically, scoring in the lowest category of satisfaction significantly drops the odds of encouraging children ($p < .01$). None of the other community measures appears to have a marked effect.

Our third model examines human and social capital resources that are relevant to the more general labor market. Our thinking here was that those with greater investments in types of capital that would provide greater success in the noncommercial fishing labor market (i.e., education, prior work experience, holding second nonfishing jobs) would be the least likely to encourage their children to take up oyster harvesting. However, the results are mixed and none of the variables in our third model yielded significant outcomes.

When we consider all variables in our full model, we find that the significance of the log odds of two of the fishing-relevant capital variables disappear (family history in fishing and years harvesting oysters). The reason for this is not evident, although it may be that adding our community satisfaction variable to the model reduced these effects. The items that retain their significant effects are ethnic identity, family involvement as crew members, and community satisfaction.

Oyster harvesting has long been an established part of the culture and way of life in communities along the Louisiana Gulf coast. However, faced with an array of problems ranging from environmental disturbances to increasing regulatory pressures, the future viability of this industry has become a concern. Because the oyster harvesting industry in Louisiana is characterized by family-owned operations that have been handed down for generations, recruitment into this occupation is an important factor with regard to sustainability. Our goal in this paper was to examine the possibility that recruitment into the industry is related to human and social capital resources and to attachment to local community. Because of the distinct ethnic composition and its historical significance in the Louisiana fishery, we paid particular attention to ethnic identity as a form of social capital. We argued that forms of social and human capital that are tied directly to oyster harvesting would increase the likelihood of encouraging children. We also anticipated that attachment to local community would be associated with recruitment. On the other hand, we argued that possessing social and human capital resources that were applicable to the broader labor market would likely act in the opposite direction.

Our results, although mixed, offer support for our suggestion that forms of social capital that are relevant to commercial fishing would affect how oystermen advise their children. Ethnic identity is of special interest in this regard. However, we had anticipated that the Croatian oystermen, for whom the oyster business appeared to be most firmly grounded in family tradition, would be the most inclined to recommend the business to their children. Not only did we find that a Cajun identity was more important in this respect, but that the Croatian oystermen were substantially less likely than all other oystermen to recommend the occupation to their children.

Beyond ethnicity, we found one aspect of social capital—other family members serving on the crew—to significantly increase the odds of encouraging children. In addition, we found that satisfaction with the local community also had a positive effect. None of the human or social capital variables that were linked to the broader labor market yielded significant results.

The finding that Cajun oystermen are less reluctant than Croatians and others to recommend the occupation to their offspring begs further attention. Our data allow us to speculate on several possible reasons for this finding. First, the relationship between resource investment and recruitment may be more curvilinear than linear. Consistent with our initial expectations (and keeping in mind that oyster harvesting is a business as well as an occupation), it is likely that those on the low end of the continuum of human and social capital investment in oyster harvesting would have few resources that would be advantageous for successful entry into the occupation. On the other hand, those with the greatest investment in the business (and the most resources to potentially pass on), may be at a relative disadvantage for sources of paid employment outside the oyster-harvesting sector. That is, oystermen with the greatest resource commitment to the industry (which includes most Croatians) also would be those with the least labor market flexibility. If this occupational rigidity is considered in the context of the severe problems clouding the future of the industry, a reasonable family strategy for this group would be to diversify, that is, to encourage children to seek other occupational avenues. Somewhere between these two poles of resource commitment would be oystermen whose livelihood is more balanced between harvesting and other sources of income, which is descriptive of many Cajun oystermen. This group may find the problems confronting the industry to be less daunting in terms of occupational security and hence would be less hesitant to recommend that their children take up the business.

In addition to the curvilinear hypothesis, our results point to other possible explanations for the differences between Croatian and Cajun oystermen. While members of the Croatian community have much higher social and human capital investment in the industry, it is noteworthy that family support (i.e., kin serving as crew members) is the one indicator of social capital for which Croatians are significantly lower. Although this type of resource may be of less absolute value than assets such as large vessels and established family businesses, the involvement of family and kin as crew members may represent a type of social capital that encourages recruitment into the industry. Put another way, this type of social capital may be indicative of a self-sustaining occupational community. Our finding that Cajun oystermen express much higher community satisfaction than do Croatian oystermen offers further support for our speculation that sustaining the occupational community may be an important motivation among Cajun oystermen.

Our line of reasoning regarding social capital differences can be extended by considering our finding for educational attainment. Although education did not turn out to be a significant factor in our logistic regression models, it may be more appropriate to consider the marked educational attainment disparity between Cajun and Croatian oystermen (revealed in our descriptive profiles) as a communal rather than individual attribute. That is, educational attainment levels may reflect (and possibly determine) normative expectations within occupational communities, and as such, contribute to how members of these communities view the prospects for their children's future. Within the Croatian community, with its relatively high educational attainment levels, alternatives to the business of commercial oyster harvesting may have become preferable for the future.

As a final note, our findings have implications that go beyond the restructuring occurring in the Louisiana oyster industry. Although local restructuring generally arises from forces beyond the control of those who are directly affected, the impacts are never even. Human and social capital resources obviously influence how individuals and families adjust to industrial restructuring, but as we have found for the Louisiana oystermen, the effects of these resources are not necessarily what we might expect. The social context, such as the existence of ethnic communities, can have a bearing on how these human and social capital resources are brought into play.

Notes

1. There are indications of a trend away from private bed cultivation. The proportion of oysters harvested from public waters has recently increased to nearly half the total harvest (Louisiana Department of Wildlife and Fisheries 1999).

2. Respondents who claimed to have no children were asked, If you had children, would you encourage them to enter oyster harvesting?

3. The number of years in business could be viewed as a measure of embeddedness, which would make it more a variable of social capital than of human capital. Because we include measures that more directly tap embeddedness (both in the community and in the industry), we felt that years of oyster harvesting would better serve as an indicator of industry-specific experience.

4. Two points need to be made here. First, although our measure may seem to be based on a low level of educational attainment, the educational levels of commercial fishermen in general is low, particularly for their parents. Second, while educational attainment would be a human capital variable for the parents

or spouses themselves, because these spouses and parents are key members of respondents' networks, education can be considered what Edwards and Foley (1998) refer to as a "social relational and structural resource characteristic of social networks"—in other words, a form of social capital.

5. Even though some of our respondents were not currently married or living with a partner, this measure should be applicable as a type of social capital because it indicates the extent to which households are linked to the paid labor force.

6. The selection of the three community attachment items was determined by factor analysis of six community-related items. Because of the propensity of respondents to respond favorably to community items, we dichotomized responses to each of the items where the most favorable response (i.e., very satisfied) was given a value of 1 and other responses were given a value of 0. This yielded a range of four possible scores ranging from 0 to 3. Given the distribution of responses, we collapsed the categories as follows: low attachment was assigned to those who scored either 0 or 1, medium attachment to those who scored 2, and high attachment to those who scored 3.

7. Although we did not include vessel size in our models, nearly all the Croatians (93 percent), compared to only about a third of other operators, own and operate vessels over forty feet long (Deseran and Riden 2000). This ownership pattern is a strong indication of the relatively high investment Croatians as a group have in the industry. We did not include this variable in our models because there were so few (N = 2) Croatian oystermen in the smaller vessel categories.

References

Blauner, R. 1960. "Work Satisfaction and Industrial Trends in Modern Society." In *Labour and Trade Unionism,* ed. W. Galenson and S. M. Lipset. London: Routledge and Kegan Paul.

Carroll, M. S., and R. G. Lee 1990. "Occupational Community and Identity among Pacific Northwestern Loggers: Implications for Adapting to Economic Change." In *Community and Forestry: Continuities in the Sociology of Natural Resources,* ed. R. G. Lee, D. R. Field, and W. R. Burch Jr., 141–55. Boulder: Westview.

Coleman, James S. 1988. "Social Capital in the Creation of Human Capital." *American Journal of Sociology* 94 (supplement): S95–S120.

Davis, Dona Lee. 1986. "Occupational Community and Fishermen's Wives in a Newfoundland Outport." *Anthropological Quarterly* 59: 129–42.

Deseran, Forrest A., and Carl Riden. 2000. *Louisiana Oystermen . . . Surviving in a Troubled Industry.* National Sea Grant Library Research Report #LSU-S-00-003, May 2000.

Ellis, C. 1984 "Community Organization and Family Structure in Two Fishing Communities." *Journal of Marriage and Family,* August.

Garrity-Blake, Barbara J. 1996. *To Fish or Not to Fish: Occupational Transitions within the Commercial Fishing Community of Carteret County, N.C.* Institute for Coastal and Marine Resources Technical Report 96–05.

Light, Ivan H. 1972. *Ethnic Entrepreneurship in America: Business and Welfare among Chinese, Japanese, and Blacks.* Berkeley: University of California Press.

Louisiana Department of Wildlife and Fisheries. 1999. "Oyster Lease Survey Section." Rev. December 1998. <http://oysterweb.dnr.state.la.us/oyster/>.

Lummis, Trevor. 1977. "The Occupational Community of East Anglian Fishermen: An Historical Dimension through Oral Evidence." *British Journal of Sociology* 28 (1): 51–74.

Margavio, A. V., and Craig J. Forsyth. 1996. *Caught in the Net: The Conflict between Shrimpers and Conservationists.* College Station: Texas A and M University Press.

McKinney, J. 1994. "FDA Committed to Seven-Month Ban on Gulf Oysters." *Advocate* (Baton Rouge), August 3.

Nadel, Jane H. 1984. "Stigma and Separation: Pariah Status and Community Persistence in a Scottish Fishing Village." *Ethnology* 23 (2):101–15.

Nadel-Klein, Jane, and Donna Davis. 1988. *To Work and to Weep: Women in Fishing Economies.* Social and Economic Papers, no. 18. Institute of Social and Economic Research, Memorial University of Newfoundland.

National Marine Fisheries Service. 1999. Office of Science and Technology Fisheries Statistics & Economics Division Web Site, http://www.st. nmfs.gov/commercial/landings/monthly_landings.html

Padgett, H. R. 1960. "Marine Shellfisheries of Louisiana." Ph.D. dissertation, Louisiana State University, Baton Rouge.

Paxton, Pamela. 1999. "Is Social Capital Declining in the United States? A Multiple Indicator Assessment." *American Journal of Sociology* 105 (July): 88–127.

Portes, Alejandro, and Julia Sensenbrenner. 1993. "Embeddedness and Immigration: Notes on the Social Determinants of Economic Action." *American Journal of Sociology* 98 (6) May: 1320–50.

Portes, Alejandro, and Alex Stepick. 1993. *City on the Edge: The Transformation of Miami.* Berkeley: University of California Press.

Putnam, Robert. 1993. "The Prosperous Community: Social Capital and Public Life." *American Prospect,* Spring, 35–42.

Richling, Barnett. 1985. "'You'd Never Starve Here': Return Migration to Rural Newfoundland." *Canadian Review of Sociology and Anthropology* 22 (2): 236–49.

Roberts, K. J., and W. R. Keithly Jr. 1993. "Transfer and Auction Procedure as Determinants of Oyster Lease Values in Louisiana." *World Aquaculture* 24 (3) (September).

Salaman, G. 1971. "Some Sociological Determinants of Occupational Communities." *Sociological Review* 19 (1): 53–76.

Van Sicle, Virginia R., Barney Barrett, Ted Ford, and Lewis Gulick. 1976. *Barataria Basin: Salinity Changes and Oyster Distribution.* Louisiana Sea Grant Publication no. LSU-T-76–02, LWFC Technical Bulletin no. 20.

Vujnovich, Milos. 1974. *Yugoslavs in Louisiana.* Gretna: Pelican Publishing.

Wacquant, Loïc J. D., and William J. Wilson. 1989. "The Cost of Racial and Class Exclusion in the Inner City." *Annals of the American Academy of Political and Social Science* 501:8–26.

Wall, Ellen, Gabriele Ferrazzi, and Frans Schryer. 1998. "Getting the Goods on Social Capital." *Rural Sociology* 63 (2): 300–322.

Wasserman, Stanley, and Katherine Faust. 1994. *Social Network Analysis: Methods and Applications.* Cambridge: Cambridge University Press.

Wicker, Karen M. 1979. "The Development of the Louisiana Oyster Industry in the Nineteenth Century." Ph.D. dissertation, Louisiana State University, Baton Rouge.

Woolcock, Michael. 1998. "Social Capital and Economic Development: Toward a Theoretical Synthesis and Policy Framework." *Theory and Society* 27: 151–208.

7

Identity of Self and Others through Work
A Life of Commercial Fishing in the Mississippi Delta

Ralph B. Brown

YOU KNOW WHEN you have arrived in the Mississippi Delta. If you travel east to west, the rolling hills that define its eastern boundary melt abruptly into a perfectly flat plane that juts to the west. All features of landscape are lost in the flatness of that land. The rich, alluvial dirt—or soil, to those whose present trappings of luxury have relied on those who work the dirt—have made the geographic Delta one of the finest agricultural regions in the world and traditionally the source of extremes of poverty and plenty.

Though traditionally cast in extremes, considerable progress in social and economic conditions has recently taken root in the Delta. Increasingly, whites and blacks have banded together to tackle the Delta's chronic social and economic woes. Despite these efforts, the demographic characteristics of the Delta still paint with broad strokes the details of its remaining extremes. By the numbers, the Delta remains behind the rest of America in almost all social and economic categories. Using U.S. census figures from 1990,[1] the estimated median household income in the United States in 1990 was $27,310, while in the Delta it was $13,684. Even more telling is that the median household income for blacks in the Mississippi Delta was only $6,190.

The percentage of families and individuals living below the poverty line in 1990 for the United States was 9.6 percent for families and 12.4 percent for individuals. For the Mississippi Delta, 37 percent of the families in the core thirteen-county area lived in poverty (56.3 percent of black families, and 10 percent of white families); and 11.5 percent were unemployed (blacks 18.6 percent and whites 3.7 percent). In 1990 African Americans accounted for 12.9 percent of the U.S. population; for the Delta, 59.7 percent. Even when compared to other black-majority areas in the United States, the Delta has fared worse economically, primarily due to low educational attainment (Doyle 2000).

Again, despite some recent improvements, social and political aspects of Delta life are still cast in extremes. Duncan (1999) found that generational life chances and social and economic opportunities of Delta residents are tied to an elite white patronage system. Failure to recognize the elite hierarchy often closes opportunities for one's self and family. She claims that "Everyone—white and black, professionals and school dropouts—can name the top five or so families that run things" (1999, 74, 75). Nylander (1998) also found that identified white leaders, in the two rural Mississippi Delta communities he examined, neatly followed an elite power structure model, while black leaders had a much more diffuse, issue-oriented leadership structure, more characteristic of a pluralistic model. Lyson (1988) notes that present-day Delta economies were created by the rural white elites, and accordingly, economic development in the Delta is controlled to the degree that human development needs are kept to a minimum. Additionally, Brown and Warner (1991) and Williams and Dill (1995) have suggested that this same rural white elite controls much of the behavior of blacks through financial dominance in banking, wholesale, and retail, and also through the legal, educational, and political life of the community (see also Gray 1991).

Such a portrait may paint the Delta as a place apart from the rest of America. Historian James C. Cobb quips, "I soon learned that I was actually but one of a host of commentators who over the years have treated the Mississippi Delta as an isolated, time-warped enclave whose startling juxtaposition of white affluence and black poverty suggested the Old South legacy preserved in vivid microcosm" (1992, vii). Indeed, the Delta's native son David Cohn, a *New York Times* journalist, described his home as a "a strange and detached fragment thrown off by the whirling comet that is America" (in ibid.). Yet what characterizes the Delta is not its apparent aloofness from the rest of America, as Cobb himself goes on to confess, "The Delta that ultimately emerged from my study was no mere isolated backwater where time stood still while southernness stood fast" (viii). What characterizes the Delta today is that it has participated in the major social changes of the past century, yet despite this participation in "the major economic, political, and social forces that have swept across the America landscape," it remains to those who live in it, versus us who analyze it, a land of extremes (viii). The extreme geological features of the land continue to be a pretext to the extreme social features of those who occupy it.

From a geographic perspective, I am technically focusing on the Yazoo River Basin. But this geographic specificity loses out to the more loosely defined, but socially identifiable, Mississippi Delta. Calling it the Mississippi Delta qualitatively shifts the emphasis from a geographic region to a sociocultural one. As Tuan explains; "Things are not quite real until they acquire names and can be classified in some way. Curiosity about places is part . . . of the need to label experiences so that they have a greater degree of permanence and fit into some conceptual scheme" (1977, 29). The Delta is a place; but it is a place where certain types of people live and where certain things have happened and continue to happen. The Delta is its own unique "place-world."

> Place-making does not require special sensibilities or cultivated skills. It is a common response to common curiosities—what happened here? . . . What people make of their places is closely connected to what they make of themselves as members of society and inhabitants of the earth. . . . Place-making is a way of constructing the past . . . it is also a way of constructing social traditions and, in the process, personal and social identities. We are, in a sense, the place-worlds we imagine. (Basso 1996, 5, 7)

Reflecting the place they inhabit, the daily combination of terrestrial and eternal pressed together in the Delta continues to breed people of extremes. The Delta is not only a place but the unique human experience of the people associated with that place. In Cohn's words, "One must be part of what is forever part of oneself" (in Cobb 1995, 103). Being from the Delta means living in a world of extremes through one's own extremeness.

When people define themselves in terms of extremes their identities become manifest in their relations to others—that is, to those who are not like them. It is this mutual definition of otherness that paradoxically binds them together. Thus, community in the place-world of the Delta is forged more by each others' sense of otherness than by people's sense of commonality. So it should be apparent that in a place-world, like the Delta, a multiplicity of communities exist within even larger communities. Consequently, both community and communities in this place-world continue to be defined in terms of extremes; defined in terms of their otherness.

Work is one of those things that both bring the extremes of the Delta into contact with each other and at the same time represents one of its extremes. It is how work represents one of these extremes and how they come together in a temporary union of interaction through one's work that is the focus of the present chapter.

Harper argues, "To understand the meaning of work, then, is to see it as a currency of community, the basis of exchange" (1987, 7). Work and community are combined and mutually supportive. They arise from each other. Bittner makes a similar argument: "Practical labor is always controlled by full regard for the timely and local features of the environment within which it takes place" (1983, 253). Specific communities of work are the outcome of the environments that spawn them.

In this chapter I follow one man's interactions in and through the various segments of his and others' "communities" through his work—fishing—and his perception of work in general. I explore Vern's (a pseudonym) place-world—his personal and social identities in the Delta—through his identity and experience of work as he, through it, interacts with others' place-worlds. Vern's interaction with others through his work illustrates nicely the combination of extremes so characteristic of the Delta place-world. Although only one person, Vern's experiences do provide a social history of a unique part of the

American landscape. His work and the social relationships it engenders reflect larger societal trends and the demise of his occupation.

Methods

My goal was to examine how Vern's occupational community—the interactions having to do with his work, who he comes into contact with, the nature of those contacts, the history behind his interactions with others through work, the regional context that surrounds his work—serves as a basis for his own identity and how he views others.

My interactions with Vern span an eight-year period. I first met him in 1993 and have continued to interview and converse with him. I formally interviewed him on three different occasions, each session lasting approximately two hours. I also accompanied him in his work on four different occasions and videotaped two of these. Finally, I talked with Vern on numerous other occasions in a more informal way to check out hunches and to put pieces of an emerging puzzle together. His story was extracted from many other possible stories in the Delta.

The data I use to examine Vern's occupational community are taken from field notes, transcribed formal interviews with Vern and others, videotapes of Vern engaged in work, and interviews and observations of others who interact with him. Much of these data were extracted from a larger data set consisting of observations of, and interviews with, local fishers in the upper Yazoo River Delta.[2]

"I Had Some Hard Knocks, but I've Enjoyed My Life"

VERN'S IDENTITY OF SELF AND OTHERS THROUGH WORK

Vern is seventy-seven years old, white, married, and has two children, both in their late forties. By profession and enjoyment, Vern is a commercial fisher in the Mississippi Delta. He has also trapped furs. He has been fishing commercially in the Delta since the early 1940s. He was born in 1923 in a little town near Indianola, Mississippi. When he was five years old he moved to Ricks (a pseudonym), a town of about three hundred people, where he resides still. He has lived his entire life in the Delta. He was married at twenty-two to a seventeen-year-old girl from Ricks. They continued to live in the Ricks area, where Vern continued to fish—an occupation that he had begun at seventeen. He has been at it for fifty-three years. Though he officially retired in 1985, when he was almost sixty-three years old, he continues to fish, only on a more limited scale.

Through the lens of his work, Vern habitually defines himself and others through the same extremes in which he finds himself. Vern's work is inseparably tied to the abundant natural resources of the Delta. Fishing brings him into daily contact with the competition between nature and man-made worlds. For Vern, there is a spiritual satisfaction in the natural character of his work that does not exist in the built world of industry, though this too increasingly surrounds him with its mechanized agriculture and pond-raised and processed catfish. Nature demands hard work and respect. Metaphorically, his descriptions of his work and work ethic are presented in extremes and his narrative telling of them communicates how he relates to others' lack of a work ethic. It is Vern's lens to his community in all its diversity.

> There ain't many folks worked as hard as, I mean, I ain't braggin', but hard as I worked all my life. . . . I had some hard knocks. But I've enjoyed it. I've enjoyed my life. If I don't live another day, I've done enjoyed my life. Nothing to grumble about. . . . If a fella works hard, he don't have no trouble sleepin'. I used to work all night long, all night long. I'd come back in for a little nap. I used to dress my fur at night. I'd be out trappin' all day. Dress 'em at night. By 10 P.M. I'd be out there skinning fur.

His descriptions of himself as a hard worker contrast with those people who he feels are not. "I've never grabbed no government checks. No. None of that junk. I footed my bills myself. . . . I've never had no food stamps or none of that junk. I was always too independent."

This contrast between himself and "others" is further illustrated by the following passage in which he describes how others see him and try to do the same things he does, fish, but without the same effort, unwilling to "lay with it" long enough to assure success.

See, in my time I've seen 'em come and go. They say, "Vern makes a livin' fishin'." They'd jump up there and run and try it—lose their britches. . . . I just laid with it. I didn't blow my money. I just saved it along. You know. 'Course my wife, she works. She used to be a cashier for a store, then she worked in another store. Her money helped buy the kids clothes. That's all she did with her money. Yeah, I've seen a lot of 'em come and go since I've been in it—fifty-three years it will be. . . . That's a long time in the same job, ain't it? But I enjoy it.

When I asked him if he now fished more for his own enjoyment or for an income, he responded, "Yeah, I enjoy it, and it's a livin' too. So if a fella's mind is occupied and he likes his job, well, there is no use in changing, is there? I got my kids a good education. I didn't get it when I was growing up."

Vern's definitions of himself, his relations to others, and his life in general are through his work. He introduced his foray into the world of work to me with the following account:

I started plowin' a mule when I was seven years old. I mean, I was plowing myself. . . . 'Course there was ten of us kids. I was the oldest boy. I had two older sisters, but they didn't know work. Really, 'cause I worked just like a man. . . . Me and my dad worked for this old woman. I plowed a row every time he did. I was thirteen years old. And when it come time to pay off, she paid him seventy-five cents for a day; she paid me fifty cents. Three days, now, that I worked for her, she paid me fifty cents a day. It made me so mad; I plowed a row every time he did. I said, "I wouldn't work for that old ___, or help her again at all." They had plenty of money anyhow. She used to have a million dollars' change when she died. Oh, that made me so ___, I didn't work for her no more.

He compares himself to those who do not value work like he does and how they cannot be trusted. Equal work demands equal compensation. People who have never worked in their lives, people of leisure, would not know how to honestly compensate others' "honest" work. Hard workers are reliable and honest. The following account of his father—a sharecropper, living as a tenant on someone else's land—illustrates this connection.

> We never did go hungry. We would raise what we eat: hogs, cows—we had cows, two cows—butter, beets. But we didn't have no money when we come up, you know. But if my dad owed you a penny, he paid you a penny. And if I owed you a penny, I'd pay you it. I can't say it about some of the rest of the bunch [his siblings], you know, but I'd say it about me, because I don't owe nobody nothin'.

In Vern's world, those who do not work hard are not trustworthy; generically they are thieves. Hard work is honesty and a natural law that if violated will incur consequences. Moral rightness will always prevail.

> I used to sell seven or eight hundred dollars worth [of fish] a month in Ricks. My wife would sell them there at the house and the kids. But there's a bunch of illegal fishin' that's come in there with them slat baskets and they undersold me and they just. . . . That's been twenty years ago I guess. . . . They used to have a good market there at home. They just catch them and give 'em away. Just illegal fishin', you know. I think they in with the game warden, they bound to be gettin' paid off; 'cause they couldn't keep it goin', you know. One of them ol' boys is at the state pen. Well, they give him twenty years for his boat ring. He got out in about a couple of years. 'Course he's kind of destitute. Walks the chalk line, you know. [If he crosses the line,] they grab him up and put him back in there. I think he's got cancer. They say.

His relationship to blacks in the region is an interesting one, though they constitute Vern's primary customer base. "I don't sell that many [fish] to whites. I've got a few white customers that want certain . . . well, yellow cats. They want a certain kind of cats." A lack of trust based on race and perceived deficiency in work ethics manifests itself in Vern's comments about blacks. Yet Vern's comments also reveal a guarded trust of blacks with whom he has a personal relationship. The common theme of hard work and trustworthiness versus slothfulness and thievery is clear in the following comments:

> I sell niggers all through here fish. A lot of 'em buy 'em, niggers, you know, well, blacks. Niggers—I call 'em niggers 'cause I'm from

"Miss'ippi" [laughs]. Hell, a lot them niggers around here, I say a lot of
'em, different ones works them fish places down there [the processing
factories], they stealin' them folks's fish by the pickup load. They'll sell
you a pickup load if you want to get in with 'em. They bootleggin' 'em,
stealin' 'em from them white folks, you know, that's got the fish market, fish ponds. You know, workin' for 'em and stealin' 'em. They'll sell
you a whole pickup load fer twelve to fifteen dollars. Let's see. A little
ol' Datsun—one 'em drove a little ol' Datsun pickup—sell a whole bed
full of 'em for so much, you know [laughs]. Stealin' them out them
ponds. Yeah.

I asked if this made it hard for him to sell his fish.

Yeah, at times. You know, they come to you peddle 'em, sellin' them.
Yeah. Them other blacks [local people] will tell you about 'em if they
like you.

After this statement I asked if those doing the stealing were local
people.

No. They just swipe 'em out of them fish ponds and sell 'em. Peddle
'em. Well, one of them drives one of their trucks, I think, that delivers
catfish; they buy a lot of them from him. They trying to steal 'em from
him too, you know. They got them freezer trucks. They steal all these.
Most of these big planters has got blacks a-workin' for 'em, you know.
They will see—well, see all of this? [He points to some shabby-looking
houses sparsely dispersed on the road side.] Belongs to blacks, and
then you got the big shots that's got these big farms. They buy all that
stuff you put on your crops, and them niggers are stealin' some from
somebody else. I've seen 'em just stop and make them folks stop who
were delivering it, and they stole it from the delivery trucks—fertilizer.
'Course it ain't none of my business [laughs]. Them white folks 'posed
to be puttin' that stuff out, you know [laughs], fertilizer and everything else. If you ever knowed or worked around a black, you know
what I'm talking about. This is Mississippi. They'll steal you blind if
you let 'em. If you ever had any dealing—well, they'll steal from you
and give to me and steal from me [laughs]. Man, it's something. In this
country they think the white folks are the ones that are living, you
know. They think every white fella's got plenty of money. You know. If
he ain't, he ought to have [laughs].

Identity of Self and Others through Work: Commercial Fishing | 165

Vern is unique in that he is the only commercial fisher in the area that consistently sells directly to blacks. Yet, like other whites in the region, Vern holds blacks generally in low regard. When I asked other commercial license holders in the area why they do not maintain an active peddling route, they voiced two main reasons. The first was that, with the exception of Vern, they used their catch primarily to stock their own freezers and to give to friends and family. Second, they would have to sell primarily to blacks. One of the most common fish consumed by blacks in the Delta that is caught with commercial gear is buffalo (see Brown and Toth 2001). The sale of these fish to blacks would constitute the major portion of a peddling business. The association of blacks with buffalo is an enduring one in the Delta (Cobb 1995). White fishers in the region consistently identified buffalo as a "black fish." "Smartest thing is we throw them back into the lake. Most of the buffalo we throw back into the lake. You can't do nothin' with 'em. You would have to have an established sales route and that's the only way you can get rid of 'em. But we throw 'em back." Those that they do keep they often give to friends to feed to their hunting dogs. One white commercial fisher commented surreptitiously that he actually preferred the taste of buffalo to catfish. The fact that it is a "black fish," however, keeps him quiet about his palate's preference.

Though a local demand for buffalo exists, it is almost exclusively from the black community. Outside of larger fish markets, who get their stocks from large commercial fishers on the Mississippi River, Vern is a primary supplier of buffalo to the black community in this region. His willingness to sell to the black community allows him to continue to fish for a living and brings him into constant contact with blacks as part of his work.

Because Vern's work brings him into direct contact with the many different groups in the Delta, his views on work act as a lens to interpret his interactions with them. His interactions with others are so mediated through this lens that even his dealings with "respectable" workers are tempered by his hypernotions of hard work and frugality. For example, in his work as a fisher, a pickup truck is essential. I asked him about his trucks and he explained that his first "truck" was actually a 1935 Ford sedan that he attached a box to. Of nineteen trucks he has purchased since 1953, he financed it and his first two pickups. He paid cash for the other seventeen. When I asked him how many miles he puts on a truck in a year, he told me sixty thousand or so. I also asked him if he had a good dealer working with him. He commented:

> Yep. I lost him one time. I mean, he lost me. Yep, I bought several trucks from him. I tried to buy my son one. A car. I "jewed" him down too. He bought a little ol' Nova, I think. I wasn't worried about it. It was fifty dollars cheaper if I bought it over at Water Valley. [So he did—the local dealer with whom he had done business every year for many years wouldn't come down fifty more dollars to match the Water Valley dealer's price; so Vern bought it at Water Valley.] "Man," he told me, "I lost you one time. I don't want to lose you again."

Nevertheless, he did. On another occasion, after having lost his business on the Nova, the same local dealer tried to meet Vern's specifications for a new pickup but could not find what Vern wanted. Even though Vern recognized and acknowledged that the man tried, effort needs to be saddled with results. So he went someplace else and has not been back to the local dealer since.

Frugality and commonsense practices are inseparably linked to a work ethic and thus also characterize Vern's ideal of himself and others. About how he raised his two children, Vern observed:

> They didn't run to the store and buy knickknacks. I said, "You goin' to eat off the table." I had a brother that raised a big family. And they was a-knickknakin' and their teeth rotted out, every one of 'em. I said, "See, my kids ain't goin' to do it." We raised our stuff mostly. We didn't buy kids junk to eat.

Everyone I talked to about Vern saw him as being far more financially successful than he actually is. In fact, by Vern's own account, he made $14,000 gross in his best year. "With expenses . . . took it down to about $10,000 or $12,000. I ain't made no money. Everybody think I made plenty of money. You know. Spent plenty of money." Clearly reinforcing Vern's view of how others see him, the owner of a small fish market who often purchased fish from Vern said this about him:

And I tell you something. I bet you the old man's got maybe two million dollars. He's got, I believe he told me, sixty-three rental properties. [He has three.] He told me that he made every penny of it fishing, and he makes good money. Fifty years of fishing. That's all he's ever done.

These insights into Vern's identity of himself and others through his work and work ethic set the stage for explaining how he goes about his work.

WHAT HE DOES: VERN'S WORK

As a commercial fisher, Vern holds a Mississippi commercial fishing license. This allows him to use "commercial gear." And it allows him to sell fish. "A licensed commercial fisherman is considered to be a producer and is entitled by law to sell his own catch to anyone or at any point within or outside the state of Mississippi" (Mississippi Wildlife 1993, 2). He is not allowed to catch and sell "game" fish. The license allows him to catch, store, and sell "bulk" fish—catfish, buffalo, drum, and carp, among others. A commercial license is thirty dollars a year plus a five-dollar "tag" for each piece of equipment (nets, lines, etc.) used. Today, Vern spends approximately forty-five dollars a year on tags because he runs eight nets. Before the 1980s, Vern used to run over one hundred nets, spending approximately three hundred dollars a year for licenses. "That was some fishin'. Well, I had over one hundred nets. I would have me about three lines of them [nets] at a time. I had forty-five hoop nets, and I would have me a line here [Tallahatchie River] and a line down, down in the Big Black River, and one in the Yalobusha." Today he runs an average of eight nets two or three times a week.

Like the other commercial fishers I interviewed in the area, Vern stores much of what he catches in his freezers for his own consumption; but he is the only one I encountered who actually made a living fishing. Vern has an amazing penchant for remembering specific dollar amounts of sales, things he has purchased, and taxes he has paid, even forty or fifty years later. This ability reinforces the idea that Vern's lens on the world filters all that comes through it by the calcu-

lus of his work. Research conducted by psychologists Nunes, Schliemann, and Carraher (1993) shows that when numbers are used in
everyday work settings, even by children—street-market boys in
Brazil—they can do the math and do it well, even when they do very
poorly on math tests in school. The math is filtered through something very meaningful and is not just an abstract concept to be mem-
orized for school (Devlin 2000). Vern's arithmetic abilities are born
from their connection to his work. Reading however, is not something that Vern needs as badly in his work.

Vern fishes all year long. Most commercial fishers who still sell some
of their catch will fish from March through June to catch the "runs" of
buffalo and catfish. He claims that by the late 1960s and early 1970s, he
could no longer secure a living through fishing.

> I used to fish the Pearl River and other rivers down there. You know,
> two months of the year I would run down there and catch a run of
> fish. I was fishing stuff, I was fishing then. I was fishing back here too
> [Tallahatchie]. But I ain't made no money fishing. I just messin'
> around. Probably ten years, I haven't made nothin' offa fishin.' I used
> to haul 'em to Memphis. . . . I ain't hauled no fish to Memphis since
> 1967 or '68 or somewhere along there. Back in the '60s, when I was
> catchin' 'em, when I was really fishing, you know, I hauled a lot of
> them up to Memphis.

Not only did his fishing activities shrink, so too did his selling sites
and options. "I had some places I'd stop. I unloaded a lot of 'em in
Grenada. I used to sell a lot of fish in Grenada. Stores, big ol' stores.
Batesville. Man, I sold to lots of stores up in Batesville."

HOW VERN FISHES

Vern still gets up at 4:30 A.M. and is on the river by 5:30 to check his
nets. The area on the river where he sets his nets covers approximately
five miles. It takes him less than two hours to run them. He has a private access spot on the river that is well hidden around a blind curve
on both sides where his sixteen-foot johnboat is moored. The boat is
well "seasoned" and camouflaged. The first time I accompanied him,

a two-foot sapling was growing out of its bow. Water filled with the detritus from fish, dirt, and leaves rarely gets cleaned out and thus makes an ideal seedbed for all kinds of plants and fungi. His boat reminded me of some overgrown Chia-Pet. Yet its "natural" coloration keeps it well hidden amid the trees and shrubs on the banks. He says he has never had a boat stolen. On one occasion somebody did "borrow" it without asking, but they later returned it.

He has driven two six-foot logs about three feet into the ground and about five feet apart to keep others from launching their boats from his spot. This had become a problem. People with four-wheel-drive vehicles had torn up the steps in the steep bank that he had made to get to his boat. They had also bent up his boat once when they launched theirs over his.

> I caught 'em down here one day; and I told 'em in a nice way, I said, "Now this is my drive, I cut this road out and graveled it, and them's my steps." And I said, "Don't come back 'round here no more and pull your boat over my boat and bend it up like you did." I said, "I don't appreciate it." I said, "Don't you come back down here no more." I said, "If you want a ramp, you go back down there and build you one like I did."

In Vern's world, there can be creation ex nihilo—something out of nothing. Work is the common factor that brings all things into being. If you want what I have, you must do what I did—work: "Build one like I did."

He does not leave his outboard motor attached to the boat; he stores it in the back of his pickup on top of an old tire. He lifts the motor out of the back of his pickup and carries it down to the boat. The path to the boat is steep and slippery. He seems to get it to and from the pickup without difficulty, however. The motor itself is not extravagant, only a 1.5-horsepower Suzuki, adequate for the job, with nothing to spare. Yet another metaphor of Vern's approach to things: frugality and functionality—your equipment needs to be enough to get the job done, nothing more.

Once in the water, Vern begins to check his nets. The hoop nets, approximately fourteen feet long, are constructed of seven wooden hoops with net between them that narrows to a tail. Vern drops the tail of the net into the water and then allows the boat to drift while he holds onto the rest of the net, periodically shaking it along from tail to head, to stretch the net out to its full length. Other fishers I observed placed indiscreet markers on the bank to allow them to "remember" where they had placed their net. Once the net is submerged into the turbid water but a few inches, it is invisible. Vern, however, uses no marks.

Retrieval of the nets occurs two days after their placement. Vern uses a six-inch metal grappling hook with four prongs approximately two inches long at the top to retrieve the nets. He fluidly moves from place to place in the river where he has placed his nets. He knows precisely the location of each net, even with no identifying marks on the banks. Amazing to me, on the four different occasions that I accompanied him to collect nets, only three times did he miss a net with the hook on the first try.

Hooking the net requires a soft touch. Pull too hard, and the net will tear. Once the net is hooked, Vern pulls the boat to the net by pulling on the rope. Then, seeing where he has hooked the net, he works his way to the mouth, shaking it as he goes, to knock any fish caught in the webbing back into the body of the net. He then positions the boat in relation to the net so that he can roll the net lengthwise alongside the boat. He does this by holding the hoops and shaking the net. He then rolls and folds the first hoop—the mouth of the net—into the boat and in the same fashion brings the rest of the net in hoop by hoop as it collapses onto itself in the bottom of the boat. The procedure reminded me of a Slinky walking down stairs. The tail of the net remains anchored to the bottom of the river.

Once the net has been retrieved, Vern lifts its tail and shakes any fish in that section down toward the head. The fish drop out of the net through the same cavity they entered it—the throat. The throat inverts, dropping the fish onto the bottom of the boat. This is where the fish stay until he docks the boat. Depending on how many fish are in the net, their size and species, the net can weigh well over two hundred pounds.

Vern knows his prey. Almost sixty years on the rivers has given him a knowledge of fish behavior. Explaining why at times he catches more in his nets than at other times, he observed, "You know, when the moon changes, it has something to do with 'em. They move a little differently. About once a month they move, you know. Some folks don't know much about the moon, but if you fish, you know that moon is making them fish move."

Repairs to nets are done on the spot. Nets can be damaged through the thrashing of fish, particularly catfish, with their barbels. Turtles are also often caught in the nets. Snapping turtles in particular will try to chew themselves free. Occasionally, beavers will also get caught in the nets and will chew their way free. Damage to the hoops is often caused by boat propellers and by the dredging barges used by the Army Corp of Engineers. Vern keeps a spool of net line in his pocket. When he finds a tear in the netting, he may first dump the fish then set to repairing it, or if it is a tear that may spread further by dumping the fish, he will tie it before emptying the net. His tying appears automatic. He typically completes his repairs within a matter of seconds. "I have to line these things about every three years. Put new stuff on; new webbing on. It don't rot, but it will wear out."

After docking, Vern puts the fish from the bottom of the truck into five-gallon buckets along with water dipped from the river with the cut-off top of an old Chlorox bottle (which he also uses as a bailer). In his truck is an old refrigerator laid on its back. The night before he checks his nets, he freezes a twenty-pound block of ice to place with the fish. It is important that the fish remain alive, because it is virtually impossible to sell a dead or "cut" fish. The ice helps them stay alive for several hours.

With his day's catch in the back of his truck, Vern immediately hits his route to sell it. His route has shrunk considerably over the past twenty or so years. Today it covers approximately seventy miles round-trip from his house. He figures that he puts over a hundred miles on his truck every day he goes fishing. The arrangements with the people he sells to have been established over years of deliveries. Thus the route is not based on its economic efficiency but on normative social expectations. He does not seem to be worried about acquiring new customers. "I peddle some through here. But I ain't catchin' that many. If I was catchin' many, I don't know where I'd sell 'em at, really.

That's one reason why I just kind of got me a route through here. Sell 'em while comin' back to home, you know." The route contains approximately seventy-five identified individual stops at private residences.

Vern pulls into the drive of his "customers"[3] and honks his horn. The typical response is a resident's yell through the screen door, "What ya got?" He proceeds to tell them what fish are available. If they are interested in the catch, they come out of the house and inspect the fish. He then weighs the fish, using a hand-held scale and metal bin. At no time in this transaction is the price per pound discussed or negotiated. The transaction is normative. Certain customers have standing orders for exotic fish or other animals. On one occasion he caught a fifty-three-pound snapping turtle in a net. When I asked him what he intended to do with it, he simply said, "It's already sold." He then delivered it to a particular house on his route.

Out of seventy-five stops on his route, there were only two white families; the rest were black. One of the times I accompanied him on his route, he stopped at nine places in an all-black community before somebody actually bought some fish. Sometimes he sells the entire catch to a black lady in the area. She often buys from him on a monthly basis. He has been selling fish to her for over forty years, and she buys two hundred to three hundred pounds a month and also pays him monthly.

Another factor that has cut into Vern's business over the years has been the proliferation of pond-raised catfish. Twenty years ago, people like Vern were the primary source of catfish consumed in the region. Now ponds have assumed that role, and "wild-caught" fish have been relegated to a nostalgic celebrity role for periodic fish fries. It appears that those who purchase wild-caught fish are of generally two distinct groups, both of which deal more with significant events and nostalgia than with everyday subsistence. The first are primarily whites who generally buy wild-caught fish in large quantities for celebrations (e.g., fish fries), with a preference for flathead catfish. The second are primarily blacks who get wild-caught fish in two distinct ways: some buy fish periodically from a peddler like Vern; others, returning home from other areas of the country for a visit, occasionally bring several hundred pounds of frozen fish back with them. Not only a taste of home, but an image of home.

For Vern, work is clearly more than just a way to earn a living. Work is the lens through which he defines his interactions with others and his own sense of identity. Work is Vern's foundation of community. It is what ties him to whites and blacks alike in a region where the differences between these groups are a lighting rod for every issue. "To understand the meaning of work . . . is to see it as a currency of community, the basis of exchange" (Harper 1987, 7). "Practical labor is always controlled by full regard for the timely and local features of the environment within which it takes place. Accordingly, one would have to say that [practical labor] . . . involves the exercise of an intelligence that comes into its own in communication with the concrete and actual realities of its natural setting" (Bittner 1983, 253). These observations further symbolize that Vern's occupational community is a product of the extremes of the environment that produces it and gives it meaning. He cannot be divorced from the context that gives meaning to him and his image of himself and others because his work, as he defines it, is a product of that context.

In the Mississippi Delta it makes sense to talk about multiple communities of work, each constructed by the boundaries that define the various extremes of social life. The irony is that the more extreme groups come into contact with each other in these conditions the more their differences are amplified. The communities remain solid in their separate but concurrent identities because their foundations are rarely challenged.

The extremes of the Mississippi Delta are indelibly ingrained in the images and approaches to work that its residents harbor. Possibly a first reaction to Vern's story will be to see him as a relic—someone from another era. I think such a perception of Vern misses the fundamental component of what he does represent: he is just one of many extremes still present in the Mississippi Delta. Even if the approach and lifestyle Vern has pursued in the Delta have changed, their essence has not. The Delta remains a land of extremes where, as work and occupational communities have changed, how people define themselves and others in this context has changed little (see Duncan 1999). As Vern and others told me on several occasions, "Nobody fishes for a livin' any more." Though the type of work pursued in the Delta has changed, the essence of work—as one of many categories by which to define oneself vis-à-vis all others—probably will not, for in the Delta, it is this very otherness that binds people together and makes community out of many separate but concurrent communities.

Notes

1. I used 1990 census data from the 1994 City County Data Book because by the time of this writing, the 2000 census figures for counties and census-designated places (STF3 files) were not yet available. While figures for U.S. and state population, poverty, and unemployment were available, they have not been disaggregated, thus limiting comparability with Delta counties.

2. I chose to focus on Vern as he was the only fisher out of all the interviewees who still "fished for a living" and whose constant engagement in his work as a fisher brought him into contact with both the white and black communities of the area on a consistent basis. Vern is clearly not representative of other males, black or white, in the region in terms of his occupation; he is the only one still doing it. I believe he is, however, representative of the numerous types of work in this area, the extreme character of that work, and the people who engage in it.

3. On the difference between customers and consumers, see Strasser 1989.

References

Basso, Keith H. 1996. *Wisdom Sits in Places: Landscape and Language among the Western Apache*. Albuquerque: University of New Mexico Press.

Bittner, Egon. 1983. "A Technique and the Conduct of Life." *Social Problems* 30 (3): 249–61.

Brown, D., and M. Warner. 1991. "Persistent Low-Income Areas in the United States: Some Conceptual Challenges." *Policies Studies Journal* 19 (2): 22–41.

Brown, Ralph B., and John F. Toth Jr. 2001. "Natural Resource Access and Interracial Associations: Black and White Subsistence Fishing in the Mississippi Delta." *Southern Rural Sociology* 17:81–110.

Cobb, J. C. 1992. *The Most Southern Place on Earth: The Mississippi Delta and the Roots of Regional Identity.* Oxford: University of Mississippi Press.

_____. 1995. *The Mississippi Delta and the World: The Memoirs of David L. Cohn.* Baton Rouge: Louisiana State University Press.

Devlin, K. 2000. *The Math Gene: How Mathematical Thinking Evolved and Why Numbers are Like Gossip.* New York: Basic Books.

Doyle, R. 2000. "Hard Times in the Delta." *Scientific American,* September, 30.

Duncan, C. M. 1999. *Worlds Apart: Why Poverty Persists in Rural America.* New Haven: Yale University Press.

Gray, P. A. 1991. "Economic Development and African Americans in the Mississippi Delta." *Rural Sociology* 56:238–46.

Harper, D. 1987. *Working Knowledge: Skill and Community in a Small Shop.* Berkeley: University of California Press.

Lyson, T. A. 1988. "Economic Development in the Rural South: An Uneven Past—An Uncertain Future." In *The Rural South in Crisis,* ed. L. J. Beaulieu, 265–75. Boulder: Westview.

Mississippi Wildlife, Fisheries, and Parks. 1993. *Mississippi Digest of Freshwater Commercial Fishing Laws and Regulations.* Jackson: Mississippi Wildlife, Fisheries, and Parks.

Nunes, T., A. Schliemann, and D. Carraher. 1993. *Street Mathematics and School Mathematics.* Cambridge: Cambridge University Press.

Nylander, A. B., III. 1998. "Rural Community Leadership Structures in Two Delta Communities." Ph.D. dissertation, Department of Sociology, Anthropology, and Social Work, Mississippi State University.

Strasser, S. 1989. *Satisfaction Guaranteed: The Making of the American Mass Market.* New York: Pantheon Books.

Tuan, Y. 1977. *Space and Place: The Perspective of Experience.* Minneapolis: University of Minnesota Press.

United States. Department of Commerce. Bureau of the Census. 1994. *County and City Data Book.* Washington, D.C.: GPO.

Williams, B. B., and B. T. Dill. 1995. "African-Americans in the Rural South: The Persistence of Racism and Poverty." In *The Changing American Countryside: Rural People and Places,* ed. E. N. Castle, 339–51. Lawrence: University Press of Kansas.

8

Sense of Place and Rural Restructuring

Lessons from the Low Country

William W. Falk

THE AMERICAN SOUTH is surely one of the most analyzed and yet misunderstood regions in all of America. It is not easily captured by any one set of descriptive terms. It is complex in geography, language, customs, cultures, and in what many people see as its most defining characteristic, race. This chapter is about one of the South's most striking places, the Low Country—a place where race (there are many historically black counties) and language (Gullah-Geechee) have had profound effects on local culture.

The Low Country is bounded by barrier islands to its east and long stretches of flat land with tidal creeks, marsh grass, and large stands of pine trees with decidedly fewer live oaks, although pictures of live oaks bedraped with Spanish moss are for many people the quintessential picture of the Low Country. (It is such a picture that graces the cover of the bestseller, *Midnight in the Garden of Good and Evil*). The Low Country's most popular places were Charleston, South Carolina, and Savannah, Georgia, but in more recent years developers have struck gold in other places—Myrtle Beach, Hilton Head, St. Simons, and others that share common traits: they are either barrier islands or right along the coast, they offer a plethora of golf courses, their economic characteristics reflect larger, socioeconomic changes, and hugely disproportionate white populations who have usually and mostly unwittingly (at least for the newcomers) displaced black people who had lived in the area for generations. This chapter focuses on one such place and addresses one broad question about it: What is the relationship between economic restructuring, demographic change, and sense of place? Phrased differently, When rural areas go through economic restructuring—and the demographic restructuring that often comes with it—how is local culture and one's commitment to it affected? Are there occasions in which a sense of place is so strong that it obviates nearly any force, local or external, that could alter it? What I learned about these things caused me, eventually, to rethink much of what I "know" about poverty, and rural people, and sociological principles more generally (things to which I return later in this chapter).

Colonial County

Colonial County (like all other names used here, this is fictitious) is like many Low Country counties—mostly rural, marshy, poor, and historically black. The county was mostly black until the mid-1980s, when a combination of black out-migration and white in-migration brought about a majority white population for the first time in nearly two hundred years. Urban areas are near, Savannah and Charleston being the closest cities. The county itself has about nine thousand people. Census data reveal a rather predictable portrait: whites are better educated and financially more solvent than blacks, but there are few people who might be described as wealthy. Like most rural places, the population is comprised of mostly young and old people, groups that are the most likely to be dependent on others (or social security programs) for their financial support. The one surprise is that proportionally more blacks than whites own their homes (Hargis and Horan 1997). For years Colonial County was one of the poorest counties in the Low Country but recent pricey real estate developments will probably alter the aggregated income data for the county while doing little for most of the long-term residents.

The county was settled in the 1700s by colonialists who brought slaves in to develop plantations. Only one former plantation remains accessible in any way and it is on a barrier island. On the mainland, the county seat is a place of about 2,500 people; its downtown buildings look like many other rural places—some occupied, others not; some businesses are new, most are old. At the opposite end of the county sits Yvonne, a crossroads community at the intersection of U.S. 17 and a county road—a road that in one direction leads to the interstate but in the other leads along the coastal part of the county (although only occasionally can the coast itself be seen), arriving after twenty miles or so at the county seat. Numerous roads lead off of U.S. 17, often ending on shell roads at recreational fishing or hunting camps or where commercial fishermen keep their boats. Despite the fact that the county has gotten increasingly white in recent years, it is possible to drive down the country road from Yvonne to the county seat and never see one white face—either alongside the road or in the cars traveling on it.

Houses in Colonial County are mostly in one of three places—in the county seat, where the density is fairly high; facing one of the county's two main roads (U.S. 17 or the county road just described); or off the road a short ways in a "spot" (a clearing in a dense grove of pine trees that hides the house from the road). Sometimes these houses rest in communities based on kin whose land has been passed through the generations to family members. The houses themselves are mostly of three types—trailers (mobile homes), block houses (made of cinder blocks), and stick-built (wooden frame) houses. "Tabby" houses are also prominent in the north end of the county, where two new, expensive waterfront developments have sprung up; tabby, made of ground up oyster shells, is unique to the Low Country and very popular with coastal architects and high-end builders. In general, though, it is axiomatic that the longer the people have resided in the county, the greater the likelihood that their house will look worn. It is common to see old stuff outside these houses—cars and trucks in various states of disrepair, boats, refrigerators, furniture, and so on.

Like many other Southern coastal communities, Colonial County has been discovered by developers and others, mostly outsiders, who have found the place attractive. And, not unexpectedly, these new-comers are disproportionately white. This raises a fundamental question, especially in a place that is historically black: As more outsiders move in, what happens to the sense of this place, which has been developed over generations for many of the long-term indigenous people, and especially for African Americans, for whom the economic gap between themselves and the increasingly white population seems to be getting bigger and bigger? Indeed, what happens to the place itself—physically and economically?

Methods

It was my curiosity about such questions that led me first to census records and other secondary data and then to actually visit selected places. I had one major criterion: All places visited had to be or have been mostly black. Such places still exist in the Black Belt, a string of counties running from Virginia's Tidewater down the coast to Georgia then turning west and running through south-central Georgia, Alabama, and Mississippi before ending in the Mississippi Delta (see chapter 7). Given the geographic and industrial variation in this region, I decided to focus on only one part of it, the Low Country. My reasons for this were quite simple. First, the Low Country has been almost entirely overlooked by sociologists and only little studied by other social scientists. Second, it was easy for me to access. By chance, I knew someone who could get me introduced to older African Americans in the area. I went for a visit and determined very quickly that the study would be workable. Third, as I spent time in the place, I decided to focus entirely on one family's experience there, although I interviewed upwards of twenty people. I decided to focus on one family because the family patriarch (described below) became my key contact and I realized I could get good access to people (even if mostly family members) through him. Given the relatively short time I had for fieldwork and given what I imagined the relative richness of my data might be, this was, I believe, a wise decision. My interviews (or equally often, more informal visits) lasted as little as one or two hours and as long as many, many hours with the family patriarch. And while my initial visit to the area lasted three months, I have subsequently returned several times and revisited both the area and the family. Fourth, the economic restructuring occurring throughout rural America was also occurring here.

A Sense of Place

For residents, Colonial County is a common touchstone, the first place named when you ask someone where they are from. Consequently it is easy to get local people to discuss the county. Whether living there now or previously, their feelings about the county run deep; it is the kind of place that inspires reverence. As the late anthropologist and rural sociologist Janet Fitchen has said of this quality in relation to rural people's lives: "People construct community symbolically, making it a resource and repository of meaning, a referent of their identity. . . . However the deeper meaning of community . . . is of the mind; the ideational or symbolic sense of community, of belonging not *to* a place but *in* its institutions and *with* its people (1991, 252; emphasis Fitchen's). For Fitchen community "is a chosen place . . . [residents'] present location represents a decision not to leave but to stay" (255).

And increasingly as geographers (Cromartie and Stack 1989), anthropologists (Stack 1996), and sociologists (Tolnay 1999) have shown, African Americans who fled the South only a generation ago are now returning in record numbers; in the 1980 census, for the first time since the Civil War, more African Americans returned to the South than left. Carol Stack refers to this accurately with the title of her book *Call to Home* (1996). While millions of African Americans may have left their Southern "home," apparently it never entirely left them.

Historian William McFeely writes about a similar phenomenon in his book about one of the Low Country's barrier islands, *Sapelo's People*. The seventy or so residents of the island are all direct descendants of former slaves there. McFeely puzzled over the fact that after the Civil War, during which Sapelo's slaves were forcibly marched inland by their owners, most of them returned to the island: "Why would people who had been forced to work the land as slaves ever want to see that dirt again? They were free now from those who had done that forcing; why did they go back to the scene of the crime? The clue to the mystery lies in the fact that the memory of the scene was as strong as that of the crime. The Sapelo people who went back saw the place as separable from the oppression that had taken place there. . . . They knew no other place as home" (1994, 82–83). "By working the island's land," McFeely says, "by laughing, weeping, praying on it, being born and dying on it, the former slaves traded possessors; they became the island's, and it became theirs" (93–94).

Dwayne Walls (1971), sounding remarkably like McFeely, although writing twenty years before him, reaches a similar conclusion: "It is in his love of land, of place, that the Southern black most readily shows his Southernness. . . . But how can this Southern sense of belonging held by native blacks be accounted for? Perhaps it is that . . . some of the toughest times of one's life—and the places where one has suffered these times—are rich because one survived and came through. . . . Whatever the reason, the attachment exists widely and deeply, and it is far more than simple nostalgia" (113–14).

Outside Capital, Outside People: A Local Place

What I found in Colonial County was a place that to nearly any outsider looks like a "poor," rural place. Its houses, schools, and storefronts give the appearance of being more than a little worn around the edges. The outsider's sense of local poverty is reinforced dramatically when reviewing census data on education, income, and poverty levels; in all these the county is among the poorest in the state. There are no good-paying jobs in the county other than those in the public sector. There is no heavy industry or manufacturing employer with more than a few employees. Like many rural counties, workers most often seek decent-paying jobs in adjacent counties. In all cases this involves commuting at least forty-five minutes to work. A common source of employment for black women remains unchanged over the past hundred years—seafood processing. But black women are also increasingly found in retail sales. One notable change, from even twenty years ago, is that black women no longer just prepare food in local restaurants; more often (than in the past) they serve it as well. For black men, timber processing and other such jobs are still common in counties to the west and south as well as in Colonial County itself. Commercial fishing has become increasingly the province of white men, although some black men may be found working on their boats. At present, so far as I could ascertain, only one black man owns his own commercial fishing boat.

The most obvious example of outside capital coming into the county is found in retail sales and residential construction. Several years ago a new outlet mall was built at the southern end of the county, on the interstate (I-95). The mall was mostly upscale retailers (e.g., Mikasa china, Polo and Tommy Hilfiger clothiers, Rockport shoes, Coach handbags). Nearby, right at the interstate exit, were new national fast food franchises, service stations, and national discount motels. On U.S. 17, the county's Main Street, a large regional grocery store chain bought out a locally owned family store that had been in business for over half a century. At the same time, a smaller regional independent grocer also closed.

At the northern end of the county, nearest a large city, two new "plantations" have been developed. In some ways, these pricey residential developments are the quintessential symbols of economic restructuring for rural, coastal areas, especially in the Low Country. The prime wooded lots are those right on the water. As an older black resident told me, "Friend, white people will kill to live by the water!" Subsequently this was confirmed by the county's first black tax assessor, who made a very similar comment. One of the county's new plantations is a "fly-in" community with its own landing strip; easily half the houses have a hangar for the owner's plane and the streets have signs saying Low Flying Aircraft Have the Right of Way, with an outline of a plane. Up the road a couple of miles from the fly-in plantation is an even pricier development with a large clubhouse. Here is a place where virtually no resident works locally. Aside from retirees, nearly all other employed people work in the nearest city, which is over one hour away; ease of access to the interstate (about a ten-minute drive) makes such a commute more tolerable than it might otherwise be.

The interstate highway and the new, wealthier white residents are good benchmarks for locating a sense of detachment from the county. The interstate mostly carries people through the county, not to it. Yet in an odd way, the travelers' sense of the place is similar to that of the newer residents—many of whom are quick to point out how little they actually do in the county besides live there. Criticism of all county services and its local officials is widespread among the newcomers, nearly all of whom have no historical ties to the place. Their roots are elsewhere and it is not clear that this will change appreciably no matter how long they "live" there. To some degree, they will always "be" from somewhere else.

The gap between the interstate travelers and the newest, affluent residents on the one hand and the local longer-term residents on the other suggests how different their sense of this place is. People whose entire lives have been lived in Colonial County have an incredible depth of feeling for the place. Although it was not uppermost on their minds as they went about their daily business, the county always provided a context for that business; it was either a place they were going to be or would be leaving from to return (shortly or much later, but always inevitably, back they came). In part, this can be explained by land ownership patterns.

One Family's Sense of Place

Immediately after the Civil War, African Americans in the Low Country were the least likely of all rural blacks to reside on the plantations that had enslaved them. Related to this, they were also the least likely to be engaged in sharecropping (working as tenant farmers). Perhaps most important, Low Country African Americans were much likelier than tenants and sharecroppers to own land (see Hargis and Horan 1997), which may help to explain their sense of rootedness in place. While they still had to deal with powerful white folk, they did so from a place where they too were owners of something other than merely their labor.

This was immediately apparent to me when I met the man who was to become my key informant and, to some degree, collaborator— AC. AC is in his mid-sixties and has a full head of salt and pepper hair, hair that is decidedly not stylish by today's standards but looks like an Afro of the 1960s. AC is solidly built, weighing around two hundred and fifty pounds, most of which is muscle from a lifetime of hard work. He lives in Yvonne, right on U.S. 17 but back far enough from the road that cars going by are unnoticed. He lives in a house that he built himself, nearly thirty years ago. It is a block house of gray, un-painted cinder blocks. The roof is the original one and like much else about this place, it looks tired on the outside. The house is joined by smaller houses on each side—one built by AC for an aunt and the other built for his mother (who "passed" a few years ago). Right next to the house sits a chicken coop. Chickens roam the yard and "lay" here and there. AC gathers the eggs when he has a mind to and har-vests chickens on occasion. A rooster struts around, crowing now and then to remind you of his domain. A small dog is tied up right next to the chicken coop, with a worn-looking doghouse for protection from sun and rain. The driveway is red dirt and the "yard" is crabgrass and whatever takes a mind to grow there. In fact, the most convenient way to get back on the highway is simply to circle through the yard along well-worn tire tracks.

Inside, furniture covered in velour and vinyl is found in both the liv-ing room and a kind of family room that occupies space once intended for a carport. A wood-burning stove helps keep the house warm in the winter, swelteringly so in the family room, where it is located. A televi-sion is the main focal point in the room, but AC seems to watch it rarely. His wife, however, watches it almost continuously, even when talking on the phone. Pictures of family members are scattered about and a picture of the "gran" they raised reflects their pride in her—a framed, formal photograph in her college graduation cap and gown.

AC has lived all his life in Colonial County. He was one of thirteen children, but one drowned as a child and one was killed (by his own wife) as an adult. In time (since my visit), two more were claimed—one by old age, the other by a lifetime of alcohol and cigarettes. His parents were from "Carolina" (meaning South Carolina) and had lived in the county since early in the twentieth century. His father worked "in the woods" (mostly in the turpentine industry) and also had chickens, pigs (which ran wild), and a substantial garden. Colonial County is the only place he has ever known as home.

We sat in AC's family room, AC wearing jeans, a flannel shirt, and slippers and sitting in a vinyl recliner. I was dressed casually and, I'm sure, having that intense look that comes from being on a mission. I realized immediately that it would take such intensity to understand what AC was telling me. His dialect reflects his deep roots in the Low Country. He doesn't speak what local people call "flat" (meaning a kind of Gullah-Geechee, especially in using local, idiomatic expressions such as *rations* for "food"), but he does speak in a dialect that is heavy with his history in this place. (I report what was said to me as accurately as possible, spelling words in ways meant to capture the local dialect and what people sound like as well as what they had to say.) After exchanging pleasantries about AC's gran and my friend who knew her, we began to talk about AC's life in Colonial County. I wondered initially about who had left and who hadn't.

I wasn't goin', no way, no how. Most of my family, goin' didn't excite us. My sisters went to get a better job but they all have intentions to come home. We love bein' 'round one another. We have barbecues, even the ones from New Yawk come. And then they take back rice, sauces, bacon with skin on it, steaks, everythin'. . . . My father always told us that Colonial County was the best place in the South you could stay. . . . Even when there was lots of discrimination, you could do pretty much what you wanted.

Now my children, three in the service. They all left Colonial County but they all comin' back. My oldest daughter, she bought a house on a hill over there [and he points behind him; *hill*, as it turns out, is a local expression for nearly any place a few feet above sea level; a place, in other words, that is drier than the marshy, boggy land common to the coastal Low Country]. She just got out of the army after twenty years, so she's back for good. The other two girls, they ain't nevah left. Lived right down the road there, near where they was bo'n. My two sons both been in the military but they's about to get out now. . . . [And recently, both did.] Them two boys love one each other; want to spend their lives near one another. [Which they also are doing; they live right across the street from one another in a new subdivision in a small city.]

Aside from the fact that all of AC's children live near him (none more than forty-five minutes away and three within five or ten minutes), virtually all his siblings live in the county. For AC, his home in the county is synonymous with family. Indeed, as I eventually learned, he is perceived by all his relatives as a family patriarch—the one to whom they turn in times of trouble and whose counsel they seek for many things. Although he left school in the fourth grade, unable to read or write or do arithmetic, he is a wise man, one who eventually learned how to read and do math.

His sisters who moved to "New Yawk" kept up their family ties by regular visits and by having food and other local items sent to them. Beyond that, though, they did what countless other African American families have done who migrated away from the South: they sent their children "home" to spend part or most of the summers. As AC tells me,

My sister sent her children here every year when they were out of school. . . . Every summer they were sent here to get them off the street. "Send you to AC," she'd tell me. They like to come, too. I tell 'em all kinda tales and stories, like my father did to me. Fixed 'em candied yams, potatoes, and bacon, then rice and eggs. They all member stayin' up waitin' fo' me to git off work [shift work at a nearby plant]. . . . Even now when they come they want me to fix my little ole special. [And he laughs, remembering those days thirty years ago or so.]

Eventually, he and his second wife (of twenty-five years) had one of these children stay permanently. Her mother had lost one child to illness and eventually decided that she would rather have her child raised "right and rural" than live in the city and be raised in daycare by strangers. This child had grown up with her grandparents and she has now gone on to graduate from college and start a family of her own, living "'cross the state" but keeping regular contact.

AC's love of Colonial County is not built on simple biology, though. It is based on relationships with this place and the people in it, especially his family and friends. A story about one of his houses epitomizes this. The house was one of the first to be "block built" in his part of Colonial County. He built the house when he was still married to his first wife, Clorice. She was from one of the county's most well educated black families, unlike AC's family. But as often happens, love conquers all, and when they were both very young, she got pregnant and they got married. Even more than twenty-five years after their divorce, they remember vividly their young lives together and what they tried to build—having five children and quite literally building a house for them. AC worked on the house in his off-hours, mostly during the days (before he started his shift at 4 P.M.) and on weekends. At the time, AC could read, but only poorly. Clorice, on the other hand, could read very well. She told me, "We got all the books on how to do it [build a block house]; how to do the concrete; how to mix the mortar. But see, AC couldn't understand those terms. He could read but he couldn't understand what the term meant. And he said, 'Will you explain it to me?' So I'd read and explain it." And her recollection of this evokes a smile and a sense of pride in what they did. "We went over the books I don't know how many times . . . and finally we started building." As AC told me, "I laid all them blocks, and I'd never done that befo'. That was the first time I tried it. And the curious thing was that as soon as I got mine built, I had three more to build. Sho did."

In time, AC's first block house was destroyed in a fire. No one was injured, but at about the same time, his relationship with Clorice also ended. AC married another woman and built a new house for them. Clorice also got married but to a man from New York, where she moved with her two youngest children. In time, though, she came "home." Her sentiment and the expression of it was common: "My whole intention was to come back. I love this place."

AC's former sister-in-law, Louise, and his sister Althea provide similar accounts. Louise, too, left the county briefly, before returning almost sixty years ago. When she visits a daughter who lives several hundred miles away, it is never long before she gets homesick. As she tells me, "When my mind say home, home I'm comin'! . . . It's nothin' but woods but I'm ready to come home to my chirren. And they happy to see me. That's my reason for stayin' here. I just love it." AC's sister Althea told me that while most of her children lived nearby, "When my husband died, my daughter and my sons in Atlanta said, 'Mama, ain't nobody home but chou. Why don't you move up heah with us?' And I said, 'Un uh. I'd rather stay right heah.' . . . I love this place. I love it. I wouldn't want to be nowheres but heah. And I been heah so long, all these many years that I can't remember anywheres else!"

AC's daughter Alice left to go into the military but she always knew where she would go afterward: home.

> I knew I would come home. Where else was there to go? Where you got and be at home? . . . My big thing is family. My mother and father was here. When I was growing up I knew my grandparents. . . . Matter of fact, I knew my great grandmother on my mother's side—and I mean *knew her*, cuz she lived right down the lane from us. Where you grown up and git up on Saturday mornin's and stuff and go help her pump the water—cuz she still had a pump—and follow her into the woods to get berries and deer tongue [a leaf that looks and smells like tobacco and can be sold] or dog tongue [very similar to deer tongue]. . . . And we'd go fishin'. I remember bein' with my mama's grandmother and spendin' time in the field—pickin' corn, butter beans, okra, diggin' potatoes. . . . This county is a good county. People love to come here.

AC's other children sound much like their older sister, their aunts, and their parents. They too never left or did so only briefly, and always with a sense of returning. Even the one sister most committed to "escaping" (who had, in fact, recently left), plans on returning. She still owns her house right up the road from her parents, her father in one direction her mother in the other; her youngest sister lives right across the road. And while she is gone, her house is occupied by her son, his girlfriend, and their young daughter. All in the family.

It is this kind of rootedness in place and their relationship to it that is absent for most of Colonial County's newer residents. Unlike the newcomers, AC and his family have not bought into a community as one more consumable good. Instead, they have built it—quite literally in some cases. AC's family has been born, raised, and buried there. This is not a retirement or second "home" for them. This is home.

I posed questions at the outset of this chapter about the relationship between economic restructuring, demographic change, and sense of place. I wondered especially how local culture and commitments to it are affected by economic and demographic change. And more specifically, I wondered about these relationships in a historically black county, a county that nearly any visitor would assume (from driving through or a casual visit) is poor.

To many sociologists, "poor people" are seen as victims—in all possible ways. As a result, they are given little power or credit; they seem too weak to ever effectively take control of their lives. They are more acted upon than initiating action; and when they do initiate action, it is often seen as leading to negative results (crime, unemployment, violence, etc.). I went to a place that nearly everyone would believe is poor, so finding victims there should have been relatively easy. Instead, I found people who had asserted considerable control over certain social spaces in their lives—their churches, schools, and especially families. My findings on these things were much like Mitchell Duneier's in his study of a "poor," inner-city, African American neighborhood in Chicago (1992). Like him, I found considerable complexity to "poverty" but in a rural area, not an urban one.

What I discovered about this rural, very "poor" place was that secondary data and "facts" can only provide a limited amount of information about it. They can, for example, tell you nothing about its soul (to use Dwayne Walls's term). But it is precisely its soul that is most at issue for understanding its strength of character, how its people coped with life locally, how they thrived on it and prospered in ways economic and otherwise. For them, Colonial County was rich in memory—of work, of play, of family, of church, of politics, of good times and bad. In all these things, local black people had played active roles. Everyone had memories of the Ku Klux Klan and racial problems, but even against such memories, including some contemporary problems in politics and the schools, people had a strong sense of kinship and belonging. Only one person (a former politician) spoke of having been victimized, and even that person had returned to the place to fight for change.

Pride in self and love of place are not often considered important in decisions about economic development. But in rural places, and especially historically black ones, such factors might bear special consideration. They suggest a depth of commitment to a place, the reverence with which a place is held in people's souls. A true love of place was repeatedly expressed and underscored, especially for older residents. But for the younger residents, some worrisome facts remain. First, as has been true for generations in rural places, out-migration of young people far outpaces in-migration or retention. Young people go where they perceive the job opportunities are greatest, and most often that is elsewhere. For those (regardless of race) who go away to college, the perceived labor market may be far beyond the borders of the county, state, or region. Second, local job opportunities (especially in the county) have changed in form but not in content. The service sector—with its notoriously poor wages and equally poor fringe benefits—has arisen as a major employer. While this has replaced more dangerous work in the timber industry and the repetitive work in the seafood-processing industry, it has done little to dramatically increase the earnings for most workers. For many in the county, disability, retirement, and other transfer payments are major sources of income. No new heavy industry has come into the county other than residential construction, and that occurs mostly at both ends of the county— with relatively easy access to nearby urban labor markets and their skilled labor forces—thus promising little for local workers. Third, and perhaps most worrisome, drugs are present in rural Colonial County, and, especially troubling, young black males are most often arrested for selling them. The local newspaper reports regularly on drug arrests in black areas of the county. Everyone seems to know places for finding drugs and those who deal them. In this sense, perceived lack of opportunity caused by economic and historical shifts is much like what is found in urban areas—and with similar consequences.

Rural residents, whether young or old, are mostly buffeted about by the winds of economic change. For some return migrants, with skills learned elsewhere, the local scene may offer opportunities not perceived by others (see Stack 1996). But for the most part, economic life in Colonial County (not unlike most rural places) is a struggle. Seemingly far removed from national and global forces, Colonial County residents are nonetheless affected by them. Whether it is goods or services or their own marketability, they must adjust to the changes around them.

We know (from secondary data) the degrees to which rural poverty exists throughout the United States. The South is still disproportionately the poorest of all regions and nowhere more so than in historically black counties (see Wimberly and Morris 1996; also Hoppe 1985 on "persistent poverty"). But this tells us nothing about the variance among these places and the presence of people like AC and his family. While no one would want to generalize from an N of one family in one place to all rural African Americans who live in similar places, Cynthia Duncan's very recent ethnographic findings (1999), coupled with those of Stack (1996) and others included in the present volume, may ultimately suggest that there is much about the Protestant ethic that still rings true. Hard work can pay off. The return migration to the South of many talented African Americans, coupled with the presence of hard-working indigenous people, may craft a future for such places that none of us can envision right now. Indeed, as legitimate economic opportunities in urban areas so radically diminish, with plants and factories moving away (see Wilson 1987, 1996), it is reasonable to posit that increasing proportions of rural residents (to include black ones) may choose to stay local to seek their futures. This only adds to the mix of possibilities and suggests the kind of power that may be found there. Not everyone will benefit equally; some will prosper while others may continue to reproduce forms of poverty that existed long before them. It is precisely such outcomes that we must better understand to unravel the ways in which local people and cultural norms are embedded in one another. And not unimportantly, we must understand these processes in a changing economic context—one in which global forces impinge on all areas to include rural ones. This is something with which even the most motivated, hardest-working people must contend; restructured local economies are affected directly and indirectly by forces far outside their own geographies. This point is well made by Duncan (1999) in her ethnographies of communities in the Mississippi Delta, Appalachian Kentucky, and New England.

For many rural counties, to include Colonial County, economic restructuring is most obvious in what George Ritzer (1999) calls "cathedrals of consumption" (malls and similar venues). Ubiquitous consumer culture suggests a radical transformation of places and the people in them. It suggests a kind of homogenizing—that knowing how things are in one place will be a great predictor of how they are elsewhere. And yet that denies the reality that places differ, markedly in many instances and nowhere more pointedly than between rural and urban locales. No matter the influence of an interstate highway or satellite television, rural, less dense places often retain a pervasive sense of their small-town ways. Thus economic restructuring does not ipso facto lead to what I will call cultural restructuring. Culture is bigger, slower to change. To be sure, the Low Country's demography has changed and no doubt will continue to do so.

It seems safe to predict that the proportion of whites in all Low Country counties will continue to grow, while the proportion of blacks will continue to decline. But will all black folk move away? Unlikely, very unlikely, I believe. Why? Because in the face of economic and political uncertainties that accompany demographic change, local black people will continue to wield power. They will continue to own land (although perhaps not as much). They will continue to disproportionately live on land that is the least valued by whites and the least susceptible to development. They will continue to provide the labor for many necessary jobs, especially those least desired by the newcomers and their progeny. They will continue to control and "own" the social spaces most crucial to them—their families, churches, and communities. They will continue to have a sense of their counties and the communities within them as theirs in ways that will be hard to replicate elsewhere and slow to be fully established by newcomers. And they will continue to fight for their rights and the very things over which they have a unique sense of stewardship.

It is well known in sociology that migration is selective. By extension, we can posit that return migration will also be selective. Since my interviews were conducted with residents who either chose to remain or left and returned at some later date, it could be argued that my findings are biased; I never interviewed out-migrants who chose not to return. Despite this limitation, it is my belief that what I found exhibits how strongly a powerful sense of place is embedded in time and space. In the face of racism and great inequalities of all sorts, African Americans in this Low Country community developed organizations, networks, and social spaces that provided forms of autonomy even during historical times of both de jure and de facto racial segregation. Owning land, having family networks, belonging to local churches, having some control over local schools, these were all components of spatially based survival strategies; they provided material and psychological resources for family survival. They were, to use a contemporary term, forms of social capital. With the end of legally mandated segregation, additional material and psychological resources (e.g., education) that were not tied to specific places became available for the next generation.

In a certain sense, the generational issues uncovered in this research represent a real paradox—the decline of *both* oppression and autonomy. In the process, the sense of community changed dramatically and with the demographic shifts documented, it is a certainty that community will remain fluid—emergent for the newest residents but in transition for all others. What will not change markedly is the proprietarial desire to hang on to those local things most valued, and none of these seems more important than the rootedness in place.

References

Berendt, John. 1994. *Midnight in the Garden of Good and Evil: A Savannah Story.* New York: Random House.

Cromartie, John, and Carol B. Stack, 1989. "Reinterpretation of Black Return and Non-return Migration to the South." *Rural Sociology* 39:514–28.

Duncan, Cynthia M. 1999. *World's Apart: Why Poverty Persists in Rural America.* New Haven: Yale University Press.

Duneier, Mitchell. 1992. *Slim's Table: Race, Respectability, and Masculinity.* Chicago: University of Chicago Press.

Fitchen, Janet. 1991. *Endangered Spaces, Enduring Places: Change, Identity, and Survival in Rural America.* Boulder: Westview.

Hargis, Peggy, and Patrick M. Horan. 1997. "The Low-Country Advantage for African-Americans in Georgia, 1880–1930." *Journal of Interdisciplinary History* 28:27–46.

Hoppe, Robert A. 1985. *Economic Structure and Change in Persistently Low-Income Nonmetro Counties.* Economic Research Service, report no. 50. Washington, D.C.: U.S. Department of Agriculture.

McFeely, William S. 1994. *Sapelo's People: A Long Walk into Freedom.* New York: Norton.

Ritzer, George. 1999. *Enchanting a Disenchanted World: Revolutionizing the Means of Consumption.* Thousand Oaks, Calif.: Pine Forge Press.

Stack, Carol. 1996. *Call to Home: African Americans Reclaim the Rural South.* New York: Basic Books.

Tolnay, Steward E. 1999. *The Bottom Rung: African American Family Life on Southern Farms.* Urbana: University of Illinois Press.

Walls, Dwayne E. 1971. *The Chickenbone Special.* New York: Harcourt, Brace, Jovanovich.

Wilson, William J. 1987. *The Truly Disadvantaged: The Inner City, the Underclass, and Public Policy.* Chicago: University of Chicago Press.

———. 1996. *When Work Disappears: The World of the New Urban Poor.* New York: Random House.

Wimberly, Ronald, and Libby V. Morris. 1996. "The Southern Black Belt." Map available from Ronald Wimberly, Department of Sociology, North Carolina State University, Raleigh.

9

Housing Labor's Unrest

Economic Restructuring and the Social Production of Scale

Jeff R. Crump

ON AUGUST 17, 1997, the former International Harvester plant in Canton, Illinois, burned in an arson fire. As word spread, residents gathered at the site, their responses a mixture of anger and grief. While many watched with tears in their eyes, others began to collect souvenir bricks and some actually welcomed the destruction of the plant that had symbolized Canton's industrial past.

Meanwhile, in Beardstown, Illinois, Mexican immigrants went to their jobs in the local pork processing plant. The wages they earned allowed many to establish homes in the town along the banks of the Illinois River. While their presence had been encouraged by the large meatpacking firm, many longtime residents resented the newcomers and fought to keep them out of "their" town. Local conflicts erupted over lack of housing and attempts to increase the number of available housing units by constructing a new mobile home park.

The economic and social changes occurring in Beardstown and Canton exemplify many of the forces shaping small towns and cities throughout the rural Midwest: deindustrialization, immigration, a restructured agricultural processing industry and a deteriorating built environment are some of the changes in the fabric of life that make the rural Midwest a very different place today than it was thirty years ago. Using a comparative case study of Beardstown and Canton, Illinois, I explore the economic, social, and spatial processes that are changing the lives of people in these places.

To begin this chapter I present my theoretical perspective on rural restructuring in the U.S. Midwest. Here, I argue that social and spatial processes are mutually constitutive and that social and spatial processes are seamlessly integrated in everyday life (Harvey 1982). I also argue that a fundamental aspect of social, economic, and spatial restructuring is a reconfiguration of geographic scale. Lastly, I emphasize that the workers of the rural Midwest are not passively accepting the changes occurring in their communities. Rather, rural labor throughout the Midwest is actively adapting, contesting, and struggling to meet the challenges posed by the restructuring of economic, social, and spatial relations both within their communities and with the outside world.

Economic and Sociospatial Restructuring and the Production of Geographic Scale

In social theory, space is often viewed as a fixed, arid backdrop for social processes. Space is portrayed either as a container for social processes or as a set of contextual variables that in some unspecified manner influence the individuals that inhabit a particular place (Smith 1993). Recently, such static conceptions of space are giving way to more process-oriented theoretical perspectives that view social and spatial processes as deeply intertwined and mutually constitutive (Harvey 1982).

Scale is a fundamental aspect of sociospatial organization. Despite its central importance in defining space and organizing human activity, relatively little attention has been paid to what scale is and how various scales are formed (Jonas 1994). In general, scale is taken for granted and it is tacitly assumed that certain geographic scales simply exist (Smith 1993). Scale is viewed as a set of rigid, preexisting boundaries that govern the size and shape of spatial containers for social action. Scale is most often treated as a methodological problem; here the major issue is said to be choosing an appropriate scale of analysis (Swyngedouw 2000).

In contrast, I argue that scale is socially produced and that a fundamental aspect of economic, social, and spatial change is the reconfiguration of geographic scale. Recent theoretical and empirical work explores the idea that scale is socially produced and that as restructuring occurs, space is itself reconfigured (Crump 2002; Smith 1993; Swyngedouw 1997). As Swyngedouw (2000) argues,

> Spatial scale has to be understood as something that is produced historically; a process that is always deeply heterogeneous and contested . . . as the power to appropriate place is always contested and struggled over, then the alliances social groups or classes forged over a certain spatial scale will shape the conditions of appropriation and control over place and have a decisive influence over relative sociospatial power positions. The continuous reshuffling and reorganizations of spatial scales are an integral part of social strategies and struggles for control and empowerment. (2000, 70)

Social conflict frequently breaks out over efforts to construct wider scales of influence and thereby increase the geographic extent of control or power. Scalar struggle may also involve actions intended to force opponents to operate in restricted geographic areas, subsequently reducing their power. For their part, actors forced to work at limited geographic scales struggle to extend, or "stretch," their scale of operation, thereby increasing their relative political power. Because it both embodies and reflects power relations, the production of scale is a profoundly political act (Swyngedouw 1997).

According to Swyngedouw (2000), current efforts to reconfigure geographic scale involve a globalization of certain types of production activities and a concomitant increase in the exploitation of local differences such as wage rates (Swyngedouw 2000). The simultaneous nature of these global-local movements is captured by his term *glocalization* (Swyngedouw 2000). Glocalization means that as the scalar structure of capitalism changes, some locations are characterized by increasingly strong ties to broader economic and sociospatial processes. Simultaneously, other places fail to find a niche in the global economy and are increasingly isolated from broader-scale processes.

The "stretching" of scale—that is, increasing ties to a wider set of locations—is occurring in many rural locations. For example, in amenity-rich rural towns in Idaho and Montana, the immigration of footloose high-tech entrepreneurs results in a growing network of linkages between those places and locations such as Silicon Valley. Consequently, an increasing number of rural locations are now subject to changes in the global market for high-tech goods or to rapid fluctuations in the NASDAQ.

At the same time, other rural areas are delinked and cut off from broader-scale processes. For example, when a factory closes, the production and distribution networks constructed by firms will be cut, leaving a community that finds itself pushed to the periphery of the global economy. The connections between workers may also be severed by a plant closing. In particular, when the union local closes, the ties forged with national-scale labor organizations are excised and workers may be left to fend for themselves.

The local outcomes of economic, social, and spatial restructuring are then extremely varied. Some places are ever more tightly bound to the global economy, while others are left behind. Although increased ties to other locations (i.e., globalization) are often viewed as a necessity, negative outcomes may result—for example, loss of community identity and local control. Although being isolated from broader-scale processes is almost always viewed as a negative outcome, it may also mean more local control. Moreover, isolation can force communities to develop local social capital, a potentially positive outcome.

METHODOLOGY

The Beardstown and Canton case studies evolved out of a desire to document the local impacts of the widespread social and economic restructuring occurring throughout the rural Midwest in the 1980s and 1990s. Initially a series of quantitative analyses, based on 1990 U.S. census data, were produced (Crump 1994). The results indicated that job and population loss was widespread, and the rapid growth of poverty, particularly among the young, reflected a high and growing level of economic and social distress in the region (Crump 1994).

Other events within west-central Illinois, notably the extended strike that pitted the United Auto Workers against the global might of the Peoria-based Caterpillar Corporation, called attention to the active agency of workers (Crump and Merrett 1998). Given the variegated and complex landscape of economic and social change that was unfolding in west-central Illinois, I concluded that detailed fieldwork, based on a case study approach, was called for.

The fieldwork phase of the research began with a broad reconnaissance of several towns and cities within west-central Illinois. During this phase of the project, informal interviews, field notes, and photographs were collected. As the reconnaissance stage proceeded, several themes began to emerge. The built environment of the entire region was in a state of deterioration, many towns were crippled by factory closings, and still others were undergoing rapid change as new immigrants began replacing the existing union workers.

Although many towns were worthy of further study, for a number of reasons I decided to concentrate on Beardstown and Canton. From a general perspective, the patterns of economic, social, and spatial change in Beardstown and Canton, reflect broad patterns found throughout the rural Midwest. The importance of new immigrants and the challenges of dealing with a rapidly changing community in Beardstown are representative of what is occurring throughout the meatpacking centers of the rural Midwest (Gouveia 1994). The devastating impact of deindustrialization, common to many rural places in the Midwest, is exemplified by Canton. In addition, both towns reflect the regional industrial specialization of much of the Midwest in meatpacking and farm implements, sectors that have undergone considerable restructuring.

In Beardstown, a change in the ownership of the large meatpacking firm brought many new immigrants to town, displacing and replacing long-term workers and residents. As the ethnic composition of the town changed, a series of dramatic events drew attention to what was happening there. The closure of International Harvester in Canton, and the later burning of the old factory, drew me to the town. Moreover, the resilience and determination of the residents of Canton seemed so important and so characteristic of rural people that it proved irresistible.

Fieldwork was conducted in Beardstown and Canton over a period of four years (1995–99). Although the major focus was on the towns, it was not restricted to their city limits. As the fieldwork progressed it became obvious that in order to capture the diversity of the region, each study area should include not only the towns but much of the surrounding countryside as well. For example, in the case of Beardstown, information was gathered on the controversy surrounding the siting of mega–hog farms in the surrounding rural areas. In the case of Canton, the long strike at Caterpillar in nearby Peoria proved to be especially relevant to employment conditions in the town.

In each town interviews were conducted with residents and public officials. These individuals were chosen because of the depth of knowledge they had gained through long experience in the community. Observations were also carried out by attending meetings of local economic development committees, visiting local schools, and spending time in local shops and restaurants. The archives of local newspapers were also investigated, and an important component of the data collection was the use of photographs to document the built environment of each town. Such visual information proved to be particularly valuable in tracking changes in the towns and in communicating research results.

REGIONAL SETTING—BACKGROUND

Beardstown and Canton are typical of many towns in the rural Midwest. The Mississippi and Illinois Rivers are important regional boundaries and the region is anchored by St. Louis to the south and Chicago to the north. The economic foundations of west-central Illinois are production agriculture and agriculturally related industries, such as meatpacking and farm implement production. The region exemplifies the Midwestern agro-industrial complex, as farming and related manufacturing and processing industries continue to be the economic bedrock (Page and Walker 1991).

The history of west-central Illinois is marked by bitter and protracted conflicts between capital and labor (Crump and Merrett 1998). The hard-fought battles between workers and companies help explain why a strong sense of working-class consciousness has evolved in the region (Crump 2002). As economic restructuring has swept the region, workers and unions have opposed efforts to cut wages and reduce benefits. During the 1980s and 1990s, strikes in Peoria and Decatur, Illinois, focused national attention on workers' efforts to resist the restructuring efforts of capital (Frank and Mulcahey 1995).

Much of the social struggle within the region revolves around geographic scale. During the union organizing drives of the 1930s and 1940s, workers fought to move beyond localized confrontations with capital. Labor unions fought long and hard to equalize wages and working conditions within particular industrial sectors and across the regions of the United States. And as companies were forced to sign industry-wide pattern contracts, significant gains in wages and benefits were achieved (Herod 1991). These efforts to construct wider spaces of engagement as a way to increase labor's power vis-à-vis capital were largely successful. Throughout west-central Illinois and the industrial Midwest, the economic prosperity of many workers and their communities derived directly from the power gained by organizing at regional and national scales.

Between the mid-1950s and mid-1970s, west-central Illinois enjoyed an era of relative labor peace and economic prosperity. However, beginning in the 1970s, confrontations between organized labor and the major companies began to increase as workers militantly demanded higher wages to match the inflation sweeping the country and employers actively resisted union demands. At the end of the 1970s, capital launched an all-out offensive against labor. A centerpiece of capital's strategy to undermine the power of labor involved efforts to end industry-wide pattern bargaining and force unions to return to local-level negotiations (Herod 1997). In many towns this scale-busting strategy left union locals on their own. In many instances, communities were pitted against each other as companies threatened to pull out of town if their demands for concessions by workers and the community were not met. Throughout the region and the country, companies were able to break down the national-scale system of labor negotiations and thereby limit the bargaining power of workers (Herod 1997).

In the meatpacking industry, old-line companies such as Oscar Mayer and Wilson closed numerous plants. The closed factories were then sold to new meatpacking firms such as Iowa Beef Packers and Excel, a division of food giant Cargill, and then reopened. These new firms, operating in an extremely competitive environment, instituted revolutionary production techniques that greatly increased productivity while at the same time, reducing the skill required to cut meat (Stanley 1994). The changes in the process of disassembly also facilitated the radical restructuring of labor relations in the industry. As the new giants of the meatpacking industry reopened the plants of the old-line meatpacking firms, they replaced unionized, skilled, high-wage workers with nonunion, often immigrant employees (U.S. General Accounting Office 1998). The new labor force was specifically recruited to provide the "lean and mean" firms with a hard-working, low-cost, tractable labor force (Ufkes 1995). These labor force strategies not only significantly reduced labor costs, they also eliminated union militancy as a force in the meatpacking industry (Griffith, Broadway, and Stull 1995). From the perspective of the new meatpacking firms, local-scale contract negotiations and an international scale of labor recruitment were the formula for increased profits in the 1990s.

Throughout the Midwest, economic restructuring has been accompanied by fundamental shifts in the scale of economic and social life. In some locations, deindustrialization has left communities outside the global marketplace. Concomitantly, economic restructuring has involved rural localities in broader nets of connections that bring the world to Main Street, USA (see also Warren 1978). These variegated trends are exemplified by the case studies of Beardstown and Canton, which not only serve to illustrate the broad social processes outlined, but also provide a view of the differences in how these processes were worked out at the level of the community.

CASE STUDY: BEARDSTOWN

Beardstown, Illinois, is located on the Illinois River. Founded in 1826, the town was built on top of American Indian burial mounds that were leveled to provide building sites. Since Beardstown is in the river's flood plain, it has been inundated numerous times, the most recent being in 1993. Currently, the Illinois River is kept at bay by a twenty-foot earthen levee supplemented by a flood wall eight feet high in the downtown area.

The major source of employment in Beardstown has traditionally been the meatpacking plant, located on the southeast edge of town. The plant was formerly owned and operated by the Oscar Mayer Company and it employed between six and seven hundred workers. The unionized labor force that worked there earned between $16.00 and $20.00 per hour, wages that enabled workers to provide their families with a decent standard of living. Another major source of local employment was a plant that manufactured heat transfer devices and employed approximately two hundred workers.

During the 1980s, Oscar Mayer closed the plant and although some workers found employment in other Oscar Mayer operations, many found themselves out of work. Another blow to the local economy occurred when the machinery plant closed. Significant job declines also hit those employed in the agricultural sector, where 17 percent of the jobs were lost between 1980 and 1990 (Crump 1994). During the 1980s the employment base that had supported a relatively large and well-off working-class population, disappeared.

Following the closing of Oscar Mayer, the plant was purchased by the Excel Corporation. When the plant reopened under Excel's management, production processes were reorganized and line speed was greatly increased. Excel's labor force strategy also departed from Oscar Mayer's. Wages were cut by approximately 40 percent, falling to the current rate of around $8.00 per hour (Crump 1997). Employment at the plant was doubled, to over fifteen hundred workers. Whereas Oscar Mayer workers came mainly from the local area, Excel relies on immigrant workers from Texas and Mexico and from other Midwestern meatpacking towns (e.g., Columbus Junction, Iowa).

By reaching outside the local labor market to meet its desire for a nonunion, low-wage labor force, Excel effectively expanded the scale of Beardstown's labor market. The increased scale of Excel's labor recruitment meant that Beardstown was now directly tied into a labor market that reached deep into Mexico and the town was now impacted by patterns of legal and illegal immigration. The local effects of this stretching of scale were quickly evident as a number of local conflicts arose over education, health care, housing, and race.

In 1993, there was only one Hispanic family in Beardstown. In a single year, this number increased to over 700 (Crump 1997). Hispanic students in the local school district went from ten to over 350 (Fimmen et al. 1998). Taken by surprise by the rapid changes in its student body, the school district initially had no way to accommodate non-English-speaking students. It took some time before administrators, teachers, and students were able to address the needs of students. One administrator commented, "In the beginning we didn't know how to take care of it. We didn't know what to do. We just had a problem, but we didn't have solutions. Now we have resources and we have solutions, and it might take us a day or two, but I don't think we are really just baffled anymore" (Fimmen et al. 1998, 15).

Initially, the non-English-speaking students were placed in regular classrooms and provided with a translator. However, the growing number of children that needed bilingual education forced the school district to develop comprehensive programs in English as a Second Language (ESL). Some staff and parents resented the development of such programs and the cost burdens associated with them.

The rapid influx of new residents also strained the capacity of the local housing market. The available housing stock, mainly comprising mobile homes and substandard houses, was not sufficient to meet the needs of the new workers. Moreover, many landlords were reluctant to rent to the newcomers, and the homes for sale were either inadequate or too expensive. In an issue tinged with racial implications, a new city ordinance to ban additional mobile homes was proposed. According to the terms of the ordinance, existing mobile homes remained legal, but any new development of mobile home parks would be outlawed. To many in the town it appeared that this ordinance was aimed at preventing Hispanics from purchasing and locating mobile homes in Beardstown.

As the immigrant population expanded, racial antagonism between whites and Hispanics became evident. In 1996, these tensions exploded, culminating in a violent killing, a cross burning and an arson fire. The spark came when a Hispanic male, living with a white woman, was beaten by her ex-husband (Fitton 1996a). Later that night, the Hispanic male encountered the ex-husband at the local Hispanic tavern. Pulling out a gun, he attempted to shoot the ex-husband. However, the shot missed its intended target and killed a friend of the ex-husband's instead (Fitton 1996a). After the shooting, the accused murderer fled to Mexico. In a bizarre twist to the tragic story, the ex-husband was killed the next day in an automobile accident (Fimmen et al. 1998). Further angering Beardstown residents was the fact that even though the accused was later apprehended by Mexican authorities, he could not be extradited, because there is currently no extradition treaty between the United States and Mexico.

Many longtime Beardstown residents were angry and frustrated that the man had escaped justice. In the days that followed, there were further racial confrontations. The owners of the Hispanic tavern and grocery store were threatened and the night following the shooting, a six-foot cross was torched in front of the tavern (Fitton 1996b). Following the cross burning, the tavern was burned to the ground (Fitton 1996a; Fuhrig 1996). The next day, the owner of the Mexican-owned grocery store, having received several threats, decided to close (Fuhrig 1996). Although cooler heads realized that the feud had been a long-standing one in which race was but one element, the killing and fires had kindled explosive emotions in the town.

Although local leaders appealed for calm and a group was formed to combat racial prejudice, the Beardstown landscape reflects continuing tension. Located in downtown Beardstown, across from the newly renovated chamber of commerce and the local post office, is a white power hangout in an abandoned bank building. Upon entering through the smashed in doors, one sees white power graffiti, swastikas, and other racist symbols covering the walls.

Just across the street is a Hispanic tavern. According to local informants, the street in between the abandoned bank and the tavern becomes a war zone at night as combatants stake out their territorial boundaries. When I asked if I should come and observe a typical Saturday night, I was told, "Stay away, you don't want to be here."

The local effects of the increasing scale of Beardstown's labor market, is evident as the U.S. and Mexican border now extends right into downtown Beardstown, Illinois. In this example, the reconfiguration of geographic scale has generated many local conflicts and created a no-man's-land in small-town Illinois.

However, several positive community actions have been taken in response to the racial tension in Beardstown. A locally organized alliance comprising political and religious leaders, along with members of the community, was formed to help promote better race relations. Although housing problems continue to be an issue, some Hispanic residents have purchased homes and are beginning to rehabilitate the formerly dilapidated structures.

The social conflicts in Beardstown are not confined to that community but have spilled over into the surrounding rural areas as well. In a related struggle, many rural residents find themselves forced to take sides in a conflict over the siting of mega–hog facilities in the area. With the meatpacking industry in place, large corporations such as Murphy Family Farms of North Carolina have found west-central Illinois an attractive location (Crump 1997). Moreover, Illinois places relatively few restrictions on large livestock operations, making it relatively easy to site such facilities.

As capital has constructed broader scales of labor recruitment, Beardstown residents find it difficult to assert any control over the forces that are changing the town and the lives of its residents. Although the restructured meatpacking industry has brought new jobs and new residents to town, it has unalterably changed its social and economic landscape.

CASE STUDY: CANTON, ILLINOIS

For over a century, the economy of Canton, Illinois, was based on the production of farm implements, especially plows. Plow production began with the arrival of William Parlin in 1840, and by 1900 the Parlin and Orendorff Plow Works (P&O) employed eight hundred workers. Local control of the factory was lost when P&O merged with

McCormick and other farm implement firms to form the International Harvester Corporation (IH), headquartered in Chicago. IH's brick factory was located near the town square and in many ways, the "works" were the center of life in Canton. Daily life in Canton was lived in rhythm with the changing shifts at the IH works, and workers were called to their jobs by the plant's whistle, affectionately known as the Big Toot.

International Harvester was one of the largest corporations in the United States. The company operated factories throughout the country and had a vast network of dealers around the world. Production also occurred outside of the country. For example, IH owned large plantations in Central America that produced fibers used to make the twine used by various types of harvesting machinery (Gilpin 1989). Therefore, when P&O merged with IH, Canton became part of a production and distribution network that spanned the globe. From 1910 until the plant closed in 1984, the Canton works produced plows sold throughout the world. Because it was a site within the IH global production system, the well-being of Canton was closely linked to regional and national markets for farm implements and conditions in the U.S. agricultural economy.

The activities of IH were not the only set of scale-stretching linkages between Canton and other places. Workers also played an important role in constructing such networks that connected Canton with the labor movement at the national scale. Active efforts to build unions by IH workers in Canton, allied with regional and national-scale union-organizing drives, provided an important set of scale-bridging networks outside capital's control. Reflecting the active coal mining in the area, the first union to represent Canton IH workers was the United Mine Workers. However, by 1946, the workers were represented by the militant Farm Equipment and Metal Workers Union (FE). Union organizing was very difficult and fraught with conflict. IH consistently maintained its opposition to unions and fought workers' demands for representation. Not only did IH's anti-union efforts fail, they helped create an attitude of militant unionism among its employees. By the end of the Second World War, the FE had won significant concessions from IH through a combination of strikes, tough negotiations, and rulings by the National Labor Relations Board (Gilpin 1992).

Between 1950 and 1955 the FE and the United Auto Workers (UAW) engaged in a bitter contest for the right to represent Canton's IH workers (Crump 2002). In the end, the UAW was victorious, and by the mid-1950s Canton's local was firmly entrenched in the national labor organization of the powerful UAW. In contrast to the system of peaceful coexistence adopted by other farm implement firms and their union workers, labor conflict between IH and the UAW remained a constant throughout the 1950s. IH stubbornly refused to accept the industry-wide pattern contracts negotiated between the UAW and other farm implement companies. Every round of contract negotiations was accompanied by strikes, and Canton workers acquired a great deal of skill at maintaining a picket line. It was not until 1961 that IH made major concessions to its UAW workers. Ironically, the long labor struggle meant that workers at IH were better organized and much more militant in pressing their demands than the workers at the company's competitors (Crump and Merrett 1998). Consequently, they ended up with significantly better contracts than their counterparts at Deere or Caterpillar (Marsh 1985).

The good wages and excellent benefits earned by years of union organizing brought prosperity and stability to Canton. The town boomed and the 1970s were especially good years, when the demand for farm implements was high, supported by a strong farm economy. By the end of the decade, however, Canton was once again roiled by labor strife. As contract negotiations opened in 1979, IH management was determined to undo the gains of the workers. These efforts were met head on by a militant labor force determined to maintain wages and benefits. Unable to reach an agreement, the UAW struck IH in a three-month strike (Marsh 1985). Christmas 1979 was a lean one in Canton, as striking workers subsisted on strike pay and patrolled picket lines.

Not only did IH management fail to win concessions, when the strike ended, the overextended company found itself teetering on the edge of bankruptcy. The impact of the Farm Crisis, which decimated the market for farm implements, was compounded by years of financial mismanagement, a rigid and inefficient management structure and outmoded factories (Marsh 1985). As the company's losses mounted, Canton's IH workers knew their jobs were endangered. The end came on December 23, 1984, when 144 years of production ceased at the Canton works.

The loss of IH was a terrible blow for the economy of Canton. Local officials struggled to find a way to replace the lost jobs, and they were able to negotiate the purchase of the plant and its equipment for a nominal fee. A locally owned corporation, Canton Industrial Corporation, was formed in an attempt to restart production. However, the efforts failed and Canton plunged into economic and social crisis as workers tried to survive and to envision their lives without IH.

The closing of the factory cut the networks that had bound Canton to broader-scale processes. The town was no longer closely linked to a global corporation or to trends in the demand for farm implements. The loss of the factory also meant the closing of the UAW local and although many workers remained active in union-related activities, the town was no longer connected to UAW national-scale contract negotiations.

In the early 1990s, the plant was sold to an out-of-town investor, Alan Wolfson (Taylor 1996). Wolfson purchased a tire-shredding machine and received permission from the Illinois Environmental Protection Agency (IEPA) to initiate a tire-recycling operation. Interestingly, the IEPA granted his request, even though Wolfson did not provide the customary financial guarantees to cover the expense of cleaning up the site should the business fail. Hundreds of thousands of tires were brought onto the IH site and shredded. The business soon went bankrupt, leaving the city with a potentially dangerous situation. The IEPA then had to clear the site of all the tires, at taxpayer's expense. Wolfson has also failed to pay his property taxes and currently owes the city of Canton over $400,000.

In August 1997 a huge blaze broke out at the IH plant. The arson fire rapidly consumed the old brick warehouse and spread to other buildings on the site. It took one week and over one million gallons of water to put the fire out. During the fire hundreds of spectators gathered to watch and tears clouded the vision of many (Dayton 1997a).

As they witnessed their past burn, residents and local officials initiated a number of actions intended to preserve some talismans of memory. As the buildings were consumed, Canton police allowed local residents to venture onto the factory grounds to collect bricks and to take pictures. City officials decided to stop this dangerous quest by using their front-end loader and dump truck to scoop up bricks, transport them to a city owned lot and allow residents to collect them in relative safety.

Although residents were upset by the fire, their reactions varied:

- The local newspaper: "Canton eyesore was once heart of the city." (Dayton and Cloat 1997, A8)
- The local police chief: "[T]hey [the residents of Canton] looked like they lost a friend." (Dayton and Cloat 1997, A8)
- A local minister: "[W]hen that building burned, I saw tears all over town." (Thorne 1998, A12)
- Former IH worker: "I hated to see (the plant) close back then. But it can burn to the ground now." (Pospechil 1997, 1)

THE WHISTLE

Since 1912 an important feature of life in Canton was the IH whistle, locally known as the Big Toot. This 325-pound steam-powered brass whistle sounded seven times daily. In 1973, the whistle was temporarily silenced by the IEPA, which claimed it violated noise regulations. Canton residents were outraged at the IEPA's decision and sponsored a petition drive that gathered over 7,000 signatures. Under intense media scrutiny (Canton was featured in an article in the *New York Times* and on ABC television) and local pressure, the IEPA relented and on January 9, 1974, the Big Toot once again sounded its clarion call. As one resident commented, "the EPA grabbed a tiger by the tail when they silenced our whistle" (Canton Daily Ledger 1974, 1).

As the IH plant was consumed by flames, Don Edwards, longtime mayor of Canton, became concerned about the whereabouts of the whistle. He gathered Canton city employees together and sent them into the burning building with the mission of rescuing the whistle (Luciano 1997). They found the whistle where it always had been—mounted on a pole four stories above the IH power plant. They climbed up and were quickly able to dismount the whistle and take it with them. The mayor reported to concerned Canton residents, "The whistle is in good shape; there are just some nicks on it" (Dayton 1997b, A9).

The rescue of this valuable symbol of Canton's past brought with it a great deal of controversy. As the IH plant is still owned by Alan Wolfson, the city had (illegally) taken bricks and the whistle from a privately owned factory. Wolfson demanded that either the city of Canton pay him $1 million or he would take possession of the Big Toot and melt it down for scrap. Given this ultimatum, the mayor responded that since the city had stolen the whistle, it should be held as evidence in the Canton police station. The Canton police have taken the whistle as evidence and it is currently being held under their protection in a steel storage shed behind the police station. Currently, the future of the whistle is unknown. However, it is almost certain that it will never be given up without a fight.

Today the plant still looms (in the most literal sense) over the city of Canton and the needed clean-up is complicated by several factors. First, after the fire the IEPA found that the plant site was contaminated with asbestos. A remediation plan was just recently finalized and two years after the fire the environmental clean-up has not yet started. Furthermore, who will ultimately bear the enormous expense associated with the clean-up is not known. The owner of the plant refuses to contribute and the city does not have anything near the required resources. Second, contradictory public sentiment towards the plant complicates planning for the future of the site. Although the IH plant is steeped in history and many residents have a deep sense of identity and memory connected with it, many also feel that it is time to move on, to bury the past and forget about the plant. This common sentiment was voiced by one Canton resident when he said, "Forget about IH, I'm tired of hearing about it. Let's tear that eyesore down and move on." As long as the plant stands, it remains a painful symbol of the struggles of Canton since 1984.

To many other residents, however, the plant still exerts a strong pull. As one longtime Canton resident said, "There's a mystique about the thing that just doesn't go away.... I have to go by there once in a while and I think about how the streets were lined with cars. . . . You just kind of visualize where the old warehouse stood" (Thorne 1998, A12).

Beardstown and Canton: Comparisons

The case studies of Beardstown and Canton provide two examples of how economic restructuring, social change, and the reconfiguration of geographic scale have impacted the rural Midwest. In both cases, the towns were connected to the broader agricultural economy, one through the meatpacking industry and the other via the farm implement industry. A broad-scale set of connections existed via the structures of the two major corporations, Oscar Mayer and IH. In both towns, the 1980s brought plant closings and severe job loss. The relatively prosperous working class in Beardstown and Canton, found their economic well-being threatened.

In Beardstown, the successful reopening of the former Oscar Mayer plant by Excel did not restore the livelihoods of former Oscar Mayer workers. The lower wages and benefits, along with the greatly increased speed of the disassembly line, kept many local workers from returning to the plant. Moreover, Excel's labor force strategy effectively undercut the position of local workers and the company was not eager to rehire former Oscar Mayer workers. Instead, it recruited a largely immigrant labor force, one that was willing to work under the new conditions of employment. The town's disenfranchised working class now coexisted uneasily with a new immigrant working class, and the town was deeply divided along racial lines.

In Canton workers also lost their jobs when IH closed down. Efforts to reopen the plant failed and the lost jobs were never replaced. The formerly strong, prosperous working class faced hard times. Many left town or sought employment in lower-wage sectors of the economy. In many cases, Canton's workers were forced to broaden the scale of their job search in efforts to find employment. The town itself was largely cut off from broader-scale influences.

In both cases, the result of plant closings had left the local working class with reduced incomes, few prospects of new employment, and a town that was sinking into poverty. In the case of Beardstown, the advent of immigration brought a challenge to community identity and fostered resentment over the local resources (e.g., ESL school programs) needed by the new residents. On the other hand, as the struggle over the whistle indicates, many Canton residents maintained their sense of community identity. Yet, their town seemed to be entering a period of long-term decline.

Beardstown has a growing and increasingly diverse population. Despite the difficulties and tensions within the community, the jobs in the meatpacking plant do bring income and people to town. Still in doubt is the town's willingness to integrate or at least accept the newcomers. In part, efforts to find suitable housing is a key aspect of giving the newcomers the opportunity to settle, feel at home, and, hopefully, become accepted by others.

Canton's population remains quite homogeneous and the town has steadily lost population since 1984. On a more positive note, civic leaders and community members have actively worked to recruit new companies, lobbied for improved highway connections, and successfully convinced the state to construct a new prison just outside town. Although it was hoped that the prison would bring many new jobs to town, this has not happened, as most prison employees come from outside the community.

I began this chapter with the argument that the rural Midwest is being buffeted by a number of forces. Job loss, a changing agricultural production and processing sector, and rapid immigration that is altering the ethnic and racial structure of many Midwestern towns all have significant local impacts. I argued that these local impacts are part of a broader restructuring in the geography of capitalism and that a critical aspect of these broad socio-spatial transformations is a reconfiguration of geographic scale. This claim rests on the idea that geographic scale is socially produced and that as socio-spatial restructuring occurs, scale is itself reconfigured.

The case studies of Beardstown and Canton, were efforts to illustrate these arguments. In the case of Beardstown, the loss of a long-time meatpacking firm undercut the economic position of the working class of the town. When a new firm was induced to reopen the plant, its reorganization of production processes and wage cuts discouraged local workers from applying for jobs. The lack of a local work force did not deter the company because the centerpiece of the firm's labor force strategy was to keep labor costs low and to avoid labor militancy by recruiting non-local workers, in this case, Hispanic immigrants, to work in the plant. This strategy linked Beardstown to an international labor market and vastly increased the scale of the "local" labor market. The local impacts of this strategy were quite severe, including racial antagonism as well as struggles over schools and in the housing market. Over the long term the influx of new residents may actually bring renewed life to a declining town. Yet, whether this occurs still remains to be seen.

In the case of Canton, a town that was part of a global production network and national-scale labor organization and had strong links to larger-scale processes, the closure of the IH factory resulted in the town being cut off from broader-scale networks. In a very real sense, Canton residents were left on their own to cope with the aftermath of the IH closing. The disastrous fire left the city to deal with a number of environmental and legal problems and strained the capacity of residents to cope. However, the case study also illustrates the great resiliency of Canton. Despite the suffering and bitterness that accompanied the economic decline of the town, residents have maintained a strong sense of pride and determination. No town in Illinois has worked harder to foster economic development and to maintain city services. In the final analysis, however, residents realize there is no way that local efforts can offset the loss of the factory.

The examples of Beardstown and Canton are emblematic of what has happened throughout the Midwest. Therefore, there are several important lessons that can be drawn from the Beardstown and Canton case studies. The first is a recognition that labor actively shapes the global structure of capitalism. In Canton, IH workers achieved a measure of well-being, not through the largesse of capital, but through their own steadfast struggles. Although their efforts are in the past, they remain a powerful example of what labor can achieve as well as a reminder that the social and spatial structures of capitalism are not shaped by capital alone. The second lesson is that when labor loses its power to negotiate with capital, community well-being often suffers. For the "old working class" of Beardstown and Canton, low wages mean working poverty for many formerly prosperous families. Third, both of these communities demonstrate a great deal of resiliency. Despite the changes the have reshaped the lives of longtime residents and newcomers alike, people strive to maintain their dignity and community.

As the new millennium dawned, Canton residents tried to come to grips with the changes that had shaken the foundations of their town. It was not simply the loss of jobs that was hard to cope with, but also the disappearance of an entire way of life. In Beardstown, new and old residents alike attempted to find common ground. Longtime residents knew that like Canton, their town would never be the same. As new immigrants joined the line of cars dropping children off at the local elementary school, a new era had arrived in the town. Perhaps, with the brightly painted homes purchased by immigrants as a backdrop, the town would come to accept the newcomers.

References

Canton Daily Ledger 1974. "Canton Fought for Its Whistle." *Canton Daily Ledger,* January 1.

Crump, J. R. 1994. "Population, Poverty and Employment in Rural Illinois: Results from the 1990 Census." Macomb: Illinois Institute for Rural Affairs.

———. 1997. "The Changing Rural Landscape of Illinois: Hispanic Immigrants in Rural Illinois." Macomb: Illinois Institute for Rural Affairs.

———. 2002. "Contested Landscapes of Labor: Rival Unionism in the Farm Implements Industry." In *Geography of Power,* ed. A. Herod and M. K. Wright, 277–307. New York: Blackwell Publishers.

Crump, J. R., and C. D. Merrett. 1998. "Scales of Struggle: Economic Restructuring in the U.S. Midwest." *Annals of the Association of American Geographers* 88:496–515.

Dayton, J. 1997a. "As IH Bricks Come Down, Canton Scoops Up History." *Peoria Journal Star,* August 9, A1, A9.

———. 1997b. "Canton Acquires Factory Whistle from Debris." *Peoria Journal Star*, August 9, A1, A9.

Dayton, J., and L. Cloat. 1997. "Factory Hisses into History." *Peoria Journal Star*, August 7, A8.

Fimmen, C., B. Witthuhn, J. Crump, M. Brunn, G. Delaney-Barmann, D. Riggins, M. Gutierrez, D. Schabilion, and B. Watters. 1998. "A Spatial Study of the Mobility of Hispanics in Illinois and the Implications for Educational Institutions." Julian Samora Research Institute, Michigan State University, East Lansing.

Fitton, M. 1996a. "Burning of Beardstown Tavern Confirmed as Arson." *Peoria Journal-Star*, August 21, A1.

———. 1996b. "Pair Held in Cross-Burning at Beardstown Tavern." *Peoria Journal-Star*, August 22, B6.

Frank, T., and D. Mulcahey. 1995. *Solidarity in the Heartland*. Westfield, N.J.: Open Media.

Fuhrig, F. 1996. "Fire Exposes More Ethnic Tensions in Beardstown." *Peoria Journal-Star*, August 19, B1.

Gilpin, T. 1989. "Labor's Last Stand." *Chicago Labor History* 18:42–57.

———. 1992. "Left by Themselves: A History of the United Farm Equipment and Metal Workers Unions, 1938–1955." 2 vols. Ph.D. dissertation, Yale University.

Gouveia, L. 1994. "Global Strategies and Local Linkages: The Case of the U.S. Meatpacking Industry." In *From Columbus to Conagra*, ed. A. Bonanno, L. Busch, W. H. Friedland, L. Gouveia, and E. Mingione, 125–48. Lawrence: University Press of Kansas.

Griffith, D., M. Broadway, and D. D. Stull. 1995. "Making Meat." Introduction to *Any Way You Cut It: Meat Processing and Small-Town America*, ed. D. Griffith, M. Broadway, and D. D. Stull, 1–16. Lawrence: University Press of Kansas.

Harvey, D. 1982. *The Limits of Capital*. New York: Verso.

Herod, A. 1991. "The Production of Scale in the United States Labor Relations." *Area* 23:82–88.

———. 1997. "Labor's Spatial Praxis and the Geography of Contract Bargaining in the U.S. East Coast Longshore Industry, 1953–1989." *Political Geography* 16:145–69.

Jonas, A. A. 1994. "Editorial: The Scale Politics of Spatiality." *Environment and Planning D: Society and Space* 12:257–64.

Luciano, P. 1997. "Mayor Issues Order for Whistle Retrieval." *Peoria Journal Star*, August 8, A1, A11.

Marsh, B. 1985. *A Corporate Tragedy, the Agony of International Harvester Company*. Garden City, N.Y.: Routledge.

Page, B., and R. Walker. 1991. "From Settlement to Fordism: The Agro-Industrial Revolution in the American Midwest." *Economic Geography* 67:261–314.

Pospechil, J. 1997. "Fire Robs Piece of Canton History." *Macomb Journal*, August 7, 1A, 8A.

Smith, N. 1993. "Homelesss/Global: Scaling Places." In *Mapping the Future: Local Cultures, Global Change*, ed. J. Bird, Barry Curtis, Tim Putnam, George Robertson, and Lisa Tucker, 87–119. New York: Routledge.

Stanley, K. 1994. "Industrial and Labor Market Transformation in the U.S. Meatpacking Industry." In *The Global Restructuring of Agro-Food Systems*, ed. P. McMichael, 129–44. Ithaca, N.Y.: Cornell University Press.

Swyngedouw, E. 1997. "Neither Global nor Local: Globalization and the Politics of Scale." In *Spaces of Globalization, Reasserting the Power of the Local*, ed. K. R. Cox, 137–66. New York: Guilford.

———. 2000. "Authoritarian Governance, Power, and the Politics of Rescaling." *Environment and Planning D: Society and Space* 18:63–76.

Taylor, J. 1996. "Alan Wolfson." *Wall Street Journal*, December 3.

Thorne, C. 1998. "Plant's Legacy Still Looms over Canton." *Peoria Journal Star*, December 14, 12A.

Ufkes, F. M. 1995. "Lean and Mean: U.S. Meat-Packing in an Era of Agro-Industrial Restructuring." *Environment and Planning D: Society and Space* 13:683–705.

United States General Accounting Office. 1998. "Community Development Changes in Nebraska's and Iowa's Counties with Large Meatpacking Plant Workforces." Washington, D.C.: GPO.

Warren, R. L. 1978. *The Community in America*. Chicago: Rand McNally College Publishing.

10

Hogs and Citizens

A Report from the North Carolina Front

MaryBe McMillan and Michael D. Schulman

FROM THE PAGES of *U.S. News and World Report* and the *Raleigh News and Observer* to the floor of the North Carolina General Assembly, the influx of large-scale, corporate hog production in North Carolina has created controversy and conflict. In March 2002, North Carolina had 9.6 million hogs in various stages of production, making it the second leading hog-producing state in the nation (NCDACS 2002a). In Duplin County, which produces the most hogs in the state, hogs outnumber people 42 to 1 and produce over 3.9 million tons of waste annually (Environmental Defense Fund 2002a). This growth is due to the industrialization and concentration of hog production. Ninety-six percent of all hog production occurs on farms with two thousand or more animals (NCDACS 2002b). The hogs are raised in enclosed buildings on slats that channel all waste into open pit lagoons. Most pork producers are no longer independent family farmers but operate facilities that are either owned or operated under contract for one of five large integrated pork production companies (Schaffer 1997).

In February 1995 the *News and Observer* published a five-part series on the North Carolina hog industry that won the 1996 Pulitzer

Prize for public service. The first paragraph of the initial article vividly describes the enormity of the waste management problem associated with large-scale hog operations: "Imagine a city as big as New York suddenly grafted onto North Carolina's Coastal Plain. Double it. Now imagine that this city has no sewage treatment plants. All the wastes from 15 million inhabitants are simply flushed into open pits and sprayed onto fields. Turn these humans into hogs, and you don't have to imagine at all. It is already here" (Warrick and Stith 1995). Months after the *News and Observer* graphically brought to the public's attention the potential environmental problems associated with large-scale hog operations, a lagoon spill at a farm in Onslow County, North Carolina, released 25 million gallons of swine waste into nearby fields and eventually drained into the New River (Satchell 1996). The event piqued public ire and sparked debate about the possible environmental impacts of such concentrated livestock operations.

The growth of corporate hog production in North Carolina is indicative of a more general trend in the structure of U.S. agriculture. Since the 1980s, the number of small family farms in the Unites States has decreased and the number of large-scale operations has dramatically increased. From 1982 to 1997 the number of farms in North Carolina decreased by 32 percent, from 72,792 to 49,406 farms. During that same period, the number of farms with sales of $100,000 or more increased 13 percent, from 8,978 to 10,146 farms (USDA 1997).

With the increasing scale of operations, the control of farming operations has shifted from the individual farmer-entrepreneur to the corporate integrators and processors. The general decline of the traditional family farm, the development of intensive farming operations, and the restructuring of rural regions raise questions about the trend toward industrialized agriculture and its consequences for the social and economic well-being of small farmers and rural communities.

The case of North Carolina's hog industry is illustrative of not only the trend toward large-scale industrialized agriculture but also the potential social and economic impacts of that transition. Although citizens generally refer to odor and potential contamination of water as their main concerns, such environmental issues are manifestations of a larger problem: the altered power structure in which citizens' concerns are subordinated to the interests of large pork producers. In their study of citizens' concerns in eastern North Carolina, Thu and Durrenberger write, "The lack of respect for their concerns and the sense of frustration with the channels of redress available to them has created a tense and stressful situation for many rural residents in the heart of North Carolina's hog industry" (1994, 22). Many citizens in North Carolina think that the government on all levels has ignored their concerns and generally favored the interests of contract pork producers. The expansion of intensive swine operations has created concerns, complaints, and conflict in eastern North Carolina.

With stricter regulation of the hog industry enacted in 1997 and a moratorium on new hog operations established in 1998, pork producers have found themselves having to defend the industry against citizens' claims and, most important, against additional regulation. The few remaining independent pork producers claim that stringent regulations will shut them down because they cannot afford new capital investments in waste control technology. With increasing numbers of citizens complaining about the industry, contract pork producers have picketed and lobbied the North Carolina Legislature as a counter to the environmental activists who seek more regulation of the swine industry (Henderson and Batten 1997). Claiming environmentalists had unfairly targeted pork producers as polluters, the political interest group of the pork producers began a public relations campaign that focused on other industrial polluters, such as municipal water and sewage treatment plants. Most producers acknowledge the need for some regulations, but they think that officials and citizens have unfairly singled them out as polluters. Producers also urge legislators to give current regulations adequate time to work before they enact more legislation.

The case of the large-scale hog industry in North Carolina is relevant to questions about the future of rural communities in regions where the industrialization of agriculture is widespread. In addition to illustrating the current transition in the structure of U.S. agriculture and its possible impacts on rural communities, the North Carolina case is also indicative of another larger sociological concern: how people react collectively to such changes in the social structure, particularly when those changes affect their livelihoods and communities.

Social-movement theorists have demonstrated that people often react to major social change by participating in collective action. Tarrow (1994) suggests that participants in U.S. social movements generally use a "rights" frame to describe their issues and claims of injustice. For example, scholars who study environmental movements note that people who live in environmentally threatened communities view themselves as second-class citizens whose rights to legal protection and home ownership have been denied (Capek 1993). This perception of second-class citizenship is often what motivates people in an environmental controversy to participate in social action (Capek and Gilderbloom 1992). The protest against corporate hog operations provides a timely opportunity to examine how various parties in the hog controversy frame issues in terms of their rights.

To study issues of community impacts and citizen reactions to changes in the structure of agriculture, we conducted a series of focus groups in Sampson and Duplin Counties (counties with many hog confinement operations) during the summer of 1998. A total of five focus groups were completed: one with community leaders, one with contract hog producers, one with Sampson County citizens, one with Duplin County citizens, and one with members of an organized anticorporate hog opposition group. To gather additional information about perceived impacts and citizen reaction, we also conducted a series of informant interviews with members of an African American community group and members of a predominantly white antihog activist group involved in fighting the corporate hog industry in North Carolina.

Focus Group Methods and Interviews

The influx of large-scale hog operations in eastern North Carolina represents a major structural transition not only in agriculture but also in rural communities. This transition has created significant social and economic changes that rural citizens must contend with. The primary research question is, How have different groups of rural residents reacted to such a structural transformation? In particular, How do groups of citizens who represent different social positions relative to the controversy vary in their reaction to structural change? How do they differ in their framing of issues, their construction of social problems, and their choice of action?

To answer these questions, we will analyze data from different social groups, all of whom are affected by the expansion of large-scale hog operations in eastern North Carolina. These groups include residents of rural communities—both those who live next to hog operations and those who do not, business and civic leaders, and pork producers, both large and small. When the expansion began in the late 1980s and early 1990s, business and community leaders as well as pork producers saw it as welcome economic development for an area that had relied on tobacco for too long. As the expansion continued, however, residents of eastern North Carolina began to raise concerns about odor, potential water contamination, and declining property values. Mainstream environmentalist organizations such as the Sierra Club also publicized their concern that the concentration of hog waste in areas in eastern North Carolina threatened waterways and wildlife. Poor people and minorities also began to discuss the disproportionate location of large-scale hog operations in their communities as evidence of environmental racism.

These various perspectives, which continue to fuel the controversy over the industry in the state, illustrate how social location in the rural community and position relative to the hog industry potentially influence how people frame the corporate hog issue. To address these questions on a broad level, we have focus group data from groups affected by the structural transition in pork production, including citizens, opinion leaders, and hog producers in Sampson and Duplin Counties and members of a statewide antihog activist organization. To further understand some of the reasons why people might oppose the hog industry, we conducted individual interviews with members of an African American community organization in Halifax County and with local antihog activists from Duplin County.

Two focus groups for this project were composed of citizens who reside in Duplin and Sampson Counties. For the purposes of this research, these people will be called Citizens. An additional focus group included members of an organization who have been active in raising concerns over hog issues. These participants will be called Activists. Another focus group was comprised of area opinion leaders from both Duplin and Sampson Counties. Participants in this focus group will be called Leaders. The final group included area hog producers from both Duplin and Sampson Counties. These people will be called Producers.

Participants in each of the groups were selected and recruited during the summer of 1998. The Duplin and Sampson county extension offices provided lists of names of local business leaders and opinion leaders. After eliminating those who were directly involved in hog production, a telephone screener verified that the respondents were between the ages of eighteen and sixty and had no one living in the household that currently raised hogs. Of the fifteen people invited, three women and nine men attended the Leaders' focus group. The Leaders' group included bankers, insurance agents, health care providers, automotive and equipment dealers, and local governmental officials.

The Duplin and Sampson County Extension Offices provided lists of hog producers. A telephone screener asked if the respondents met the following qualifications: (1) were between the ages of eighteen and sixty; and (2) currently raised hogs commercially. We invited fifteen producers selected at random from these lists. Ten men and three women attended the Producers' focus group session. All participants were white. Given the dominance of contractual integration in the industry, we assume that they were all contract producers.

The participants in the two Citizen focus groups were selected through a procedure known as random digit dialing, which randomly generated lists of phone numbers from existing lists of telephone exchanges—one from northern Duplin County and one from southern Sampson County. During the initial telephone call, interviewers screened respondents for those who lived outside city limits, were between the ages of eighteen and sixty, and had no one living in the household that currently raised hogs. Sixteen citizens of Duplin County were invited from the random lists, with three women and six men attending the focus group. Of the nine Duplin citizens in attendance, six were white, two were African American, and one was Hispanic. These people worked in various industries throughout Duplin County: two were teachers, one was a homemaker, two were farmers (but not livestock producers), and four worked for various public service agencies. Thirteen citizens of Sampson County were invited, with five women and two men attending the focus group. These citizens, who worked in various industries throughout Sampson County, included one teacher, one health nurse, a waitress, a carpenter, a pastor, and two homemakers. The Sampson County citizens were all white.

The final group included people selected from membership lists from several citizen groups who have actively raised concerns about the hog industry. The Activist group was the best attended of any group. Initially nineteen people were invited. However, when ten men and eleven women actually attended the focus group, we included them all in the discussion session.

The meetings of the focus groups were held in three different restaurants within Duplin and Sampson Counties. A dinner and a small stipend were provided to each focus group participant. A moderator and an assistant moderator conducted each of the focus group sessions and made audiotapes of each discussion. Two independent readers summarized the tape transcripts into key themes.

In addition to the focus group with members of an anticorporate hog group, we interviewed individual anticorporate hog activists from two counties in North Carolina: Halifax County and Duplin County. Halifax ranks twenty-third among North Carolina counties in hog production. A local anticorporate hog group was successful in getting the county to pass a set of regulations that restricted the location of large-scale confinement agricultural operations. Informants in Halifax County were African American members of a community group that was at the core of the local organizing effort against the corporate hog industry. Duplin County is the number one producer of hogs in North Carolina and is home to several of the largest integrated pork production companies. Duplin County activist informants were predominantly white and members of the Alliance for a Responsible Swine Industry, a state-level opposition group.

The Citizens in Duplin and Sampson Counties, where there are large numbers of intensive hog operations, voice complaints about odor, health problems, and environmental effects and express anger toward the government for their lack of oversight of the hog industry. As one would expect, odor tops the list of Duplin and Sampson County Citizens' complaints about the large-scale operations. One Duplin County Citizen exclaims, "The odor is horrendous!" Another Duplin County Citizen elaborates:

> It's every day. I mean, I went and bought the [air freshener] plug-ins. I've got them in every room in my house. Every morning I go through my house with a spray and try to eliminate the odor. It's that bad. My son would come home from work and he would come to the door gagging because the only way to come to our house is right past all of the hog houses. I mean, it's dangerous. It's everywhere. There's not a day that goes by that you don't smell it.

Duplin and Sampson County Citizens described numerous sources of odor, including lagoons, dead hogs, and the trucks that haul mortalities away.

The Duplin and Sampson County Citizens also complain that they can no longer enjoy being outside in their yards because of the odor and flies. According to one Duplin County Citizen, "You can't sit on your porch anymore, you can't have cookouts, and for me, what really makes me mad is that our little girl can't play outside. She has a swing set and she hasn't swung on it three times, and she can't because the flies just eat her up."

Aside from not going outside because of the odor and flies, Duplin and Sampson County Citizens are also concerned about the effect of hog waste on the environment and, consequently, their health. One Duplin County Citizen explains, "I feel like the waste is just floating into the air, and you're breathing it." A Sampson County Citizen comments on the possible health effects of lowered air quality: "Some people have asthma problems. They have a strong ammonia around where they spray the waste. They have problems breathing." Participants in the two citizen focus groups contend that the incidence of asthma and other respiratory diseases have increased among people they know who live near large-scale hog operations.

Duplin and Sampson County Citizens expressed sympathy for the economic plight of farmers and understand how the hog industry was initially a way to boost the economy of the region and keep farmers in business. A Sampson County Citizen expounds on the need for economic development:

> A lot of industry has moved away from here and so the people were looking for a way to survive and that's the way that they did it . . . We have the capacity to feed the world but the farmers are the ones who are being ruined and run out of business. Their only alternative was to turn their land over to hogs or turkeys. And I cannot blame a farmer for doing that.

For most Citizens, they do not oppose hog production per se. They are instead opposed to the current large-scale and integrated structure of the industry.

While the Duplin and Sampson County Citizens recognize the need for industry and agriculture to flourish in their area, they are angry that the hog industry expanded so rapidly and without regard to its effects on neighbors and residents. As one Duplin County Citizen angrily declares, "We are supposed to accept this because somebody is making a living. My children can't go out and have a picnic or go out and play because of the flies. It's ridiculous."

Other Duplin and Sampson County Citizens assert that, in addition to halting the rapid expansion of the industry, there is need for better regulation of the existing operations. A Sampson County Citizen discusses the need for regulation: "We just need to regulate what we've got. And in the next ten years, you've got a management problem as to what to do with that wasted land. You're talking about not just the farmer but the farmer's children, you know. We want to protect the environment as well as provide an income for the future." Citizens in all focus groups emphasize that more regulation of large-scale operations might eliminate some of the problems associated with the industry.

Most Duplin and Sampson County Citizens blame the lack of enforcement on the limited resources of the state regulatory agencies. A Sampson County Citizen explains, "They don't have enough people, enough manpower to go around, to really inspect the farms that are in error." Another focus group participant hints at not only the limited resources of the state regulatory agencies but also what they perceive as the agencies' close relationship to the integrators and the consequent reluctance of officials to enforce the regulations.

Given their frustration over the smell, flies, and change in their lifestyles, combined with their contention that the pork companies have corrupted government supervision of the industry, the Citizens of Duplin and Sampson Counties are angry with pork producers and feel betrayed by their neighbors. To the Citizens, neighbors would not create such problems for other neighbors nor would they create such divisiveness in the community. Several Citizens talked about the conflict in the community that the controversy over the large-scale hog operations has created. They mention neighbors, relatives, and friends who no longer talk to each other because they have opposing views about the hog industry.

The pervasiveness of the hog industry in Duplin and Sampson Counties means the many people have friends or relatives involved in pork production. Citizens generally think that absentee owners of large-scale operations are less invested emotionally and, to some extent, financially in making sure the facility operates according to the regulations and in a way that does not bother neighbors. The experiences of Citizens suggest, however, that even when locals own the operations, they do not always respect their neighbors, which makes for more community conflict.

Most Duplin and Sampson County Citizens are incredulous that better waste and odor management technology do not exist. They stress the need for more effective waste management practices that will protect the environment and their health. Since they think that the hog industry can manipulate the government, they want a neutral person or group to develop technological solutions to the current controversy. One focus group participant explains: "Appoint someone or a group of people that are scientists, that specialize in this particular field, that is not affected by megamoney. An independent counsel to study this. To come up with suggestions to improve this. Not someone who's going to be bought off. Someone who's going to be fair and impartial and who will come up with a solution."

One Duplin County Citizen explains why he thinks the industry cannot continue to expand: "Something in the biological structure is going to break down, if it hasn't already. . . . There's going to be some type of calamity, for lack of a better term, of disease because of the concentration of people and hogs."

Community Leader Focus Group

Unlike the Citizens who participated in the focus group, Duplin and Sampson County Leaders are quick to extol the economic benefits of the hog industry. One Leader deems the industry "economic salvation" and "one of the best things that's happened to Sampson County." Another Leader expounds on the economic growth he has seen in the area. He believes this growth is a result of the expansion of the hog industry: "I personally have seen the growth in ten years. Ten years ago, the people didn't have that kind of income. . . . It's been great for us."

Even with the glowing testimonials about the economic development of their counties, the Leaders acknowledge that the hog industry cannot continue as the region's economic savior. One Leader explains, "We need the swine industry, but we need something besides swine."

The Leaders also realize that citizens and other community leaders, especially those who are not involved in agriculture, will focus on the hog industry's negative aspects, such as odor and noise. "There's no way in the world anybody would say that hog odor smells good," says one.

Given such problems, the Leaders think more effort should be put into technological development to improve odor and waste management. While most Leaders are confident that the technology can be developed to reduce or even eliminate hog odor, they recognize that pork producers need to take steps now in order to be more responsive and considerate of citizens' complaints. One Leader states: "I think that it might be very important to talk about corporate leaders here working with their growers and their contractors to be a little more responsive to their neighbors' needs. If it's a Saturday afternoon or a Sunday afternoon, try not to pump [spray liquid hog waste on fields] when the neighbors might be having a barbecue. Don't do it when the wind is blowing thirty miles per hour. Do commonsense type of things. And 90 percent of them do, but you always have bad apples in every bunch."

The Leaders think that the hog industry needs to take steps to improve its image, particularly because they think that the media has portrayed the industry in an especially negative light. One Leader comments: "I personally think that the state has allowed the media to take some bad shots at the hog industry. I'm disappointed, as important as agriculture is to this state, that the people in Raleigh have not been more forceful in supporting the industry. . . . I really think the government could help out a lot considering the importance of agriculture in North Carolina, and also it [government] takes some of the heat off and corrects some of the things that are being presented incorrectly by the media."

From the view of these community and business Leaders, the hog industry and the state government should take an active role in projecting a better image of pork production and countering the negative publicity in the media.

Producer Focus Group

Like the Leaders who participated in the focus group, the Producers contend that the hog industry has helped economically depressed counties in eastern North Carolina prosper, especially in the wake of the decline of tobacco. One Producer describes the changes in the area, such as the growth of county infrastructure, that have occurred since the hog industry has expanded: "When we came to this county nine years ago, most of the people were leaving the county for health care because the hospital was too small and didn't have enough doctors. We have doctors now, and a new wing on the hospital. . . . We have three or four new schools funded by the county taxpayers." Another Producer comments, "People [now] have spending money. I think that's quality of life."

Producers reject Citizens' claims that their quality of life has declined due to nearby hog farms and dismiss their concerns about water contamination, illness, and excessive odor as "irrational" and unfounded. Against Citizens' allegations of environmental degradation, Producers emphasize that they need clean water and fertile land in order for livestock production to continue. They argue that this dependence on the environment for their livelihood makes farmers conscientious environmental stewards. One producer explains:

> I just feel like the hog people, or farmers in general, are stewards of the land. They live here. They don't want water screwed up. We drink the water, we use the water, we're the ones that have the greatest interest in the water quality being good, but nobody seems to recognize it. Nobody is informed of that. . . . The media and the politicians have just led people astray. And maybe the biggest part of it is the smell of it, that creates it [the media attention], and they just got to strike at something.

Other Producers point to their environmental record as one of the best among agricultural or industrial enterprises. A participant in the focus group comments: "The fact is, if you look at the research and the inspections that have occurred since 1995, the bottom line is that less that one percent of the swine operations have been found in violation. . . . I would challenge any other industry in this state to have that record. Again, all you read about is that the swine industry is destroying the environment, it's destroying the water quality in this state. It's just not there."

The Producers think that the Citizens' claims are greatly overstated and do not reflect the concern that producers have for the environment and their diligence in trying to operate their facilities according to the regulations. Producers blame the media for much of the public concern about odor, water quality, and health. A Producer explains,

"Every time you hear the news, it's about hog farmers polluting groundwater. Somehow the media needs to be straightened out and educated that we haven't found the groundwater polluted yet." One participant in the Producers' focus group explains:

> My concern is basically politicians and the media. I think that politicians are causing public hysteria about the hogs, the environment. I think they play the public for the vote. I think that they've created this scare of the environment going bad because of the hogs, because there are more voters out there that don't have hogs than those that have hogs. It's like a lot of the people moved into the area. The hogs didn't move to them, they moved to the hogs and the politicians recognized that and they played on that. They make issues out of it to get the votes. The media follows up with them and blows it completely out of what the reality is.

This statement also reflects the view of Producers that the people complaining about the hog operations are new to the area and to agriculture.

Producers want local residents to visit their operations to see that they are trying to run the facility in the best way possible. A Producer explains, "A lot of times if people would come out and see what you all do, and how you do it, they're amazed. But get them there. You just can't; they just won't come." Given the outcry from citizens regarding the industry, Producers hope that lawmakers will not be swayed by their emotional pleas to enact more regulation. Another Producer explains, "I think members of the General Assembly . . . need to realize and be sure that they know what they're doing with the issue. . . . They need to make decisions based on science and not emotion."

Activist Focus Group and Antihog Informant Interviews

Like the Citizens in the focus groups, Activists who participated in the focus group are concerned about the impact of the hog industry on health, the environment, local economic opportunities, and community neighborliness and cohesion. While the hog industry has contributed to economic growth, the abundance of hogs has hurt other industries. One member of the Activist focus group states: "That's how the economy of hogs works. One man gains, one man loses." Another explains that "most of that [hog] money is going out to the fat cats and not spent [in the county], and . . . we've seen many, many jobs being taken up and other people coming up and our social services have been taxed, our schools are taxed, our welfare programs are taxed."

The Activist focus group also thinks that the hog industry has a negative impact on the environment and on human health through the contamination of drinking water from animal waste, odor, and airborne particles. One Activist states, "It terrifies me when I think about between twenty and twenty-five thousand hogs in our community radius, the waste from these hog operations, all of them large . . . and they are polluting our air, our water." Odor is constant: "there's two times that we smell hog manure in our house and that's if it's light and if it's dark."

The Activist focus group wants better technology to control odor and flies, but most important, they want fundamental changes that would end large-scale confinement operations and replace them with a "family farming" model where the owner-operator lives on site. "What you can do is help our situation is to go back to family farms," one Activist explains. Activists think that the hog industry cannot sustain itself given current conditions and technology.

The themes from the Activist focus group mirror the concerns expressed by the antihog informants in the individual interviews. The African American informants from the Tillery community in Halifax County voiced concerns about odor, groundwater contamination, and negative health impacts due to airborne bacteria and water pollution. For example, one informant asserted, "There's a lot of sickness behind this mess [hog farms]. It is blowing in the air and getting into our water. You don't want to worry about this when you are old." The Tillery informants were also concerned about the economic impact of the hog industry. One, an ex-farmer, raised a few hogs, but "then the corporate hog farms came in and put the small farmers out of business." Most informants think that the industry only benefits the owners of operations who do not live in the community. The Tillery informants also asserted that large-scale hog operations, like prisons, hazardous-waste facilities, and landfills, are purposively located in poor and minority communities, a practice that they claim constitutes environmental racism.

The white antihog informants from Duplin County had specific grievances that resulted from their personal experiences of living near hog operations. According to many informants, the hog industry is a threat to their traditional rural quality of life. Health problems, including allergies and respiratory problems, were common complaints, along with concerns about the contamination of drinking water from animal waste. While acknowledging that some may have benefited from the rapid expansion of the hog industry in Duplin County, antihog informants contended that the dominance of the hog operations has discouraged other industries from locating in the county, has hurt tourism, and has driven small farms out of business. Informants also feel that the power of the hog industry in the county has created a company county, characterized by fear, stifled opposition, and corrupted local government. For the Duplin County antihog informants, the fight has escalated beyond local grievances to one that pits them against the industry and state and local government.

The views of Citizens from Duplin and Sampson Counties who participated in the two focus groups were generally negative about the impact of large-scale hog operations on their quality of life. They believed that the hog industry wields power and influence over the state and local governments. Citizens attributed the lack of regulatory enforcement to the political power of the large integrators. Duplin and Sampson County Citizens thought that the divisive controversy over the industry had fractured the local community and violated American ideals of freedom, liberty, and protection of their rights. Citizens suggested that producers and government officials come visit their houses and experience the odor and flies for themselves. Citizens thought that continued expansion of the industry without improved technology would eventually lead to environmental problems so great that the industry will no longer be able to sustain itself.

The Leaders had a mixed opinion of the hog industry. While they saw the industry as benefitting their counties economically, they acknowledged that the publicity and problems associated with the hog industry could prevent further economic development of the area, particularly in terms of tourism. For this reason, the Leaders urged policy makers and producers to put resources into developing better technology and improving the public image of the industry. The Leaders encouraged pork producers to reach out to neighbors and residents who live near their operations, become considerate of their concerns, and offer to work together to find solutions to problems.

Producers were quick to point out the economic benefits that the hog industry had brought eastern North Carolina, a region that has had the most poverty in the state. Additionally, they countered claims of environmental degradation by asserting that, as farmers, they depended on the land for their livelihood so they work to protect it. Producers attributed much of the public concern to the media, which they alleged has exaggerated the threat to the environment that hog operations pose. Given the misinformation in the media, Producers asserted that educating citizens about the pork production process is one way to resolve the controversy. Finally, Producers stressed that legislators should fund technological developments rather than passing more regulations.

All parties involved in the controversy about large-scale hog production framed issues in terms of their rights to resources and a special rural quality of life. Various definitions of rights to fundamental resources, particularly land and all that it symbolized, pervaded the discussions—pro or con—of the hog industry. Tarrow (1994) contends that participants in American social movements use a "rights" master frame to define their concerns and their claims of injustice. The particular definitions of rights and responsibilities used by the combatants in the North Carolina hog "wars" reflect the embeddedness of race and class in the local rural economy and social structure.

The African American antihog informants from Tillery felt they had a right to continue farming on their land, and they had a right to clean air, water, and uncontaminated land. Furthermore, as African Americans, they saw the location of hog farms in poor, minority communities as environmental racism. Their battle for environmental justice implies that they have a right to live in communities that are not threatened by hog farms or other noxious facilities. They have a right to safe, healthy communities, just as whites do. Ultimately, the movement to keep the industrialized hog farms out of Tillery was a fight for justice and civil rights. The African American informants wanted a guarantee of the same civil and civic rights as whites: the right to land, housing, and safe communities and the right to government protection from any type of discrimination.

Like the African American Activists, the white antihog informants believed that they had a right to breathe clean air, drink clean water, have good neighbors, and keep their land safe from contamination. As middle-class whites, they believed that the government would protect their rights. Then the hog farms came into their backyards and threatened the air, the water, and their quality of life. Eventually, however, the hog farms threatened much more than that—the ensuing controversy over the hog industry challenged the white Activists' assumptions about government and democracy. When, according to the white antihog informants, government officials did nothing in response to their concerns, they felt their civic rights as Americans to life, liberty, and happiness had been violated. The battle expanded from shutting down the hog operation next door to defending their rights to government protection and ensuring that no one suffered the same indignities.

Like the white Activists, Citizens thought they had a right to clean water and air. In addition, Citizens believed they had a right to enjoy their property. Unlike the African American and the white Activists, Citizens did not feel like their constitutional rights had been violated. Like the other parties in the controversy over hogs, the Producers also framed issues in terms of their rights. Producers believed that property owners had a right to do with their land whatever they wanted and that citizen outcry was threatening their right to earn a living from the land. Similarly, the Leaders also believed in people's right to make a living, whether by farming or in industry, as long as in the course of their business they do not threaten others' right to make a living. Their concern was that the citizen outcry and the negative side effects, like the odor and flies, associated with the hog industry threatened residents' right to earn money by deterring other industries from locating in the region and lessening opportunities for economic growth.

The various groups' framing of the hog issue intertwines the moral rhetoric of rights with the entitlement of resources, not only the natural resources of land and the environment but also the less tangible ones that citizens associate with life in a rural community, such as the reciprocity and respect of one's neighbors and an appreciation of farming and the land. The different perspectives point to the inextricable link between the economic and social sectors and how they affect each other. Naples explains, "The processes by which economic restructuring is affecting the social relations within rural communities in the Midwest are contoured by historic and on-going patterns of social relationships, contradictions of agrarian ideology, and the class, racial-ethnic, and gender dynamics of particular communities" (1994, 131). The groups in this research had different ideas about what their rights were. These differences depend largely on group members' perceived social position and collective identity. This collective identity informs a moral economy: a repertoire of interpretations that group members draw upon to define what is right or wrong, fair or unfair in various situations, including defining what their rights were. Collective identity is related to group members' race and class, which in turn are related to the actors' position relative to the controversy—essentially whether they reap the rewards of the hog industry or they bear its costs.

The industrialization of agriculture threatens not only the environmental sustainability of the rural landscape, but also the social sustainability of rural communities by taking power away from small farmers and rural citizens and giving it to a few agricultural elites. The controversy in eastern North Carolina is ultimately not about the concentration of hogs but the concentration of power in the hands of a few corporations and the government officials who, according to citizens, too often protect corporate interests. The Environmental Defense Fund (2002b) argues that solutions to factory hog farms involve the establishment and enforcement of strict standards about the location of farms, waste management technology, and pollution control. In addition, citizens and local governments need to have more power:

the power to zone hog factories, the power to require public notice and hearings on proposed permits for hog factories, and the power to assess the impact of industrial hog production on local social, economic, and environmental conditions.

Note

The research was supported by Grant LS97–85 from Southern Region SARE to the Center for Sustainable Systems and North Carolina State University. Additional support was received from the North Carolina Cooperative Extension Service and the North Carolina Agricultural Research Service. The authors thank Tom Hoban and William Clifford from North Carolina State University and Yevonne Brannon of the NCSU Applied Research Group for their assistance.

References

Capek, Stella M. 1993. "The 'Environmental Justice' Frame: A Conceptual Discussion and Application." *Social Problems* 40:5–24.

Capek, Stella M., and John I. Gilderbloom. 1992. *Community Versus Commodity: Tenants and the American City.* Albany: SUNY Press.

Environmental Defense Fund. 2002a. "1997 Rankings: Animal Waste in Duplin County." <wysiwyg://main.65/http://www.score.../county.tcl?fips_county_code=37601>.

———. 2002b. "Hog Watch." <http://www.hogwatch.org>.

Henderson, J. B., and Taylor Batten. 1997. "Hunt Urges Hold on Hog Farms." *Charlotte Observer,* April 9, A1, A17.

Naples, Nancy A. 1994. "Contradictions in Agrarian Ideology: Restructuring Gender, Race-Ethnicity, and Class." *Rural Sociology* 59 (1): 110–35.

NCDACS (North Carolina Department of Agriculture and Consumer Services). 2002a. "Hog Inventory Up." <http://www.agr.state.us/stats/livestoc/anihgio3.html>.

———. 2002b. "Hogs and Pigs: Number of Operations & Percent of Inventory by Size Group, North Carolina 1999–2000." <http://.www.agr.state.nc.us/stats/livestoc/anihigyr.htm>.

Satchell, Michael. 1996. "Hog Heaven and Hell." *U.S. News and World Report*, January 22, 55–59.

Schaffer, Michael. 1997. "Boss Hog." *Washington City Paper*, October 10, 21–30.

Tarrow, Sidney. 1994. *Power in Movement: Social Movements, Collective Action, and Politics*. Cambridge: Cambridge University Press.

Thu, Kendall, and E. Paul Durrenberger. 1994. "North Carolina's Hog Industry: The Rest of the Story." *Culture and Agriculture* 49:20–23.

United States. Department of Agriculture. 1997. *Census of Agriculture*. Vol. 1, part 33, chap. 1. North Carolina State-Level Data. <http://www.nass.usda.gov/census/census97/volume1/nc-33/toc97.htm>.

Warrick, Joby, and Pat Stith. 1995. "New Studies Show Lagoons Are Leaking." *Raleigh News and Observer*, February 19, A1.

11

Does Welfare to Work Work?

Rural Employers Comment

Julie White, Ann R. Tickamyer,
Debra A. Henderson, and Barry Tadlock

WELFARE REFORM IN the United States was implemented at the height of the economic boom of the 1990s. In the midst of an economy that created more than 20 million new jobs, it is not all that surprising that welfare-to-work programs were heralded as a success. Not only was job placement facilitated by these improved economic conditions, but welfare-to-work programs provided many employers with the low-cost labor they require for continued profitability in a context of otherwise rising labor costs.

Yet the benefits of this booming economy were not universal. Global economic restructuring means that extractive industries and manufacturing jobs, formerly the bread and butter of many rural economies, have relocated to developing countries (Billings and Tickamyer 1993; Tickamyer and Duncan 1990). Thus restructuring has had a disproportionate negative impact on rural areas, and economic growth has done little to compensate for these losses. In light of this, the opportunities for employment that are presumed by advocates of welfare-to-work programs are often absent. Where there are jobs, basic employment support (child care, public transportation, workforce training, etc.) tends to be less available in rural than in metro-

politan areas, making the transition from welfare to work more difficult (Shelton et al. 2000).

This chapter presents a study of the impact of welfare reform in four
Appalachian counties in southern Ohio. While welfare-to-work pro-
visions are the centerpiece of restructuring the welfare state, there has
been little research investigating how those who are expected to supply the jobs view the situation. We focus here on interviews with local
employers, supplementing these with surveys of employers in the same
region. Our findings have both conceptual and policy implications.

Conceptually, the employers' accounts seem to challenge assumptions about poverty and welfare dependency that fueled widespread
support for welfare reform. Most recent work follows a long tradition
of depicting "cultural" explanations as *alternatives* to structural explanations, with the concept of a culture of poverty providing the account that resonates with the public and policymakers alike.[1] Kathryn
Edin and Laura Lein note, "According to this view, the problem of
welfare dependency arises from the values of the individual recipient,
not from the larger social and economic system. It is assumed, therefore, that even among unskilled and semiskilled parents, those who
choose welfare do so primarily because they lack the correct values"
(1997, 194). The employers we interviewed generally voiced support
for welfare reform and frequently framed that support in terms of
concerns about work ethic and the character of dependence. As they
talked about their experiences as employers in the region, they attributed local poverty to "Appalachian culture," a culture that produced
laziness and a lack of ambition.

That employers would frame much of their discussion of poverty
in the terms of a "culture of poverty" is hardly surprising given the
broader public discussions of welfare over the last ten years (Gilens
1999; Gingrich 1994; Katz 1993; Polakow 1993). The programmatic defense of welfare-to-work policies took culture-of-poverty explanations
for granted. However, what is interesting is that none of these employers, even those who worried about generational laziness, felt the
problem could be straightforwardly reduced to culture-of-poverty
explanations. These employers see two coexisting explanations for
poverty and welfare dependence. While they often attributed the

causes of poverty to the character of the poor, they also made references to structural obstacles to employment. As a consequence, while employers generally supported the effort at welfare reform, they also predicted limited long-term success due to problems they saw as particular to rural environments with underdeveloped infrastructure and historically high unemployment rates.

Taken together, these employer perspectives have implications for policy. Common themes include commitment to economic development, the need for some government investment in transition programs, and the tradeoffs between saving tax dollars and the goals of welfare reform. We elaborate on these policy implications in the final section of this chapter.

Method

Our study of rural employers is part of a larger project assessing the impact of welfare reform in rural areas. In 1998 we began by collecting baseline data on the twenty-nine counties constituting the Appalachian region of Ohio. We looked at their labor markets, unemployment rates, and dependence on transfer payments. We also conducted interviews with Department of Human Services (DHS) directors in each of these counties. Extrapolating from the baseline data, we then selected four showcase counties that represent the spectrum of socioeconomic conditions in the twenty-nine-county region. We conducted focus groups and surveys with welfare recipients in each of the four counties. Employers in the four counties were also surveyed with 144 responding of the 381 surveys mailed (37.8 percent response rate). This was followed by semistructured interviews with forty-eight recipients and twelve employer interviews in the area, as well as with the DHS directors in each county. Focus groups with DHS case managers were also conducted, as were interviews with county commissioners.[2]

In the following sections we focus on our work with employers.[3] Local employment is dominated by manual labor or service work, reflected in the employers we interviewed. We spoke with three nursing home directors, two hotel owners (who were interviewed together), the owner of a lumber yard, a manager in a food-processing plant, a furniture manufacturer, a bank manager, the manager of a thrift shop, a school superintendent, the director of a placement service for nursing personnel, and the director of the Council on Aging in one of the counties. We selected employers from each of the four counties that are the focus counties in our study. Often the county Department of Human Services would recommend local employers. The format for our conversations was a semistructured interview. Interviews lasted from thirty-five minutes to almost two hours. In several cases we found interviewees were enthusiastic about the opportunity to discuss both their experience and their own policy recommendations for welfare.

We were interested in employers' experiences of welfare to work both in their role as participant employers and as community members. Since one of the employers we interviewed and most we surveyed had not actually participated in the welfare-to-work program, their responses offer insight into possible explanations for employer reluctance to participate. In addition, we asked questions about how employers would assess the impact of welfare reform on the community beyond the workplace. In response, several employers talked about the difference between their employer perspective and what one woman identified as her "human" perspective on the problems of poverty and unemployment. Where these perspectives diverged, employers often identified obstacles recipients faced and simultaneously felt it was beyond the scope and power of their position as employers to address them. Understanding employer reluctance to participate as well as the frustrations of those who participated has important policy implications, and we elaborate on these in the final section of the chapter.

Training and Infrastructure

Most employers we spoke with, as well as the vast majority of survey respondents, saw welfare-to-work programs as a positive aspect of welfare reform. Of the 144 surveys of employers in the region, 67 percent of respondents said they either supported or strongly supported welfare reform when it was first proposed at the federal level. Yet when they were asked about welfare reform and its implementation at the county level, 61 percent of those surveyed said it was either unsuccessful or very unsuccessful. Only 8 percent were willing to label welfare reform at the county level successful. Similar positions were reflected in the interviews; the sentiment most often voiced is best captured in the comment of one nursing home director: "I think welfare reform was a good idea, an honorable idea—I just don't think they [policy makers] did their homework." She added that "they are setting these people up for failure."

As policy, welfare reform, and the welfare-to-work programs it required, assumes that the chief obstacle to employment is the character of the unemployed. The logic of the policy assumes that if we could only encourage a greater sense of personal responsibility, work rather than welfare would be the rational choice of recipients. Much of what employers said in the course of interviews suggests that they shared this view. Yet the interviews also reflected a recognition that there were substantial populations who wanted to choose work over welfare but for whom the work was simply not there. Employers generally offered accounts of the underlying causes of poverty and unemployment that were more complex than a lack of personal responsibility on the part of the unemployed. Most employers recognized the limitations on employment opportunities in the local area. Thus, while they were optimistic about what could be accomplished with welfare-to-work programs on a national scale, they also consistently felt policymakers failed to take account of obstacles to job expansion that were particular to their rural areas.

Employers were supportive of the broad agenda of welfare-to-work programs. In particular, both hotel managers and the nursing home directors we spoke with openly acknowledged that welfare-to-work programs were providing them with a labor force they would not have had otherwise. Statewide, as unemployment rates dipped to 4 percent, finding workers for their low-paying, entry-level jobs was a challenge. In fact certified nursing assistants were in such high demand that Certified Nursing Assistants (CNAs) frequently traveled from southeastern Ohio to Columbus, a two- to three-hour drive, because the labor shortage there had driven wages up to between $11 and $12 per hour to start.

In comparison, nursing homes in the counties we studied paid somewhere around $5.50 per hour. One nursing home director saw the potential of welfare-to-work programs in the following terms: "the type of people [that] are on welfare basically is the same type of people we use as nursing assistants, housekeepers, dietary aides, and so forth. Mostly low education level, and a lot of them are single parents, single mothers, and so forth and I can see a lot of potential for us to use these people." The hotel managers also identified their housekeeping units in similar demographic terms. They said that in their industry demand for welfare-to-work participants was high. One nursing home director openly acknowledged that his CNA jobs were desirable only to those who had few other options. He guessed that he had already lost about forty of the eighty-eight people he had hired that year. And he added, "Nursing aid is a low-pay, hard-work, burnout job—that's endemic. It is a rough job and an unappreciated job." Another nursing home director admitted he didn't know whether he could himself handle the work of a CNA. Recognizing that the work was difficult both emotionally and physically, however, did not translate into an increase in wages to draw workers. Most of these directors felt they were already operating businesses at the margins of profitability. Two of the directors insisted they simply couldn't afford to pay higher wages and stay in business. In this context, mandatory welfare-to-work programs were critical to keeping them in business.

A real concern for the nursing homes, as well as for the representative from the Council on Aging, was that their businesses currently pay the cost of training and certifying CNAs. One director suggested that the cost could be justified, but he was the exception; all the others felt that the Department of Human Services should be helping with the cost. And one nursing home director emphatically stated that requiring certification for nursing assistants was the worst thing the state could have done; in his mind, it contributed to a labor shortage in the midst of high local unemployment. The other two nursing home directors and the director of the council on aging all said that while there was considerable financial strain involved in footing the bill for training, the payback was questionable. One director estimated that about fifty percent of those who began the training program stuck with it, and there was no guarantee that they would come to work for the employers who paid for the training. However, the shortage of certified assistants required training. "The training part, the advantage to us is we get first shot at hiring them. . . . and hiring them, it relieves a lot of our problems as far as having bodies to take care of the patients."

From the employers' perspective, the disadvantage of subsidizing training was that employees, especially those who were new to the work, were quick to look for better jobs elsewhere, especially in the Columbus area, where wages were often double. But locally, welfare-to-work requirements provided a steady stream of "bodies" in the context of what was often a desperate shortage of nursing home labor.

The limited access to training and certification programs was clearly a problem for some of the employers we interviewed. But the difficulty most often identified by employers in managing new employees was the obstacle of reliable transportation. One nursing home director commented of participants: "A lot of them have transportation problems. I know one class we taught, there were only one or two that drove, out of the eight in the class, and we had to help find transportation to get them to the class."

Similarly, the school superintendent commented, "if you're gonna get a job here in this county, you're gonna drive someplace . . . and if you don't have a decent vehicle to do it then you can't, and I . . . we've had that situation. . . . I know of people personally who had to quit their job cause they couldn't afford to buy a different vehicle and their vehicle just wasn't capable of maintaining that drive, you know, . . . even to, even as close as Athens. I mean Athens or Parkersburg, Gallipolis to a certain degree, are probably the closest places to get jobs around here and, and Athens is what, twenty-five, thirty miles away."

And the director of the county's Council on Aging suggested that the issue of transportation was one she felt totally frustrated by as an employer but completely sympathetic about as a fellow human being:

It's very frustrating also to know that there are jobs available and, and people simply are not willing to work. That is my feeling as an employer. Now, as a human being, I can see all the other sides of the issues. I understand that, you know, if you don't have enough money to get a car—you have to have a car in this business . . . if you're gonna be a home health aid you gotta get there. So it's catch-22. They don't have a car. They don't have enough money to get the insurance. You've gotta have a telephone in the home 'cause you got to be able to get a hold of 'em . . . so they can't get ahead far enough to get all these things in place . . . so they can hold down the job, so I understand the whole issue. So, you know, it sounds real cold and calculating when I say they don't make good employees. However, as a human being, I understand.

She recognized that as an employer the temptation was to reduce the issue to a simple lack of adequate will power, of personal responsibility on the part of the employee, but as a human being she understood that it was a lot more complicated than that.

Others we interviewed recognized that the problem of transportation went beyond the problem of individuals owning reliable cars to get to already existing jobs; the relatively underdeveloped system of roads presented an obstacle to drawing new business and new jobs to the area. The school superintendent commented:

You know, we, everybody, wants a Toyota plant . . . and it wouldn't do any good to bring a Toyota plant to this county. Yeah, we got a lotta unemployed people but they couldn't do the jobs. . . . But, you know, given the time frame it takes to build a Toyota plant . . . we could have a lotta people trained. You're gonna attract people in but, you know, in an area like this, with very minimal transportation ability, minimal infrastructure . . . you know, to support a large business, a small, ten- to fifteen-employer type . . . is far more important to us than keep tryin' to attract the big name, you know, big factory or whatever.

Underdeveloped infrastructure, whether the educational infrastructure required for certification and training, or the transportation infrastructure for moving employees and drawing new employers, was a pervasive obstacle to connecting potential employees with jobs. One nursing home director said that he had had to turn down clients for home health care because he didn't have the aides and he couldn't hire them. He said that the jobs as nursing assistants were available but that "these people have never worked before." But in the course of conversation the fact that these people hadn't worked before was not in his view merely a consequence of a crisis of will or a lack of individual responsibility. Because there was no local certification program, nursing aides were being hired from the surrounding counties. And he acknowledged, "You can't drive too far and make a living. If we could hire local they'd stay." He had to turn to other counties for employees because there was no local certification program. And he thought other counties had certification programs because they had stronger K–12 systems: "Education isn't that good here. There is more in other counties. . . . You got to be trained to operate a backhoe these days—you can't even dig ditches without qualifications. It doesn't matter how much you want to work if you don't have the qualifications."

Even in areas where certification was not an issue (e.g., housekeeping or retail), employers felt that DHS should provide some kind of job readiness training in order to prepare recipients to deal with the public appropriately in their capacity as service workers. The two employers that defined their work as "unskilled labor" that was not service work—food processing and lumber yard work—were the most insistent that there were jobs for anyone willing to work. When initially asked, they saw little need for government support even in transition to work programs, but on further questioning there were concessions to the important safety net government must provide at times. The manager of the food processing plant offered the following response:

INTERVIEWER: Do you think the people who are still on welfare rolls—do you think there are jobs out there for them if they wanted them?

EMPLOYER: I truly do for most of them.

INTERVIEWER: Ah, so the major factor in success is an individual's desire to work?

EMPLOYER: I think that's a lot of it. 'Cause most, you know, like I said, our jobs are physical. You know, but, but they're not complicated or technical in any way. So people with little training, or no training really, can come work, you know, in this environment if they have the initiative to . . .

INTERVIEWER: What is going to happen when the economy slows and there are fewer jobs?

EMPLOYER: . . . I think you're gonna see those rolls, welfare rolls increasing again and, you know, probably not because that's what people desire but they're probably not going to have any other alternative.

While she felt that the employment opportunities were available at present, she, like most employers with whom we spoke, did not deny the role that the overall health of the economy played in constraining options for employment. For instance, she acknowledged that many of her employees commuted up to an hour to work, because there simply were no jobs available any closer to home.

Similarly, when we asked the manager of a local bank about whether the county economy could produce jobs for everybody then on welfare, he responded, "No. The problem is not with the employer and it's not with the welfare recipient. The problem is that economic opportunity needs more employers starting businesses. It's limited. Limited I would say by the fact there's no sizable water supply in here like the Hocking River. Limited in the fact that there's almost no four-lane highways running through this county. Those are just general economic factors." He continued, "You know, we would like to see more industry come in here. What we're told is that this is discouraging to them . . . transportation, water. It's the basics to be able to operate an industry."

When we look at the general demographic picture, when we assess the transportation and communication infrastructure in these rural areas, the obstacles to creation of new jobs are formidable. Employers' lack of optimism about the prospects for welfare reform in the long term are grounded in an accurate assessment of employment opportunity. According to one study, there are between two and four workers in need of low-skilled jobs for every low-skilled job opening in Ohio. And in southeastern Ohio, where our case study counties are located, between four and eight workers are seeking every job.

Moreover, if we limit the jobs available to those that pay at least poverty wages (which in 1997 was $12,278 for a family of three), the worker-to-job ratio is 23 to 1 across the state (Kleppner and Theodore 1997).

Assessing the Performance of Welfare-to-Work Participants

Because the dominant rhetoric of welfare reform assumed that work ethic was a key problem, we were interested in employer perceptions of work ethic among participants in welfare-to-work programs. A typical response is captured by the assessment of welfare-to-work participants by the manager of a food processing plant: "Their actual performance on the job is probably equal to most because our jobs are not technical in nature, you know, they're just repetitive. So as far as the job, they do as well as most." Similarly, one nursing home director, when asked if he thought welfare recipients were comparable in terms of general job skills, commented, "Most of them are. We'll run into one every now and then that is not.... But for the most part . . . they're comparable to the other people we've been hiring. . . . we have two-thirds, half to two-thirds good results with recipients participating in welfare-to-work." And again, the survey research suggests that these are typical results; the majority of respondents felt welfare-to-work participants were as good as or better than their other workers.

But the interviews also suggest that while job performance is comparable across these populations, absenteeism is more of a problem with welfare-to-work participants. As one nursing home director commented of his employees generally, "They may be here three months and decide they don't like it and we work them too hard, and they go down the street and find out that the work's just as hard there and they go to the next place." For most, absenteeism was the single most frequent criticism of participants in welfare-to-work programs, although for some employers, dealing with increased absenteeism was compensated for by the fact that welfare-to-work participants did not tend to job-hop as much as other employees, perhaps because of control exercised in case management.

In assessing the performance of these participants, the issue of employee reliability is complicated. First, while the problem of absenteeism was more pronounced with the welfare-to-work participants, several employers noted that the problem of workplace loyalty was more pronounced among the general employee population. Second, employers pointed to simultaneous but potentially competing explanations for absenteeism. Eleven of the twelve employers we interviewed attributed the problem of absenteeism directly, though not exclusively, to transportation issues. And most identified it as the critical obstacle to regular work for many people in the county.

Analyzing employer assessment of welfare-to-work participants, we get a mixed picture. The survey results suggest that the majority of employers feel that job readiness (68 percent), job skills (61 percent), job education (77 percent) and worker dishonesty (94 percent) were NOT significant problems for welfare-to-work participants. The majority also said that work ethic was not a problem (52 percent)—a surprising finding given that the public debate has focused so heavily on this as an explanation for welfare dependence. The only problem identified by the majority of employers responding to the survey was worker reliability (58 percent). The interviews help us make sense of the reliability problem. Employers saw welfare-to-work participants as competent and comparable to other workers in their competence, but they identified absenteeism as a key problem. When pursued in the course of interviews, employers attributed problems of worker reliability to problems of transportation as well as to work ethic. The discussion of work ethic often prompted references to a kind of Appalachian culture of poverty, but there were also competing accounts that stressed a strong work ethic as defining the culture of the region.

In the following section we turn to explore the meaning of *Appalachian* in greater detail. The stories of Appalachian culture reveal constructions of heroes and villains, of insiders and outsiders, stories of who is to blame and who is a victim, when there is simply unavoidable misfortune and when there is active injustice. The contested meaning of *Appalachian* reveals the complexity of the larger social context in which welfare reform is to be implemented.

In reviewing the transcripts of interviews for this project, we noticed a frequent and unanticipated theme. In assessing both regional economic potential generally, and in assessing welfare-to-work recipients in particular, reference was repeatedly made to the role that Appalachian culture played in shaping work ethic. And, interestingly, there seemed to be competing accounts. On the one hand, Appalachians were depicted as a hard-working and loyal people. On the other, Appalachian culture was depicted as a culture of poverty that produces laziness and parochialism. In the first case, Appalachian history became the history of hard work and hard luck. In the second, that same history became the story of an unworthy people.

Dwight Billings and Ann Tickamyer note that this schizophrenia about the meaning of Appalachia is an enduring one: "Images of Appalachia have taken on almost mythic proportions in popular perception, the media, and even policy circles (Shapiro 1978). These images vary from highly pejorative to intensely partisan, often on the basis of the same attributes. The region is variously depicted as a cesspool of grinding poverty and human misery, a throwback to pre-industrial and pioneer standards of self-sufficiency and strength, the quintessential example of internal colonial exploitation, a testimonial to the endurance of the human spirit, a hillbilly backwater" (1993, 7).

Almost all our employer interviews contained descriptions that recognized unfortunate circumstances beyond the control of individuals in the region. But this was sometimes accompanied by a description of *Appalachian* that emphasized the strength of character it takes to endure these conditions, sometimes by a depiction of an Appalachian hillbilly culture that created and perpetuated conditions of poverty.

When it came, for instance, to absenteeism, many employers simultaneously attributed it to a cultural lack of familiarity with work and to a material issue, like lack of transportation or availability of adequate health care for the employee or family members. For example, one nursing home director believed that welfare reform was "working fairly well for the health care industry." He also understood the reluctance of employers to participate in welfare-to-work programs and he attributed that reluctance to concerns about a pervasive culture of poverty in "this area":

> I think that a lot of them see this as—this area, as I said when we started, is high welfare area, high, high human services usage area, and it's been grandfather, father, son . . . right on down the line. It's been handed down, you know. People around here joke when the kids aren't in school, what these kids [are] doing out of school. Well they're training for when they grow up on welfare. That's typical in this area. You drive down the street in the daytime and mom and dad and the kids are all sitting on the front porch when they should be working around and in school and, ah, I think it's gonna shift but it's just gonna take time. But a lot of people see that as the culture . . . and they see these people won't work. They've never worked out; we've hired them before. You know, we hired his grandmother twenty years ago and she wouldn't do it, so I know he's not gonna do it 'cause he's been bred up to, brought up that way, and it's inbred into him.

One longtime resident and director of a nursing home similarly commented, "It's almost like welfare is part of their genetic makeup." And he added that a lot of people in the county were third- and fourth-generation welfare families. "Policymakers don't understand poverty, period. You have a mind set in this county, in Appalachia generally—generational welfare. . . . Some women have been drawing welfare so long, they don't have the will to work." But even this picture was complicated. He went on to acknowledge that there were very few jobs in the area but then added, "I don't know—you got to try—you can't give in to hopelessness and despair. What do you have left if all the smart people leave Appalachia?"

Another employer said that a representative from the local welfare-to-work program had come by to explain some common assumptions about the pool of workers he might be getting. The representative explained that transportation and childcare are going to be issues that cause absenteeism:

> So she did kinda tell us that and she explained things—how this is more like of an Appalachian characteristic. Which I'm Appalachian too so . . . I don't think it's true for everybody, but just how they don't

identify with work as much. It's not really important to them, like where they work . . . what they're doing, as much. And then the other thing which I've seen for sure is just like what I call kinda like a culture of crisis. . . .

You know, where just the same things don't happen in our non-WEP [Work Employment Program] workers, employees' lives. I mean a lot of some of the absenteeism is sort of understandable and it's re-lated to crises like cars blowing up all the time . . . relatives' houses burning down, and, you know, lots of open-heart surgery . . . just more crises . . . And I mean stuff like my home life is just tame . . . you know, empty of incidents compared to what we've experienced or seen.

When asked about the causes of this culture of crisis, he remarked, "I don't know. Well, a lot of it's just, you know, like I can afford a new car . . . so car problems are never going to be an issue." Here *Appalachian* seems to refer to both cultural and material circumstance. But what separates the Appalachian employer from the welfare-to-work participant is in the end not culture but the fact that he can afford a new car.

Appalachia was also frequently defined as a region relatively iso-lated from other regions, and Appalachians were seen as uniquely parochial. In an era of globalization, one in which cosmopolitanism is embraced by the mainstream, this is a damning cultural characteris-tic. As the school superintendent commented to us in the interview, "it would probably blow you out of the water, you know, the number of people who won't go beyond Athens [twenty miles away]."

Yet it was not clear that he associated this parochialism with a problem of work ethic. The superintendent noted that if the jobs were available locally, the unemployment rate would be just as low as it is in Columbus (2–4 percent). "It's an issue, . . . it's an issue of availabil-ity of jobs. . . . it's also an issue of our culture." He noted that there had been a migration to Columbus, that there were whole subdivisions of Appalachians up there. But, he argued, if people had a choice they would be "here," in Appalachia. "This is their home, you know, and people will do what people have to do . . . they don't wanna starve to death . . . and there is, I think, a strong work ethic in this part of the state; people want to work. . . . But, like I said, when you can earn more sittin' at home doin' nothing than you can working, what is the incentive to work?" And a similar response speaks to work ethic: "after a while, you know, you're like third-generation welfare down here. I mean, you, you . . . it's a family thing, and if my mom and dad or my grandparents can survive on those monthly checks, why should I do anything different?"

When asked to compare the performance of welfare-to-work participants with the performance of people who move into jobs directly from other jobs, the director of the Council on Aging said, "it's hard sometimes to assess, because of course you can't ask if they have come off the welfare rolls . . . et cetera, but sometimes you have a real sense of that because of cars, their cars . . . and all those kinds of issues, you know, . . . and sometimes just general attitude, to be honest." And she argued that DHS should provide mandatory courses on work ethic. But simultaneously she acknowledged important success stories:

> Oh, we've hired, we've hired a lot of people over the years, I have, I've got a couple real success stories right now that were here in the agency working off-hours. We hired 'em. Because they showed all of the skills and the work ethic and the willingness to do whatever somebody wants, and what can I do to help them?
>
> . . . they're poor for so long. I think it's kinda like the single factor that you're trying to climb a ladder, you know, and you always get to the top and something happens and you fall down again, and every time it's gonna be a little bit harder. And it's not because—you know, a lot of these families, *I don't think it's ever because they don't want to* [her emphasis]. It's just that some people, or some families, seem to go around with a black cloud over their head . . . kind of, and it just becomes too much . . . to keep trying, to keep climbing.

Several employers offered accounts like these; accounts that both seemed to argue that there was a problem of work ethic for which Appalachians themselves were to blame and yet also to argue that the story of the region was one of a hard-working people who had suffered great misfortune.

This story of misfortune offers a particularly stark contrast with the story line about the economy beyond Appalachia. Yet again there are both material and cultural ways of talking about this isolation. While some employers commented that the parochialism of the region resulted from geographic isolation, others saw it in social terms as well:

> Let me just say, I came into this county in 1973 and I'm still an outsider. I will always be an outsider. . . . and we're not related to anyone . . . we're not related to anybody, how could we ever belong? . . .
>
> Even in almost the year 2000, there are certainly very strong pockets of people who resent and resist people such as yourself . . . [directed to researcher]. I mean, you sense that, you see that, I'm sure. I mean, I see that with my own staff sometimes. It's just a, it's kind of like an intangible thing . . . like a people not knowing they're prejudiced but they really are; maybe they sit and tell you they're not prejudiced until they have a mixed marriage in their own family . . . and then they discover they are. That's the only way I can explain it, it, it's just there. It's Appalachia; it's the culture.

Depictions of Appalachia as an isolated and perhaps isolationist culture were also present in interviews with other employers. One of the employers we interviewed came from southern Ohio but had set up a business in the Columbus area. She offered a placement service for health care employees, coordinating with one of the certification-training programs in the Appalachian region in order to respond to a desperate shortage of nursing assistants in the Columbus area. She was aware that many of the graduates of the programs would be reluctant to come to jobs in Columbus. She recounted her own fears the first time she had a job outside the area around her rural home. As a consequence she often offered to set assistants up to car pool together and helped them get rooms together so they could work weekend shifts. She could work to overcome their reluctance to work in the city because having herself experienced it, she understood it. She credited much of her success at placement to this shared experience. Assistants placed through her were earning $11 to $12 per hour, often more than twice the starting wages for nursing assistants in our four case study counties. It seemed by her account to be a winning situation for everyone.

Everyone, that is, except the rural nursing homes in southern Ohio. I asked if any of the nursing homes in the four-county region we studied had tried to use her services to remedy their own shortage of employees. Her responses reflected an interesting view of Appalachian culture:

> They can't afford the buyout [the payment a placement agency like this employer's would charge a nursing home]—to begin with, and they can't afford to even—well, let me say they won't allow themselves to afford to make a comparable wage. And it's just not feasible at this point. I think this is something that hit them really hard. They weren't expecting it. But that area is so Appalachian. . . . They, you know, $5.35 is minimum wage or whatever—$5.65 is minimum wage, that's what you're gonna get paid, like it or leave it . . . because there's somebody waiting in line to take your job if you don't like it.

From her perspective, "Appalachian" employers had not made a smart response to an inevitable labor shortage in this field. But where the people she hired were described as Appalachian, this clearly had all positive connotations:

> the people that work for me from Meigs County and the Southeastern Ohio area, I would rather any day work with those people than I would people from Columbus, the Delaware area.[4] Because they want to work, number one—they don't call in sick. They don't show up on their shifts late. They don't treat me as an employer like, "Well, I can just go to any other old agency in town and get a job." They're very loyal. They . . . have been very loyal to me and I really appreciate these people.

In the course of these interviews, when *Appalachian* was invoked it was used to clearly distinguish insiders from outsiders. It wasn't always clear who counted as an insider and who counted as an outsider, who was a victim and who was a villain. What is clear is that once insider and outsider had been distinguished, outsiders were clearly a source of suspicion and distrust.

Does Welfare to Work Work? Employer Perspectives

Welfare reform was marketed to the American people on the basis of two related claims: first, the Personal Responsibility Act was supposed to remedy the problem of individual irresponsibility presumed to be the primary cause of welfare dependence; second (and indirectly), by cutting spending on welfare, allowing in turn for cuts in taxes, welfare to work was supposed to stimulate economic growth (Gingrich 1994, 72). Is welfare reform then the answer to persistent rural poverty, underemployment, and unemployment?

These employers seem to believe that while it might be a part of the answer, the explanation for persistent rural poverty is complicated, and solutions must recognize that. Many employers, in both the surveys and the interviews, expressed concern that welfare itself has contributed to a culture of irresponsibility and laziness that is reproduced generationally. This was often reflected in their discussions of the meanings of *Appalachian*—employers often seemed to be describing a culture of poverty. But in a departure from much contemporary work on the culture of poverty (Katz 1993), this explanation often coexisted with structural explanations that attributed the plight of poor and dependent individuals to forces that transcended individual and culture—for example, the lack of physical infrastructure (access to highways (complicating transportation) and water) and structural unemployment. As one employer put it, even though she saw jobs out there now, she could foresee a time when "you're gonna see those rolls increasing again and, you know, not because that's what people desire, but they're probably not going to have any other alternative." In response to the question, "Can your county produce jobs for everybody currently on welfare?" another employer responded, "No. You're kidding yourself. The problem is not with the employer and it's not with the welfare recipient. The problem is that of economic opportunity." In this sense, to the extent that they are using "culture-of-poverty" style explanations, most employers recognize that "cultural" explanations are not an alternative to but are situated within larger political and economic structures.

While work by others has failed to find a significant difference between rural and urban/suburban employers (Owen et al. 2000), our own preliminary findings suggest that our employer discussions differ from urban employers on this score. Work by Joleen Kirschenman and Kathryn Neckerman (1991) and William Julius Wilson (1996) with the Urban Poverty and Family Life Study documents that

Chicago employers view the meaning of race through the lens of a "culture of poverty." There is little evidence that they recognize structural barriers to employment. As Wilson suggests, this is hardly surprising. Survey research consistently documents that individualistic explanations for poverty (lack of effort or ability, poor morals, poor work skills) are overwhelmingly favored over structural explanations (lack of adequate schooling, low wages, lack of jobs, and so on). "Americans remain strongly disposed to the idea that individuals are largely responsible for their economic situations" (Wilson 1996, 159). In this sense, the attitudes of urban employers seem simply to reflect that widely shared disposition. And such attitudes may be the underlying explanation for the low level of support for government intervention reflected in our surveys. But interviews with rural employers paint a more complex picture. For these employers clearly do recognize circumstances beyond an individual's control as potential obstacles to employment.

This difference between urban and rural employers may be in part attributable to the fact that urban employers were clearly identifying problems that pertained to "others." By contrast, our rural employers seemed to have an ambivalent relationship to the meaning of *Appalachian*. On the one hand, *Appalachian*, like *inner-city*, was often used as shorthand for lazy, uneducated, unemployable. And, as in the classic formulations of the culture of poverty, interviewees frequently talked about these attributes being passed from one generation to the next. But they also sometimes identified themselves as Appalachian, and in this sense the relationship of these employers to *Appalachian* differs from the relationship of urban employers to *inner-city*. One employer simultaneously used *Appalachian* to describe the backward approach of nursing home owners in the area, but she also spoke approvingly of Appalachians as having a strong work ethic and strong sense of community—a community of which she was herself a part. This sense of community as a positive attribute of Appalachian culture was referenced in several other interviews. When asked about whether he had hesitations about hiring welfare recipients, one bank manager commented, "No. We don't think of sheeps and goats. We don't think in terms of this is a welfare, this is not a welfare." Though he acknowledged problems of work readiness and professionalism and he thought there were people who "just can't really perform," he also stressed that in his day-to-day life kids in the community all went to school together, adults all played in the softball league together. He seemed to be suggesting that the community was simply too small, too intimate, for such divisions to be of real consequence.

Our focus groups with recipients paint a very different picture, a picture that suggests that there are "sheeps and goats." Cynthia Duncan's work in Appalachia (1996) also supports the recipient perspective; she argues that the patterns of class relations are marked by rigid stratification. But the perception on the part of employers that they too are Appalachians does have consequences for how they see their role with respect to the community; at least in the interview process they often saw themselves as advocates of a sort. Class differences between employers and workers are mediated by a shared regional identity.

Both the employers and the local DHS directors we interviewed frequently claimed that the whole southern region of Ohio was being overlooked by the state due to its lack of political clout. Several employers expressed concern that economic development dollars were not being fairly allocated, and they touted the potential of the area for tourism and recreation if initial state investments were made. Given this, the evidence cited earlier—that while the majority of employers think welfare reform is a good idea, the majority also think it isn't working very well in their counties—becomes meaningful. Shifting the incentives to work rather than welfare only matters if there are jobs at which to work.

Many employers recognize that addressing welfare dependence and local poverty will require job creation as well as instituting local training programs to create a fit between labor and existing employment opportunities. Who should bear responsibility for such training? Our survey put this question to employers, offering as options the employee, the employer, and local, state, or federal government. Over half said that the employee and the employer bore responsibility; there was little support for a role for government in ensuring skills training or job fit. Yet again our interviews suggest a different picture. Without the suggestion of alternatives, employers often argued that there was a need for

DHS training and job readiness, and some role for the agency in certification programs. They saw a role for public investment. Several explicitly argued that the goal of welfare should not be to save state dollars but to invest them differently—in economic development and job training, for example. One employer offered, "As a tax payer . . . [I'm] thinking that the welfare reform seemed to be a better way to spend the dollars that are going to be spent. They are always gonna need to be spent and I don't have a problem with that."

In the two-pronged defense of welfare reform, the vast majority of employers, both those surveyed and interviewed, see welfare-to-work programs as having the potential to remedy the problem of individual irresponsibility, to create a cultural shift. But the interviews suggest some skepticism toward the claim that welfare reform is going to reduce government expenditure. Rather some employers argued that employment-training and support programs, economic development dollars, and the recognition that there will always be those who need welfare, may mean little overall reduction in government expenditure.

Making Rural Welfare to Work Work

Employers recognize that rural labor markets differ in significant ways from their urban counterparts. Yet these differences have not been consistently taken into account in the course of designing welfare-to-work programs. Making these programs work will require public policy that recognizes contingencies of place.

A critical difference recognized by employers as well as recipients and DHS personnel is quite simply the absence of jobs in which to place people. Given this, it is particularly imperative to link welfare reform in these rural areas with an economic development strategy designed to produce jobs. This will require public investment—indirectly in infrastructure and more directly in development funds. While there were a few employers who could not hire the labor they needed, jobs that pay a living wage are in very short supply.

Access to training and certification programs is also very limited. When combined with the problem of reliable transportation, this often presents an obstacle to access to the jobs that are available. If welfare to work is to work in these rural contexts, training and certification programs must be developed locally. It is ironic that in the midst of high levels of local unemployment, nursing home directors have to go outside the county to hire CNAs. If certification is going to be a continued requirement, the resources for obtaining certification will have to be provided locally.

Finally, the success of welfare-to-work programs hinges on developing adequate systems of support for the transition to employment. This support must take a variety of forms but, again, some support systems are made necessary by the unique conditions faced in rural environments. For example, all our rural employers recognized that reliable transportation was a critical obstacle for many of the participants in welfare-to-work programs. They also recognized that few of these participants had the material resources to overcome this obstacle on their own. County Departments of Human Service are beginning to develop programs to subsidize private-vehicle ownership, to extend loans, and to provide reimbursement for repair. More successful policy will require a more systematic approach to the problem of transportation and this will require public investment. And in both rural and urban environments support for the transition to work must also include a longer period of continued medical benefits until private coverage is a realistic option. One of the nursing home directors insisted that this was the critical obstacle to keeping her CNAs, most of whom were women with children. The hotel owners faced similar problems.

Successful economic development will require a two-pronged approach. First, it requires the involvement of locals in the design and implementation of such programs. Given the suspicion of outsiders, getting insiders involved in such programs is critical to their legitimacy at the local level. At the same time, economic development and employment support systems of the kinds described will require some state support. While employers embrace welfare reform as an institutional remedy for a culture of poverty, they also recognize structural barriers to employment, barriers welfare reform itself doesn't address. If welfare reform is to work in their counties, economic development, training programs, and support for transition to work, must all be addressed. The employers expressed concern that it was both beyond their capacities as employers and beyond the capacities of prospective employees to address these issues on their own. Our interviews suggest many rural employers recognize that creating good private-sector workers requires some public investment.

Notes

Support for this research comes from grants from the Joyce Foundation, the National Research Initiative of USDA, and Ohio University.

1. Michael Katz (1993) argues that in its original inception, Oscar Lewis's account of a culture of poverty (1968) did not converge with claims about an "undeserving poor," though he acknowledges that this conflation is often made now. A closer look at Lewis's own account reveals the tension between a cultural and a structural focus. He writes, "The culture of poverty is both an adaptation and a reaction of the poor to their marginal position in a class-stratified, highly individuated, capitalistic society. . . . Many of the traits of the culture of poverty can be viewed as attempts at local solutions for problems not met by existing institutions and agencies because the people are not eligible for them, cannot afford them, or are ignorant or suspicious of them. For example, unable to obtain credit from banks, they are thrown upon their own resources and organize informal credit devices without interest." But he goes on to suggest that this culture, though it begins as an adaptation to objective conditions of the larger society, reproduces itself from generation to generation even when those structural conditions change. In this situation, members of the subculture, "are not psychologically geared to take full advantage of the changing conditions or increased opportunities that may occur in their lifetime" (188).

2. For an account of our work with Department of Human Services Directors and recipients, see Tickamyer et al. 2000.

3. Quotes presented in this paper were lightly edited to remove redundancies while still preserving the speech pattern and grammar of the interviewees.

4. Delaware is a white, middle-class suburb of Columbus.

References

Billings, D., and A. Tickamyer. 1993. "Uneven Development in Appalachia." In *Forgotten Places: Uneven Development in Rural America*, ed. T. Lyson and W. Falk, 7–29. Lawrence: University Press of Kansas.

Duncan, C. M. 1996. "Understanding Persistent Poverty: Social Class Context in Rural Communities." *Rural Sociology* 61 (1): 103–24.

Edin, K., and L. Lein. 1997. *Making Ends Meet.* New York: Russell Sage Foundation.

Gilens, M. 1999. *Why Americans Hate Welfare: Race, Media, and the Politics of Antipoverty Policy.* Chicago: University of Chicago Press.

Gingrich, N. 1994. *Contract with America.* New York: Times Books.

Katz, M. B. 1993. "The Urban 'Underclass' as a Metaphor of Social Transformation." In *The "Underclass" Debate: Views from History,* ed. M. B. Katz, 3–26. Princeton: Princeton University Press.

Kirschenman, J., and K. M. Neckerman. 1991. "'We'd Love to Hire Them, But . . .': The Meaning of Race for Employers." In *The Urban Underclass,* ed. C. Jencks and P. E. Peterson, 203–34. Washington, D.C.: Brookings Institution.

Kleppner, P., and N. Theodore. July 1997. "Work after Welfare: Is the Midwest's Booming Economy Creating Enough Jobs?" The Job Gap Project: Chicago Urbana League and The Office for Social Policy Research, Northern Illinois University.

Lewis, O. 1968. "The Culture of Poverty." In *On Understanding Poverty,* ed. D. Moynihan, 187–200. New York: Basic Books.

Polakow, V. 1993. *Lives on the Edge: Single Mothers and Their Children in the Other America.* Chicago: University of Chicago Press.

Shelton, E., G. Owen, A. Bush Stevens, J. Nelson-Christinedaughter, C. Roy, and J. Heineman. 2002. "Whose Job Is It? Employers' Views on Welfare Reform." In *Rural Dimensions of Welfare Reform,* ed. B. Weber, G. Duncan, and L. Whitener, 345–74. Kalamazoo, Mich.: W. E. Upjohn Institute for Employment Research.

Tickamyer, A. R., and C. Duncan. 1990. "Poverty and Opportunity Structure in Rural America." *Annual Review of Sociology* 16:67–86.

Tickamyer, A. R., D. A. Henderson, J. A. White, and B. Tadlock. 2000. "Voices of Welfare Reform: Bureaucratic Rationality versus the Perceptions of Welfare Participants." *Affilia: Journal of Women and Social Work* 15:173–92.

Wilson, W. J. 1996. *When Work Disappears: The World of the New Urban Poor.* New York: Vintage Books.

Part III

Reaction and Resistance

Survival Strategies of Rural People

12

The Bus from Hell Hole Swamp

Black Women in the Hospitality Industry

Susan E. Webb

INLAND FROM THE South Carolina cities of Charleston and Myrtle Beach is the Hell Hole Bay Wilderness Area. It is part of the Francis Marion National Forest at the junction of Berkeley, Clarendon, and Williamsburg Counties. The surrounding region, known as Hell Hole Swamp, is a sparsely populated rural area dotted with ramshackle wooden houses, dilapidated mobile homes, tiny brick ranch houses, and occasional small farms. Secondary roads and narrow state highways wander miles through pine forests and toward a few small crossroads communities and towns. Hell Hole Swamp was first mentioned in early grants and land sales, and it appears on a 1775 map printed in London, most likely because there were productive colonial plantations in the area (Shemanski 1984, 170). Today the plantations are long since gone, agriculture is declining, and poverty, unemployment, and dependency rates are significantly higher than in other parts of the nation (Washington 1994). There are few jobs in the area and the Francis Marion Forest region is one of rural America's "forgotten places" (Lyson and Falk 1993), bypassed by economic growth and trapped in poverty. For many of the black women in Hell Hole Swamp, the only opportunity to earn an income requires traveling by bus several hours each day to work as maids, laundry workers, fast food servers, and kitchen help in Myrtle Beach.

The bus system that transports the workers from Hell Hole Swamp to Myrtle Beach, over a hundred miles away, began in the 1960s. Small groups of black women in rural areas adjacent to Myrtle Beach traveled there to work as hotel maids. As the resort, and worker demand, grew, they recruited friends, relatives, and neighbors and pooled resources for transportation. First old trucks and vans, later school buses, were purchased, often by church groups, and informal transit systems were started. In Kingstree, South Carolina, near Hell Hole Swamp, the Williamsburg County Transit Authority was formed in the early 1970s by local black leaders who contacted Senator Strom Thurmond and were assisted in locating funding to buy buses and establish a regional transit system.

Throughout the year, black women living in Hell Hole Swamp begin gathering at 5:00 A.M. at local churches and crossroads to board the system's buses for their long journeys to work on the Grand Strand. As the buses rumble toward the coast, they stop at country stores, at churches, and at transfer points in small towns, where they are met by vans of additional passengers. In Georgetown County, en route to Myrtle Beach, more workers board. As they enter the first section of the sixty-mile coastline of the Grand Strand, the buses begin to stop every few blocks to discharge workers. The return trip, which begins at the northernmost part of Myrtle Beach, starts around 2:30 P.M. The last passengers leave the bus at Hell Hole Swamp between 5:30 and 6:00 P.M.

On summer mornings hundreds of refurbished school buses, regional transit buses, and vans of all sorts and conditions join the buses from Hell Hole Swamp and converge on the hotel-lined boulevards of Myrtle Beach. A few buses and vans transporting rural black women to their jobs on the beach are modern, air-conditioned masstransit vehicles compliant with current federal requirements. Most, though, have no contemporary safety features or amenities, and many are aged, recycled school buses and government surplus vans. A half-dozen or so of the vehicles are owned by hotels and provided at no cost to the riders. The majority are owned by black entrepreneurs and by regional transit groups organized by black citizens. While some of the larger buses make trips back and forth to rural counties throughout the day, most of the vehicles are parked at Myrtle Beach during the day. Many drivers also work housekeeping, maintenance, or groundskeeping jobs in addition to driving commuters.

Church networks play a role in the commuting of rural black women to the Grand Strand. In the 1960s black ministers in Clarendon and Williamsburg Counties used church vans to transport workers. One of them led the effort in the early 1970s to obtain the state and federal funding for the Williamsburg County Transit Authority, which today has eighteen buses and over thirty vans transporting hospitality workers. The bus from Hell Hole Swamp is among these vehicles. The "county" transit system crosses county lines into Clarendon County to pick up Hell Hole Swamp passengers and passes through Georgetown County as it transports workers from areas without jobs to work at the beach in Horry County.

Other regional transit systems, most with black leadership, transport workers to Myrtle Beach. One system of over a dozen old school buses and vans is privately owned by a black woman who is head of housekeeping for several hotels and not only hires but also transports her staff from her rural county. Depending on the ownership and the distance traveled, passenger costs for van or bus trips range from $2.50 to $6.00 daily. Some of the women boarding buses miles from the beach have already traveled by van to central pickup points. Van rides to bus stops also cost workers, typically $1.50 to $2.00 a day.

In the winter two to three hundred hospitality workers commute from rural inland counties, and throughout the year the number varies by day with changes in resort occupancy rates. Beginning in March, with Myrtle Beach's annual Can-Am Festival, which brings over ten thousand Canadians to the beach for a week, and swelling with the first big influx of a quarter million or more tourists for the Easter holiday, the number of women journeying to work increases. At the peak of the summer season, thousands of black women commute as much as 175 miles each way from Black Belt counties to employment in the hospitality industry at Myrtle Beach.

The Study

The research reported here is part of an ongoing study of black women employed in a growing sector of the emerging services economy, namely the hospitality (travel, tourism, and entertainment) industry. Primary observations and secondary data analyses indicate a majority of the black women working in Grand Strand hotels, motels, resort condominium complexes, campgrounds, amusement businesses, restaurants, and fast food establishments travel from distant communities in rural areas to their jobs at the beach. The project focuses on black women who commute from Black Belt counties to work in South Carolina's Myrtle Beach–Grand Strand resort area. In the Black Belt, "a social and demographic crescent of Southern demography containing . . . higher-than-average percentages of black residents" (Wimberly and Morris 1997, 2), counties have black populations of 30 percent or higher.

Project data include audiotaped, transcribed interviews with government officials; community leaders; hotel, motel, and restaurant owners and managers; and black women commuting to work at the beach. The project has also involved surveys of workers; field observations to obtain counts of buses, vans, and workers; and analyses of demographic and labor force data from a variety of sources. Since 1992, Coastal Carolina University sociology majors have been invited to participate in the research, and several dozen have completed group and individual projects. Key informants in the study are ten black women who were students (now graduates) in Coastal's sociology program and worked in Grand Strand hotels and motels with their grandmothers, mothers, aunts, sisters, cousins, and friends during their younger years. Their written reflections on their work as hotel maids shape the feminist standpoint (Naples and Sachs 2000) of this ethnographic research. Surveys and interviews developed and conducted by these students and their families and friends in hospitality jobs added participatory research to the study and shaped my understanding of the scope of the issues involved. The key informants introduced me to community leaders, bus system owners, housekeeping supervisors, and workers. The snowball sampling process continues as the research tracks trends affecting black women in the Grand Strand hospitality industry.

Black Women and Employment

There is compelling evidence that work in menial, poorly paid jobs with few fringe benefits remains a reality for the majority of black women in the United States. Women made up 43 percent of the labor force in 1967 and 56 percent by 1997, and the proportion of women of color in the labor force is increasing. The labor force participation rate for African American women was 61.7 percent in 1997. Yet "even as the status of some women of color improves, many will remain stuck in low-wage service and clerical jobs" (Malveaux 1999, 663). In her extensive analysis of Census and Current Population Survey data, Woody (1989) documents the concentration of black women in various sectors of the emerging services economy. Historically, the majority of employed black women worked as domestic servants or as agricultural laborers. As Malveaux points out, in 1940 "a full 70 percent of all African American women worked in domestic and personal service jobs, mostly in private homes" (1999, 668–69). Through the 1960s black women continued in these occupations and their numbers gradually increased in low-pay factory work. Several converging forces—declining employment in agriculture, the end of legal discrimination, general shifts in the occupational structure of the American labor force, increasing numbers of female-headed households, and expanded occupational opportunities for women and minorities—led to a steady decline in the proportion of black women working in farming or as domestics in private households. The numbers employed in clerical jobs, in retail trade, and in human, personal, and business services, especially in government jobs, has continued to increase.

By 1992, when this study began, 19.7 percent of the overall black labor force were employed in managerial and specialty occupations; 31.0 percent were in technical, sales, and administrative support positions;

25.1 percent were in service occupations; 23.8 percent were in production, craft, repair, operator, fabricator, and laborer positions; and only 0.5 percent worked in farming (U.S. Department of Labor 1993). Yet these figures are deceptive, particularly with regard to the participation of black women in the labor force. Data from the Equal Employment Opportunity Commission's Job Patterns for Minorities and Women in Private Industry (1991) revealed the occupational concentration of black women in low-status, low-pay occupations. The 1990 EEOC report (based on the mandated Employer Information Report from private employers with one hundred or more employees or those with fifty or more employees and federal ties) reveals that for black women employed in large private industries, the largest group (35.8%) worked in service industries, with retail trade (16.5%) and manufacturing of nondurable goods (13.9%) the second and third largest segments of employment for black women. More significant for my study, within service industries 41.8 percent of black women were employed as service workers (U.S. EEOC 1991, 1–5). In 2000 national EEOC data tracked 3,361,319 employed black women in private industries. Of these, 719,401 (21.4 percent) were service workers. In South Carolina, 31.7 percent of the 105,328 black women covered in the reports were service workers (U.S. EEOC 2001).

Research on black women in the hospitality industry is quite limited, and even though the positions held by black women in the industry are marginal jobs, part of the secondary labor market, "proportionately more [black women are] employed in hospitality service occupations than in any other" (Farrar and Gyant 1998, 134). Indeed, hospitality service work is both racialized and gendered (136). The black women of Hell Hole Swamp, whose hospitality employment is concentrated in janitorial, housekeeping, laundry, kitchen help, and fast food service occupations, are representative of national trends in their employment. Unlike most black women nationwide, however, these women, and thousands like them throughout rural South Carolina, work away from their home counties and commute long distances for low income and marginal and contingent employment. Round-trip journeys of two hundred miles or more, with commuting times of four or more hours a day, are common.

Commuting, Black Women, and Labor Market Areas

Most research on commuting has concentrated on urban areas. In these studies, it has been found than men typically commute greater distances, with more commute time, than women, that blacks and Hispanics have longer commutes than whites (partly explained by their greater use of public transportation), that the gender differences are less when black men and women are compared, and that long commutes are associated with higher-wage, higher-status positions (for reviews of this literature, see McLafferty and Preston 1991, Taylor and Ong 1995, and White 1988). In their study of work-trip duration for the twenty-four counties of the New York Consolidated Metropolitan Statistical Area, McLafferty and Preston found that the general association of higher-status occupations with longer commutes applied to white men and women, black men and most black women, and Hispanic men and women. "Particularly noteworthy is the exceptionally long commuting time for black women in personal service industries. This finding could reflect the concentration of black women in domestic jobs that require long trips to distant, high-income areas" (1991, 11). Also relevant are the findings of Garkovich (1982), who analyzed commuting patterns in a Kentucky study of nonmetropolitan counties. Although Garkovich does not disaggregate her data for race, she defines commuting as traveling to another county for work and found that blue-collar workers were significantly more likely to commute for employment than white-collar workers. In their analysis of commuting among welfare recipients, Ong and Blumenberg comment, "It is unlikely . . . low-skilled workers will accept minimum-wage jobs that require round-trip commutes of 50 miles or more, because the time and expense of commuting will significantly reduce or even exceed wages from employment. Hence, employment requiring long commutes is only viable if there are offsetting benefits such as higher wages" (1998, 77). However, the women on the bus from Hell Hole Swamp commute more than a hundred miles each way to low-skill, low-pay work. In most cases, work at the beach is the only opportunity for wage labor for these workers.

Bloomquist (1990) defines labor market areas (LMAs) by the spatial organization of commuting behavior in an area and notes that Southern labor markets differ historically from other labor markets in that job opportunities are much more concentrated in specific industries and occupations. Ranking LMAs by types of industries in the area and density of population (urban versus rural LMAs), Bloomquist concludes, "Black women's employment opportunities are the most concentrated in all LMA types, but the difference from white women decreases within larger, more densely populated LMAs" (1990, 206). Because their job opportunities are limited, black women in rural South Carolina commute long distances despite their reliance on the low-skill, low-pay work concentrated in hospitality services. The LMA for many extends 150 miles or more from their homes.

Hell Hole Swamp: The Place and the Metaphor

Women riding the bus from the Hell Hole Swamp area travel from three of South Carolina's nonmetropolitan counties: Clarendon, Williamsburg, and Georgetown. Of the three, only Georgetown County is adjacent to the Myrtle Beach metropolitan area. Table 12.1 compares population characteristics of these sending counties to Horry County, site of the Myrtle Beach Grand Strand, and to South Carolina as a whole. Compared to the rest of the state, the Myrtle Beach area has more high school graduates, a larger population over age 65, a lower unemployment rate, higher per capita personal income, and a largely white population (81.0 percent). While South Carolina overall has a 29.2 percent black population for 2000, Horry County is 15.5 percent black. Clarendon and Williamsburg counties have black majorities (53.1 percent and 66.3 percent, respectively) and Georgetown County is 38.6 percent black.

The three nonmetropolitan counties have dispersed populations. Compared to 133.2 people per square mile for South Carolina overall, Williamsburg County, home of the transit system sending the bus from Hell Hole Swamp, has a sparse 39.8 persons per square mile. This is consonant with the geographically large labor market area for

Table 12.1

Population of Hell Hole Swamp, Grand Strand, and South Carolina

| Characteristics | Hell Hole Swamp Counties | | | Grand Strand | |
	Clarendon	Georgetown	Williamsburg	Horry County	South Carolina
Population, 2000	32,501	55,797	37,217	199,629	4,012,012
Pop. change, 1990–2000	14.2%	20.5%	1.1%	36.5%	15.1%
Population, age 65 + up	14.0%	15.0%	13.0%	15.0%	12.1%
Black population, 2000	53.1%	38.6%	66.3%	15.5%	29.2%
White population, 2000	44.9%	59.7%	32.7%	81.0%	67.2%
Persons per sq. mi., 2000	53.5	68.5	39.8	173.4	133.2

Source: U.S. Census Bureau 2002.

black women and indicates the obvious necessity of transportation for work. Information from the 1990 Summary Tape File 3 (STF3) Census samples for South Carolina counties, shown in table 12.2, provides a measure of a problem reported by many of the hospitality workers in this study: the lack of a private vehicle. Over a quarter of the South Carolina black households sampled in 1990 reported that they had no vehicle (2000 STF 3 data is not yet available for the counties in this study). These families had to depend on others for transportation and were therefore limited to the job destinations available.

The counties sending black women to work in the hospitality industry on the bus from Hell Hole Swamp differ from Horry County and the state on a number of indicators (table 12.2). Unemployment rates for 1999 range from 7.8 percent in Clarendon County (where many residents no longer attempt to find work) to 12.9 percent in Williamsburg County, compared to the 3.9 percent unemployment rate in Horry County. Per capita incomes for 1996 in Georgetown County are within $775 of Horry County levels, but are $6,467 less in Clarendon and $6,873 less in Williamsburg County. Home ownership rates, however, are higher in the Hell Hole Swamp counties than in Horry County (73.0 percent) or in South Carolina as a whole (72.2 percent). In Hell Hole Swamp they range from 79.1 percent to 81.4 percent.

Hell Hole Swamp is not only a specific location that sends workers to Myrtle Beach, it is also a metaphor for the rural, persistently poor, underdeveloped Black Belt counties inland from the South Carolina coast. As Duncan comments, "cheap labor was important to plantation owners in the deep South, and the social, political, and cultural consequences of maintaining it are still evident throughout the region" (1996, 111). Jensen, in his review of employment hardship and rural minorities, concludes that "there is reason to believe rural places with high minority concentrations may be particularly disadvantaged in their efforts to generate or maintain local employment" (1994, 134). Initially slaves on plantations and later sharecroppers and farm laborers, today the black population "hardly at all participates in agriculture" in the Black Belt (Wimberley, Morris, and Bachtel 1992, 80). There is compelling evidence that blacks in the rural Black Belt are

Table 12.2
Economic Characteristics of Hell Hole Swamp, Grand Strand, and South Carolina

Characteristics	Hell Hole Swamp Counties			Grand Strand	South Carolina
	Clarendon	Georgetown	Williamsburg	Horry County	
HS grads, 25 + up, 1990*	54.9%	63.9%	55.6%	74.3%	68.3%
Home ownership, 2000*	79.1%	81.4%	80.5%	73.0%	72.2%
Unemp. rate, 1999**	7.8%	8.6%	12.9%	3.9%	4.5%
Persons below poverty*	26.8%	18.6%	28.3%	14.4%	14.9%
Children below poverty*	38.2%	29.9%	39.0%	25.1%	23.0%
Median HH income*	$23,906	$30,915	$22,448	$31,312	$33,325
Per capita income, 1996**	$13,804	$19,490	$13,428	$20,271	$19,898
Black HHs w/ no vehicle, 1990***	26.0%	33.4%	34.4%	28.8%	25.6%

*U.S. Census Bureau 2002. Poverty and income measures estimated from 1997 model.
**SCESC 2001.
***Calculated from U.S. Census Bureau 1990. 2000 STF3 for these counties not yet available.

burdened by tremendous economic disadvantage (Falk and Rankin 1992; Wimberley and Morris 1997). The region is characterized by high rates of poverty, unemployment, dependence, and single parent households. Yet "ties to the land and to place are hard to break" (Falk et al. 1993, 71). A majority of the black women in Hell Hole Swamp are home owners (see table 12.2) and are unwilling to relinquish property ownership and relocate. With no jobs nearby and often no transportation of their own, these women turn to bus transportation to the beach as their only chance to earn incomes. Malveaux noted that in discussions of welfare reform "women of color are prominently highlighted, but mainly in terms of failure to work" (1999, 666). The black women of Hell Hole Swamp want to work; the failure is not theirs but instead a failure of economic restructuring and the persistence of inequality.

Hell Hole Swamp is typical of the Black Belt counties of the coastal plains and midlands region of South Carolina. These areas have experienced dramatic declines in agricultural employment—from 1980 to 1990 there was a 21.4 percent drop in agriculture, forestry, fisheries, and mining employment in Clarendon County, while Williamsburg County saw a 27.8 percent decline. Nationally, economic restructuring has meant not only declining farm work but also a loss of manufacturing jobs. And this has been true for all of South Carolina. In 1980 manufacturing was 41.9 percent of total private employment; by 1995 it had fallen to 28.2 percent, and plants continue to close. Textile mills, once a mainstay of the South Carolina economy, represented only 6.7 percent of employment by 1995. In the Hell Hole Swamp area, these changes have had less impact than elsewhere in the state, simply because there have never been textile mills offering local employment and few manufacturers have located in these counties.

Working on the Beach

The South Carolina Grand Strand stretches southwest about sixty miles from the North Carolina state line to the northern limits of the old seaport town of Georgetown, encompassing the towns of Little

River, North Myrtle Beach, Atlantic Beach, Briarcliffe Acres, Myrtle Beach, Surfside Beach, Garden City Beach, Murrells Inlet, and Pawleys Island. In the eighteenth and nineteenth centuries, wealthy South Carolina planters built their summer homes on Pawleys Island and among the small lodges and seafood markets in the fishing villages of Little River and Murrells Inlet. The 1900 construction of a railroad from the Waccamaw River at Conway, South Carolina, fifteen miles inland, provided access to what is now Myrtle Beach and made development as a summer resort possible. The area's first golf course, Pine Lakes International, was completed in the early 1920s. The first public accommodations, the small Seaside Inn, was joined in 1926 by the Ocean Forest Hotel; that same year the streets of Myrtle Beach were laid out (Edgar 1998). Between 1930 and 1950 the Grand Strand grew slowly but steadily as the oceanfront became lined with beach cottages and hotels and motels were built in the city of Myrtle Beach. Cleaning hotel rooms and cottages provided work opportunities for black women in the area and, more significant, for commuting workers.

Today an estimated 13.5 million tourists visit the Grand Strand annually (MBACC 2002). They sleep in 460 hotels with 37,000 bedrooms; resort condominiums and rental homes account for another 15,000 bedrooms (L. Taylor 2001). In 2000, Grand Strand tourism revenues were in excess of 2.25 billion dollars and an estimated 36,360 people were employed as a direct result of resort visitors (South Carolina Parks 2000). Totals for 2000 Myrtle Beach MSA employment showed 13,760 people in food preparation and serving-related occupations and 6,810 in the cleaning and maintenance of buildings and grounds (Bureau of Labor Statistics 2002). The black women of Hell Hole Swamp, working mostly in fast food jobs and housekeeping, are part of these numbers.

Since the beginnings of the Grand Strand resort, maids have played an important role. Single-family beach cottages, which once blanketed the coast, are fast disappearing from the Grand Strand and only a few remain in some isolated areas. An interesting standard feature of beach cottage architecture on the Strand was a "maid's room." Most beach cottages are built on pilings, and the main living and sleeping quarters are situated over parking areas underneath. Typically the maid's room is adjacent to the parking area and contains a bed and small bathroom, often with cold water only. Through the 1960s, middle- and upper-class families in the Carolinas brought their maids with them when they came to the beach. Although live-in domestic help was uncommon after the 1940s, private household domestics continued to cook, clean, and do laundry six or seven days a week, to wear uniforms while working, to serve as baby-sitters when parents were away for evenings or overnight, and to accompany the family on vacations. On the Grand Strand, black women were a sizable but often invisible presence. Although the texture of the resort area grew and changed, the place of black women remained essentially the same: to clean and to cook for white vacationers. In the past, visitors brought their maids with them from inland. Today, the majority of maids still travel from inland to the beach.

Through the early 1960s, low-density beach cottages prevailed on the Grand Strand, but beginning in the mid-1960s, more and more cottages were demolished to make room for large hotels and condominium complexes. In the 1960s black women in Hell Hole Swamp began to commute to jobs as maids in Myrtle Beach hotels. Describing her first hotel job at age fourteen, in 1966, a former maid told of traveling in an old Ford pickup truck:

> As I rode for an hour and a half, and sometimes two hours, I would think how blessed I was finally to be out of the hot sun of the only work I had experienced [in tobacco fields]. I heard that the rooms would be air-conditioned, and I had only been in an air-conditioned area in the stores and the houses where my mother worked as a maid. I felt that I had reached the mountaintop!
>
> It did not bother me that we were packed like sardines on the back of a canvas-covered, half broken down, air-polluting hazardous wreck. I was glad that Mrs. Catherleen was able to give me a ride. The truck had three rows on it that consisted of homemade board benches. We would sit with our backs to the side of the canvas on the two sides of the truck. Down the middle we would straddle the bench. The older women would sit in the back of the truck, giving the front part to the younger children. There was no ventilation in the truck. The younger children would hold the flap of the edge of canvas to avoid and control the air flow into the back, where everyone was seated.

. . . Wages for cleaning for a day was seven dollars. One dollar of your pay would be for ride money. We worked seven days a week. Many times after a day's work, I would sleep on the ride back home. There were other times when we were happy, mostly on payday. There would be laughter and singing all the way home until the last rider would jump down from the cab of the truck.

For the black women from Hell Hole Swamp, working on the beach has changed little over the decades, and they remain embedded in long-standing structures of inequality. Field observations and reports of students working at the beach indicate that black women are overwhelmingly concentrated in housekeeping and janitorial positions, in fast food jobs, and in cooking and cleaning positions in larger restaurants, entertainment complexes, and retail establishments. The faces that tourists see waiting tables, clerking in stores, and working behind desks in Grand Strand hotels, motels, campgrounds, and condominium complexes are white. They are the faces of high school and college students and, increasingly, white retirees.

Like the domestics of earlier eras, the uniformed black women on South Carolina's Grand Strand today work behind the doors of kitchens and laundry rooms or enter lodging, entertainment, and eating places to clean when they are unoccupied. While the details of employment have changed for black women in tourism, two overwhelming continuities characterize their work. First, the pattern of traveling to carry out personal services for white vacationers continues. Second, the work continues to be low pay, low skill, and low status. In 1992 wages on the beaches of South Carolina for housekeepers, who "supervise work activities of cleaning personnel, . . . inspect work [and] investigate complaints regarding housekeeping service and equipment" averaged $5.10 an hour (SCESC 1993, 161). Janitors and cleaners other than maids averaged $5.02 an hour, and maids and housekeeping cleaners averaged $4.90 an hour. For 1998 housekeeper wages averaged $8.51 an hour, janitors and cleaners, $7.09, and maids and housekeeping cleaners, $6.66 an hour (SCESC 2000).

The number of housekeeping staff needed, and working, varies as a function of season, day of the week, and occupancy rates. As a result of fluctuating demand, the number of women who are paid to work changes each day. In the peak summer season, most cleaning staff work seven days a week. Layoffs of housekeeping staff are frequent and are associated with declines in occupancy rates from season to season and the varying duties associated with the numbers of guests checking out versus the number staying over several nights. The average workweek of hotel maids is under 35 hours; thus the work remains part time even though it may be seven days a week. Typically, housekeeping staff clock in at 9 A.M. and clock out at 2 P.M., with a half-hour lunch break. Despite the short work schedule, workdays are long because of the two- and three-hour trips to and from work on the beach.

Grateful for the Work

Over the decades since the 1960s increasing numbers of black women have been commuting to the Grand Strand from more distant locations. In the last few years bus routes have been added from Black Belt counties that experienced layoffs and plant closings in manufacturing. Like migration streams, the flow of workers is tied to pulls from family members, friends, neighbors, and sister church members who provide information and referrals to the transportation systems and the employment opportunities. The salience of extended kinship and community networks in the lives of black women is well documented (Stack 1974; R. Taylor et al. 1990). Many of the black women working on the Grand Strand today are the third generation of their families working as housekeepers in the hotel or motel to which they commute. Following their older relatives, young women often begin traveling to the beach for summer work before they are old enough for legal employment. A Coastal student looked back and explained, "I started at the age of fourteen. And I was introduced to this line of work through one of my sisters-in-law. At that time she would take me along with her and she would train me, and then that next summer I started out on my own." Numerous workers told of starting informally and accompanying older relatives as helpers before beginning actual employment. The process of gaining employment is casual, as this hotel housekeeper remembered:

Going to work on the beach was exciting for me. All that was required was someone taking you to work one day with them when they needed extra help or when the motel was hiring new maids. There were no applications, instructions, or training involved in this type of work. One only needed to know that they were to be sure the room would be cleaned to the expectations of the boss man. The older women would show the young newcomers how to clean the toilets, make beds, vacuum and clean the kitchen when one was present.

Another respondent, whose grandmother, mother, aunts, and sisters have been working at the same oceanfront hotel for forty-eight years, began traveling to work with them each summer when she was eight. For her help, her grandmother and great-aunts would pay her a small allowance. Most of the housekeeping staff interviewed had family members working in the same hotel or motel. A majority first worked on the beach assisting their relatives without pay until they became employees themselves. Because of ties to family and community in the workplace, one former maid remembered, "Everybody would help each other as much as possible with whatever means they could."

In some cases, bus drivers or owners are also (black female) housekeeping supervisors with hiring and firing authority. Describing housekeeping arrangements in three hotels owned by the same man, one worker explained the hierarchy in this fashion:

What he does is that he has a supervisor. She's the top supervisor, and what she does is she finds his workers for him. And so everybody who works there works under her, and just wherever she needs help, at whichever hotel, she'll send you to that one. . . . She, the lady, the supervisor, she has four buses and that is used as the mode of transportation for the workers. . . . he buys the buses for her and I guess whatever comes along after that she takes care of, like taxes and stuff like that. . . . They're hers and she charges to ride her bus to the motel and you owe $3.50. She really doesn't like anybody—you know if you're working for her she wants you to ride her bus. . . . if you wanted to drive for a week or so you have to pay her for that week. Even though you drove your own car you have to, that's how she has it. You have to still pay her whether you're on that bus or not. So I guess it's a thing—she wants to prosper also.

Often the hotel owner or manager delegates all responsibility for hiring and firing to the housekeeping supervisor, who brings people from her family and community into the place she works. Controlling transportation also controls access to employment. Several hotel owners at the beach, like the owner described above, have provided buses to their housekeeping supervisors. Most, though, are owned by local transit groups, black entrepreneurs, and private individuals. Bus owners and drivers also work in hospitality positions, often in supervisory roles. The link between transportation and hiring and firing means that the maids at the beach tend to be grouped by geographical area of origin; most hotels have staff who live in the same community. The ties between homeplace and workplace are long-standing and intergenerational. A local resident who managed a large hotel at Myrtle Beach for over twenty years indicated that for almost fifty years the black women working there have come from Hell Hole Swamp. A group of five hotels owned by one family employs workers who are direct descendants of slaves and later sharecroppers on the hotel owner's ancestral plantation in the rural community from which the workers commute.

Such long associations with communities and several generations of families have led in some cases to strong paternalistic attitudes on the part of hotel and motel owners. There is evidence that at least some hotel and motel owners maintain the status quo through restrictive hiring. Asked if she had worked with whites or other minorities in housekeeping, one maid interviewed in 1992 replied, "No. To be honest he [the owner] doesn't like anyone else there working, just colored people. They have had a couple of Caucasians come in but he never allows them to work." A college senior now in her early forties looked back on her years as a maid in Myrtle Beach motels (1969–75) and commented,

> When I went into that type of service I knew that was not what I wanted to do, but during the time when I was coming up finding a summer job . . . it was hard for a black female to go into a grocery store or somewhere and find a job as cashier. So we more or less, we knew, during the summer that this is what you had to do if you wanted to make some extra money. But I always knew that when I graduated

from high school and got some type of training I would never go back there. . . . Like I said, I had a negative attitude that entire time that I worked as a maid, but it was bringing in money, income was coming in, so I did what I had to do. I felt like it was degrading to me. If I had grown up in a society where both sides were doing it, black and white, then maybe, you know, it wouldn't have affected me the way it did.

For this woman, now a college graduate and social services professional, the bus from Hell Hole Swamp was a temporary means to income and part of a process of inter- and intragenerational mobility spanning a number of years. Like the low-income single mothers studied by Dill (1998, 410), working as a hotel maid was a means to "a better life" and a necessary part of the "struggle for self-sufficiency" in a racialized, gendered environment.

Economic Restructuring and Economic Opportunity

Bolstered by strong ties of kin and community on the journey to work and in the workplace, the women riding the bus from Hell Hole Swamp are traveling the long, slow road of social mobility. A black minister whose Hell Hole Swamp church is a gathering place for bus riders said,

They have a desire. They want to work. So the people give them a job over to the beach. It's different now than when it was back yonder. People did not have jobs. They only worked in the house, only in the kitchen. Now they can get out and with that they learn a lot. By being on the job as a maid, they learn to make friends with other people, people that they have never seen. . . . I'm glad the Lord put it into some people to get something to help the people. There are a lot of people out there that need help and are not able to help themselves. Some people want to go to the beach to work and just don't have no transportation to get there. By the Lord blessing someone else with transportation, then that person was able to get on the bus and go and make a day. I feel like they feel good they can go out and work.

As Dill notes, the strategies low-income black women use to improve their lives "are contingent upon the structure of economic, political and social resources within their immediate environment" (1998, 421). Rural communities do not have a sufficient base of resources and so rural residents do without or look outside the community for work, trade, education, and other services (Wilkinson 1991). For black women in Hell Hole Swamp, community and work are joined on the long bus ride to hospitality employment. And, as one former maid, now a schoolteacher, explained, "People who worked as maids were grateful for the work. . . . . Our mothers, aunts, and everyone who came to work as a maid, had little or no other choice. Jobs and transportation were very hard to come by. There was simply no opportunities. . . . Maid work was rewarding and served its purpose well for the thousands of women who traveled from near and far for employment." For this woman, who was the first college graduate in the family, working on the beach was a means to an end and was left behind as better economic opportunities arose. For many women in Hell Hole Swamp, there is still "little or no other choice." Nevertheless, the bus offers an alternative to no work at all.

Economic restructuring at the state and national level results in gains in some types of employment. However, "the expansion of social services, health services, business services, government and selected industries . . . occurs mainly in, or very near, nonmetro cities" (Adamchak et al. 1999, 95). In more isolated, rural areas, there is little expansion and there may even be declines in low-skill services (Steinacker 1998). Further, there is regional consolidation of retail activities as large national chains drive out small independent businesses (Adamchak et al. 1999). Thus not only have Black Belt residents lost wage opportunities in farming, there are unlikely to be local alternatives when these jobs are lost.

Paradoxically, economic restructuring represents growing economic opportunity for black women in Hell Hole Swamp. The growth of tourism has meant jobs, even though the jobs are miles away. "Tourism and allied service sector activities are frequently heralded as one component within economic restructuring and regeneration" (Butler and Baum 1999, 25). Much of the work in tourism is labor intensive and relatively unskilled. Because the jobs are seasonal, they are what Nelson (1999, 26) classifies as "bad jobs" in her analysis of economic restructuring and informal work. Following their grandmothers and mothers in working as maids in the hospitality industry, the black women riding the bus are caught in the social reproduction of long-standing patterns of domestic service to whites. It is tempting and consistent with concerns about economic restructuring to focus on the negative dimensions of the social capital, journeys to work, and employment conditions they experience. Yet in a larger framework of survival strategies (Dill 1998; Nelson 1999) and in their embracing the only available opportunity for employment, their lives exemplify commitment to social mobility, concerted community effort, and determination to earn wages. The black women in the hospitality industry who ride the bus from Hell Hole Swamp are evidence of the desire for self-sufficiency, the need for good jobs, and, perhaps more important in rural areas, the necessity of public transportation systems to give people access to work. Their lives are a testament to the power of community networks in the face of relentless obstacles.

References

Adamchak, D. J., L. E. Bloomquist, K. Bausman, and R. Qureshi. 1999. "Consequences of Population Change for Retail/Wholesale Sector Employment in the Nonmetropolitan Great Plains: 1950–1996." *Rural Sociology* 64:92–112.

Bloomquist, L. E. 1990. "Local Labor Market Characteristics and the Occupational Concentration of Different Sociodemographic Groups." *Rural Sociology* 55:199–213.

Butler, R. W., and T. Baum. 1999. "The Tourism Potential of the Peace Dividend." *Journal of Travel Research* 38:24–29.

Dill, B. T. 1998. "A Better Life for Me and My Children: Low-Income Single Mothers' Struggle for Self-Sufficiency in the Rural South." *Journal of Comparative Family Studies* 29:419–28.

Duncan, C. M. 1996. "Understanding Persistent Poverty: Social Class Context in Rural Communities." *Rural Sociology* 61:103–24.

Edgar, W. 1998. *South Carolina: A History.* Columbia: University of South Carolina Press.

Falk, W. W., and B. H. Rankin. 1992. "The Cost of Being Black in the Black Belt." *Social Problems* 39:299–313.

Falk, W. W., C. R. Talley, B. H. Rankin, K. Little. 1993. "Life in the Forgotten South: The Black Belt." In *Forgotten Places: Uneven Development in Rural America,* ed. T. A. Lyson and W. W. Falk, 53–75. Lawrence: University Press of Kansas.

Farrar, A. L., and L. Gyant. 1998. "African-American Women, Family, and Hospitality Work." *Marriage and Family Review* 28:125–41.

Garkovich, L. 1982. "Variations in Nonmetro Patterns of Commuting to Work." *Rural Sociology* 47:529–43.

Jensen, L. 1994. "Employment Hardship and Rural Minorities: Theory, Research, and Policy." *Review of Black Political Economy* 22 (special issue: Blacks in Rural America): 125–45.

Lyson, T. A., and W. W. Falk, eds. 1993. *Forgotten Places: Uneven Development in Rural America.* Lawrence: University Press of Kansas.

Malveaux, J. 1999. "Women of Color in the Labor Market." *Quarterly Review of Economics and Finance* 39:663–78.

McLafferty, S., and V. Preston. 1991. "Gender, Race, and Commuting among Service Sector Workers." *Professional Geographer* 43:1–15.

Myrtle Beach Area Chamber of Commerce (MBACC). 2002. "Myrtle Beach Area Statistics." <www.myrtlebeachinfo.com/chamber/stats/index.htm>, retrieved April 19, 2002.

Naples, N., with C. Sachs. 2000. "Standpoint Epistemology and the Uses of Self-Reflection in Feminist Ethnography: Lessons for Rural Sociology." *Rural Sociology* 65:194–214.

Ong, P., and E. Blumenberg. 1998. "Job Access, Commute and Travel Burden among Welfare Recipients." *Urban Studies* 35 (1): 77(17). <http://web5.infotrac.galegroup.com>, retrieved July 9, 2000.

Shemanski, F. 1984. *A Guide to Fairs and Festivals in the United States.* West Port, Conn.: Greenwood Press.

South Carolina Department of Parks, Recreation, and Tourism. 2000. "Direct Impact of Tourism by County 2000." <www.discoversouthcarolina.com/gir/girresearchstatsannual.asp>, retrieved April 19, 2002.

South Carolina Employment Security Commission (SCESC). 1993. South Carolina Annual Labor Market Report 1992. Columbia: SCESC Labor Market Information Division.

————. 2000. "Labor Market Information, Occupational Employment Statistics Program (OES)." <www.sces.org/pears/>, retrieved September 14, 2000.

————. 2001. "Labor Market Information." <http://www.ors.state.scu.us/abstract_99/chap8/emp19.htm>, retrieved April 19, 2000.

Stack, C. 1974. *All Our Kin.* New York: Harper and Row.

Steinacker, A. 1998. "Economic Restructuring of Cities, Suburbs, and Nonmetropolitan Areas, 1977–1992." *Urban Affairs Review* 34:212–29. <http://web5.infotrac.galegroup.com>, retrieved November 29, 2000.

Taylor, B. D., and P. M. Ong. 1995. "Spatial Mismatch or Automobile Mismatch? An Examination of Race, Residence and Commuting in U.S. Metropolitan Areas." *Urban Studies* 32:1453–73.

Taylor, L. D. 2001. "Myrtle Beach Accommodations Study." Center for Resort Tourism, E. Craig Wall Jr. College of Business Administration, Coastal Carolina University, Conway, South Carolina. Unpublished research.

Taylor, R. J., L. Chatters, M. B. Tucker, E. Lewis. 1990. "Developments in Research on Black Families: A *Decade Review*." Journal of Marriage and the Family 52:993–1014.

United States. Bureau of the Census. 1990. *Census of Population and Housing.* Census Detailed Tables, Sample Data (STF3). <http://factfinder. census.gov/>, retrieved September 26, 2000.

————. 2002. "State and City Quick Facts." <http://quickfacts.census.gov/qfd/states/45/>, retrieved March 16, 2002.

United States. Bureau of Labor Statistics. 2002. *2000 Metropolitan Area Occupational Employment and Wage Estimates. Myrtle Beach, SC MSA.* <www.bls.gov/oes/2000/oes_5330.htm>, retrieved May 10, 2002.

United States. Equal Employment Opportunity Commission (EEOC). 1991. *Job Patterns for Minorities and Women in Private Industry 1990.* Washington, D.C.: Government Printing Office.

————. 2001. *Job Patterns for Minorities and Women in Private Industry, 2000.* <www.eeoc.gov/stats/jobpat/2000/>, r etrieved April 14, 2002.

Washington, B. 1994. "Business Development in Depressed Rural Counties. (South Carolina Institute on Poverty and Deprivation)." Paper presented at the annual meeting of the Southern Sociological Society, Raleigh, April 8.

White, M. J. 1988. "Sex Differences in Urban Commuting Patterns." *American Economic Review* 76:368–72.

Wilkinson, K. P. 1991. *The Community in Rural America*. The Rural Sociological Society. Classic Studies in Rural Sociology. Madison, Wis.: Social Ecology Press, 1999.

Wimberley, R. C., and L. V. Morris. 1997. *The Southern Black Belt: A National Perspective*. Lexington, Ky.: TVA Rural Studies.

Wimberley, R. C., L. V. Morris, and D. C. Bachtel. 1992. "New Developments in the Black Belt: Dependency and Life Conditions." In *New Directions in Local and Rural Development*, ed. N. Baharanyi, R. Zabawa, and W. Hill, 76–84. Tuskegee, Ala.: Tuskegee University.

Woody, B. 1989. "Black Women in the Emerging Services Economy." *Sex Roles* 21:45–67.

13

Stretched to Their Limits

Rural Nonfarm Mothers and the "New" Rural Economy

Cynthia Struthers and Janet Bokemeier

RURAL FAMILIES ARE challenged by changes associated with the restructuring of the rural economy. Rural nonfarm mothers, the focus of this study, actively balance the demands of the labor market and their responsibilities for much of the day-to-day activities of family life. Their patterns of balancing work and life reflect ideological preferences regarding parenting, employment, childcare, and gender roles.

The impact of economic restructuring on rural places cannot be taken out of the larger context of social, economic, and political disadvantage experienced by rural regions compared to urban places in the United States (Lyson and Falk 1993). Rural places have consistently lagged behind urban places on a number of economic and social indicators (Brown and Warner 1991). Still, rural people and places continue to survive even if they fail to thrive (Falk 2000).

The households in this study rely on an economic mix of service and manufacturing jobs. Our sample's demographic characteristics are similar to those in other rural counties in the Midwest. The respondents are white, non-Hispanic, married, and predominately working class. The study site is a nonmetropolitan county in Michigan. Many people in the research county commute to an urban area to work but the county is not adjacent to a Metropolitan Statistical Area.

The Restructured Rural Economy, Changing Families, and Ways of Life

A number of concurrent trends make the study of rural nonfarm family life timely.

TREND 1: THE RESTRUCTURING OF THE ECONOMY

Restructuring has had a powerful impact on rural places both in the kind of work that is done and the gender distribution of the labor market. Agricultural productivity has increased while the number of farms and farm families has decreased. Rural nonfarm families are an increased proportion of rural residents. Rural counties that previously had agriculturally dependent economies have become more economically diverse. Within the manufacturing sector, jobs have changed from higher-paying skilled jobs to lower-paying unskilled jobs (Flora et al. 1992). As manufacturing jobs have changed, women have entered these newer, less secure positions and are hired at lower wages than men. In addition, the service sector has expanded in predominately female fields, such as the hospitality and health industries (Amott 1993). These industries are growing in those rural counties with recreation or retirement amenities. However, rural counties dependent on service industries are more economically and socially distressed than farm-dependent counties (Albrecht 1998).

TREND 2: THE INCREASED EMPLOYMENT OF RURAL MARRIED WOMEN WITH YOUNG CHILDREN

Historically, rural married women with young children were unlikely to enter or remain in the labor market because of the difficulty of combining paid employment with family responsibilities (Kessler-Harris 1982; Tilly and Scott 1989). Currently, married women with young children in both rural and urban places are entering the labor market in increased numbers (Ollenburger, Grana, and Moore 1989). Some rural women (e.g., farm women) always engaged in a range of productive and reproductive activities, but their productive contributions were often overlooked (Rosenfeld 1985; Sachs 1983). Today, women's paid employment is usually necessary to maintain a household. Women across social classes are increasingly likely to work outside the home. Previously the productive labor of rural women was hidden; it is now increasingly visible.

TREND 3: CHANGES IN RURAL PATTERNS OF MARRIAGE AND FAMILY

Rural and urban household composition has changed over time, but rural families are still more likely to be white, married, and older than urban households (Dolbeare and Strauss 1997). Though divorce rates in the United States have stabilized, they remain high. It is estimated that half of all children will spend some time in a single-family home (Zill and Nord 1994). Though marriage remains the most common marital status among rural households, the number of single-parent families is growing and rural family arrangements are increasingly similar to urban households (Lichter and Eggebeen 1992). Marital status and family size can encourage or restrain participation in the labor market but so too might rural residence.

Restructuring has increased the likelihood that married women will enter the labor market even though women retain primary responsibility for home and family (Hochschild and Machung 1992). Women's responsibilities for child and family care are implicitly and explicitly reinforced in some rural economic development strategies, suggesting that there has been little change in rural places in the emphasis placed on the appropriate roles for women (Gringeri 1994). The question is not whether women will be workers or mothers, but how they reconcile tension between these roles.

Labor market factors alone do not shape people's perceptions of the place in which they live. Even as the nonfarm population increases, rural people's relationship to the land, nature, and self-provisioning activities remains strong and are applied to all rural residents (Struthers and Bokemeier 2000). Overall there is a tendency to ignore certain realities of rural life, such as the economic disadvantage that rural people and places face (see Willits and Luloff 1995). Positive images of rural places remain quite powerful and rural residents still continue to adhere to an agrarian ideology even as rural family structure and rural economies change (Bell 1992; Naples 1994).

Beliefs about rural living as a more wholesome environment for families and as a desirable alternative to urban life can influence how women understand their roles as mothers and workers. Kathleen Gerson (1985) used a typological approach to analyze and categorize how urban women came to define themselves as mothers or as competent paid workers. She found that where women end up is often the result of unexpected satisfaction or dissatisfaction with the actual experience of having and raising children or working. But whether women remained in the role they had "planned" for themselves either as mothers or workers were ultimately determined by factors such as marital instability, frustrated work aspirations, or unexpected job advancement and rewards or emotional fulfillment. The typological approach can help us understand how women make sense of their roles at home and in the labor market. We differ from Gerson in that we use a sample of rural women. We also differ from Gerson in that not having children did not appear to be a conscious option for the women we interviewed, suggesting that they start at a different psychological and physical place than women in the Gerson study. Working outside the home may be optional but having children appears to be less so for women in rural places.

Rural areas persist and rural families get by. In this study, we will examine how and why this is possible. We examine not only women's labor market experiences but also their consciousness of place and family responsibilities. Being stretched to one's limits but able to support one's family is what separates rural families from other families. Comments made by the rural Michigan women we interviewed often reflect the value placed on marriage and hard work.

Methods and Sample

TELEPHONE SURVEY AND CENSUS DATA

We used several methods to collect our data. Our goals were to develop a comprehensive case study of the county and to describe the complexity of rural life for families with elementary-age children. The project involved a random sample of county residents using random digital-dialing telephone sampling methods ($N = 300$). County residents were asked a broad range of questions about their household and financial well-being, their perceptions of the county, the amenities and services available to them, and their views on men's and women's roles at work and home.

The county was originally settled in the mid-1800s, when the lumber industry expanded southward across the state. Agriculture developed after the forest was cleared, but today only 4 percent of the working population over the age of sixteen works in agriculture, forestry, or fisheries. The economy consists of some light manufacturing and service jobs.

This county would not be considered especially remote when compared to other rural counties in Michigan. It has one urban place, the county seat, with a population of 12,000 full-time residents. Although the county did grow in population from 38,000 in 1990 to 40,553 in 2000, it remains classified as a nonmetropolitan county because the total population is less than 50,000. A major interstate highway runs north and south through the county, linking residents to a highly urbanized area in the southwest part of the state. Many of the female respondents we interviewed indicated that they or their spouses or partners drive from forty-five to sixty minutes to get to work.

One distinct feature of the county is the presence of a regional state university. It is the largest employer in the county, with over

1,600 workers. But the university has been struggling to maintain a viable educational mission and has had a difficult time securing consistent leadership. Service jobs are prevalent on and around campus. Though a growing service economy has increased the number of jobs available, it has not reduced the amount of poverty in the area.

The county is relatively poor when compared to Michigan as a whole. County residents lag behind state residents on key economic indicators. Average incomes of families with children, married couples, and female-headed households were lower in the county and poverty rates were higher than in the state as a whole. At the same time, county residents have higher rates of education, dropout rates are lower, and there are fewer births to teens with less than high school education than in the state. Rather than growing or slipping further into poverty, this county appears to be stagnating.

The telephone survey data are analyzed to establish the general, defining ideologies of the rural context within which rural mothers create household strategies and personal beliefs and preferences. This exploratory analysis will show that rural residence is characterized by conflicting themes regarding women and mothering. A strong traditional view of motherhood and family type shapes rural attitudes. Respondents question nonfamilial childcare, even though intense pressure is placed on rural women to economically provide for themselves and their children. Indeed, rural places offer mothers few alternatives to their own work efforts and limited resources for support of their children. Furthermore, rural places have few childcare and transportation alternatives.

FACE-TO-FACE INTERVIEWS

In addition to the telephone survey, we constructed a purposive sample of families from the rural school district. Households were chosen from a list of second- and third-graders. Each household had at least one child who was eight to ten years old. This child became the target child; we asked mothers questions around the life of the child and about their employment and family decisions. During the fall and winter of 1995–96, thirty households participated in intensive face-to-face interviews and completed a self-administered question-naire. Only mothers' comments are used in this analysis (N = 29).[1] For the face-to-face interviews, mothers were asked about the charac-teristics of their jobs and family, aspects of their children's lives, and their household's economic situation.

Most respondents in the telephone survey and the face-to-face in-terviews live in married couple households. However, important varia-tion exists among the twenty-nine women we interviewed: six of the twenty-nine mothers were divorced or separated at the time of the in-terview though two were living with a boyfriend, and eight of the married mothers are in second marriages. Mothers in the intensive-interview sample said they had been married from less than a year to more than twenty years.

The job opportunities currently available to county residents are in service or manufacturing industries. Among the women inter-viewed face to face, even those with college educations work at jobs in health care or the schools, fields traditionally dominated by women. Local manufacturing jobs pay less than similar jobs in nearby urban-ized counties. So, if possible, women with less than a high school education work out of county in manufacturing jobs. Among the women that participated in intensive interviews, most were working for hourly wages rather than in salaried positions. Most husbands and fathers in the interview households worked for hourly wages as well.

Twenty-five thousand dollars per year was the approximate me-dian income for county residents. Among the intensive-interview families, half the households with incomes less than the median had only one wage earner. Individual and household characteristics deter-mined whether mothers worked outside the home. Of the eleven stay-at-home mothers in the intensive-interview families, half had babies or preschool children at home while the others had physical or less tangible disabilities that kept them out of the labor market. Gen-erally, potential wages have to be greater than the costs associated with employment for these rural mothers to be employed. Childcare and transportation are not only costly for residents but also difficult to find. In our intensive-interview sample, when the target child's mother was disabled, the household was dependent on a sole male wage earner. Although families with disabled adults are prevalent among the face-to-face-interview sample (17 percent), very little is known about the economic strategies of rural households with disabled adults.

The intensive personal interviews allow us to examine the employment patterns of mothers with children at home and how they articulate the work ethic and their sense of responsibility for their children. Rural mothers stretch their own physical and emotional resources to provide for their children. The interviews are the basis for identifying the different patterns by which rural mothers develop their beliefs about work and home commitment.

Analysis

WHAT COUNTY RESIDENTS BELIEVE

In the telephone survey, county residents were asked questions relating to their attitudes on family and work responsibility, reasons why women work, and the availability of quality care and whether childcare is harmful. Three statements asked residents about appropriate gender roles and the distribution of work and family responsibility. When asked whether "it is much better for everyone if the man earns the main income and the woman takes care of the home and family," 29 percent of county residents strongly agreed with the statement and 25 percent somewhat agreed. When asked if "in today's world, women have as much responsibility as men to provide financially for their family," 54 percent strongly agreed with the statement and 32 percent somewhat agreed. When asked if "both husband and wife work full time, they should share household tasks equally," 85 percent strongly agreed and 11 percent somewhat agreed. Though the support is not overwhelming, many respondents still support the male breadwinner/stay-at-home mother ideology even as they believe women have an increased responsibility to provide for their children. It is important to note that though there is overwhelming agreement that housework should be shared when husbands and wives both work within this sample, in reality there is little parity in actual behavior.

When asked whether residents thought the main reason most women work outside the home is because they need the money to support their families or for personal satisfaction, two-thirds of the sample believed it was because their families needed the money. Only 11 percent said women worked solely for personal satisfaction, though 22 percent believe women work for both economic and personal reasons. The strongest message we can garner from these responses is that women are expected to and need to provide financially for their families. But these beliefs are difficult to reconcile with the persistence of the breadwinner ideology. In the absence of a breadwinning husband or father, women are expected to be both mother and breadwinner.

County residents were far more divided in opinions about whether quality day care is available and whether young children are harmed by nonfamilial care. When asked if "there is plenty of quality day care for children in the county," 24 percent strongly agreed and 28 percent somewhat agreed. Twenty-two percent somewhat disagreed with the statement and 18 percent strongly disagreed. When asked "if children under three years old are not harmed by all day childcare in a licensed center," only 15 percent strongly agreed, 28 percent somewhat agreed, 28 percent somewhat disagreed, and 22 percent strongly disagreed.

Because we are interested in the interrelationship between the characteristics of households and opinions about the availability and impact of day care, we constructed a variable that combined the number of incomes that respondents reported (either 0, 1, or 2) with the number of adults present in the household. This allowed us to identify households with no employed adults, single-earner households with one or two adults, and two-earner, two-adult households. We found that households with no income from employment were most likely to agree with the statement about the availability of quality care. Those most likely to disagree were those in two-income, two-adult households. One-income households were evenly split between agreeing and disagreeing. One-income, one-adult households were most likely to disagree that young children are not harmed by all day care. Though we cannot completely explain this result, it is possible that one-income, one-adult households feel they have little option but to use what care is available even if they are not convinced their children are not harmed by it. There is a weak but positive correlation between those that agree women should provide for their families and those that feel day care is harmless. The correlation analyses found that those who agree that men should be the main provider and women should care for the family are more likely to think childcare is harmful for children.

A tension exists between the economics of rural places and the realities of family life that rural mothers face. Regardless of how women feel about working or staying at home, they face increased pressure to work outside the home.

Typology of Patterns of Work and Life among Rural Mothers

Data from the intensive face-to-face survey and a self-administered questionnaire allowed us to construct a typology of work and life patterns for the mothers we interviewed. Other typologies have been offered to account for women's decisions about work and family. Gerson (1985) illustrates how women's early choices about work or family must be reconciled to their current commitment in time and energy to family or employment. A typology of men's involvement in career and family can be found in Gerson (1993). The underlying premise of Gerson's work is that even though women and men plan to commit themselves to a career or family their opportunities may be constrained, and that leads them to commitment to the opposite.

The typology we present expands this work by examining how rural restructuring constrains or encourages a commitment to the labor market or home. One factor that surfaced regarding commitment to work or home was the presence of a disability. The typology emerged as we contrasted women's accounts of how they perceive their choices related to the work-life balance through the early stages of marriage and childbearing. We asked them to describe their work and family commitment around the life of the target child (eight to ten years old). The patterns reflect what mothers told us about their work history before and after the birth of the target child, the types of jobs they had held, their total household income, and their education and skills.

Six different work-life patterns emerge among the rural mothers we interviewed. We describe women with different work-life patterns as either: (1) provider mothers, (2) modern traditionalists, (3) disjointed workers, (4) nouveau provider mothers, (5) hearth-committed by choice, or (6) hearth-committed by circumstances (table 13.1). The first four work-life patterns involve employment outside the home that is more or less stable and involves varying use of childcare. The other two categories are women who express strong desires and preferences to devote their time and effort to home-related work. These work-life patterns reflect not only the cultural messages women receive but also the opportunities available to them in the rural labor market.

PROVIDER MOTHERS

The provider mother pattern is one of the most common and accounts for about a quarter of the mothers we interviewed. These mothers have a stable work pattern and marriages of long duration similar to Rubin's settled-living working-class households (1992). Provider mothers describe a continuous work history through their adult years. They worked before the birth of the target child and returned to work after a very brief period following the birth. Two-thirds of provider mothers had working mothers themselves. Provider mothers and their husbands labor in blue-collar occupations and their combined income keeps their family at or above the county median of $25,000. Provider mothers describe wage labor as an extension of their responsibility as mothers. Provider mothers are keenly aware of their responsibility to provide for their families and see their financial contribution as necessary for a decent standard of living. They have arranged for safe and dependable childcare from the time their children were infants. Their households do not live

Table 13.1

Selected Household Characteristics of Families in Face-to-Face Interviews and Employment/Home Category

Family #	Marital Status	Household Size	Employment Status	Reported Household Income
Provider moms				
5	remarried	4	full-time	$ 20–25,000
6	married	5	full-time	40–45,000
7	married	4	full-time	25–30,000
11	married	4	full-time	20–25,000
14	divorced*	6	full-time	10–15,000
15	married	4	full-time	35–40,000
29	divorced	3	full-time	10–15,000
30	married	4	full-time	45,000 +
Modern traditionalists				
1	married	4	part-time	45,000 +
9	married	4	part-time	35–40,000
10	married	4	part-time	45,000 +
20	married	5	full-time	45,000 +
23	remarried	6	part-time	45,000 +
Disjointed worker moms				
13	divorced	4	full-time	10–15,000
17	married	6	full-time	30–35,000
25	divorced	5**	full-time	10–15,000
Nouveau provider moms				
2	married	6	unemployed	30–35,000
18	married	4	part-time	20–25,000
22	remarried	3	full-time	30–35,000
Hearth-committed mothers				
By choice				
4	remarried	5	unemployed	40–45,000
8	remarried	4	unemployed	20–25,000
21	remarried	6	unemployed	15–20,000
24	married	6	unemployed	15–20,000
26	divorced*	6	unemployed	25–30,000
By circumstances				
12	divorced	4	unemployed	10–15,000
16	remarried	4	unemployed	10–15,000
19	remarried	5	unemployed	25–30,000
27	married	11**	unemployed	15–20,000
28	married	3	unemployed	20–25,000

* Unmarried-couple household.
** Multiple-family households.
Source: U.S. Census Bureau 2002.

extravagantly, but achieve a balance between needs and wants. Three-fourths of provider mothers are in first marriages of long duration and they mentioned this as a source of pride. Only two households in this group had more than two children.

What distinguishes this category from the others is the consistent importance of their income to the household. Remaining in the labor market has given provider mothers steady household incomes. Though their jobs in factories and services are not exceptionally satisfying, they are committed to working because of the lifestyle they help provide. They avoid overtime work because they want to be home with their families in the evenings and on weekends. Provider mothers are devoted to their children and feel an intense responsibility for them.

MODERN TRADITIONALISTS

Another fairly prevalent work-life pattern we describe as the modern traditionalists. With industrialization and urbanization, women entered the labor market and remained until they married. A more recent pattern is for women to enter or reenter the labor market once their children have entered school. Modern traditionalist mothers work before having their children but stay home throughout the childbearing stage. They do not return to the labor market until their youngest child has begun school. Perhaps the most important factor related to this pattern is the difficulty the mothers had finding childcare that they considered safe and dependable. Also, modern traditionalist mothers believe their presence at home is more important than the income they would generate if employed. Modern traditionalists describe being home as easier than constantly arranging childcare. These mothers have more education on average than the rest of the sample, as do their husbands. Modern traditionalists know they can find high-paying jobs once they reenter the labor market, and did report reentering the labor market on their own terms.

What distinguishes the modern traditionalists from the provider mothers is social class. With more education and income, working part-time is a viable option for these mothers and allows them time to be more involved in their children's school and extracurricular activities. Like the provider moms, modern traditionalists were in first marriages of long duration and had only two children, generally. The modern traditionalist mothers report the highest average household income of all women interviewed.

NOUVEAU PROVIDER MOTHERS

Like modern traditionalists, nouveau provider mothers delay employment and take first jobs only after their target child has started school. Unlike the modern traditionalists, nouveau provider women planned to be stay-at-home mothers, but marital instability and economic need have forced them to enter the labor market. Two of the nouveau provider mothers have been married less than five years, indicating that their target child had been born before marriage or within a previous marriage. Marital instability has forced nouveau provider mothers to invest in additional training and to find jobs in order to provide for their children. Currently, their income makes an important contribution to the household. One mother mentioned that she was making more money than she ever could have imagined. Though she is concerned about leaving her daughter in day care, she is quite proud of her ability to financially provide for her. Nouveau provider mothers are more ambivalent about working outside the home than mothers in the first two groups. Provider mothers and modern traditionalists represent a largely stable work and family pattern, while nouveau provider mothers have more recently adopted employment and marriage patterns that could have a long-term stabilizing effect.

DISJOINTED WORKERS

This pattern includes mothers whose work histories can best be described as disrupted. Disjointed worker mothers had children during lengthy periods of unemployment. None of them have graduated from high school and consequently they have extremely limited job opportunities. Disjointed workers have worked at a series of low-wage and low-skill jobs and lack economic security or confidence.

Factory jobs are the only available jobs that pay some semblance of a living wage. In our sample, disjointed worker mothers commute to work outside the county.

Disjointed worker mothers are the sole support of their families because they are either divorced or married with an unemployed husband. The advantage of having an unemployed husband is that it saves the family from having to purchase childcare. One mother in this category is currently living with her mother and stepfather, who help her with childcare and living expenses. The women with disrupted work histories have quite precarious economic and family situations. All are living in households with incomes less than $25,000. Their interviews suggest that these women had faced economic hardship in their family of origin. They were very young, even still in high school, when they had their first child. All feel responsible for providing for their children but they struggle daily to make ends meet. They work hard in what they describe as dead-end jobs. These mothers, though very dependent on the labor market, suffer more discord about working than women in the provider group who also work in factories.

HEARTH-COMMITTED MOTHERS

The most prevalent work-life pattern among the intensive-interview sample is stay-at-home mothers or what we term hearth-committed. About one third of the mothers interviewed were not employed and indicated a preference for being in the home full-time. During the face-to-face interviews, we found they had very different reasons for being home full-time. All hearth-committed mothers had some work experience—in factories, babysitting, home sales, or various casual or day labor jobs; only one mother had never worked outside the home. Hearth-committed mothers do not speak of any sustained commitment to the labor market before having the target child. Among the hearth-committed mothers, about half are home by "choice" while others are home by circumstances.

Hearth-committed moms who are home by choice have husbands who work in factories or construction. Several were married previously.

Once remarried, their new husbands agreed that they should stay home full-time to raise the children and care for the home. Being able to stay home may be a condition under which these women chose to remarry. Other studies report that women who were dissatisfied about working in a previous marriage seek partners who allow them to remain at home (Pyke 1994).

All of the mothers committed to the hearth by choice have three or more children. They often said they could not afford to take a job because childcare, transportation, and a work wardrobe would cancel out their wages. As long as their husbands can provide for them, they do not expect to enter the labor market. The jobs these mothers have held were difficult to combine with family life. Their comments indicate that when they had worked, the options available to them were not pleasant. Many worked a shift different from their partners to reduce the need for childcare and most said they had worked "midnights." Rather than continuing with bad work arrangements, they opted to commit to full-time motherhood. Most households in the choice group have incomes below $25,000. Two mothers in this category no longer have preschool-age children at home that prevent them from working. The others could potentially enter the labor force, though two of these mothers have less than a high school education. Mothers with the lowest levels of education face the poorest working conditions. Though we might question whether these mothers truly have a choice—whether to stay home, given their family and prior work experiences—they resolve any ambivalence they feel by saying this was what they chose.

Some mothers committed to the hearth by circumstances have physical or developmental problems that prevent them from working outside the home on a regular basis. Four of the mothers in this group have physical conditions that prevent them from working full-time. One mother said she had had surgery for carpal tunnel syndrome and was unable to find factory work because of it. She had gotten some additional training in medical record keeping but still could not find a job and was advised to take courses in medical transcription. Currently she was unemployed and looking for work but could not afford to have a telephone. Three mothers have chronic physical conditions that keep them out of the labor market. This category of women would have a difficult time supporting their children through paid employment, but more important, employment is unavailable to them. Only one household in this category has an income above $25,000.

Being remarried is the most common marital status for all hearth-committed mothers. Those with smaller families were older mothers that had been remarried for ten or more years, and longer marriages provide important stability even though some of these mothers have very low incomes. Hearth-committed mothers describe raising children as their job. This suggests they are influenced by the emphasis being placed on mothers to work outside the home. A mother hearth-committed by circumstances described raising her daughter as her "purpose in life." This mother best articulates the pressures that rural women feel to work and yet raise their children: "I have been really contented since Lilly moved in and I have the pleasures and agonies to raise her and being here and taking a whole different look because when I was working at my mom's, even though I was only there four to five hours a day because of my physical problems, I had a hard time keeping up with things at home. . . . It took me a long time to figure out my purpose—why can't I work like other women? Since Lilly came along it's all come together."

Three work-life patterns existed among grandmothers of the target child. Just less than a third had been home full-time. Of those who worked outside the home, about half did not start working until their daughters entered junior high or high school. Two important generational distinctions existed between grandmothers and their working daughters. A number of grandmothers entered the labor market only once their daughters were older and well established in school. The mothers we interviewed entered the labor market when their children were younger and they worked before the birth of their children. Even more salient to the younger mothers was an experience of downward mobility that was most keenly felt by those who had a stay-at-home mother and provider father. Their own family could not conform to this pattern because they "had" to work outside home and, for some in two-earner households, they could not provide their children with the economic security they felt they needed. There are few jobs that allow rural women to be the sole support of their children and stagnant and lower wages mean it is often difficult for rural dual-earner households to obtain a middle-class standard of living.

"New" Patterns of Work and Family, or a Rural Trade-Off?

By examining the concrete aspects of women's daily lives, we see how they resolve the tensions they face in their lives. Women speak about their struggles to balance their obligations to provide economically for their children, with their preferences either to stay at home to care full-time for their families or to work outside the home in jobs that contribute to a stable family income and personal satisfaction. Their preferences regarding employment, ideal childcare arrangements, and marriage are mixed, much like those identified by the county survey. Clearly some women adhere to traditional family and gender norms of "male breadwinner and female homemaker." Some question the quality of childcare available to them or are concerned about children's well-being when in childcare (or both). Others believe women can and should be employed while holding family and childcare as important. The skills and experiences women bring to the rural labor market often do not fit with what the labor market can offer them. This issue of fit influences rural mothers' patterns of work and home commitment.

We find that rural nonfarm mothers distance themselves from urban women by emphasizing their role as mothers rather than as working women. Part of this may rest in long-held but erroneous beliefs about the traditional roles of rural women. Today few rural families live on farms and even fewer depend solely on farm income for survival. Rather rural households, whether farm or nonfarm, are dual-earner households and depend on jobs off the farm. Still, even when women make essential, stable contributions to their household incomes, emphasis remains on their responsibilities for family. These factors seem to guarantee a status for women as secondary earners.

For provider mothers, working outside the home is necessary in order to meet the basic needs of their children. Like farm women before them, these mothers do not distinguish where family work or paid employment begins or ends (Rosenfeld 1985). Provider mothers describe themselves as good and hard workers on the job and see their economic responsibilities as part of being a good mother. One stated, "My family always comes first. I'd like to go back to school. . . . But as far as being able to go back now, I can't because I can't afford it. I can't take a part-time job and go to school because I need a full-time job."

They are keenly aware that they are expected to assume full responsibility for their children. Working hard is consistent with their family expectations and is also a condition of many of the employment opportunities available to them. They consistently reconcile the demands of their families with that of the rural labor market. One provider mother claimed, "I did go do some factory work for a while through a temp agency and . . . I got home at a nice time at 3:30 in the afternoon [so] I was home before they got home. I loved that. . . . But it didn't really work. They cut back now and it was just temporary, and then I found a job up here in Baldwin and I'm now a purchasing assistant. Which I love, being in the office but not all the clerical stuff. But the hours are 7:30 to 5:00 and it is thirty-three miles from here." Another said, "I want to do more at work but my job is limited. There really isn't any chance for advancement unless I get some kind of college degree in banking."

Modern traditionalists are able to reconcile a desire for rural residence with the comforts of a more urban orientation. They are often stretched to their limits in time and energy, but seldom are they financially wanting. Rather than merely balancing wants and needs, these families are able to access what they want. New-traditionalists stress their roles as wives and mothers, but they also have more resources with which to shape their work and family life. One said, "I'm proud of being able to juggle everything that goes on. [My husband] really doesn't have to worry about having clean clothes in his closet; they are usually there. He doesn't have to ask. Or is dinner on or is there food in the house or are the kids clean or gone to the doctor. I seem to handle that."

What the patterns of women's work and life reveal are not only the opportunities available to them but also a willingness to work hard to preserve a way of life. Most mothers mentioned that they were willing to forego urban amenities in order to give their children a more wholesome and natural environment. A nouveau provider mom offered, "I think kids need a place to run, and there are places they can go, you know, by the house where there is woods and experiences that they can develop that way. We're close enough to town where we can get things we need and don't have to drive forever. There's not all [the] hassle of living in the city. . . . We have space from our house to the neighbor's house where we aren't constantly being bothered by other people . . . we have our privacy." And a provider mother said, "The good part is that children have more freedom here [from] the hustle and bustle. It's not so stressful; there are some bad points because you have to go far for everything, but we like being out in the country. There are more pluses than minuses."

Stay-at-home mothers can justify their preference for rural residence in ways that fit their version of the agrarian way of life. Having a working husband allows them to reject the view that women have to work outside the home to be involved in necessary work. They adopt a language of work to describe raising children. A mother committed to the hearth by choice stated, "My husband was just saying last night, I work more than my girlfriend does and she works forty-plus hours a week. But because I do the cooking, the cleaning, and the laundry and everything else, he says, You run more than she does. I said, Yeah, the only thing is, she gets paid and I don't, but I've got my family around me. Being home, raising my kid, that's the ideal job." Because the local labor market pays them poorly, there are times in the family life cycle that working outside the home simply does not make economic sense.

At issue though is what happens in the absence of a male provider. Stay-at-home mothers have little legitimacy without a provider husband since mothers are increasingly expected to financially provide for their children. With few resources available to them in rural places, single-parent families have little with which to provide for themselves or their children. Though marriage may no longer provide a long-term survival strategy, it is very important for short-term financial survival. Nouveau provider mothers and disjointed worker mothers have experienced this harsh economic reality. Women with less than a high school diploma and those who are the sole support of a family are most vulnerable to the whims of the labor market, and they have little time or energy to invest in more education or training.

An irony of rural residence is that women who have a high school education and some college increase their incomes only marginally when they change jobs. Changing jobs is a strategy used to better coordinate work and family responsibilities. Rural mothers are stretched thin trying to support their families on low wages with no chance of advancement. All the working mothers we interviewed indicate that they do not have time to put in extra work hours, even when their families need extra income:

> The only thing I do is take extra trips or sports trips or field trips but not outside of bus driving. [modern traditionalist]

> I work overtime if I need a little extra. [provider mom]

> No, I don't have the time. I'd like the money, but I don't have the time. [disjointed worker]

Rural residents have few alternatives to poor-paying jobs, especially if they lack dependable transportation. Because many rural parents rely on hourly wages, their weekly economic situation is tenuous, and not being able to get to work is a disaster. Low-skill factory and service jobs do not vary much, whether you live in a rural or urban area, though rural areas tend to get the lowest-paying jobs in both sectors (Findeis and Hsu 1997). Restructuring reinforces women's dependence on the labor market, but rural residence strongly emphasizes their role as mothers. It is a trade-off they are willing to make to raise their children in an environment they believe is better for them.

RESTRUCTURING AND RURAL NONFARM FAMILIES

Economic restructuring has had important impacts on rural households and will increasingly redefine rural places. Currently, however, tenets of the agrarian ideology remain strong. Some generational differences are observed between our mothers and their mothers, but there is a fairly similar pattern of work or staying at home. A number of the women we interviewed experienced downward mobility when they entered the labor market. They moved from the middle to the working class in part because the rural labor market offered few opportunities to get ahead. And though we do not find working-class families slipping into poverty, two adult earners are necessary just to remain in place. Women that grew up in poor households remain poor even though they are now working outside the home.

Marriage and employment patterns reveal important aspects of the agrarian ideology. Though most families do not conform to a breadwinner-and-housewife pattern, remnants of that pattern remain. Duration of marriage can be extremely important to providing economic stability for women and their children. What these work-family patterns reveal is a tremendous amount of economic and marital uncertainty for half the mothers we interviewed. Unmarried mothers can maximize their income by marrying, remarrying, or doubling up (combining households) but this offers no long-term guarantee of financial stability.

Maternal employment provides economic stability for some families. However, the conditions and opportunities available for women do not allow them to fully support a family. Unless rural parents moonlight, they cannot substantially increase household incomes beyond a dual-earner capacity.

When rural women work outside the home, they also support the low-paying rural industrial economy and service sector. As long as their labor is expected to provide for their family, employers have a steady and dependable workforce. In the restructured rural economy, women experience competing pressures. Their family requires the income the labor market can provide and the labor market seeks employees that accept lower wages. The same factors that draw families to rural places or that compel them to remain lock them into a particular set of economic and familial relations. They adopt a work ethic that reflects the amount of effort required to sustain a family. Rural residence also reaffirms traditional gender roles and in so doing provides little impetus to change the quality or rewards the labor market offers women. The quality of rural jobs and the rewards offered in the rural economy may provide rural nonfarm men and women incentives to marry and remarry in order to support themselves and their children.

While restructuring increases economic hardship for rural families, it does not change the overall dynamics of rural family life. Employment and economic struggles reinforce beliefs about parental responsibility and shape how households balance issues of work and home. So rural residence creates a conundrum, even as the economy is stagnant or declines, it strengthens resolve about family and gender patterns. Being stretched to one's limits characterizes rural people, families, and places.

Note

1. Thirty-one parents participated in the interviews. In one household both husband and wife participated in the interview and in another household only the father participated.

References

Albrecht, D. 1998. "The Industrial Transformation of Farm Communities: Implications for Family Structure and Socioeconomic Conditions." *Rural Sociology* 63 (1): 51–64.

Amott, T. 1993. *Caught in the Crisis: Women and the U.S. Economy Today*. New York: Monthly Review Press.

Bell, M. M. 1992. "The Fruit of Difference: The Rural-Urban Continuum as a System of Identity." *Rural Sociology* 57 (1): 65–82.

Brown, D., and M. Warner. 1991. "Persistent Low-Income Nonmetropolitan Areas in the United States: Some Conceptual Challenges for Development Policy." *Policy Studies Journal* 19 (2): 22–41.

Dolbeare, C. H., and L. R. Strauss. 1997. *Rural Housing and Welfare Reform: HAC's 1997 Report on the State of the Nation's Rural Housing*. Washington, D.C.: Housing Assistance Council.

Falk, W. 2000. Discussion, Communities, and Work sessions. Rural Sociological Society, Washington D.C.

Findeis, J., and W. Hsu. 1997. "Employment." In *Encyclopedia of Rural America: The Land and People,* 2 vols., ed. G. A. Goreham, 1:227–30. Santa Barbara, Calif.: ABC-Clio.

Flora, C., J. Flora, J. Spears, and L. Swanson. 1992. *Rural Communities: Legacy and Change.* Boulder: Westview.

Gerson, K. 1985. *Hard Choices: How Women Decide about Work, Career, and Motherhood.* Berkeley: University of California Press.

———. 1993. *No Man's Land: Men's Changing Commitments to Family and Work.* New York: Basic Books.

Gringeri, C. 1994. *Getting By: Women Homeworkers and Rural Economic Development.* Lawrence: University Press of Kansas.

Hochschild, A., and A. Machung. 1992. *The Second Shift: Working Parents and the Revolution at Home.* New York: Viking Press.

Kessler-Harris, A. 1982. *Out to Work: A History of Wage-Earning Women in the United States.* New York: Oxford University Press.

Lichter, D., and D. Eggebeen. 1992. "Child Poverty and the Changing Rural Family." *Rural Sociology* 57 (2): 151–72.

Lyson, T., and W. Falk, eds. 1993. *Forgotten Places: Uneven Development in Rural America.* Lawrence: University Press of Kansas.

Naples, N. 1994. "Contradictions in Agrarian Ideology: Restructuring Gender, Race-Ethnicity, and Class." *Rural Sociology* 59 (1): 110–35.

Ollenburger, J. C., S. J. Grana, and H. A. Moore. 1989. "Labor Force Participation of Rural Farm, Rural Non-Farm, and Urban Women: A Panel Update." *Rural Sociology* 54 (4): 533–50.

Pyke, K. D. 1994. "Women's Employment as a Gift or Burden? Marital Power across Marriage, Divorce, and Remarriage." *Gender and Society* 8 (1): 73–91.

Rosenfeld, R. A. 1985. *Farm Women: Work, Farm, and Family in the United States.* Chapel Hill: University of North Carolina Press.

Rubin, L. 1992. *Worlds of Pain: Life in the Working-Class Family.* New York: Basic Books.

Sachs, C. 1983. *The Invisible Farmers: Women in Agricultural Production.* Totowa, N.J.: Rowman and Allanheld.

Struthers, C. B., and J. L. Bokemeier. 2000. "Myths and Realities of Raising Children and Creating Family Life in a Rural County." *Journal of Family Issues* 21 (1): 17–46.

Tilly, L. A., and J. W. Scott. 1989. *Women, Work, and Family.* New York: Routledge.

Willits, F. K., and A. E. Luloff. 1995. "Urban Residents' Views of Rurality and Contacts with Rural Places." *Rural Sociology* 60 (3): 454–66.

Zill, N., and C. W. Nord. 1994. *Running in Place: How American Families Are Faring in a Changing Economy and an Individualistic Society.* Washington, D.C.: Child Trends.

14

Earning a Living and Building a Life

Income-Generating and Income-Saving Strategies of Rural Wisconsin Families

Ann Ziebarth and Leann Tigges

THE GLOBALIZATION AND restructuring of the industrial economy have had a major impact on the everyday lives of rural Americans. While agriculture and natural resources remain important economic sectors, much of the employment in rural areas today is based in part-time and seasonal work, insecure manufacturing, and low-wage service jobs. Using findings from focus group discussions in four rural Wisconsin communities, along with results from a statewide survey of nonmetropolitan families, we examine the influence of social and contextual factors on the way in which households earn their livings and build their lives. Our goal is to illustrate the meaning of economic restructuring for the everyday lives of rural families, to find out what adjustments they make and how they perceive the benefits or costs of these strategies.

Wisconsin's economy in the mid-1990s was frequently portrayed as vibrant. In 1995, when our case study began, standard business measures indicated that the state had experienced growth in total income and employment and that the unemployment rates were among the lowest in the nation (Dresser, Rogers, and Whittaker 1996). Yet the benefits of this economy fell unevenly between working families and an elite group of business owners and professionals. The voices of rural Wisconsin workers reflect a darker side to the vibrant economic statistics that emanated from the state's development agencies and business organizations.

Since [my former employer] is closing down, I've had a real hard time finding a job that pays similar to what I was making there, even without the benefits.

I know a few employers here [tend] to hire somebody part-time, so they get out of workmen's comp and stuff like that. Twenty hours a week and off with you and we'll get somebody else in here, and there you have three guys taking up one guy's full-time job.

I even offered to work for less money because [the employer] was looking at other people. I don't know if it was good for me or not, but I got it, and I [had] wanted a full-time job.

These quotes are more in line with the facts assembled by the Center on Wisconsin Strategy in its 1998 report *The State of Working Wisconsin*. The report noted that even after the long economic expansion between 1989 and 1997, Wisconsin's 1997 median hourly wage of $10.63 was 8.4 percent below 1979's median hourly wage of $11.61 (in 1997 dollars). Among full-time workers, wages fell more than 10 percent between 1979 and 1997 (Dresser, Mangum, and Rogers 1998).

Economic restructuring differentially affected metropolitan and nonmetropolitan areas. Unlike the rest of the nation, Wisconsin's manufacturing employment did not decline in the 1980s. However, it did shift location—from the unionized metro areas of the southeastern region to nonunionized, lower-wage suburban and rural locations, and with that shift came a decline in manufacturing wages (Dresser, Mangum, and Rogers 1998, 49). As is true nationally, Wisconsin nonmetropolitan areas' earnings per job and per-capita income are well below metro levels (by about 25 percent in 1997) and their unemployment rates are higher (4.1 percent vs. 3.0 percent for metro areas) (USDA 2000). Not surprisingly, rural residents are disproportionately represented among Wisconsin's working-poor families with children, due in part to the concentration of seasonal and part-time jobs in nonmetropolitan industries (COWS 2000).

Neoclassical economists would expect people facing poorer employment opportunities in rural areas to migrate toward better conditions. Migration is seen, in this perspective, as the result of calculated cost-benefit decisions; people decide to move to take advantage of better employment and income opportunities (Massey et al. 1994). Alternatively, people may choose to relocate to areas where the cost of living is lower. Those who move to reduce living expenses may decide to keep their jobs but commute longer distances to work. Relocation, however, typically entails both social and economic costs that make it prohibitive for many.

Among those families who choose not to relocate, traditional strategies of "getting by" are common (Jensen, Cornwell, and Findeis 1995). Households find ways of earning income on the side. Holding multiple-jobs (moonlighting), obtaining seasonal or part-time jobs (or both), and earning money through the informal economy are common strategies for enhancing the economic well-being of the household. Householders also become adept at cutting expenses with frugal spending and do-it-yourself activities.

The income-generating and cost-cutting strategies of rural households help these families enhance their quality of life, make their housing more affordable or suitable, and build security in an insecure world. Together these strategies are ways families earn a living and build a better life. We argue that nonmetropolitan family households have employed a wide variety of strategies to improve their financial situation or increase their sense of security, and that these strategies are embedded in the local context and social ties of these families.

The embeddedness perspective contends that economic action is constrained and facilitated by ongoing social relationships (Granovetter 1985). By highlighting the social embeddedness of economic action, we illustrate how economic situations have social content. In adopting this framework, we emphasize that social relationships of community and family are important for understanding the survival strategies of rural households. The householders' ability to adopt income-generating strategies relies in part on the employment opportunities in the local area and in part on their human capital, or skills. But it also depends on the information they get, the social connections they have, and the support of family and friends. Strategies that decrease household costs also rely on location and social networks.

Theoretical Framework: The Embeddedness of Family Strategies

Our research has been guided by the concept of social embeddedness, the way in which social relationships influence individuals' actions and outcomes. Social embeddedness acknowledges that the adaptive strategies that households employ are frequently based on social connections of family, friends, and acquaintances. Social capital—the resources inherent in social relationships (Bourdieu 1986)—is often key to the deployment of these strategies. Various kinds of social support and information flow from these relationships, facilitating actions that might not otherwise be readily available. People draw on their social connections to find employment, adjust childcare to irregular work schedules, or exchange services through loose systems of bartering and swapping. However, reliance on connections with friends and family has differential outcomes, with greater benefits going to those of higher status (Smith 2000).

In this chapter, we study the ways households in different types of rural economies try to make ends meet and have a "good life." We pay special attention to the ways in which social relationships affect and are affected by these strategies. Also important for our study is the locational context of rural Wisconsin communities. Locational context refers to the aspects of a particular place that influence the employment and quality of life of working families. In advocating for locality as a focus for labor market research, Lobao defines localities as "settings of social interaction, specific to time and place, where structures and institutions shape and are shaped by the activity of their inhabitants" (1993, 25). Thus, locational context helps determine the options available to families as they respond to larger economic conditions. These options reflect the resources of the local community, the natural environment, and the labor market itself.

The focus on locational context is evident in several recent analyses of restructuring and regional decline. Studies by Davidson (1990) and Fitchen (1991) illustrate the power of this framework. Working within the classical tradition of community sociology, Davidson and Fitchen describe how the departure of educated young people and the arrival of low-wage firms undermined rural communities in the Northeast and Midwest. Communities undergoing population or employment losses experienced a declining tax base and a loss of public infrastructure, especially schools. These changes led community leaders to desperately attempt to attract industries of any type.

Locality is especially important for understanding how rural people are affected by changes in economic activity and economic relationships. Although *rural* lacks a clear definition, density and scale are important dimensions of space that uniquely affect rural residents' economic opportunities and social relationships. Small communities and sparsely settled areas limit the employment options available within commuting distance, affecting workers' ability to find jobs that match their skills and limiting their bargaining power with employers (McLaughlin and Perman 1991). Residential density also influences informal economic activities. Jensen, Cornwell, and Findeis (1995) found rurality was a strong predictor of informal economic activities done for money or barter outside the household. They suggest that the relatively small number of formal employment opportunities in rural areas may lead people to seek informal activities as a means of increasing their income or decreasing their household expenditures, or both.

Methods

We began our study in early 1995 with a series of focus group discussions held in four rural Wisconsin communities. These communities were selected to represent different economic bases, providing locational context for this part of our study. One community was oriented primarily to dairy farming and had experienced a decline of good jobs in manufacturing in the previous decade. Another also had lost manufacturing jobs but was close to a relatively large metropolitan area and to a strong and growing tourism area. The third community had a strong economic base in high-end, producer services. The final community was in a forested area where timber harvesting provided the traditional economic base, but the area had recently experienced an influx of newcomers building vacation and retirement homes.

In each community, six to ten residents discussed the economic changes they saw in their communities and the effects on local families.[1] To facilitate open discussion, our groups were composed of either all men or all women and socioeconomic differences were minimized (Krueger 1994). Women were interviewed in the agricultural and tourism communities, men in the service and timber communities. The thirty participants came mostly from the working or lower middle class in these communities with family incomes at or below the median for their county. Most participants were home owners; all but one had completed high school and seven were college graduates; all were married and parents of school-age or younger children; all were non-Hispanic whites. Of the seventeen women, five were full-time homemakers; most of the rest held traditional female occupations in service industries. Three of the thirteen men were farmers, seven worked in blue-collar jobs, and the rest held white-collar jobs.

The discussions were loosely structured, guided by the facilitator to focus on changing economic conditions in the locality, on how families were responding to those economic conditions, and on community services and supports for families. Each discussion session lasted about two hours. Discussion session tapes were transcribed and analyzed to better understand the strategies used by rural Wisconsin families to enhance their economic well-being and housing affordability. Information from the focus group sessions was also used to inform the development of a telephone survey questionnaire, which was administered for us by the University of Wisconsin Survey Center.[2] In the discussion that follows, we draw on both kinds of data to help us understand who uses particular strategies, why particular strategies are used, and how they are viewed. Statements from the focus group discussions are placed into context using summary findings from analyses of the survey data.

Basically, households employ two types of strategies to improve their economic well-being. First, they may attempt to increase their cash income either through expanding formal employment or through paid work in the informal economy. Second, they may take actions that reduce the cost of living. We use our discussion group and survey data to consider each of these types of strategies in turn.

INCOME-GENERATING STRATEGIES

One common way households increase their income is to maximize the employment of family labor. Rather than relying on a single breadwinner, multiple family members join the labor force. According to our survey data, three-quarters of nonmetropolitan Wisconsin couples had both partners in the workforce and one-quarter reported that at least one partner worked more than one job.

Traditional values regarding women's maternal responsibilities were strongly voiced and noncontroversial in both the women's and men's discussion groups. Men and women expressed a desire to have mothers stay home—not just to care for young children but to be there when older ones came home from school. Several of the women had infants and had quit work to care for them. Working mothers with school-age children reported holding part-time jobs during school hours. Despite these values and the consensus that women held primary responsibility for raising children, many mothers did work outside the home. Often this work was legitimated by the economic needs of the family. The legitimacy of women's paid work was especially strong if her job provided health insurance.

> My wife works out [of the home], and if she didn't work out, we wouldn't make it either.

> The [neighbor] lady had a job at the co-op—which doesn't pay a lot except they've got a terrific health insurance plan. . . . Literally, everything she made went for day care and a little bit for clothing and gas. But her net income . . . was nothing, except she was providing the health insurance.

When she got an offer for full-time work she jumped at that chance. She works primarily for the health insurance.

Over the years, I have found that the wives have all had to leave the farm. I was fortunate—I didn't have to, but most of them have had to for the insurance end to keep things going.

Because men's jobs generally pay more than women's, the "economically rational" couple allows his job to take precedence. Comments such as those below make it clear that this rationality is situated in a value context in which domestic responsibilities fall on women's shoulders.

Around here, as far as the woman going to work and the man staying home, there's not a lot of professional work for women where they can make enough money to offset what a man could make.

My wife went to work last year for the first time in seventeen years, since we got married, and there was no way she could afford to work for minimum wage and with day care and something like that. . . . Once the kids were in school she could have went to work. I kind of like the idea of her being home for the kids when they got there, and stuff like that. So we just kind of suffered through those eight, ten years. Now she's back to work.

Although couples are sometimes making a cost-benefit analysis of formal work, other less quantifiable values (such as taking care of the home and children) enter into their decisions as well. Most of our participants thought that families need a parent at home with the children. One mother argued that children need guidance more as they get into their teenage years, when they are facing relatively important decisions. She remarked that anyone can change a diaper, but it takes a lot more skill to communicate with a teenager. This comment illustrates the variety of values that guide what might otherwise seem to be purely economically rational decisions.

Discussion group participants pointed out that the multiple-earner strategy came at a cost to the family and the community, particularly when the couple works different shifts.

I know a lot of families that are kind of ships passing in the night. You know, one comes home, says hi, gets supper going, and the other one is taking off, and [in the morning] they come home, get breakfast, get the kids up while the other parent gets down and tries to get their sleep. It's just incredible the juggling they have to do.

You never see [my neighbors], because one works days and one works nights.

Although the telephone survey data show nearly 60 percent of two-earner couples have both partners working the day shift, sequential scheduling is not uncommon (see also Hanson and Pratt 1995; Presser 1994; Preston et al. 2000). The most common sequential arrangement, occurring for two out of ten working couples, is for the wife to work the day shift and the husband to work at some other time. In addition to sending both partners into the labor force, households sometimes try to increase income through moonlighting. One-fourth of survey respondents indicated that one of the heads of the household held at least two jobs.

Focus group participants were well aware of the ways in which people pieced together employment in order to support their families—often combining full-time jobs with part-time, seasonal, or occasional work—and the personal costs associated with these strategies. A woman who said, "My husband sometimes works three jobs: pouring concrete, bartending, working the night shift," described herself as a single mom during the week. Others commented on the strain associated with workdays and workweeks that are too long.

They [a catalog retailer] have seasonal help, so some people will work full-time at other jobs and then drive [there] like for the second shift maybe or sometimes the third shift, for four or five hours, maybe six.

Like one guy I know, he's a plumber, five days a week, and then on weekends he'll go and put someone's plumbing in for them, so he doesn't even have a day off. He works more on weekends than he does during the week. I did that for four months . . . [worked a] full-time week job and then worked on weekends.

As the last quote suggests, paid work is not limited to formal employment. In addition to working in the formal economy, many rural households do a variety of informal activities for extra cash. Informal work for pay can take a number of forms, including selling firewood and garden produce, plowing snow, or holding garage sales. Nineteen percent of survey respondents reported that their household income is supplemented by some informal activity. Focus group participants talked about informal income-generating activities as a strategy households use to make ends meet:

> During tourist season the garage sales are everywhere. That's a steady income for some people, they run a garage sale every weekend.

> The firewood racket is a standard up here. If you've got a pickup truck and a chainsaw, you cut firewood and sell it by the pickup load.

Survey respondents and discussion group participants alike noted that very little income came from these activities. For example, one woman in the discussion groups reported buying T-shirts, embroidering designs on them, and selling them to earn additional cash for the household. The difference between the cost of the materials and the sale price, however, was so small that the value of her labor was almost zero. Another participant discussed growing, picking, and selling berries and other garden produce but, again, indicated that this did not substantially increase family income.

> My wife was selling Discovery toys on the side, but people would rather spend $30 a weekend in the pool leagues and darts than just $6 on their kid. And we were driving and delivering local shopper [papers] just to get some extra money. The wear and tear on the vehicle— just ended up it was a break-even type deal. You don't get ahead doing [that] stuff.

INCOME-SAVING STRATEGIES

Focus group participants generally thought that exchanging goods and services was an important way that people enhanced their living standards. However, drawing a clear line between the informal activities that involve working for their families and those that involve working for other people is difficult. As discussion participants described the processes by which a room was added to the house or broken things got repaired, it was clear that informal exchange often accompanied self-provisioning. Those with market-valuable skills (weekend carpenters, mechanics, or makers of crafts) kept busy with their own projects and were called on to help neighbors, friends, and family. Babysitting and other services also were exchanged frequently.

While the general impression given in the focus groups was that bartering and exchange were important strategies for rural families, less than 5 percent of surveyed households reported exchanging goods and services as a means of improving their economic situation. It is possible that bartering or exchanging services did not show up much in the survey because people think of it at as being done for social or personal reasons, rather than economic ones. Levitan and Feldman's (1991) research in rural New York suggests the importance of social networks (friends and relatives) in informal economic relations. Their work shows that both social and economic factors can influence exchange relationships. For example, in describing the rules of barter exchange, they mention that characteristics such as gender or age can waive the requirement of reciprocity. Also, social relationships among participants can extend the time for "repayment" of bartered goods or services. Other ethnographic studies of both rural and urban communities document the complex networks of exchange where kinship and friendship interact with needs and provision of goods and services (Harvey 1993; Spencer 1992; Stack 1974).

Nelson and Smith report "differences in how women and men engaged in household exchanges. Men more often than women engaged in barter, where 'the exchange of goods and services of comparable value' required clear terms about how and when repayment would occur. . . . Women's casual assistance to others took the form of long-term, diffuse obligations" (1998, 92; for a discussion of the gender differences apparent in our Wisconsin focus groups, see Tigges 1998; Tigges, Ziebarth, and Farnham 1998). The following quotes, the first from a man and the second from a woman, illustrate this point.

> There's a certain amount of bartering going on. You know, I know how to fix your car; you know how to shingle my roof. My brother-in-law has a farm. . . . I go down every summer on a weekend and help him make hay. In return, he gives me half a beef, you know, so it's a barter system.

For childcare, you're finding more [parents] trying to find friends and family for favors back and forth, rather than paying that extra money out.

As families work to make a living and build a life within their changing social and economic environments, one of the most important goals is obtaining and maintaining their homes. Regardless of where they live, their income level, or how secure their employment, a basic need among all households is a decent affordable place to live.

Affordable housing is obtained when families are able to meet their housing needs without an excessive burden on their household budget. The affordability of housing is often measured by the ratio of housing cost to household income. The cost of housing within a local market is often thought to be the driving factor for affordable housing. As a result, lower-cost housing in nonmetropolitan areas is often assumed to assure that housing is affordable. However, income level also affects housing affordability; lower housing costs are offset by lower rural incomes. Housing affordability is further influenced by household strategies to increase income and decrease costs.

Like the vast majority of families in rural America, most of our survey respondents live in single-family homes. Of the more than 80 percent who were homeowners, 20.5 percent owned their home "free and clear," without any mortgage payments. With the average monthly mortgage payment of $374 and an average rental payment of $324, only a small proportion of respondents would be considered to be burdened by housing costs. Among homeowners, only 5 percent of survey respondents spent over 30 percent of their income on housing.

The high level of housing affordability in rural Wisconsin may be the result of a housing market that effectively matches housing costs and household income or it may be due to the strategies the nonmetropolitan households have employed that improve affordability of their housing. Our focus is on the activities of rural family households that enhance housing affordability and household and community factors associated with those strategies.

More households engage in informal strategies designed to decrease their costs than in strategies that increase their incomes. Our survey indicated that almost two-thirds (63 percent) of households did one or more informal activities to save money, while less than one-fifth did something informally to make more money. Cost-saving strategies adopted by households range from lowering food costs by gardening to lowering housing costs by relocating.

Self-provisioning is a common strategy for affordable living and extends far beyond gardening, hunting, and fishing. Do-it-yourself home repair, remodeling, and building are means of lowering housing costs and increasing housing affordability among homeowners. Eleven percent of the respondents were owner-builders who, in the previous year, either worked on constructing their own homes or were doing a remodeling project with their own labor. Nearly one-third (29 percent) of respondents reported doing their own home repairs.

Resources necessary to participate in home repair, remodeling, or construction include not only the financial resources and property ownership but also time, skills, and available labor power. One measure of available labor is reflected in the composition of the household, since not all household members contribute equally to demand and supply. Additional children may create a demand for larger space, but young children obviously do not help remodel or build an addition. Pahl and Wallace (1985) find that the more adult members a household has, the more likely it is to participate in self-provisioning. Offe and Heinze (1992) conclude that single-person households are the least likely to participate in self-provisioning and that "complete families" are the most likely to do so.

In our focus groups, many participants discussed do-it-yourself strategies to improve homes or make them more affordable. They felt that the improvements they and their neighbors had made not only reduced housing costs but also improved the overall economic situation of the community.

> I know a lot of people up here that built their own home. Several of them built a home with no mortgage; they just built it as they went. And that's one way people get by. I didn't build mine, I moved mine in, but did a lot of rework on it.

We bought a house when we moved up here; that's been my primary project. [We were] fortunate enough to own it outright and so we've been putting lots of time and effort into it.

You see more remodeling going on, a lot more people adding on garages or an extra room here and there.

For some households, containing living costs required fairly drastic means of obtaining affordable housing. Approximately 15 percent of the survey respondents indicated that at some time in the past five years someone from outside their household had lived with them or they had moved in with someone else. The most common reason given for sharing housing was that it was in response to an "emergency situation" such as divorce, job loss, or major medical expenses. However, some respondents indicated that they could not find affordable housing. In focus group discussions, participants identified doubling up as a cost-saving strategy, especially among lower-income households.

My son tried to find a job and all he could find was minimum wage, but then he'd have to live at home.

I had to help a friend out when I first moved to town a couple of years ago—give her a place to stay with her two children, for like two months.

SOCIAL EMBEDDEDNESS AND LOCATIONAL ADVANTAGE

The focus of this study is not only on strategies employed to enhance economic well-being but also the embeddedness of a household within the local community or area. The idea of making a living *and* building a life is that quality of life depends on more than income. It is the result of community supports for families, networks of family and friends, and the ability to call upon friends or family for support when necessary. One measure of embeddedness is that of being rooted. Following Hanson and Pratt (1995), we define rootedness as the household obtaining the land or house through a connection with a family member. Almost one-fifth of survey respondents (18 percent) reported that their home or land is or was owned by a family member. Over half of farm households were rooted in this way.

Of survey respondents who had moved to their community within the past ten years, half said that a job or school had been important or very important in the decision to locate there. Similarly, half of recent movers to the area said that the cost of housing or land had been important.[3] One-fifth of movers (22 percent) reported that access to employment opportunities in the area was important in their decision to live there. As significant as these economic factors are in location decisions, survey respondents evaluated lifestyle reasons as even more influential. Nearly half (48 percent) said lifestyle considerations were very important in their decision to locate in an area, and another 23 percent rated lifestyle as important. Discussion group participants confirmed the importance of lifestyle and locational advantages in their choice to move or stay in the rural area:

> We came to [this community] because it had affordable tracts of land that didn't have a lot of stipulations on them. We own forty acres and we have our chickens and our big garden and we hope to put in an orchard.

> I think [my community] may be a little more fortunate than other towns of similar size in the state. I think that by virtue of being half way between [two small cities], at least in the village, we see a lot of people that live in the village, work in one of those two cities.

> There's very few young people that were my age and decided to stick around and stay here. We knew we weren't going to get rich staying here, it's just the type of lifestyle that we like. It's laid back, not a lot of crime, no problems, good fishing and hunting. And like I said, I for one knew I wasn't going to get rich, but because of the area and the people here, I decided to make it my home.

Finally, social relationships were key reasons for households to move or stay in their rural community. Among the 70 percent of survey respondents with any relatives in the area, the median number of relatives was seven. Nearly three in ten recent movers said that being near family or friends was an important reason for living in the area. Although we did not explicitly ask about local kinship ties in the discussion sessions, their importance was evident from comments made by many participants. One woman referred to the after-school child-care her mother-in-law provided; another talked about how her parents helped her manage her children at church; one man worked in his father's business; another rented from his mother; a loan official worried about having to foreclose on her parents' farm.

> I've got an eleven-and-a-half-year-old, she's in the sixth grade, and we live in town but my mother-in-law lives out of town on a farm. My daughter's able to ride the bus home out to the farm. Therefore, if I'm not home, she's able to be somewhere where someone is. I don't have to have her go through town to some babysitter. She can ride the bus right out to the farm and she's out there with family.

> I moved to this area about twenty years ago, and being brought up close to Chicago . . . , I am so thankful to live in a community like this, and to be able to raise my children [here]. . . . Maybe we don't have what the bigger cities have, but . . . the sense of community is just wonderful and the safety, and I wouldn't trade it for the world. . . . Everybody looks out for everybody else.

PAYING THE PRICE

Despite the advantages they noted, respondents were well aware of the limitations of rural locations. Wages in rural areas tend to be lower than in urban areas. People in our study earned less than many urban residents and often received fewer fringe benefits. Participants in discussion sessions linked the difficulties of getting by with this disparity in pay.

> In a bigger city you've got more places, more options to work, with better conditions and better benefits. Where here, there's probably three places that would have benefits that would be worthwhile—one the paper mill, the other would be the foundry, and I'm not too sure about the truck operation over there. . . . The benefits and everything in a bigger city are much better.

> I know a lot of employers that just lost touch. They've been up here for such a long time and you lose touch with wages in [big cities] and every year it proportionately gets farther and farther apart. The job that will pay $12 an hour in Minneapolis is paying $7 an hour here.

There's more jobs available than there ever were, but they're not top-line jobs. Minimum-wage jobs—sure they're booming right now with Hardee's and motels and things like that. But you keep hearing about different towns trying to attract more technical businesses—you know, factories, high-tech manufacturing, these types of things. [This community] really hasn't done anything to try and attract those types of businesses. You know, they're still looking at lumber or tourism, and that's it. And those two often conflict with each other.

Right now, I'm looking for part-time jobs. It isn't very easy [to hold one] without having to drive thirty-five to forty miles every day. . . . There just aren't that many available jobs. . . . Very few are advertised. It's mostly always filled by association and a lot of them are part-time, so that you don't get benefits.

The costs of strategies that families employ to get by affect more than just the household; they influence the social-capital resources of the community as well. Participants in our discussion sessions clearly noted the loss of community resources as more time and energy are absorbed by families' own efforts at earning a living. Even in the village we studied with a mere five hundred residents, our focus group participants did not all know each other. There was a lot of gossip exchanged at the discussion session, but it was clear that the circles of the participants' lives did not intersect often. Community relationships seemed to have become a victim of the shortage of time.

Well, I really don't take time to look at somebody else's [life] when you're trying to shove yours along, you know. It probably doesn't sound too neighborly, but nowadays everything is so tight as it is, you really don't have time to worry [about others].

A lot of these organizations take a lot of volunteer work. . . . I belong[ed] to the . . . board for a few years and it was a lot of fun but it just got to be too much. I didn't have enough time for it and it's really tough to find people to take the time for all these things.

In this chapter we examined the variety of strategies used by non-metropolitan families to improve their financial situation or increase their sense of security. We focused on ways in which these strategies are embedded in the local economic and social context. Job information and social support are both facilitated and limited by connections with family and friends. The resources of the community, surrounding natural environment, and labor market characteristics provide a locational component as well. The choices families make are constrained by their economic situation and local employment opportunity structures. Households members' human capital resources may further limit potential employment.

We began by exploring income-generating strategies. Access to formal wage and salary jobs relies in part on the local employment opportunity structure and in part on the human capital, or skills, of labor force participants. Alternatively, strategies that rely on informal sources of income and strategies that decrease household costs frequently depend on factors of location and social networks. The connections between household and community illustrate how strategies of income generation and cost containment help families enhance their quality of life, make their housing more affordable or suitable, and build security in an insecure world. At the same time, our findings raise questions about the sustainability of these strategies for rural families and the impact they have on rural communities.

Our discussion group participants were overwhelmingly working- and middle-class people. Nearly all had high school diplomas and many held college degrees. They had strong networks of support through families and friends. The rural economies within which they were embedded were undergoing restructuring, but not a major crisis. Throughout the 1990s the Wisconsin economy remained robust, with overall family income rising slightly, but improvements in family incomes were the result of increased working hours, not higher wages (Dresser, Mangum, and Rogers 1998). One-fifth of rural Wisconsinites we surveyed disagreed with the statement, "Our needs are met and we have money left over." Almost one in five of those who did any informal activities said that the money saved or earned from these extra activities made the difference "between making it or not in terms of paying bills, putting food on the table, et cetera." Our focus group participants indicated that the resources families have to earn a living and build their lives are becoming squeezed tighter and tighter.

But few participants in our discussion groups expressed a sense of being stuck in the rural economy. Some had made a conscious choice to relocate to the area, while others were bound by lifestyle considerations or kinship ties. Social relationships with friends, neighbors, and business people added value to the assessment of community. For example, in one discussion group, three of the six participants reported that local professionals had not charged for services or had delayed collection of bills when people were having financial troubles. Small-town life also offers safety. Discussion participants stressed the positive nature of their social relations with neighbors and others within the community.

Our case illustrates that even with these advantages, working families are being stretched nearly to their limits. With households maximizing the employment of family members in the paid labor force and workers holding multiple jobs, there is little flexibility in terms of adding earnings to the household. Given the nature of rural economies, they have little chance of obtaining better-paying employment in the area. They are getting by primarily because they are working very hard. These extra efforts by families leave little time and energy for community contributions. Volunteer efforts fall on a few who are quickly overloaded, which may lead them to stop contributing at all. Few people are available to support an elderly neighbor or provide respite for those who do. Parents have less time to be involved in their children's schools.

Locations that are more rural in character and those with a stronger base in traditional rural industries are less amenable to dual-earner couples and more amenable to informal work. Yet the choices families can make, regardless of where they live, are limited. Families on their own have relatively little power to change the structure of employment opportunities. Also, the characteristics of their social resources may depend more on their position in society than on their geographic residence. Thus, while the detailed economic context within which they are embedded may vary, the strategies available to respond to economic changes are limited.

The case of Wisconsin's rural families provides a snapshot of the ways in which working people earn a living and build their lives within the context of rural economic restructuring. Regardless of where they lived, the families struggled to generate higher incomes by maximizing the family labor through having multiple family members in the labor force, moonlighting with seasonal work opportunities, holding multiple jobs, working overtime, and doing informal paid work. They supplement these income-generating strategies with a wide variety of cost-saving measures as well. We have highlighted the ways in which both kinds of strategies are embedded in the opportunity structure of the local economy and facilitated by social networks.

Yet for families—and rural communities—these efforts are realized at a high social cost. That cost is borne unevenly throughout the household and the community. Women working outside the home continue to work the "second shift" at home, with primary responsibility for cooking, cleaning, and caring for children. Cost-saving and self-provisioning strategies—hunting for bargains, clipping coupons, gardening—add to their work in the second shift. At the community level, children whose parents have too little time to become engaged in their socialization or educational or extracurricular activities may lack the social capital that would enrich their lives. If community social resources are depleted through the shortage of volunteers or are skewed because only wealthier residents have the time to participate in voluntary associations, then poorer and working-class residents will suffer disproportionately, both from the lack of assistance and from the lack of representation of their concerns or needs. It is neither realistic nor reasonable to expect families to work harder in the formal or informal economy to earn a living and build a life. Community leaders must assume more responsibility for the quality of jobs and the quality of life in the area.

Notes

1. We first contacted the school districts to get lists of families with children enrolled in the local schools. This strategy proved fruitful in two counties. For those groups we solicited our participants by randomly calling families on the school district list. In another county, we relied on contacts suggested by the

county extension agent with responsibilities for family programs. In the smallest community, the village clerk provided names of families with children.

2. The telephone survey was conducted between November 1995 and April 1996. Random-digit dialing and a set of screening questions were used to produce a representative sample of 1,610 working-age families in Wisconsin's fifty-two nonmetropolitan counties. The response rate was 58 percent. The respondents, 725 men and 886 women, represented households headed by couples with or without children and by single mothers with children aged eighteen or younger in the household (N = 121). Approximately 65 percent of households had children present.

3. Respondents were asked to indicate the relative importance of various reasons to locate in their community. More than one item could be rated highly important. For convenience, we group together as important those indicating the factor had been either very important or important.

References

Bourdieu, P. 1986. "The Forms of Capital." In *Handbook of Theory and Research for the Sociology of Education,* ed. J. G. Richardson, 241–58. New York: Greenwood Press.

Center on Wisconsin Strategy (COWS). 2000. *Barely Getting By: Wisconsin's Working Poor Families.* Joint report of the Center on Wisconsin Strategy, the Institute for Wisconsin's Future, and the Wisconsin Council on Children and Families 2000. <www.cows.org/cows/pdf/index/poor-ful1080100.pdf>, retrieved February 6, 2001.

Davidson, O. G. 1990. *Broken Heartland: The Rise of America's Rural Ghetto.* New York: Doubleday.

Dresser, L., S. Mangum, and J. Rogers. 1998. *The State of Working Wisconsin.* Madison: Center on Wisconsin Strategy, University of Wisconsin.

Dresser L., J. Rogers, and J. Whittaker. 1996. *The State of Working Wisconsin.* Madison: Center on Wisconsin Strategy, University of Wisconsin.

Fitchen, J. 1991. *Endangered Spaces, Enduring Places: Change, Identity and Survival in Rural America.* Boulder: Westview.

Granovetter, M. 1985. "Economic Action and Social Structure: The Problem of Embeddedness." *American Journal of Sociology* 91:481–510.

Harvey, D. L. 1993. *Potter Addition: Poverty, Family, and Kinship in a Heartland Community.* New York: Aldine de Gruyter.

Hanson, S., and G. Pratt. 1995. *Gender, Work, and Space.* New York: Routledge.

Jensen, L., G. T. Cornwell, and J. L. Findeis. 1995. "Informal Work in Non-metropolitan Pennsylvania." *Rural Sociology* 60:91–107.

Krueger, R. 1994. *Focus Groups: A Practical Guide for Applied Research.* 2d ed. Thousand Oaks, Calif.: Sage Publications.

Levitan, L., and S. Feldman. 1991. "For Love or Money: Nonmonetary Economic Arrangements among Rural Households in Central New York." *Research in Rural Sociology and Development* 5:149–72. JAI Press.

Lobao, L. 1993. "Renewed Significance of Space in Social Research: Implications for Labor Market Studies." In *Inequalities in Labor Market Areas,* ed. J. Singelmann and F. A. Deseran, 11–32. Boulder: Westview.

Massey, D. S., J. Arango, G. Hugao, A. Kouaouci, A. Pellegrino, and J. E. Taylor. 1994. "An Evaluation of International Migration Theory: The North American Case." *Population and Development Review* 20:699–752.

McLaughlin, D. K., and L. Perman. 1991. "Returns vs. Endowments in the Earnings Attainment Process for Metropolitan and Nonmetropolitan Men and Women." *Rural Sociology* 56 (3): 339–65.

Nelson, M. K., and J. Smith. 1998. "Economic Restructuring, Household Strategies, and Gender: A Case Study of a Rural Community." *Feminist Studies* 24:79–114.

Offe, C., and R. G. Heinze. 1992. *Beyond Employment: Time, Work, and the Informal Economy.* Philadelphia: Temple University Press.

Pahl, R. E., and C. Wallace. 1985. "Household Work Strategies in Economic Recession." In *Beyond Employment: Household, Gender and Subsistence,* ed. N. Redclift and E. Mingione, 189–227. New York: Basil Blackwell.

Presser, H. 1994. "Employment Schedules among Dual-Earner Families and the Division of Household Labor by Gender." *American Sociological Review* 59:348–64.

Preston, V., D. Rose, G. Norcliffe, and J. Holmes. 2000. "Shift Work, Childcare, and Domestic Work: Divisions of Labor in Canadian Paper Mill Communities." *Gender, Place, and Culture* 7:5–29.

Smith, S. S. 2000. "Mobilizing Social Resources: Race, Ethnic, and Gender Differences in Social Capital and Persisting Wage Inequalities." *Sociological Quarterly* 41 (4): 509–37.

Spencer, J. C. 1992. "An Open-Country Social Economy." Ph.D. dissertation, University of Missouri, Columbia.

Stack, C. B. 1974. *All Our Kin: Strategies for Survival in a Black Community.* New York: Harper and Row.

Tigges, L. M. 1998. "Constructing Gender and Rural Lifestyles in the American Heartland." In *The Social Construction of Gender in Different Cultural Contexts,* ed. G. Franberg, 143–55. Stockholm: Fritzes.

Tigges, L. M., A. Ziebarth, and J. Farnham. 1998. "Social Relationships in Locality and Livelihood: The Embeddedness of Rural Economic Restructuring." *Journal of Rural Studies* 14 (2): 203–19.

USDA. Economic Research Service. 2000. *Wisconsin Fact Sheet.* <www.ers.usda.gov/epubs/other/usfact/wi.htm>, retrieved September 29, 2000.

15

Livelihood Strategies of Farmers in Puerto Rico's Central Region

Survival in the Context of Economic Restructuring and Policy Change

Viviana Carro-Figueroa and Gwyndolyn J. Weathers

OPERATION BOOTSTRAP, the name given to Puerto Rico's development strategy inaugurated in the 1950s, was aimed at attracting export-oriented U.S. industries in order to sustain internal economic growth. For agriculture, the transformation spurred by the new programs was dramatic. In 1950 the agricultural sector employed 35 percent of the island's labor force and accounted for 19 percent of its gross domestic product (GDP). By 1970 agriculture contributed 3 percent of Puerto Rico's GDP and employed only 10 percent of its workers; by 1998 it accounted for less than 1 percent of GDP and employed less than 3 percent of the island's laborers (P.R. Dept. de Agricultura 1998; P.R. Junta de Planificación 1976).

The increasing marginalization of agriculture is not exceptional for the Caribbean or the Third World in the last five decades. As McMichael (1996) has shown, the decline of agriculture, increased food imports, and industrialization were all distinctive features of the postwar "development project" implemented by newly independent nation-states and other less developed countries. The peculiarity of the Puerto Rican experience, as Weisskoff (1985) has argued, resides less with the actual path followed by its economy than with the absolute magnitude of the changes undergone. By 1980 Puerto Rico had the smallest agriculture and the largest manufacturing and service sectors in the Caribbean region.

The extent of Puerto Rico's agricultural demise was such that the sector's prospects, structural shifts, and changing role in the economy of rural areas were rarely analyzed in studies of the Puerto Rican economic transformation after 1970.[1] Yet, if agriculture was no longer the principal industry of most rural communities, in the central region of Puerto Rico—the rural stronghold of the island—farming has remained a vital economic activity, affecting resource use decisions and conditions, and the broader development perspectives of each locality. In this context, and given the continued structural predominance of small and medium farmers in the central region's agriculture, two questions arise: Which mechanisms encouraged surviving farmers to negotiate macroeconomic policies generally unfavorable to them? How has globalization affected the prospects and livelihood options of rural areas in which farming remains important?

This chapter focuses on the impacts that agricultural restructuring and socioeconomic changes had on farming households in Puerto Rico's central region (see fig. 15.1).[2] Our principal argument is that policies (agricultural and otherwise) have had a differential impact on rural social classes. In turn, the strategies that farming households adopt to negotiate change depend on their socioeconomic characteristics, their farm resources, and on the institutional arrangements developed historically in the different regions of the island. These arrangements are a reflection of historical politico-economic struggles and decisions that still impinge on the future of rural areas, and they largely determine who benefits, loses, or survives the current instability of global and local economies. From a theoretical point of view, our intention is to ground the transition from the "development to the globalization project" (McMichael 1996) as it is being experienced in Puerto Rico's central region. Focusing on particular subnational or transnational regions is an effective way of revealing both the structural inequalities and policy outlooks emerging from current global transformations and realignments (Tardanico 2000).

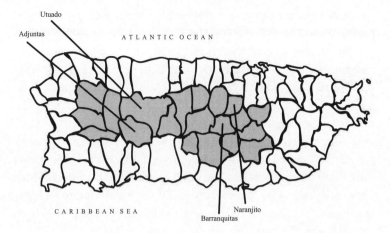

Fig. 15.1. Puerto Rico's central region and four case study municipalities. Not pictured are the municipalities of Culebra (Island) and Vieques (Island).

In the first section of this chapter we outline the consequences of Operation Bootstrap and other policies subsequently adopted by the state for the modernization of agriculture. With this policy overview as a general background, we then present our analyses of the changes in the agricultural and industrial structure of the central region since 1978 and the results of a survey examining the livelihood strategies followed by different types of farming operations in the early 1990s. The final section of the chapter attempts to situate our conclusions in a comparative perspective, taking the U.S. South and the Caribbean region as reference points, and discusses the principal policy implications we derive from this analysis.

Operation Bootstrap, State Reformist Policies, and the "Modernization" of Agriculture: An Assessment from the Perspective of Agriculture and Rural Areas

The development strategy followed in Puerto Rico after 1948 was based on three principal components: industrialization, external migration, and political reform (CEP 1979). Industrialization—based on the attraction of foreign capital through tax exemption, low wages, free access to the U.S. market, and complementary government investment in the needed physical and social infrastructure—can be divided into three broad stages: the first, running from 1948 until the mid-1960s, was geared toward the attraction of labor-intensive light industries; the second, implemented from the mid-1960s until the mid-1970s, was based on the promotion of capital-intensive industries such as petrochemical and pharmaceutical complexes through tax exemptions and access to cheap foreign oil and to the U.S. market for processed products; and the third, from the mid-1970s until the early 1990s, was principally directed toward the attraction of high-tech export manufacturing and service industries (Marqués-Velasco 1993; Pantojas-García 1990).

While economic growth during early Operation Bootstrap was rapid, the new jobs created absorbed only a fraction of the surplus labor generated by parallel reductions in agricultural employment. Massive migration, officially promoted to reduce the size of the labor force, was responsible for the model's initial success at improving the material conditions of the population (CEP 1979). Politically, the juridical relationship between colony and metropolis was also transformed during this process, and although the island remains an unincorporated territory of the United States, the Commonwealth status negotiated with the U.S. Congress effectively framed the transition from an agriculturally dependent colony to an industrialized "modern colony" (Grosfoguel 1997). In this process the economy of the island became so integrated with that of the United States that it is considered by many analysts as a differentiated U.S. regional economy rather than as an autonomous economic formation (Benson-Arias 1997). As a regional economy, however, Puerto Rico has consistently lower incomes and standards of living than even the poorest mainland states.

Rising wages in the 1960s, and later the extension of the U.S. minimum wage to Puerto Rico, undermined one of the principal attractions of the island to foreign investors. As light industries became more difficult to attract, the government strategy changed to promote the establishment of capital-intensive industries. The government expected that labor-intensive forward linkages would be generated after their establishment. This never happened. By 1973 the combined effects of oil import quotas and the oil embargo exhausted the possibilities of this economic growth strategy. In spite of increased local public investment, the island's GDP suffered its first postwar decline; as the rate of investment declined, unemployment mounted. It is in this context that federal legislation came to the rescue of both the poorest citizens of the colony and of corporate capital (Marqués-Velasco 1993).

Federal transfer payments to the poor increased tremendously with the extension in 1974 of the Food Stamp Program (FSP) to the island. Concerned about the expansion of the FSP in Puerto Rico, the U.S. Congress voted in 1982 to substitute food stamp allocations with a fixed block grant equal to 75 percent of the anticipated food stamp cost for fiscal year 1982 ($825 million). These monies were to be distributed, under the newly created Nutrition Assistance Program (known by its Spanish acronym PAN, which also means "bread"), as cash checks instead of food coupons. Corporate capital, on the other hand, benefited from the 1976 reform of the rules governing federal tax exemption for corporations operating in U.S. possessions—section 936 of the new internal revenue code—which allowed them to repatriate profits immediately to their corporate parents, tax free. The government of Puerto Rico, fearing a massive exodus of the capital accumulated in the island, enacted a tollgate tax over profits repatriated, which could be reduced if firms spaced out the movement of capital over several years. These dispositions, along with FSP money, boosted local deposits, underwriting a broader portfolio of activities for local banks (NACLA 1981).

Section 936 provided the basis for restructuring the economy. The new model devised by the government relied on the promotion of tourism, capital-intensive agroindustrial operations, international services, high-tech industries and finance as the engines for spurring economic growth. Subsidiaries of high-tech industries—pharmaceuticals in particular—and commercial banking proved to be among the main beneficiaries of this process (Pantojas-García 1990). Rural areas, never the preferred sites for industrial establishments, were hard hit by these changes, experiencing a decline in incomes and rising unemployment (Rivera-Batiz and Santiago 1990).

The neglect of agricultural development during the heyday of the industrialization program is often mentioned as being at the root of Puerto Rico's problems in the 1970s and early 1980s. Some fifteen years ago Weisskoff, in what is still perhaps the best indictment of the policies of this period and the consequences on the island, summarized the argument: "The glaring historical fact remains that it was the dismantling of the plantation sector and, with it, the small-farm food grower that led to the great exodus of the Puerto Rican people in the fifties and sixties, to the continuing high rates of unemployment in the seventies, and currently to the dependence on federal subsidies. . . . Thirty years of anti-agrarian policy have ruined the countryside; food stamps are merely the coup de grace" (1985, 138–39). Yet, if agriculture and rural areas had become increasingly marginalized from the rest of the economy—eventually affecting the continued viability of the development path followed—it is also true that this process was not without contradictory policy interventions that attempted to halt declining trends. Partial rehabilitation programs, subsidies, and incentives, were periodically enacted, but a comprehensive development program along the lines of the one prepared by Koenig in 1953, under the auspices of the local and federal Departments of Agriculture, was never implemented. Regardless of its limitations, for rural municipalities in the center of the island, continued government intervention in support of agriculture proved vital for maintaining a relatively stagnant but socioeconomically important farming sector. As figures 15.2 and 15.3 show, after 1969 there was a shift in the continuous decline trend in farm numbers experienced in Puerto Rico and in its central region. In the central region, once the 1978 Census of Agriculture data is transformed according to the changed 1982 farm definition, the prevailing trend is toward an increase in farm numbers, particularly of small farms of less than twenty *cuerdas*.[3]

In 1978, as part of a new government strategy directed toward incorporating the lagging Puerto Rican economy into new global capital trends, a plan for the modernization of the island's agriculture was devised. The creation of a modern agricultural sector was largely

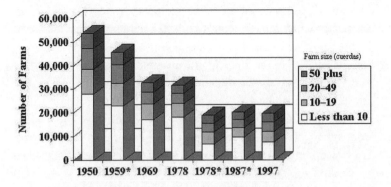

*Change in farm definition according to the Census of Agriculture.

Fig. 15.2. Number of farms by size, Puerto Rico, 1950–97

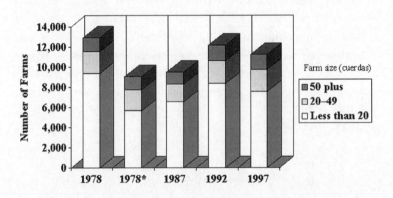

*Change in farm definition according to the Census of Agriculture.

Fig. 15.3. Number of farms by size, central region, 1978–97

predicated upon bypassing the existing farm economy, mostly concentrated in the island's central region, and substituting it by new
coastal, agro-industrial, fruit, vegetable and rice concerns, which
eventually failed or remained highly unstable (Raynolds et al. 1993).

By the early 1990s the limits of the latest stage in the economic
transformation of Puerto Rico were evident. Preferential and free-
trade agreements such as the Caribbean Basin Initiative and NAFTA
eroded the regional competitive advantage Puerto Rico had enjoyed.
The enactment in 1993 of a ten-year phaseout of the tax benefits held
by "Section 936" corporations signaled the prospective withdrawal
from the island of their productive operations.[4] The imminent
modification of federal welfare-state benefits complicated the pano-
rama faced by the government of the island, since restructuring
cycles had still left more than 50 percent of families dependent on
some type of transfer payment (Aponte 1999, 350). Taking a different
approach toward the development of Puerto Rico's agriculture, new
laws were enacted to promote private investment, tax exemptions,
and regulation of the sector through a local kind of marketing board
organized by commodity group (Kantrow-Vazquez, 1998; Revista
Agroempresarial 1998). The farmers of the central region, largely
neglected during the former twelve-year policy cycle, were again increasingly left on their own to negotiate the changes that local policies
and new global conditions were imposing over their farm operations
and their livelihoods.

Data and Methods

This work is a collaborative effort, bringing together results and insights gained from two projects conducted by the authors during the
1990s. Under the title "Agricultural Restructuring in the Central Region of Puerto Rico and the Changing Policy Context for Mountain
Farmers in the Island" (Project H-364, Puerto Rico Agricultural Experiment Station, 1997), Carro-Figueroa examined, through comparative case studies, what happened to Puerto Rico's interior farms
during the period when coastal farming and the promotion of tech-

nologically sophisticated agroindustrial projects became the local government's agricultural policy priority, neglecting the conditions of highland producers. The municipalities of Adjuntas, Barranquitas, Naranjito, and Utuado, representative of the central region's structural diversity, were selected as study sites for her project. A total of one hundred farm operators were personally interviewed in these municipalities on the farm's and household's socioeconomic characteristics, farming problems, farm prospects, and on several agricultural and environmental policy issues. For analytical purposes Carro-Figueroa classified farms into the following categories that combined a size in cuerdas with a sales class definition: (1) Residential Minifarms— farms of less than 3 cuerdas and less than $1,200 a year in farm sales; (2) Small Farms—farms of less than 3 cuerdas and between $1,200 and $7,499 in farm sales, or from 3 to 19 cuerdas and less than $7,500 in farm sales; (3) Medium Farms—farms between 20 and 49 cuerdas and less than $20,000 in sales, or of less than 50 cuerdas and between $7,500 and $19,999 in farm sales; (4) Large Farms—farms of 50 cuerdas or more, or of $20,000 or more in farm sales. Results from this survey were used to document the arguments presented in this chapter on livelihood strategies.

In her graduate research project for the sociology department of the University of Maryland, College Park, Weathers (1999) used Public Use Microdata (PUMS) data for 1980 and 1990 to examine the occupational and industrial differences between urban and rural areas on the island. For our present purpose, this analysis was supplemented with descriptive statistics from the 1990 Census of Population and Housing to provide information on the defined Central Region, on the four case studies municipalities studied by Carro-Figueroa, and on Puerto Rico as a whole.[5]

Industrial Restructuring and Rural Survival: Livelihood Strategies of Farming Households in the Central Region

By 1990, 29 percent of the island's population lived in rural areas, and less than one percent of Puerto Ricans resided on a rural farm. As tables 15.1 and 15.2 show, agriculture as an industry and occupational category involved less than 3 percent of the island's population, while service became the single most important industrial sector, followed by trade, manufacturing, and public administration. The central region—our proxy for rural areas—showed a different industrial composition from islandwide trends in which manufacturing remained more important, whereas trade and service sectors were slightly smaller. Levels of public administration in the region and islandwide were almost identical. Agriculture remained, nevertheless, more important to the economies of the central region than to the island as a whole.[6]

Occupationally there were differences as well. Managerial and tech-

Table 15.1
Employment by Industrial Sector in Case Study Municipalities, Central Region, and Puerto Rico (percent)

	Case Studies	Central Region	Puerto Rico
Agriculture	10.5	8.0	2.8
Manufacturing	10.6	19.6	16.7
Trade	18.4	17.5	20.2
Service	25.8	24.9	27.9
Public Administration	16.0	13.9	13.8

Source: Census of Population and Housing, STF3A, Puerto Rico, 1990.

Table 15.2
Employment by Occupational Category in Case Study Municipalities, Central Region, and Puerto Rico (percent)

	Case Studies	Central Region	Puerto Rico
Farming	8.8	6.7	2.3
Managerial	19.1	18.6	22.8
Tech/Sales/Admin	24.1	22.5	29.8
Service	16.4	15.7	14.5
Blue-Collar	31.7	36.6	30.6

Source: Census of Population and Housing, STF3A, Puerto Rico, 1990.

nical, sales, and administrative occupations were fewer in the central region than in Puerto Rico. While blue-collar employment actually declined in rural areas during the 1980s, coinciding with a marked decline in the manufacturing sector between 1980 and 1990, blue-collar occupations were more widespread in the central region than in Puerto Rico, a factor directly related to the type of manufacturing industries found in these respective areas.

The labor market impact that the different restructuring cycles of the Puerto Rican economy were having on the central region is more evident when unemployment rates for the 1970 to 1990 period are examined. After 1970, the average unemployment rate in the central region was more than 5 points over the islandwide rate, reaching 25.7 percent in 1990 (table 15.3).[7] The percent of the central region's population under the poverty level in 1990 was 71.9; islandwide, this percentage was 58.9.[8] An overview of household income sources for the case study municipalities, the central region, and Puerto Rico in 1990, points to the use of multiple sources of income to make ends meet (table 15.4). As the percentage of rural residents increases, greater levels of public assistance are utilized by households. Thus, in the central

Table 15.3
Unemployment and Poverty Rates in Case Study Municipalities and
Puerto Rico, 1970–1990 (percent)

| | Unemployment Rate | | | Population under |
	1970	1980	1990	Poverty Level, 1990
Adjuntas	8.75	20.14	28.44	81.50
Barranquitas	7.98	32.61	26.58	74.24
Naranjito	6.17	16.72	21.31	71.64
Utuado	8.60	23.38	29.10	76.29
Central Region	7.70	20.90	24.90	71.89
Puerto Rico	5.57	15.22	20.43	58.90

Source: P.R. Junta de Planificación 1990.

Table 15.4
Distribution of Households by Income Sources (percent)

	Public Assist.	Farm Self-Empl.	Earnings	Wages or Salary	Social Security	Retirement
Adjuntas, Barranquitas, Naranjito, Utuado	50.7	2.2	58.9	54.8	33.0	7.2
Central Region	45.0	1.7	62.3	58.7	33.1	7.0
Puerto Rico	30.8	0.5	66.3	63.2	30.0	8.3

Source: Census of Population and Housing, STF3A, Puerto Rico, 1990.

region the figure was 45 percent, while islandwide it was 31 percent. Relatively fewer households in the central region and the municipalities of the case studies have income from "earnings" or "wages or salaries" than in the island. Rivera-Batiz and Santiago, in an analysis of the labor market changes experienced in Puerto Rico during the 1980s, summarize the situation of rural areas as follows: "There was a noticeable bias in the 1980s against rural employment and rural earnings. The Puerto Rican economy continues to gravitate toward urban non-farm activities, leaving the rural sector marginalized from the rest of the economy" (1996, 107).

According to Weisskoff (1985), the small family farm sector, historically accounting for over 50 percent of the island's farms (depending on the sector's definition), has traditionally acted as a buffer to the negative effects that industrial restructuring cycles have had on rural areas, reabsorbing workers at critical times, providing them with a place of residence, and supplementing their livelihoods, both in cash and in kind. Until 1992 the trend was toward stable or increasing small-farm numbers and a small increase in the land resources commanded by them. Census data suggest that it is from the land resources of the large-farm category that the other strata are gaining land (see figs. 15.2, 15.3, 15.4).

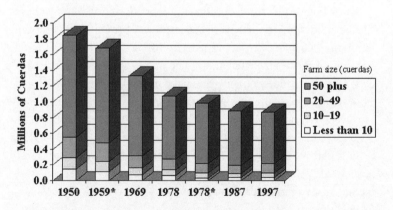

*Change in farm definition according to the Census of Agriculture

Fig. 15.4. Amount of land in farms by size, Puerto Rico, 1950–97

Our case studies, conducted in 1995, in which different types of farming households were surveyed, illustrate some of the mechanisms by which farmers were negotiating these restructuring processes and show their variations by type of farm. First, it should be established that the central region of Puerto Rico is not homogenous in terms of physical or socioeconomic characteristics. There are important differences between the eight most western municipalities and the twelve included in the eastern part. The western section has been the principal coffee-producing area of the island, while tobacco predominated in the east until its disappearance in the late 1980s. The cultural characteristics of these two crops and their different trajectories explain many of the problems and prospects faced by farming in each subregion today.

In Adjuntas and Utuado, relatively large municipalities of the central-western section selected for in-depth study, coffee is the most important crop, but oranges, plantains, bananas, and root crops are also important. Barranquitas and Naranjito, the selected municipalities from the central-east, are smaller in land area and have, on the average, a more diversified agricultural economy (Carro-Figueroa 1997). A brief depiction of some of the average farm and socioeconomic characteristics of the different types of operations surveyed is important to illuminate their survival strategies.

According to our survey results, the average size of what we have labeled residential minifarms (a subcategory of small farms housing semiretired farmers and part-time farm workers) is 1.5 cuerdas (based on six interviews). They sell an average of $604 yearly in farm products, cultivate coffee as their principal commodity, do not use hired labor, and do not receive any wage subsidy from the government.[9] The average residential farm household has a family size of three. Its principal source of income is unrelated to the farm and it derives less than 25 percent of its income from agriculture. Fifty percent of these households receive Social Security payments, while 33 percent have income from a retirement pension.

Small farms (35 interviews) had on the average 7.2 cuerdas, sold $3,571 yearly in farm products, were principally dedicated to coffee, hired an average of 3.7 workers, and in 64 percent of cases, received a wage subsidy payment from the government. Twenty-nine percent of these farms did not hire any laborers. Small-farm households had an average of 3.7 members, their principal source of income was unrelated to agriculture, and 68 percent of cases derived less than 25 percent of their income from the farm. PAN and Social Security payments were extremely important for the small farm households; 49 percent of them received the PAN cash subsidy, and 46 percent received Social Security payments.

Medium farms (29 cases) were classified according to their farm sales rather than to the land resources controlled by them. They were the group with the highest percentage of part ownership in the sample, with 31 percent reporting they owned only part of the farm operated. Thus the average picture of a mid-size farm emerging from our survey is that of an operation with a small land base averaging 17.9 cuerdas in size, having average annual sales of $8,967, and less specialized than residential or small farms in terms of commodities produced. While 55 percent of these farms had coffee as their principal commodity, 27 percent were dedicated to the growing of plantains, roots and tubers, vegetables, and fruit, and 17 percent to hogs and livestock operations. Access to additional labor was critical for these type of farms—only 10 percent reported not hiring any workers—but the average number of laborers employed was similar to that in small farms, 3.8 workers. Eighty-one percent of these operations were receiving wage subsidy payments. Family size averaged 3.8 member in medium-farm households. The majority of medium farms derive 25 percent or more of their income from agriculture (51 percent of cases derive 74 percent or more). Nevertheless, given their low average sales, transfer payments were as significant for medium households as they were for small farms. Forty-five percent of medium farm households were participating in PAN and 45 percent received Social Security payments. Moreover, only 10 percent of households did not receive any transfer income—the smallest percentage among all farm categories.

The large-farm operators included in the survey (30 interviews) had farms that averaged 72.8 cuerdas and farm sales of $36,185. Similar to mid-size farms, 20 percent of large operators were part owners and 13 percent, the largest proportion in the sample surveyed, were tenants. In contrast with the other farm types, large farms were not specialized in any particular crop or commodity. Seventeen percent were dedicated to plantain and banana farming, 14 percent to coffee, 17 percent to hogs, eggs, or livestock, and the rest to a diversity of fruits and vegetables (including root crops). All of them depended on hired labor for their operation, hiring an average of 11.5 workers per farm. Eighty-seven percent were receiving wage subsidy payments; those not receiving the subsidy were disqualified because they were not hiring labor by the hour. The sale of farm products was the principal source of income for 73 percent of these farms. Fifty-one percent of large farm cases informed us that 75 percent or more of their income was derived from agriculture. Social Security payments were received in 30 percent of the large farms. Twenty-three percent of cases, those with a relatively large land base but with low farm sales and family income, were participants in PAN.

Coffee cultivation is perhaps the principal risk-aversion strategy followed by all types of the central region's farmers, gaining in importance as the scale of the farm diminished. While 47 percent of large farms reported coffee as their principal commodity, 80 percent or more of residential and small farms reported the same. There are several reasons accounting for this: coffee is the only crop in Puerto Rico protected since the 1930s, it has well-established marketing channels, prices are relatively good and regulated by the government, and until recently, considerable incentives and subsidies were available to most farmers. Besides, given the steepness of many of the region's farms, many farmers believe it is the only crop that can grow well on their land.

Cultivating only a fraction of the available farmland is also a tactic followed by all farm types to cope with market- and weather-related instability. Survey data showed, however, that while residential, small, and medium farms had more than 50 percent of their land under cultivation, large farms had cultivated only 39 percent of their total acreage. Several of the large farmers commented, when questioned about the changes undergone by their farming operation during the last ten years, that limiting the amount of land under cultivation was their response to rising operational costs, due in part to hurricane-associated damage and problems with the availability of labor.

Access to an adequate labor supply was the most important problem identified by all types of operators, probably conditioned by the concentration of these farms into coffee production. It was more critical for large farms, which require more laborers, and for small farmers, who lacked the capital to attract more workers to their farms. To secure the needed labor, particularly during harvest, incentives other than wages were provided to the workers, such as shortening the length of the workday to five or six hours, providing breakfast, and in some cases, also lunch and transportation. Smaller farms showed a tendency to depend on paid family labor that, due to the kinship relationship, remained loyal to the farmer. Participation of the farmer's wife (95 percent of operators in this survey were men) in many of the farm tasks was reported by 53 percent of operators, being more important for both large farms (60 percent reported their contribution) and small farms—the two categories more hard pressed by labor scarcity. Mid-size farms, probably because of their more diversified commodity structure, were the ones providing more permanent employment (five months or more) and having fewer problems with labor availability.

Rising labor costs in Puerto Rico, resulting in part from the gradual application of federal minimum-wage laws to the island and the implementation in 1982 of the Nutrition Assistance Program as a cash transfer payment, have aggravated the production squeeze faced by Puerto Rican farmers. Although the 1969 Wage Subsidy Program was enacted by the local government to ease the detrimental effects that wage increases were having on agriculture, our survey data suggest that this subsidy is biased in favor of higher-income, larger employers of labor. The percentage of farms receiving wage subsidy increased with the scale of the farm, from 64 percent in the case of small farms, to 87 percent of large farms. Larger operators seem more likely than smaller farmers to have the ability to fill out the forms, pay Social Security and labor insurance, and meet all the legal requirements for the subsidy.

Over two-thirds of the farmers interviewed said that agriculture was their principal occupation, meaning that they did not work outside their farm at any time during the year. Holding multiple jobs is apparently not a strategy easily followed by farm operators in the

Central Region. In the residential farm category,[10] however, seasonal migration to the United States or informal activities like raising fighting cocks were mentioned as important. Over half the farm operators surveyed obtained their principal source of income from the sale of farm produce or farm-related income; 43 percent reported their principal source of income as unrelated to the farm. Again, the scale of the farm is key in this equation: the smaller the farm, the greater the percentage increase generated by nonfarm income sources.

Family incomes provided by the respondents showed about two-thirds to be below the poverty threshold in 1993.[11] As is the case with the general rural population, reliance on the state via transfer payments formed an important income strategy for many of those surveyed. A little less than one-third of the sample did not receive any income from transfers. PAN and Social Security income were the most important payments received. While Social Security was received by 41 percent of all households, retirement pensions were received by only 14 percent. Other forms of transfer payments, such as welfare and unemployment benefits, were not a major source of income for these families—only 2 percent reported having income from such a source.

Irrespective of the forces obstructing the continued viability of the different types of farms portrayed in this analysis, or favoring the regeneration and stability of each stratum, the majority of those interviewed envisioned themselves farming for the next ten years. When asked about prospects for the farm after their retirement, less than one-fifth said they would sell the farm, and about half responded that their relatives would continue to run it. The remaining third were equally divided between those who thought the farm would be converted to a nonfarm use and those who did not know what would happen to the farm upon their retirement.

Globalization, State Policies, and Agricultural Change

The postwar economic transformation of Puerto Rico closely followed international capital trends. Operation Bootstrap's initial industrialization policies were so successful at stimulating economic growth that the island became a "showcase" for what the American development model could offer to the Third World (Grosfoguel 1997). But if the "development project's" Keynesian-based ideas of public investment and state economic intervention (McMichael 1996) effectively framed Puerto Rico's early economic success, agricultural decline and increasing rural marginality seem to have been the unintended consequences of the process.

Rapid agricultural demise was not exceptional within Puerto Rico's regional context. As Marsden (1997) portrays it, in the Caribbean the "managed" decline of agriculture has given local governments the freedom to choose other development and capital accumulation paths, more attuned to the interests of powerful local elites. The devalorization of food and agriculture in the regional policy outlook and their substitution for imported fresh and processed foodstuffs has also been present in the case of Puerto Rico. This process, however, has not been linear. The web of reformist policies implemented by Puerto Rico's government after 1969, coupled with the limited protection already in place or negotiated over the years, had the effect of reducing the pace of decomposition and even supporting the partial emergence of a fragile but relatively stable family farm sector. The moderate expansion of a family farms' distribution program, the establishment of the Wage Subsidy Program, and the availability of credit and incentives for new types of operations like poultry production, were all partial mechanisms supporting the survival of existing operations and the emergence of new farming types. Yet, as our study suggests, it was perhaps the increased extension of federal transfer payments to the island—particularly of the FSP and PAN—that allowed small farmers to survive in spite of little farm production and market instability. These food-and-cash subsidy programs affected the diverse strata of Puerto Rico's agricultural structure differently. While they could not support the expanded reproduction of small farmers, they did allow for the continued farm residence and survival of a significant sub-commercial, subfamily farm sector that played a stabilizing role in rural areas. At the same time, however contradictory, they worked against the viability of medium and large commercial operations, whose ability to compete was affected by the heightened cost and reduced availability of labor (the unintended effects of these programs) (Weisskoff 1985).

Increased global economic integration, the wholesale adoption by local governments of prevailing market-oriented ideas, and associated globalization trends in food and agriculture—be they in the commodities traded, in consumption patterns, or in the organization of production and retailing—may aggravate the agricultural and rural marginalization trends in Puerto Rico. Analyzed from a regional framework perspective, the prospects faced by Puerto Rico in the "new global order" (Tardanico 2000) are both similar and different from those faced by the U.S. South and by other Caribbean islands.

The recent transformations experienced in neighboring islands such as Barbados or the Dominican Republic, where schemes for the penetration of external markets and agricultural diversification strategies based on production of fruits and vegetables have proved to be highly unstable and biased against small farmers (Marsden 1997; Raynolds 1994), are similar to Puerto Rico's experience with the 1980s agricultural modernization policies and the 1990s attempts at reform and "orderly regulation" of commodity production and marketing. As in these cases, the implementation of new agricultural policies and development schemes in Puerto Rico was also biased in favor of larger, coastal, agroindustrial operations and provoked conflicts over the control and distribution of scarce resources, credit, and access to markets (Raynolds et al. 1993). Puerto Rico indeed seems to follow closely the Caribbean prototype in terms of being part of a "dependent space" characterized by the "growing scarcity and marginalization of environmental and agricultural resources" (Marsden 1997, 183), the dissociation between local food production and consumption, and the instability of nationally based agricultural initiatives. Its case is nevertheless special because the island's political relationship with the United States has, until now, provided it with special access to financial markets and federal subsidies not available to its Caribbean counterparts (Deere 1990). Restructuring pressures associated with the debt crisis in most of Latin America and the Caribbean were not experienced similarly in Puerto Rico. As our studies depict, the island's population probably had a broader array of coping strategies to deal with economic restructuring than those available in the rest of the region.

Postwar economic growth in the U.S. South, while impressive, has also reproduced patterns of inequalities and rural marginalization. According to Glasmeier and Leichenko (2000) the postwar ascendancy of the South, largely based on the attraction of low-wage industries, was possible because it concentrated a great share of federal subsidies and was able to negotiate favorable trade protection for its industries. A reduction in the infusion of federal government resources at a time when trade liberalization policies are also expected to influence negatively the ability of an important segment of the South's industrial base to remain competitive, may precipitate a new crisis in the region, particularly affecting the conditions of unskilled laborers and rural areas. In Puerto Rico, the phaseout of section 936 benefits to U.S. corporations, coupled with prospective modifications in welfare regulations, and changes in the local government's policies toward agriculture, leaves subnational areas such as the Central Region, with its concentration of small farmers and unskilled workers, in a very vulnerable position to negotiate impending changes. Thus, both in the U.S. South and Puerto Rico macroeconomic policies need to be tailored to the particular conditions of disadvantaged localities.

In the case of Puerto Rico, Aponte (1999) has suggested the need to articulate and institutionalize a "strategic industrial policy" focused on the "production process" and the "firm," as an alternative path for facing the current challenges of the island. In this analysis, particular subsectors within the targeted industries of agriculture, manufacturing, and services were identified as having the greatest potential for spurring economic growth. Within agriculture, coffee and poultry production are the subsectors that, given their spatial concentration, their structural composition—in which local ownership and small and medium producers predominate—and the integration between different aspects of production and marketing, have the greatest potential to stimulate regional economic development (Alvarez 1993; Aponte, Alamo, and Carro 1992). A strategic industrial policy targeted toward building up linkages between agricultural subsectors and the flourishing food industry offers great potential for strengthening the economies of rural areas and meaningfully reembedding agriculture and food in their local settings. The analyses presented in this work on the characteristics of different types of farming operations and their livelihood strategies is a necessary starting point for the design of alternatives that could incorporate disadvantaged peoples and places into a more sustainable economic development strategy.

Notes

We thank Edna Droz, UPR-PRAES, for sharing with us the manuscript of her forthcoming publication "Sectors Providing Sources of Employment and Income-Generating Activities for Agricultural Families and Residents of Rural Communities." Her description of thirty-six farming households in four Title VI communities in the municipality of Orocovis provided a countercheck for some of the arguments developed in this work.

1. Exceptions to these trends were the studies by the U.S. Dept. of Commerce (1979), Weisskoff (1985), and Marqués-Velasco (1993).

2. For the purpose of this study the central region of Puerto Rico includes the following twenty municipalities: Adjuntas, Aguas Buenas, Aibonito, Barranquitas, Cayey, Ciales, Cidra, Coamo, Comerío, Corozal, Jayuya, Lares, Las Marías, Maricao, Morovis, Naranjito, Orocovis, San Sebastián, Utuado, and Villalba.

3. One cuerda equals 0.9712 acre. In 1982 the Census of Agriculture adopted a new farm definition that eliminated all farms with less than ten cuerdas and selling less than $500 in agricultural products during the year. Farms of ten cuerdas or more that sold less than $100 during the census year were also left out. When this definition is applied to the 1978 census data, farm numbers decline by 40 percent.

4. Indeed, preliminary analysis of the Census 2000 figures for Puerto Rico shows declines in the manufacturing sector (represented by the number of jobs in this industrial sector) from 16.7 percent to 13.5. The decline in manufacturing is also seen in the case study municipalities and the central region, although declines here do not appear to be as sharp as those islandwide. Additionally, the central region remains much more heavily dependent on the manufacturing sector for employment than our case study municipalities or the island as a whole.

5. Data from the 2000 Census for Puerto Rico became available late in the chapter revision process. We provide a preliminary analysis of these data in relevant endnotes to provide some sense of the trends over the 1990s.

6. Preliminary analysis of census data from 2000 indicates a continuation of the same patterns noted in the relationship of various industrial sectors to the central region and the island. Employment in agriculture, manufacturing (see note 4), trade, and public administration continued to decline. The service sector as an industry appears to have experienced sharp growth, however. For example, in Puerto Rico as a whole, service sector employment increased from around 28 percent in 1990 to approximately 38 percent in 2000. In the central region, services grew from 25 percent to 34 percent. With regard to occupations, there appears to have been an increase in Puerto Rico as well as in the central region in managerial positions, although the central region still has fewer of these jobs than the island as a whole.

7. Census data seem to indicate that unemployment rates dropped quite dramatically during the 1990s, to less than 10 percent for Puerto Rico as a whole and for the central region. The gap in poverty rates, however, remains (see note 8). Important to note are the debates surrounding these unemployment figures. Some economic analysts have suggested that these figures may reflect a large number of people dropping out of the labor force, having given up looking for work in increasingly difficult straits. Alameda-Lozada notes that between 1997 and 1998 the unemployment rate dropped from 13.4 percent to 13.2 percent but that decline was due to the fact that 36,000 people left the labor force: "In 1996 employment increased by 38 thousand [jobs]; in 1997 by 20 thousand and in 1998 by only 4 thousand." Such figures, he states, denote "significant reductions in the capacity to generate jobs . . . , a lack of dynamism in the labor market to absorb the new people entering the labor force and a loss of the competitive locational advantage of Puerto Rico especially with regard to manufacturing" (1999). Thus, the official level of recorded unemployment could indicate not an improvement in conditions but a worsening of the economic crisis discussed in this chapter.

8. The poverty rate in Puerto Rico appears to have declined significantly over the 1990s, according to Census 2000 data, although it remains very high. The poverty rate in the central region also appears to have declined, but remains much higher than the overall rate. An initial look at rates of public assistance reflects noticeably large declines at this time. However, given the remaining high levels of poverty, the decline in people receiving public assistance as income is perhaps due to changes in welfare regulations rather than moving out of poverty. Further analysis is needed to fully explore the dynamics of assistance program participation and poverty rates in the 1990s.

9. In 1969 the government of Puerto Rico implemented an agricultural wage subsidy program that, with certain limitations and restrictions, reimbursed farm operators part of any minimum-wage increases over what they were paying in

1968–69 (U.S. Dept. of Commerce 1979). In 1997 the minimum wage in agriculture was increased to $4.25/hr. and the subsidy was raised to $2.12/hr. To qualify for the program benefits, the farm operator must have evidence of compliance with other labor market regulations, like social security and worker's disability insurance payments, and submit a copy of his payroll quarterly. Only workers on hourly wages qualify for the wage subsidy.

10. Only a few cases in our sample fell into this type, but interviews with extension agents and other key informants suggest this category is increasing in importance with the aging of the farm population, the high land prices, and the instability of markets.

11. In 1993 the poverty threshold for a family of four with two related children was $14,654. The family incomes stated as being below the poverty threshold include the category of $10,000–$14,999, the cutoff for which is slightly higher than the poverty threshold.

References

Alameda-Lozada, J. I. 1999. "¿Transición o crisis?" *El Nuevo Día Interactivo.* http://www.endi.com, 20 May.

Alvarez, C. A. 1993. "Evolución de un proyecto autóctono dentro de un sistema importador de capital." Presented at the Caribbean Encounter of Production, Work, Management, and Organizational Alternatives, December 5–11, La Habana, Cuba.

Aponte, M. 1999. "Política industrial estratégica, producción y empresas en Puerto Rico." In *Futuro Económico de Puerto Rico,* compiled by F. E. Martínez, 345–85. San Juan: Editorial de la Universidad de Puerto Rico.

Aponte, M., C. Alamo, and V. Carro. 1992. "Hacia una política agrícola y agroindustrial estratégica para la industria cafetalera en Puerto Rico." Unpublished working paper presented to the Coffee Sector of the Farmers Association of Puerto Rico.

Benson-Arias, J. E. 1997. "Puerto Rico: The Myth of the National Economy." In *Puerto Rican Jam: Essays on Culture and Politics,* ed. F. Negrón-Muntaner and R. Grosfoguel, 77–92. Minneapolis: University of Minnesota Press.

Carro-Figueroa, V. 1997. "Agricultural Restructuring in the Central Region of Puerto Rico and the Changing Policy Context for Mountain Farmers in the Island: Status and Prospects of Different Types of Farming Operations." Presented at the annual meeting of the Rural Sociological Society, August 15, Toronto, Canada.

Centro de Estudios Puertorriqueños (CEP). 1979. *Labor Migration under Capitalism: The Puerto Rican Experience.* New York: Monthly Review Press.

Deere, C. D. (coordinator). 1990. *In the Shadows of the Sun: Caribbean Development Alternatives and U.S. Policy.* Boulder: Westview Press.

Droz, E. Forthcoming. "Sectors Providing Sources of Employment, and Income-Generating Activities for Agricultural Families and Residents of Rural Communities." Río Piedras, P.R.: Agricultural Experiment Station, University of Puerto Rico.

Glasmeier, A. K., and R. M. Leichenko. 2000. "From Free-Market Rhetoric to Free-Market Reality: The Future of the U.S. South in an Era of Globalization." In *Poverty or Development: Global Restructuring and Regional Transformations in the U.S. South and the Mexican South,* ed. R. Tardanico and M. B. Rosenberg, 19–39. New York: Routledge.

Grosfoguel, R. 1997. "The Divorce of Nationalist Discourses from the Puerto Rican People: A Sociohistorical Perspective." In *Puerto Rican Jam: Essays on Culture and Politics,* ed. F. Negrón-Muntaner and R. Grosfoguel, 57–76. Minneapolis: University of Minnesota Press.

Kantrow-Vazquez, M. 1998. "Recomienda Agricultura medidas exención tributaria." *El San Juan Star,* 18 December.

Koenig, N. 1953. *A Comprehensive Agricultural Program for Puerto Rico.* Washington, D.C.: U.S. Government Printing Office.

Marqués-Velasco, R. 1993. *Nuevo Modelo Económico para Puerto Rico.* Puerto Rico: Editorial Cultural.

Marsden, T. 1997. "Creating Space for Food: The Distinctiveness of Recent Agrarian Development." In *Globalising Food: Agrarian Questions and Global Restructuring,* ed. D. Goodman and M. J. Watts, 169–91. London: Routledge.

McMichael, P. 1996. *Development and Social Change: A Global Perspective.* Thousand Oaks: Pine Forge Press.

NACLA Report on the Americas. 1981. "Tax Exemption: Basic Terms." *NACLA* 15 (2):33–34.

Pantojas-García, E. 1990. *Development Strategies as Ideology: Puerto Rico's Export-Led Industrialization Experience.* Boulder: Lynne Rienner Publishers.

Puerto Rico Departamento de Agricultura. 1998. *Anuario Estadístico de la Agricultura de Puerto Rico 1998*. San Juan, P.R.: Departamento de Agricultura.

Puerto Rico Department of Labor and Human Resources. 2002. *Labor Force and Unemployment Data by Labor Market Areas Average 2001*. San Juan, P.R.: Department of Labor.

Puerto Rico Junta de Planificación. 1976. *Informe Económico al Gobernador*. Santurce, P.R.: Junta de Planificación.

———. 1990. *Indicadores Socioeconómicos por Municipio, 1990*. San Juan, P.R.: Junta de Planificación.

———. 2001. *Indicadores Socioeconómicos por Municipio, 1996*. San Juan, P.R.: Junta de Planificación.

Raynolds, L. T. 1994. "The Restructuring of Third World Agro-Exports: Changing Production Relations in the Dominican Republic." In *The Global Restructuring of Agro-Food Systems*, ed. P. McMichael, 214–37. Ithaca: Cornell University Press.

Raynolds, L. T., D. Myhre, P. McMichael, V. Carro-Figueroa, and F. H. Buttel. 1993. "The 'New' Internationalization of Agriculture: A Reformulation." *World Development* 21 (7):1101–21.

Revista Agroempresarial. 1998. "Como va el ordenamiento de los sectores agrícolas en Puerto Rico." *Revista Agroempresarial* (Oct.–Dec. 1997/ Jan.–Feb. 1998):42.

Rivera-Batiz, F. L., and C. E. Santiago. 1990. *Island Paradox: Puerto Rico in the 1990s*. New York: Russell Sage Foundation.

Tardanico, R. 2000. "Poverty or Development?" In *Poverty or Development: Global Restructuring and Regional Transformations in the U.S. South and the Mexican South*, ed. R. Tardanico and M. B. Rosenberg, 257–80. New York: Routledge.

United States Census Bureau. 2002. Census 2000 Summary File 3 (SF 3)— Puerto Rico. (Internet version) <http://factfinder.census.gov/servlet/ DatasetMainPageServlet?_lang=en> Accessed January 14, 2003.

United States Department of Commerce. 1979. "Agriculture, Food and Rural Living." In *Economic Study of Puerto Rico*, report to the President prepared by the Interagency Task Force coordinated by the Department of Commerce. Washington, D.C.: U.S. Government Printing Office.

Weathers, G. J. 1999. "Rural Development, Industries and Occupations: Bootstraps and De Facto Policies in Puerto Rico and the U.S. (Mainland) South." Paper presented at the annual meeting of the Rural Sociological Society, August 4–8, Chicago, Ill.

Weisskoff, R. 1985. *Factories and Food Stamps: The Puerto Rico Model of Development.* Baltimore: Johns Hopkins University Press.

16

Older Workers and Retirement
in Rural Contexts

Nina Glasgow and Alan Barton

THIS CHAPTER INVESTIGATES work and retirement characteristics and economic well-being of nonmetropolitan older residents. The U.S. population is aging rapidly, making a focus on older workers and retirement especially important at this juncture in American history. Labor economists have predicted that the rapid aging of the population will lead to shortages of workers in the coming years. Due to overall job-growth, the U.S. already experienced a tight labor market during the latter half of the 1990s. Journalistic accounts suggest that increasing numbers of older persons are remaining in the labor force into their late eighties and even their nineties (Brewer 2000). The economic well-being of rural residents, however, is hampered by the structure of rural labor markets because lower-wage, lower-skill jobs in peripheral industries are more concentrated in rural than urban areas (e.g., Bloomquist et al. 1993; Doeringer 1984; Lyson et al. 1993; McGranahan 1988; Singelmann and Deseran 1993). America's restructuring from a predominantly manufacturing to a predominantly service economy has resulted in greater availability of higher-wage producer service jobs in urban areas and predominantly lower-skill, lower-wage service jobs in rural labor markets (Fuguitt, Brown, and Beale 1989). Employment opportunities are limited in rural labor markets, and rural workers have limited paths to career advancement.

Significant questions remain regarding whether older individuals will increasingly remain in the labor force past the typical retirement age; this would increase the labor supply and counteract projected shortages of workers when the large Baby Boom cohorts reach retirement age (between 2010 and 2030). Here, we investigate the extent to which older individuals participate in the labor force, whether the propensity to do so varies by place of residence, and whether that has changed over time. To explore these issues, we use national-level Current Population Survey (CPS) data to evaluate changes over time in labor force attachment and occupations of older workers and to assess whether their well-being is adversely affected by residence in rural labor markets. We then use case study data to analyze labor force participation and retirement among rural older people in upstate New York.

The Timing of Retirement

We interpret our findings using a life course perspective, an approach that emphasizes the dynamic processes through which work and retirement occur over time (e.g., Moen et al. 2000). The life course approach calls attention to the cumulative advantage or disadvantage of older workers and retirees based on such characteristics as age and gender, which affect life chances over time, and current characteristics reflecting individual circumstances. A life course perspective views individuals' lives in the *context* of macrostructural events and changes, such as economic restructuring, and how particular cohorts are affected differently than others. Gaining an understanding of cohort differences provides a framework for understanding the *context* of individuals' lives across time and space.

Cohort differences are one factor influencing the timing of retirement. Birth cohorts share common life experiences, including opportunity structures that may be unique to events that occurred during their productive years. Shared experiences shape worldviews, including attitudes about work and retirement, and may affect when members of a particular cohort decide to retire. The presence or absence of opportunities for work during the life course and the terms and quality of available employment influence one's ability to choose retirement over continued work that might be necessary, if previous employment has not provided the means to support oneself. Opportunities for assuming new social roles during retirement (through volunteering, for example), input from family members, and health are other factors that may influence the timing of retirement, and that may correlate with cohort effects.

Data Analysis

The emphasis on process in the life course approach includes the importance of timing of significant events such as retirement (Moen et al. 2000). While we interpret our findings in light of insights from the life course perspective, our approach is better described as a life *stage* analysis. We use indicators that capture event timing and birth cohort effects to assess the labor force attachment of older Americans. A life course perspective in entirety would use panel data to follow the same individuals over time; however, such data are unavailable to us.

Instead, we use data from the Current Population Surveys of 1980, 1990, and 2001 (the most recent year for which data are available) to compare variation in labor force participation and the occupational composition of jobs among nonmetro and metro workers aged 55–64 and 65 and older. We then analyze case study data from a 1995 survey of a representative sample of 737 persons aged 65 and older living in Cortland and Seneca Counties, New York. We do so to gain a more detailed understanding of older persons' labor force attachment in a particular rural context that has undergone substantial economic transformation in recent years. The case study data were collected through a telephone survey in which 75.8 percent of eligible respondents participated.

Labor Force Activity of Metro and Nonmetro Older Americans, 1980–2001

The *New York Times* recently reported that the proportion of older Americans (aged 55 and older) working full-time increased in the five years between 1995 and 2000, following decades of decline or holding steady (Brewer 2000). That account, however, did not indicate whether increased participation is characteristic of both rural and urban older residents. Data from the 1980, 1990, and 2001 CPS confirm that older male and female workers are an important part of the nation's workforce in both metro and nonmetro areas, but increased labor force participation has occurred primarily among women aged 55–64 (table 16.1). By 2001 over two-thirds of men and over half of all women aged 55–64 were in the labor force, as were over one-sixth of men and approximately one-tenth of women age 65 and above.

Among preretirement-age men (55–64 years), labor force participation was consistently but only slightly higher for metro than for nonmetro males. Differences between metro and nonmetro were negligible among men aged 65 and older. From 1980 to 2001, the proportions of employed females increased among both nonmetro and metro women, especially in the 55–64 age group (table 16.1). By 2001 over half of women aged 55–64 were in the labor force, as were one in ten women aged 65 and over. *These data show that the recent upward trend in labor force participation among older Americans is being fueled more by increased labor force participation among women than men, with both metro and nonmetro women contributing to the trend.*

In summary, since 1980 labor force participation of women aged 55 and over has converged somewhat with that of men. Preretirement-age and older women account for most of the rise in labor force attachment among persons aged 55 and over in both metro and nonmetro areas. Still, men were and are now more likely than women to be employed, regardless of age or place of residence.

Table 16.1

Labor Force Participation by Age, Gender, and Residence, United States, 1980, 1990, and 2001 (percent)

Year, Age, and Residence	Total		In Labor Force				Not in Labor Force	
			Employed		Unemployed		Retired, Other	
	Male	Female	Male	Female	Male	Female	Male	Female
1980								
55–64 years								
Metro	74.4	43.2	71.8	42.2	2.6	1.0	25.6	56.8
Nonmetro	69.5	39.4	67.4	38.3	2.1	1.1	30.5	60.6
65 years and older								
Metro	19.0	8.2	18.5	8.0	0.5	0.2	81.0	91.8
Nonmetro	19.4	8.7	18.9	8.3	0.5	0.4	80.6	91.3
1990								
55–64 years								
Metro	68.7	46.6	65.7	45.3	3.0	1.3	31.2	53.4
Nonmetro	63.7	42.1	60.4	40.7	3.3	1.4	36.2	57.8
65 years and older								
Metro	17.6	8.9	17.2	8.7	0.4	0.2	82.4	91.0
Nonmetro	17.2	9.1	16.7	8.8	0.5	0.3	82.7	90.9

Year, Age, and Residence	In Labor Force						Not in Labor Force	
	Total		Employed		Unemployed		Retired, Other	
	Male	Female	Male	Female	Male	Female	Male	Female
2001								
55–64 years								
Metro	69.2	54.6	67.0	53.2	2.2	1.4	30.8	45.4
Nonmetro	65.8	51.2	63.2	50.0	2.6	1.2	34.2	48.9
65 years and older								
Metro	18.6	9.7	18.0	9.4	0.6	0.3	81.3	90.3
Nonmetro	19.0	10.4	18.4	10.1	0.6	0.3	81.0	89.7

Source: U.S. Bureau of the Census, Current Population Survey, 1980, 1990, and 2001.
Due to rounding, row percentages for males and for females may not total exactly 100.

What kinds of jobs do older workers hold, how has this changed over time, and how does this affect their economic well-being? CPS data (not shown)[1] indicate that the majority of employed older persons in the United States, regardless of residence, occupy white-collar jobs and that dependence on these types of jobs has increased since 1980. This is especially true among workers aged 65 and older, particularly females. Since 1980, service jobs have increased as a source of employment among workers of all ages in the United States, but dependence on service jobs remained relatively stable among older male workers and declined among older women during this period. Farming and other extractive pursuits employ only a small percentage of persons in the United States, and this proportion remained relatively stable since 1980 among preretirement-age older workers. Such jobs, however, increased in importance among nonmetro men and women aged 65 and older. The proportion of older workers employed in skilled, semiskilled, and unskilled production jobs declined in both metro and nonmetro areas and among both women and men. This may reflect overall restructuring of economic activities that occurred in the United States in the '80s and '90s, but over one-quarter of the jobs in nonmetro economies are still in manufacturing, with older persons' involvement in such industries lower than that of younger workers.

In summary, our findings suggest that *older persons are most apt to remain in the workforce if they hold higher-status, well-paying jobs.* Older men and women who live in metro areas, however, are substantially more likely to occupy white-collar professions than their nonmetro counterparts.

The economic well-being of older workers, as measured by income, varies by residence due largely to the types of jobs that are available (data not shown). Higher-paying occupations in the managerial, professional, technical, sales, and administrative sectors are concentrated in metro areas, giving older metro working men and women an advantage over nonmetro workers. By the same token, nonmetro older men and women are more likely to be employed in lower-paying jobs in farming, forestry, and fishing, or as operators, fabricators, and laborers. A higher proportion of metro older workers is employed in service jobs than their nonmetro counterparts. Given that higher-paying producer service jobs are concentrated in metro areas and that the U.S. economy is increasingly comprised of service jobs, this may be yet another indicator of metro over nonmetro advantage among older workers.

The increase in labor force participation has been more rapid among women than men during the last two decades, but men and women continue to be concentrated in different occupational categories (data not shown). Men are more likely to be employed in managerial, professional, extractive, and production jobs, while women are concentrated in sales, administrative, and service jobs. This situation is similar to that of younger men and women (see, e.g., Reskin and Roos 1990). Sex segregation and the crowding of older women into particular occupational categories is evident, while older male workers are more evenly spread across occupational categories. Older working women are considerably more likely to be employed in lower-wage service occupations than are their male counterparts. Nationally, higher proportions of older male than female workers hold managerial and professional jobs, but fairly high proportions of both men and women are employed in management and the professions. Earnings in professional occupations traditionally occupied by women, however, are lower than earnings in men's professional occupations (Reskin and Roos 1990).[2]

Case Study: Upstate New York

In this section we present an economic and demographic profile of Cortland and Seneca Counties, New York. Then, we analyze data on labor force activity from our case study in rural upstate New York and compare those data with patterns shown in the nationally representative Current Population Surveys. The comparison between our case study and national-level findings places our case study into a broader context. Moreover, it grounds societal-level trends in the reality of a particular place.

While the U.S. economy grew during the latter half of the 1990s, the upstate New York economy has not fully recovered from the U.S. recession of the early 1990s (Eaton 2000). Overall, both rural and urban areas of upstate New York have lost jobs and population, although particular places within the region now have growing economies (Hirschl and Heaton 1999). In fact, Hillary Clinton, bidding successfully in 2000 to become U.S. senator from New York, made the lagging upstate economy a major issue of her campaign.

Like many upstate areas, Cortland and Seneca Counties (located approximately thirty-five miles apart) experienced plant and other firm closings shortly before and during the 1995 data collection for our case study. For example, the relocation of Smith-Corona's manufacturing plant from Cortland, New York, to Tijuana, Mexico, began in 1992 and concluded in 1995. Smith-Corona's work force peaked at 5,000 in the 1960s; 4,000 were employed in 1981; and 1,200 were employed at the factory in 1992, when the relocation decision was announced (Beneria 1998). During the next three years, all employees except those in marketing and sales were permanently laid off (over 850 employees). Consequently, Cortland County lost its largest employer of many years. The city of Cortland mobilized, and many laid-off workers got additional education, job retraining, and job placement assistance. But the majority of those workers' new jobs paid them less, and women workers lost a larger percent of their income than did men (Beneria 1998). Before the plant layoffs, Smith-Corona was an important source of employment for women. Approximately two-thirds of Beneria's sample of former Smith-Corona workers were women.

Beginning in the 1970s and continuing through the 1990s, several of Seneca County's largest employers closed their doors. The closings included the Willard Psychiatric Center, the Seneca Army Depot (with one thousand military and civilian jobs lost), the Samson State School, and a community college (Hill 2000). Only in 2000 did KidsPeace, a 360-job facility for troubled youth, and Five Points Correctional Facility, a 700-job state prison, open on the land the Seneca Army Depot occupied before closing. The proportion of the workforce of correctional facilities located in rural areas that is hired locally remains a question (Hill 2000). Nonetheless, Seneca County officials believe the local economy is turning around for the better. The two case study counties exemplify economic restructuring issues that many rural communities in the United States have faced during the last two decades.

AREA DEMOGRAPHICS

Cortland and Seneca Counties are officially designated as nonmetropolitan, and respondents' residences range from open-country rural to villages and small towns to small cities. The city of Cortland is the largest place in the two counties, with a 1990 census population of 19,801 and a 2000 census population of 18,740. Seneca Falls, the largest town in Seneca County, had a 1990 census population of 9,384 and a 2000 census population of 6,861. Declines in the populations of both cities between 1990 and 2000 may have been due to former residents moving elsewhere in search of better job opportunities. In 1995, Cortland County's overall population size was 49,052, of whom 12.2 percent were aged 65 and older; Seneca County's population was 32,593, with 14.7 percent aged 65 and older (U.S. Census 1996). By 2000 Cortland County's population was 48,599 and Seneca County's was 33,342. Although impossible to determine from census data, the decline in Cortland County's overall population may be related to the county's economic restructuring during the 1990s. Seneca County's population, on the other hand, increased slightly. Mennonites have moved into rural areas of Seneca County to farm. That group may have offset population losses due to economic restructuring and firm closings.

CASE STUDY ANALYSIS

Labor Force Participation

Fifteen percent of the sample of Cortland and Seneca County residents aged 65 and older were employed in 1995 (data not shown), which included 16.6 percent of the older males and 9.9 percent of the older females (table 16.2). Males and females aged 65–74 were more

Table 16.2
Labor Force Participation and Occupation by Age and Gender, Nonmetropolitan New York, 1995 (percent)

Age and Gender	In Labor Force Employed[a]	Not in Labor Force Retired, Other
65 years and older		
Males	16.6	83.4
Females	9.9	90.1
65–74 years		
Males	20.0	80.0
Females	14.0	86.0
75 years and older		
Males	10.4	89.6
Females	4.4	95.6

Age, Occupation[b] and Gender	In Labor Force	Not in Labor Force
65–74 years		
White-Collar		
Males	46.3	54.1
Females	86.1	81.3
Blue-Collar		
Males	53.7	45.9
Females	13.9	18.7
75 years and older		
White-Collar		
Males	54.5	47.5
Females	87.5	68.5
Blue-Collar		
Males	45.5	52.2
Females	12.5	31.5

Source: Survey of representative sample of persons age 65 and older in Cortland and Seneca Counties, New York, 1995.

[a] Unemployed was a response category in the question on labor force status and would have been shown as a separate category under In Labor Force, but no survey respondents reported being unemployed.

[b] If in the labor force, respondent's occupation is the current occupation. If not in the labor force, respondent's occupation is that held prior to retiring or dropping out of the labor force.

likely to be employed than were males and females aged 75 and older. By comparison, 18.4 percent of nonmetro males aged 65 and older were employed nationally in 2001, and 16.7 percent were in 1990 (cf. table 16.1). Among U.S. nonmetro females aged 65 and older, 10.1 percent were employed in 2001, and 8.8 percent were in 1990 (cf. table 16.1). *The case study respondents live in areas that experienced recession, economic decline, and restructuring, and even with that their labor force participation is similar to that among older nonmetro residents nationally.*

Occupations

Our *N* of 737 cases was reduced for occupation because slightly over 6 percent of the sample had never participated in the labor force. Working respondents, retired respondents, those who had become disabled and unable to work, and respondents who had worked but without continuous attachment to the labor force were asked what their occupations are or were. Respondents "in the labor force" were asked to identify their current occupation. The "in labor force" group is comprised of two categories of workers—the "working and never retired" and "retired and working" respondents (those who had retired from a career job but had reentered the labor force by 1995). Respondents "not in the labor force" were asked to identify their former occupation. An examination of occupations based on a detailed set of categories showed some cells with few cases; because of this, we compare occupations based on white-collar/blue-collar status only (U.S. Office of Personnel Management 1998).

"In the labor force" younger-old (age 65–74) males are more likely to work in blue-collar than white-collar occupations, whereas a higher proportion of males aged 75 and older are employed in white-collar than blue-collar occupations (table 16.2). Among men of more advanced age, current job holding is probably easier in white-collar than blue-collar occupations. The finding for older-old men is consistent with national-level findings on type of job holding among older workers. Among former workers, younger-old men's occupations were more likely to have been white-collar than blue-collar, but a higher proportion of older-old men held blue-collar than white-collar occupations.

The white-collar occupational advantage of younger-old compared with older-old men "not in labor force" probably reflects cohort differences in educational and occupational attainment during the men's working years.

Among women "in the labor force," slightly over 86 percent of those 65–74 years of age and, similarly, 87.5 percent of those 75 years and older hold white-collar occupations (table 16.2). Among women "not in the labor force," over 81 percent of younger-old but only 68.5 percent of older-old women were employed in white-collar occupations. White-collar occupations confer an advantage to older women remaining in the labor force. Age group differences among older women "not in the labor force" probably reflect cohort differences in educational and occupational attainment. As in other studies, older women are or were more likely than men to hold white-collar occupations, but many "women's" white-collar occupations, such as secretarial work, pay relatively low wages (Collins 1991).

Reasons for Retirement

More than 73 percent of the sample of rural older people reported being retired (data not shown). We asked reasons for retirement among both "retired and not working" and "retired and working" respondents, and the reasons displayed in table 16.3 pertain to all respondents who ever retired from a career job. When asked their reasons for retirement, "retired" respondents were permitted to indicate all reasons that applied to their decision. Percentages, therefore, add to more than 100 (table 16.3). Respondents' reasons for retirement reflect push-pull motivations, and they call attention to the *process* of making a major life course decision and transition to retirement.

On the questionnaire, retirees were asked their reasons for retirement in random order, but here we have grouped reasons by positive, negative, and neutral ("beyond one's control") answers (table 16.3). Higher proportions of retired individuals were positively rather than negatively disposed toward retirement (e.g., they wanted to retire or had sufficient income to do so).

Table 16.3
Reasons for Retirement among Age 65 and Older Males and Females, Nonmetropolitan New York, 1995

	Percent indicating reason was important[a]	
Reason for Retirement	Male	Female
Wanted to retire	80.6	77.4
Wanted to do other things	69.6	58.7
Had sufficient income	58.9	49.2
Offered early pension	22.1	10.1
Reached mandatory retirement age	21.7	19.6
Laid off	10.6	11.0
Unfavorable employer policy on older workers	3.1	3.4
Didn't like work	5.7	6.7
Didn't get along with boss	2.7	2.4
Effort not appreciated	2.7	3.7
Spouse retired	8.4	15.6
Poor health	14.1	14.7
Family member's health	4.2	15.9
Other	8.4	8.3

Source: Survey of representative sample of persons 65 and older, Cortland and Seneca Counties, New York.

[a] The questions on reasons for retirement were based on a four-point scale. Here, the *important* category has been recoded to include respondents who answered "very important" or "moderately important."

Among potentially negative reasons, however, about 22 percent of men and about 10 percent of women retired because they were offered an early retirement pension (table 16.3). Firms often offer early retirement pensions when downsizing. Early retirement programs are an unusual combination of incentives and coercion, and individuals who retire early because of job insecurity express greater dissatisfaction with the retirement transition than retirees who exercise greater control (Hardy and Quadagno 1995). Slightly less than 22 percent of men and almost 20 percent of women retired because they reached mandatory retirement age; they may have retired because they had to rather than because they wanted to. Approximately 11 percent of both older males and females retired after being laid off from a job. These three negative, or potentially negative, motivations for retirement may have adversely affected the economic well-being of retired rural older people. In the next section we investigate whether incomes are lower among retirees who may have been pressured or forced out of their jobs. Other "negative" reasons for retirement were relatively unimportant (table 16.3).

More than 14 percent of older men and women retired due to health problems, suggesting circumstances "beyond their control" (table 16.3). Almost 16 percent of women retired because of the health of a family member, whereas only about 4 percent of men did so for that reason. Women's traditional role in informal caregiving is an indicator of women's social reproduction responsibilities in society, which contribute to women's cumulative economic disadvantage (cf. Moen et al. 2000; Schulman and Anderson 1993). Moreover, a higher proportion of women than men retired because their spouse retired. Such reasons reflect traditional gender roles that restrict women's lifetime earnings. Men, on the other hand, were more likely to retire because they had sufficient income, suggesting men's cumulative advantage over women in earnings during the working stage of the life course.

Income

A life course perspective leads us to expect that older individuals' employment histories and different pathways into retirement will affect their economic well-being. Hence, we examine household income for the total sample, those currently in and out of the labor force, as well as among those who retired for selected reasons suggesting employer pressures to retire. The "in the labor force" group is comprised of "working and never retired," as well as "retired and working" older individuals. The "not in labor force" group includes "retired and not working" respondents, the disabled, those not continuously attached to the labor force during the working years, and those who never worked for pay. We limit our analysis of income among respondents who retired for "negative" reasons to "retired and not working" individuals, although a small number of older persons who retired for "negative" reasons were "retired and working" in 1995. Elimination of "retired and working" respondents from the analysis of household income among "negative" reasons respondents provides a clearer picture of the effect of being pressured from one's job on level of income during retirement. We, however, investigated income among "retired and not working," as well as "retired and working" respondents who retired from a career job for "negative" reasons (data not shown). Not surprisingly, "retired and working" have higher incomes than "retired and not working," "negative-reasons" older rural residents.

"In the labor force" respondents have higher incomes than "not in labor force" older persons (fig. 16.1). Household income is comparatively low among laid-off retirees and among those who retired because they reached mandatory retirement age. For example, only 3.2 percent of "mandatory retirement age" and only 6.0 percent of "laid-off" retirees have yearly household incomes of $40,000 or more. Low incomes (under $10,000 per year) characterize "mandatory retirement age" retirees (23.2 percent), more so than any other group in the analysis (fig. 16.1). Although the reason is unclear, it may be that "mandatory age" retirees are older on average and have used up some of their retirement income resources. By contrast, those offered an early retirement pension have higher household incomes than any other group, including currently working older persons (fig. 16.1). Simply having held a job that qualified former workers for a pension seems to have assured them of higher than average household incomes. The "in the labor force" group, on the other hand,

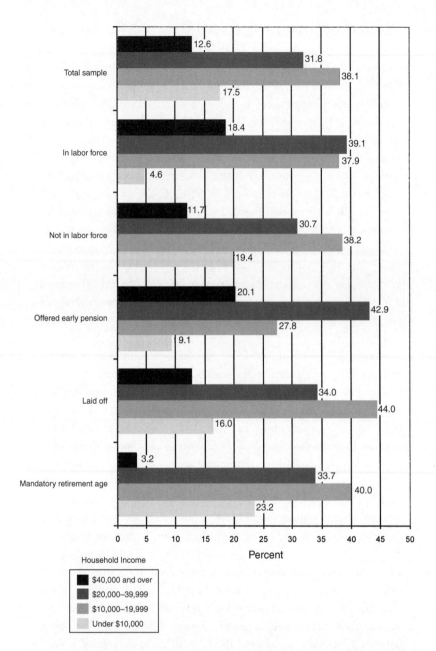

Fig. 16.1. Household income for total sample, by labor force status, and by selected "important" reasons for retirement, nonmetropolitan New York, 1995 (in percents). *Source:* Survey of representative sample of persons age 65 and older, Cortland and Seneca Counties, New York.

undoubtedly is comprised of individuals with pension benefits and those without.

Explaining Older People's Labor Force Attachment

Nonmetro older persons who remain in the labor force have higher incomes than most of their counterparts who have ceased working (fig. 16.1). But what factors are associated with remaining in the labor force? Older people's likelihood of working is determined by multiple factors, which may include their human capital, social capital, health, and driving status. We hypothesize that labor force participation among older individuals also depends on the level of urbanization of their place of residence; this should affect the diversity of opportunities available in local labor markets. We include variables representing these domains in our discriminant analysis.

HUMAN CAPITAL

Human capital theory focuses on workers' characteristics, especially education, as increasing their value to employers (Becker 1964). Individuals' investments in human capital are expected to increase their success in the labor market. Workers with higher levels of human capital get better jobs, experience greater job mobility, and become more economically secure. But do the advantages conferred by higher human capital persist in old age? Mutchler and colleagues (1997) found that labor force participation among older men was related more to need than to human capital endowments, but little research has been done on the topic.

Proponents of human capital theory often assume that education, training, and experience affect employment and earnings unhampered by discrimination based on age, race, and gender, and that geographic location does not affect one's labor market success. Returns to education, however, are lower for women, minorities, and those working in nonmetropolitan areas (e.g., McLaughlin and Perman

1991). Here, we compare the discriminating utility of human capital variables (education, occupation, and self-assessed economic well-being) versus workers' age and gender. Older age and female gender are individual-level opportunity-structure variables based on the division of labor in society that constrain their work lives (e.g., Schulman and Anderson 1993). Employment discrimination against women and older people is common. Thus, we assess the relative importance of each type of variable in predicting older persons' labor force participation. Given that nonmetro counties in upstate New York have largely white populations, we exclude variables on race or ethnic minority status.

SOCIAL CAPITAL

Granovetter (1973, 1983) theorized about the "strength of weak ties," proposing that secondary social ties—friends, neighbors, and relatives—are important sources of information about jobs. Conceptualized at the individual level of analysis, social capital refers to benefits accruing to individuals by virtue of their ties with others (e.g., Portes 2000). Hence, we label informal social network and formal organization networks "social capital." We hypothesize that higher informal and formal social participation will be positively associated with employment during old age because those individuals should have the connections to find and keep jobs during old age.

CONTROL VARIABLES

Health status and driving status are controls in our discriminant analysis. We hypothesize that health status and whether or not older individuals drive will affect their access to work. Poor health frequently is a reason for dropping out of the labor force, and Glasgow's (2000) bivariate level analysis found a significant relationship between driving and working. Public transportation availability is limited in our nonmetro case study area, and driving should facilitate older individuals' access to work.

We include contextual variables in the discriminant analysis to investigate whether employment during old age varies in relatively more and less urbanized areas. Given that the case study was conducted in two nonmetropolitan counties in upstate New York, geographic variation is limited. Nonetheless, we are able to assess variation in labor force participation by county of residence (a proxy for size of county), size of actual place of residence, and type of residence. The study counties differ in population size and other characteristics, and residents differ in the sizes of place and types of residence in which they live within their respective counties. We hypothesize that residence in Cortland County (the larger county) will be positively associated with labor force participation and that size of place and type of residence will distinguish between older people who work and those who do not. Larger communities are associated with greater social and economic complexity, which should enhance employment opportunities. Type of residence, in town versus the countryside, may also enhance access to jobs.

DISCRIMINANT ANALYSIS OF LABOR FORCE PARTICIPATION

The variables and operationalization of variables used in our discriminant analysis are described in an endnote.[3] We use discriminant analysis to investigate individual and contextual factors associated with labor force participation among older rural residents. Because very little past research has focused on determinants of labor force participation among older rural residents, we performed a stepwise discriminant analysis, which is appropriate for exploratory analyses (Klecka 1976). Discriminant analysis is also an appropriate method for this research because of the skewed distribution of the probability of being in the labor force (15 percent in vs. 85 percent not in).

We first conducted a discriminant analysis with all "not in labor force" respondents included in the analysis. We then conducted the analysis with "disabled" and "never worked for pay" individuals excluded from the "not in labor force" group because of our interest in the labor force participation of older individuals who are a potential pool of workers. Disabled older persons are unable to work, and it is unlikely that individuals could find or would start work during old age, if they never before worked for pay. The same variables were significant and the percentage of correctly classified cases was almost the same between the two discriminant analyses. Below we report the results of the discriminant analysis in which we restricted the composition of the "not in labor force" group to retired and not working, as well as respondents discontinuously attached to the labor force.

Our multivariate discriminant analysis of two known groups, "in labor force" and "not in labor force," produced one significant discriminant function (table 16.4). Statistical tests of the function show an overall Wilks' Lambda of .934 and a chi-square statistic of 43.595 with 4 degrees of freedom, which was highly significant ($p > .000$). The canonical correlation (.258) suggests a function that discriminates reasonably well between the two groups, as does the statistic showing 64.1 percent of correctly classified cases. Stepwise discriminant analysis adds the variable with the lowest Wilks' Lambda one step at a time. The threshold limit for F to Enter was 3.84 and for F to Remove was 2.71, which are the default positions in SPSS.

Four variables produced sufficient discriminating ability to be included in the stepwise model (table 16.4). Health status was the first variable included and the strongest predictor of labor force participation, followed by age, county, and gender. None of the social capital variables was significant in the discriminant analysis, and the human capital variables—education, occupation, and self-assessed economic well-being—were also nonsignificant in the model. Higher educational attainment and perceived economic well-being do not explain why some older rural residents are more likely to be in the labor force than others are. Gender was significantly related to labor force participation; older men were more likely than were women to work. This finding is consistent with past research on gender differences in labor force participation (e.g., Reskin and Roos 1990; Tickamyer et al. 1993). Net of health and other factors associated with age, we found that relatively younger-old persons were more likely to work than relatively older-old. Age is a factor in the division of labor in society, with older

Table 16.4
Discriminant Analysis of Older Nonmetropolitan
Residents' Labor Force Participation

Discriminant Variables and Statistical Tests	Standardized Discriminant Coefficients[a]
Human capital/opportunity structure	
Age	−.589
Gender (female/male)	.329
Occupation (blue-collar/white-collar)	—
Education	—
Self-assessed economic well-being	—
Social Capital	
Formal social networks	—
Informal social networks	—
Religious social networks	—
Living arrangements (alone/with others)	—
Control variables	
Health status	.573
Driving status (Non-driver/driver)	—
Level of urbanization	
County (Seneca/Cortland)	.362
Size of place	—
Type of residence (countryside/in town)	—
Stepwise descriminant analysis statistics	
Wilks' Lambda	.934
Canonical correlation	.258
Chi-square	43.595
Significance	.000
Percent cases classified	64.1
Group centroids[b]	
In labor force group	.645
Not in labor force group	−.110

Source: Survey of a representative sample of persons age 65 and older in Cortland and Seneca Counties, New York, 1995.

[a] Only coefficients for variables that were significant in the stepwise discriminant analysis are shown in the table.

[b] The centroids represent the groups' mean on the discriminating variables.

people constrained from participation in paid labor (Schulman and Anderson 1993). Riley, Kahn, and Foner (1994) argue that older people in general have a greater ability to contribute to society than they have structural opportunities for participation (the structural lag hypothesis). More recently, however, retirement has become normative and anticipated favorably by many older people as a stage in the life course (cf. table 16.3; Moen et al. 2000).

The significant effect of county showed that more of Cortland than Seneca County's older residents participated in the labor force. Residence in the larger county, as hypothesized, afforded older residents greater opportunity for employment. By contrast, the lack of an effect of size or type of place of residence on labor force participation indicates that older people respond to opportunities throughout the county rather than in their particular place of residence. Using the same survey data used here, a previous study by Glasgow (2000) showed that 87 percent of employed older people drove themselves to work. Hence, they are not limited to their own locale when choosing a place of work.

Older workers comprise an important part of the nation's work force in both metro and nonmetro areas. Most of the recent increase in labor force activity among older people in both areas is attributable to increased participation among women, although older women still are less likely than older men to be employed. Although similar proportions of metro and nonmetro older residents work, older metro people hold higher-status, better-paying jobs than do their nonmetro counterparts, and their incomes are higher.

National-level patterns characterize the labor force activity of older nonmetro residents of upstate New York. Analysis of our case study show that older people living in two relatively low-income nonmetro counties, which have undergone substantial economic transformation, were as likely to be economically active as were older people nationally. Our findings also show that nonmetro older people are more likely to be employed if they are in better health, are relatively younger, live in a relatively larger labor market area, and if they are male. *Human capital endowments and social connections, which may be important determinants of labor force participation among younger people, did not increase the labor force participation of non-metro older people in our case study.* Factors associated with labor force participation may differ at different stages of the life course. Moreover, nonmetro areas offer fewer returns to human capital than metro areas (McLaughlin and Perman 1991). The restriction of our analysis to nonmetro older residents may account for the nonsignificance of the human capital variables.

We used a life course perspective to investigate work and retirement among older nonmetro residents because the perspective focuses on the *processes* through which both occur over time. A life course perspective calls attention to cumulative advantage and disadvantage among particular groups based on characteristics such as age and gender. For example, our research showed significant age differences in occupational status among older workers. Among both women and men, relatively older individuals held lower-status jobs prior to retirement, reflecting cohort differences in educational and occupational attainment during their lifetimes. From a life course perspective, individuals' lives are viewed in the broader context of macrostructural historical events and social change (such as economic restructuring) specific to particular cohorts. Cohort differences indicate changing dynamics in the labor force participation of older rural residents. Moreover, the *context* of individuals' lives is a focus, thus providing a framework for understanding variations across space and social situation. For example, our study showed that older women were four times more likely than older men to retire because of their spouse's poor health. The implication is that many older women could remain in the work force if not for their social role as caregivers. A life course perspective extends theories of labor market structure to incorporate the combinations of structural and individual characteristics across space and time that determine the sum of local conditions. Older workers in our case study, or elsewhere in nonmetro America, cannot be treated as an undifferentiated population. Their current economic activity is affected by differences in current geographic and household context and by educational, familial, residential, and occupational choices they have made throughout their lives.

Choices are often constrained, however, and public policies to promote work opportunities for rural and urban older residents could enhance economic well-being among both groups. Such policies could help alleviate projected shortages of workers when the Baby Boom generation retires and allow older workers to reach their productive potential. Age discrimination in employment is common, however, and we need enforcement of policies that address the issue. Older women workers have closed the gap in labor force participation between themselves and their male counterparts to some extent, but parity has not been achieved. And sex segregation into particular occupational categories remains relatively high. Thus, policies to address gender differences in education, job training, hiring, and promotion opportunities continue to be needed in our society.

The discrepancies between rural and urban older residents in employment, occupational attainment, and income are likely to be best addressed by policies focused on strategies for rural economic development. The federal government does not have a comprehensive policy for rural economic development. The political will to improve the quality of rural jobs and the level of wages those jobs pay is more likely to be found at state and local levels of government. While promoting job growth and improved job opportunities for younger workers, public officials could also promote employment opportunities for older workers.

Notes

This research was partially funded by the Cornell University Agricultural Experiment Station under Regional Research Grant 1596340 and by the National Institute on Aging, Contract no. AG11171–05. The Cornell Gerontology Research Institute, an Edward R. Roybal Center on Applied Gerontology, provided an institutional framework for completion of the research. The research is also partially an outcome of Nina Glasgow's participation on the S-259, Rural Labor Markets in the Global Economy, Regional Research Committee. We thank David L. Brown for comments on earlier drafts of the chapter and Joe Francis for advice on the discriminant analysis.

1. The CPS data are available from the senior author upon request.

2. While we only discuss CPS findings on occupation in this chapter, a comparison of the industrial composition of metro versus nonmetro older workers produces a similar picture of greater concentration of women in "peripheral" industries and of overall advantage among metro versus nonmetro older workers. Those findings are available upon request from the senior author.

3. Human capital or opportunity structure variables include age (measured continuously in years, ranging from 65 to 97), gender (female = 0, male = 1), occupation (blue-collar = 0, white-collar = 1), education (8-point scale measure ranging from "eight years or less" = 1 to "doctorate or professional degree" = 8), and self-assessed economic well-being (4-point scale ranging from "not too well" = 1 to "very well" = 4). Social capital variables are formal social networks ("no," "yes" additive measure of club member and volunteer), informal social networks (frequency of face-to-face visits with relatives, friends, and neighbors, with each variable measured on a 4-point scale and used to form an additive measure), religious social networks (4-point scale of frequency of religious participation), and living arrangements (alone = 0, others = 1). Control variables in the analysis include health status (5-point scale ranging from "poor" = 1 to "excellent" = 5) and driving status (nondriver = 0, driver = 1). The contextual variables in the analysis are county (Seneca = 0, Cortland = 1), size of place (continuous measure of population size of the local township, village, or city jurisdiction in which respondent resided), and type of residence (countryside = 0, in town = 1).

References

Becker, Gary S. 1964. *Human Capital: A Theoretical and Empirical Analysis, with Special Reference to Education.* New York: National Bureau of Economic Research.

Beneria, Lourdes. 1998. "The Impact of Industrial Relocation on Displaced Workers: A Case Study of Cortland, New York." Community Development Research Briefs and Case Studies 6 (1). Ithaca: Cornell University, Cornell Community and Rural Development Institute.

Bloomquist, Leonard E., Christina Gringeri, Donald Tomaskovic-Devey, and Cynthia Truelove. 1993. "Work Structures and Rural Poverty." In *Persistent Poverty in Rural America,* ed. Rural Sociological Society Task Force on Persistent Rural Poverty, 68–105. Boulder: Westview.

Brewer, Geoffrey. 2000. "Out to Pasture, Greener Pasture: Older Workers Are Thriving in Tight Job Market." *New York Times,* June 21, Business Pages 1, 9.

Collins, Randall. 1991. "Historical Change and the Ritual Production of Gender." In *Macro-Micro Linkages in Sociology*, ed. J. Huber, 109–20. Newburg Park, Calif.: Sage.

Doeringer, Peter B. 1984. "Internal Labor Markets and Paternalism in Rural Areas." In *Internal Labor Markets*, ed. P. Osterman, 271–89. Cambridge, Mass.: MIT Press.

Eaton, Leslie. 2000. "Truth in Two Forms: Clinton and Lazio Both Right on Upstate." *New York Times*, October 29, pp. 33, 36.

Fuguitt, Glenn V., David L. Brown, and Calvin L. Beale. 1989. *Rural and Small Town America*. New York: Russell Sage Foundation.

Glasgow, Nina. 2000. "Transportation Transitions and Social Integration of Nonmetropolitan Older Persons." In *Social Integration in the Second Half of Life*, ed. K. Pillemer, P. Moen, E. Wethington, and N. Glasgow, 108–31. Baltimore: Johns Hopkins University Press.

Granovetter, Mark. 1973. "The Strength of Weak Ties." *American Journal of Sociology* 78:1360–80.

———. 1983. "The Strength of Weak Ties: A Network Theory Revisited." *Sociological Theory* 11:201–33.

Hardy, Melissa A., and Jill Quadagno. 1995. "Satisfaction with Early Retirement: Making Choices in the Auto Industry." *Journal of Gerontology: Social Sciences* 50B (4): S217–28.

Hill, David. 2000. "Prison Represents Hope for Romulus." *Ithaca Journal*, August 28, 1A & 5A.

Hirschl, Thomas A., and Tim B. Heaton, eds.. 1999. *New York State in the Twenty-First Century*. Westport, Conn.: Greenwood.

Klecka, William R. 1976. *Discriminant Analysis*. Beverly Hills: Sage Publications.

Lyson, Thomas A., William W. Falk, Mark Henry, JoAnn Hickey, and Mildred Warner. 1993. "Spatial Location of Economic Activities, Uneven Development, and Rural Poverty." In *Persistent Poverty in Rural America*, ed. Rural Sociological Society Task Force on Persistent Rural Poverty, 106–35. Boulder: Westview.

McGranahan, David A. 1988. "Rural Workers in the National Economy." In *Rural Economic Development in the 1980's: Prospects for the Future*, ed. D. L. Brown, J. N. Reid, H. Bluestone, D. A. McGranahan, and S. M. Mazie, 29–47. Rural Development Research Report no. 69. Washington, D.C.: Economic Research Service, U.S. Department of Agriculture.

McLaughlin, Diane K., and Lauri Perman. 1991. "Returns versus Endowments in the Earnings Attainment Process for Metropolitan and Nonmetropolitan Men and Women." *Rural Sociology* 56 (3): 339–65.

Moen, Phyllis, Vivian Fields, Heather E. Quick, and Heather Hofmeister. 2000. "A Life-Course Approach to Retirement and Social Integration." In *Social Integration in the Second Half of Life,* ed. K. Pillemer, P. Moen, E. Wethington, and N. Glasgow, 75–107. Baltimore: Johns Hopkins University Press.

Mutchler, Jan E., Jeffery A. Burr, Amy M. Pienta, and Michael P. Massagli. 1997. "Pathways to Labor Force Exit: Work Transitions and Work Instability." *Journal of Gerontology: Social Sciences* 52B (1): S4–12.

Portes, Alejandro. 2000. "The Two Meanings of Social Capital." *Sociological Forum* 15 (1): 1–12.

Reskin, Barbara F., and Patricia A. Roos. 1990. *Job Queues, Gender Queues.* Philadelphia: Temple University Press.

Riley, Matilda W., Robert L. Kahn, and Ann Foner, eds. 1994. *Age and Structural Lag.* New York: Wiley.

Schulman, Michael D., and Cynthia D. Anderson. 1993. "Political Economy and Local Labor Markets: Toward a Theoretical Synthesis." In *Inequalities in Labor Market Areas,* ed. J. Singelmann and F. A. Deseran, 33–47. Boulder: Westview.

Singelmann, Joachim, and Forrest A. Deseran, eds. 1993. *Inequalities in Labor Market Areas.* Boulder: Westview.

Tickamyer, Ann, Janet Bokemeier, Shelly Feldman, Rosalind Harris, John Paul Jones, and Dee Ann Wink. 1993. "Women and Persistent Rural Poverty." In *Persistent Poverty in America,* ed. Rural Sociological Society Task Force on Persistent Rural Poverty, 200–229. Boulder: Westview.

United States. Bureau of the Census. 1996. USA Counties, CD-ROM. Washington, D.C.

United States. Office of Personnel Management. 1998. *Federal Civilian Workforce Statistics: Occupations of Federal White-Collar and Blue-Collar Workers.* Washington, D.C.: Government Printing Office, September.

17

The Social and Economic Context
of Informal Work

Ann R. Tickamyer and Teresa A. Wood

ECONOMIC RESTRUCTURING AND associated changes in labor markets during the last quarter of the twentieth century have generated new interest in informal economic activity within fully mature industrial economies. Informal work more often has been the object of intensive study in developing societies, where it frequently is the dominant mode of economic activity. Only recently have social scientists who study work and labor markets recognized its widespread presence in Western, industrial and postindustrial societies. As informal work becomes increasingly visible, it joins other, better documented changes in patterns of work and employment that include a shift from manufacturing to service sector jobs, an increase in small businesses, the wide-scale holding of multiple jobs, rising female labor force participation, and an increase in all forms of marginal employment.

While there is growing interest in the extent to which informal work supplies an important source of income-generating or subsistence activity within advanced economies (Portes, Castells, and Benton 1989), numerous problems impede its systematic investigation. These begin with a precise definition of the term and extend to conceptual, theoretical, and methodological issues. There is wide variation in the literature as to what constitutes informal work, what activities make up the informal economy, where these activities are located, and what functions they serve (Portes 1994). Explanations for informal labor typically evoke different work and labor market strategies as part of larger constellations of family and household livelihood practices, but they vary by specific research tradition. An emerging picture of broad engagement in work outside the labor market has not been accompanied by specification or tests of different theoretical explanations for this activity. Finally there is a lack of systematic data available to investigate these forms of work. A few macro-level studies have attempted to assess the importance of informal activity for the economy as a whole (Smith 1987); numerous case studies provide extensive documentation of specific examples in particular times and places. Yet there is little information at a middle range—information that can answer questions about who does this work and under what circumstances; information that can be generalized beyond specific case studies to larger populations.

In this chapter, we investigate the social and economic context of informal work activity using data from a statewide telephone poll in Kentucky that was designed to explore the feasibility of using telephone survey methods to study informal work (Tickamyer and Wood 1998). The purpose is to determine who engages in informal activity and how it relates to formal labor market work for a sample that extends beyond localized case studies or restricted population groups. We examine competing theoretical claims about whether informal work functions primarily as a substitute for or a supplement to formal employment and how that reflects on livelihood practices for different groups. We conclude with a call for broader, more systematic study of informal labor as an important component of understanding changes in the intersections of work, families, households, and communities.

Conceptual Issues: Specifying Informal Work

One obstacle to a more systematic investigation of informal work is wide variation in how it is conceptualized and defined. Typically, informal activity is defined by what it is not: it is not part of the formal economy; it is not regulated; it is not counted in official statistics and national accounting schemes. Thus Castells and Portes define it as "a process of income-generation . . . unregulated by the institutions of society, in a legal and social environment in which similar activities are regulated" (1989, 12). A precise definition remains elusive, resulting in great variation in characteristics that distinguish between formal and informal work. These include type of activity, type of market, type of sanction, type of regulation, and type of exchange medium (Cappechi 1989; Castells and Portes 1989; Feige 1990; Pahl and Wallace 1995; Roberts 1994). Some analysts argue for a multiplicity of informal economies (Miller 1987) or for their inherent variability by specific context (Gaughan and Ferman 1987).

Empirical studies of informal activity identify a wide range of actual practices. Although specific operationalization varies, the most common criteria classify informal activity by type of exchange relationship and the specific kinds of goods and services transacted. Thus goods and services can be exchanged for money that goes unreported in any official venue, as exemplified by the house cleaner who gets paid in cash that is neither taxed nor reported by either employer or employee. Goods or services may be traded or bartered directly for the same or other goods or services, as in the trade of childcare services or childcare for firewood. They may be supplied and consumed to save money or to self-provision, as when members of a household raise a garden and preserve food for home consumption.

Specific goods, services, and activities vary from place to place. Urban dwellers are unlikely to raise livestock or cut wood for home consumption, but they are equally likely as rural residents to engage in the myriad of activities from childcare to household and auto repair that make up everyday life (Tickamyer and Wood 1998). Sweat shops and street vendors are most likely to be found in large urban labor markets (Gaber 1994; Sassen-Koob 1989), but industrial subcontracting and home assembly operations are well established in rural communities as well (Gringeri 1994).

One of the problems in specifying types of informal activity is in distinguishing informal from related forms of work and exchange, especially at the margins. For example, it may not be easy to distinguish between a formally conducted home business and one that largely or totally exists in the informal economy (Jurik 1998). Similarly there is a very fine line between recreational gardening versus self-provisioning. Informal labor overlaps with many other forms of waged and unwaged labor, including social and generational reproduction, self-provisioning and subsistence activities, consumption work, and community service as well as simple commodity production, self-employment, and subcontracting. Rather than representing informal work as completely distinct from formal labor market activity, it is better conceptualized as one end of a continuum. Given the blurred boundaries, most empirical studies examine a circumscribed subset of all possible forms of informal work. In this chapter we focus on a broadly representative number of specific work activities performed as any one of three types of exchange relations: the payment of money under the table, barter or trade, and savings or self-provisioning.

Theoretical Issues

Explanations for informal work focus on economic development status, locational factors, and the labor market opportunities available to particular population groups. In the United States, separate research traditions have developed among rural and urban social scientists as well as those who study immigrant populations and ethnic enclaves (typically in urban places). Women also are viewed as particularly likely to engage in informal labor.

For example, social scientists who specialize in rural social forms and processes tend to assume that informal activity is most prevalent in rural areas as extensions of long-held traditions of barter, exchange, and self-provisioning that are the legacy of a less commodified work, family, and community life traditionally associated with rural areas (Levitan and Feldman 1991). A slowly accumulating body of work on particular rural communities and regions illustrates the importance of various informal exchanges for agricultural communities and households (Lyson, Gillespie, and Hilchey 1995), among poor families

(Duncan 1992; Fitchen 1981, 1991,), and in particular regions (cf. Campbell, Spencer, and Amonker 1993, on the Ozarks, and Jensen, Cornwell, and Findeis 1995, on rural households in Pennsylvania).

Similarly, recent work by urban specialists on the importance of informal work in large metropolitan areas, particularly among the urban poor, ethnic enclaves, and recent immigrants often makes it seem that urban areas are most likely to display extensive forms of informal work (Edin and Lein 1997; Gaber 1994; Sassen-Koob 1989; Stepick 1989; Waldinger 1996). This impression has been reinforced by popular-media exposés of sweat shops, child labor, and other exploitative violations of labor law and workplace protections in large metropolitan areas.

Despite these different research traditions, there is little empirical evidence of rural-urban differences in the amount of informal work reported, although specific types of activity may vary (Tickamyer and Wood 1998). Race and ethnicity effects are often so closely tied to location as to be indistinguishable, as exemplified by studies of ethnic economies cited above. While there is evidence that gender shapes the type of informal work activities performed, there is less basis for the frequent assumption that women do more informal work than men (Hoyman 1987; Nelson 1999; Tuominen 1994). The prevalence of specific case studies provides little opportunity to determine if family and household structure, age, race, ethnicity, or region influence participation beyond the specific context studied in each case.

Perhaps even more important, there is much speculation about the economic circumstances that foster informal work. Thus relatively little is known about the relationships between informal activity and formal labor market participation for different groups, although most analysts agree that informal economies, sectors, activities, and labor can only be understood in relationship to their formal counterparts (e.g., Roberts 1994). There is no such thing as an informal economy in the absence of a formal economy. Theoretical and empirical work on economic restructuring and globalization suggests that informalization is a common outcome of the trends toward the deregulation, downsizing, and increased competition that these social and economic transformations bring. "Good jobs" that are full-time, secure, and provide benefits decline, while forms of contingent and marginal employment increase, even in times of relative prosperity. More and more people seek some form of contingent or informal labor. Thus informal work either substitutes for formal labor force participation when jobs in the formal economy are scarce or it may serve as a means to stabilize income when formal work is uncertain (Nelson 1999; Portes and Sassen-Koob 1987; Tickamyer and Bohon 2000). Which outcome is more prevalent and for whom is at best currently determined only for particular cases and locations.

The different approaches are captured in the form of linked questions: Is informal work a substitute for or a supplement to formal labor market employment and under what circumstances? Rural and community studies tend to portray informal work as supplemental work to other forms of income generation. Thus informal activity typically is portrayed partly as a means to augment income and partly as a way of life in rural communities. On the other hand, urban studies and those that focus on populations with a history of labor market disadvantage (minorities, recent immigrants, women) depict informal work as a substitute for formal and protected work. Thus off-the-books work provides income when other more desirable or less dangerous jobs are unavailable. Some research shows a complex combination of income-generating strategies that include formal and informal employment and self-provisioning, linked by the embedded relations between families, communities, and work. However, these studies are restricted by location, type of economy, or community (Gringeri 1994; Jensen, Cornwell, and Findeis 1995; Nelson 1999; Ziebarth and Tigges in this volume). In the research reported here, we explore the relationships between formal and informal work.

Methods

Most of the research on the informal economy uses labor-intensive case studies, qualitative methods, or intensive interviewing techniques, producing rich and detailed information on the activities of a relatively small number of peoples and places but restricted in its generalizability to broader populations and areas. Thus there is only limited information about the relative prevalence and location of informal activity and its relationship to social, economic, and formal labor market work across different populations and places. In comparison, telephone surveys can produce a large, geographically and demographically diverse data set quickly and inexpensively. However, phone surveys rely on short interviews composed of structured questions and therefore are limited in their ability to investigate complex issues that do not readily lend themselves to questions with simple, predetermined responses. It is often assumed that informal activities are examples of these issues that are hard to structure and quantify.

Additionally, it has been common wisdom that information on informal work is not amenable to structured survey techniques because of a combination of unwillingness and inability to answer questions about such activity on the part of survey subjects. The elusive nature of much informal activity, its often semilegal status, and the seeming lack of awareness of respondents of the extent of their participation in informal work—without using extensive probes—are seen as major obstacles to use of structured research methods. Recently, however, common wisdom has been questioned in the form of studies that demonstrate effective data collection on informal work and income-generating activities using structured surveys (Jensen, Cornwell, and Findeis 1995), random-digit dialing (RDD) telephone surveys (Tickamyer and Wood 1998), and multimethod research that demonstrates the reliability and mutually reinforcing nature of survey and interview data (Nelson 1999; Tigges and Ziebarth this volume). In this chapter, we build on the demonstrated validity of survey data to study informal work and to argue for yet more extensive use of these techniques.

We examine the relationship between social and demographic characteristics and between formal employment and income-generating activities and informal work activities using an RDD telephone survey conducted in 1994 in Kentucky. A statewide survey is certainly not representative of or generalizable to the entire U.S. population, and Kentucky is subject to particular limitations, such as a lack of racial and ethnic diversity; nevertheless, our study is more inclusive of geographic, demographic, and economic diversity than studies that intensively focus on a small number of communities, counties, or restricted population groups.

In the survey, in addition to standard questions about formal labor force participation, a series of closed-ended questions were asked to determine whether any household members engaged in any of a variety of informal work activities. These data permit investigation of the social and economic contexts of informal work, including whether and how respondents and their households combine formal and informal economic activities.

Data for this study come from the fall 1994 administration of the Biannual Kentucky Survey, a telephone poll of noninstitutionalized adults in the state of Kentucky that is administered each fall and spring by the University of Kentucky Survey Research Center to assess public opinion in the state. The sample was generated using the GENESYS Sampling Systems software package, which uses a list-assisted approach to generating a random sample of all working residential telephone lines in any defined geographic area. The phone numbers generated from this program include unlisted and newly assigned phone numbers. The fall 1994 survey included 649 completed interviews and a response rate of 42 percent.[1] The margin of error is approximately 3.5 percent (at the 95 percent confidence level). Table 17.1 provides information on sample characteristics.

Informal Work

A group of core questions are asked during each administration of the survey. In the fall of 1994, the series of questions on work and household composition were revised in an effort to better measure changes in labor force participation and household composition. Detailed questions were added to the survey to cover home-based work and

Table 17.1
Sample Characteristics of the Fall 1994 Kentucky Survey ($N = 649$)

Variable	Percentage
Gender	
Male	49.8
Female	50.2
Race/Ethnicity	
White	94.6
African American	3.6
Hispanic	.5
Other	1.4
Education	
Less than high school	23.1
High school graduate	37.7
Some college	18.7
Graduate work	7.7
Marital Status	
Married	66.3
Unmarried	33.7
Community Type	
Farm	14.5
Rural-nonfarm	21.1
Small town	39.2
Suburb	9.9
City	15.3
Median Household Size	2.6
Median Household Income	$27,500
Median Age	47
Kids (1 or more)	62.6
Employed outside the home	54.5
Number of Informal Activities	
Income/exchange	36.2
Income/exchange/savings	70.6

businesses, multiple job holding, and informal economic activity, as well as the standard questions about respondent's current employment status, self-employment, and job seeking. To construct structured measures of informal activity suitable for survey research, it is necessary to specify the types of activities and economic exchanges. Lists of specific activities were generated from the literature, local informants, and pretesting. They include holding yard sales, raising animals, and household and automobile repairs. (For a complete list, see table 17.2). A more difficult issue is how broadly to define the types of economic exchanges included in informal work. As indicated above, the literature includes examples of many different kinds of activities and exchanges, but a common approach includes work for money that is not reported, work in trade for the same or other goods and services, and work to save money or to self-provision. Typically, work done for a hobby or recreation is not considered part of the informal economy, but drawing the line between such avocational and vocational pursuits is not always easy. This study relied on respondents' understanding of their motives to make this distinction.[2] Illegal activities such as drug sales were not included in this study.[3]

Respondents were asked to indicate if they or anyone in their household performed each of seventeen informal activities "to save money, earn extra money, or in exchange for something else?" They were asked not to include "doing something purely for recreation or as a hobby." Results are reported separately for each of these types of exchanges. In addition to listing each of the seventeen specific informal activities, all informal items are summed to create measures that show the extent the sample engages in any form of informal work, regardless of type. Finally, two summary measures are constructed that combine any type of exchange (for money or trade or for money, trade, or savings) for each activity. These summary measures create dichotomous variables that when summarized for the entire sample indicate the proportion of the respondents who engaged in at least one of the activities. The exact wording of the questions is found in the appendix. Table 17.2 shows the seventeen activities and types of exchanges that were investigated in this study and the percentages of the sample who report engaging in each.

Table 17.2
Participation in Informal Work Activities by Type of Exchange ($N = 649$) (percent)

Exchange for Activity	Money	Trade	Savings	Money/ Trade	Money/ Trade/ Savings
Household repair	4.2	1.8	25.3	6.0	31.3
Auto repair	2.5	0.8	18.2	3.2	21.4
Personal service	5.5	1.4	6.0	6.9	12.9
Raise farm animals	2.8	0.3	3.4	3.1	6.5
Raise nonfarm animals	0.8	0.1	0.5	1.8	2.3
Garden/sell produce	0.6	0.5	21.1	1.1	22.2
Can/freeze/preserve	0.4	0.5	34.5	0.9	35.4
Handcrafts	3.5	0.6	4.1	4.2	8.3
Cut wood	2.0	0.6	7.9	2.6	10.5
Yard sales	16.0	0.6	1.0	16.6	17.6
Yard work	4.5	0.8	18.5	5.2	23.7
Take in boarders	1.5	0.3	0.2	1.8	2.0
Sewing	0.8	0.2	5.4	0.9	6.3
Tutoring	2.3	0.5	0.1	2.8	2.9
Bookkeeping	1.5	0.2	5.4	1.7	7.1
Typing/computer	1.7	0.8	1.8	2.5	4.3
Paint/wallpaper	2.2	0.8	18.0	2.9	21.0
1 or more activities	32.2%	8.5%	60.1%	36.2%	70.6%
Mean no. of activities	0.5	0.1	1.7	0.6	2.4
Standard deviation	2.0	0.9	0.5	1.1	2.4
Maximum	7	5	10	8	12

In this analysis we examine distributions of measures of informal activity in the total sample and in conjunction with a variety of demographic and socioeconomic measures, including gender, age (in years), current marital status, presence of children in the household, rural-urban residence, household income and its sources. Employment and income sources included employment status (employed/unemployed, full-time/part-time), whether looking for a job, whether respondent has more than one job, presence of other earners in the household, whether health insurance is a benefit of the job, and whether anyone in the household receives transfer income (welfare, social security, disability, unemployment compensation, etc). All variables except age and income are measured as dichotomous dummy variables. Depending on the analysis, age is grouped by decade or allowed to vary its full range, and income is trichotomized into less than $15,000, $15 to $30,000, and above $30,000. We then examine the relationship between informal work and formal labor market participation in a multivariate analysis to determine the relationship between formal and informal work, net of other social and economic influences.

Findings

Table 17.2 provides participation percentages for each specific informal activity and whether that activity entailed an exchange for money, for trade for goods or services, or whether it was used to save money. Rates of reported informal activity vary greatly, as demonstrated in the first three columns of the table. As should be expected, the savings or self-provisioning activities (seen in the third column) has the highest rates of participation, as do individual examples of work for savings. Slightly over 60 percent of the sample report saving activity in their households, with food preservation (can/freeze/preserve), household repair, yard work, auto repair, and home decoration (paint/wallpaper) having the highest rates, varying from 18 percent to a high of 34.5 percent for food preservation. Other activities do not attain percentages in the double digits. Although much lower than saving, work for money (first column), taken as a whole, also has substantial participation rates, with 32.2 percent of the sample reporting at least one of these activities. However, the individual work-for-money activities have much lower rates than saving, with only yard sales having close to a comparable rate (16 percent). Personal service, yard work, and household repair follow in the 4 to 5 percent range. Trade, or exchanges for goods and services (second column), are much lower, with a total of 8.5 percent of the sample reporting at least one activity.

In order to assess the prevalence of informal activity, table 17.2 also reports participation rates for the two different summary measures described earlier. The last two columns in the table show the combinations of money and trade (fourth column) and money, trade, and savings (fifth column). More than two-thirds of surveyed households report engaging in some form of informal economic activity. The fifth column demonstrates that the majority of the respondents reported that someone in their household had engaged in one or more of the activities either for money, in exchange for something of value, or in order to save money. When a stricter definition of informal work that combines only money and the trade of goods and services (fourth column), the results show a still substantial proportion (more than a third) of the population does at least one activity. These respondents are evenly split between those that report one activity and those reporting more than one (figures not shown). Adding savings increases the numbers sharply to a large majority of the sample. These summary measures demonstrate the widespread participation in some form of informal work.

Table 17.3 uses the three indicators of informal work—the sums of money, trade, and savings—to investigate the social and economic context of informal exchange. The first part of the table examines the relationships between demographic and household variables and informal work; the second half shows measures of employment and income generation. The results differ for the three measures of type of exchange: work for money, trade, and saving display different patterns of significant influences in t-tests and chi-square tests with only a few examples of consistent influences across two measures and no cases where all three display the same patterns.

Table 17.3
Participation in Informal Work by Social and Economic Characteristics

Characteristics	Percent Reporting 1 or More Informal Work Activity for		
	Money	Trade	Savings
Gender			
male	36.5*	9.6	60.1
female	27.9	7.4	60.1
Age			
18–29	45.3***	7.8**	52.3
30–39	46.4	16.4	63.6
40–49	35.7	5.0	61.4
50–59	18.7	8.0	61.3
60–69	15.2	8.7	68.5
70+	11.1	1.4	54.2
Marital status			
married	32.6	8.6	65.3***
unmarried	31.5	8.2	49.8
Children in household			
0	30.5	5.8*	66.7**
1 or more	33.3	10.1	56.2
Residence			
rural	32.5	10.0	66.7**
urban	31.9	7.7	56.6
Health insurance			
yes	36.6*	8.1	59.0
no	29.0	8.8	60.9
Employment and Income Variables			
Household income			
< $15,000	29.9	7.5	59.2
$15,000–30,000	36.4	9.8	56.4
> $30,000	34.3	8.8	67.6
Employment			
employed	38.4***	8.5	60.5
unemployed	25.2	8.5	60.2
full-time	37.2	8.8	60.1
part-time	44.6	7.1	62.5
Seeking job			
yes	50.0*	15.4	46.2
no	31.5	8.2	60.7

Table 17.3 (continued)

Characteristics	Money	Trade	Savings
More than 1 job			
yes	39.5	21.1**	63.2
no	31.8	7.7	59.9
Other earners in household			
yes	37.9**	9.5	66.6***
no	26.8	7.5	53.9
Home business			
yes	50.6***	15.7**	65.2
no	29.5	7.4	59.6
Transfer income			
Yes	22.6***	8.1	57.4
no	37.7	8.7	61.6

* $p < .05$, ** $p < .01$, *** $p < .001$

Gender, age, and health insurance through one's job show significant effects on money exchanges. Men are more likely to report informal work for money, but there are no significant gender differences for the other types of exchange. Age appears to be a strong influence, with reported participation rates peaking in the respondents' thirties and then steadily decreasing among older respondents. These differences attenuate for trade and disappear for saving. Household variables appear to be more important influences on saving activities. Married respondents and those in households without children are more likely to engage in at least one saving activity. Having kids also has a small effect on trade, but in the opposite direction. Rural-urban differences appear only for the measure that includes saving.

Differences in the relationships also occur when employment and income-generating activities are related to informal exchange. Respondents who are employed outside the home, who are looking for work, who have other earners in their household, and who report running a home business are more likely to report informal money exchanges. Those who receive transfer income are somewhat less likely to report informal exchange for money. Only those with more than one job and those with a home business are slightly more likely to report informal trade exchanges. The only variable among this group to influence saving is having other earners in the household. There are no income effects for any form of informal exchange. This is apparent when income is divided into three categories (as shown in table 17.3). These results hold when the full array of income categories are examined (not shown). For each income category, there is very little difference in proportions of households that report some informal work and those that do not.

Apart from the different patterns for different informal exchange indicators, these results suggest that informal work for money is more associated with employment and income-generating factors; saving is more influenced by household factors. The much smaller participation rates for trade and the few significant effects make these findings less definitive. The relationship between informal work and formal employment appears somewhat equivocal, especially for informal work for money. On the one hand, it appears that participation in informal work coexists with formal labor market activity, since there are higher rates for those who are employed and for those with more than one job (statistically significant only for informal trade). On the other hand, there are significantly higher rates for those seeking a job and those who have a home business, suggesting greater participation when employment is problematic. There are also higher rates among part-time workers, although these differences aren't significant, but lower rates for those with additional earners in the household and those who receive transfer income.

To sort through these disparate results, we further examine these relationships in a multivariate analysis. Each measure of informal exchange is used as the dependent variable in logistic regressions to test multivariate models that include both social context (demographic and household variables) and economic variables (employment and income sources). Table 17.4 shows analyses using the three measures of informal exchange as dependent variables in models that include as predictors the variables suggested by past research and the bivariate analysis : gender, age, marital status, presence of children, rural residence, whether employed outside the home, running a home business, the presence of other earners in the household, receiving health insurance through a job, receipt of transfer income, and job seeking. Other

Table 17.4

Logistic Regressions of Informal Work on Selected Social and Economic Variables

Variable	Money		Trade		Saving	
	B	Exp (B)	B	Exp (B)	B	Exp (B)
Gender (female = 1)	−0.15	0.86	−0.27	0.76	0.08	1.09
Age (years)	−0.04***	0.97	−0.02	0.98	0.01	1.01
Marital Status (1 = currently married)	−0.11	0.90	0.03	1.03	0.40*	1.50
Children (1 = kids in household)	−0.08	0.93	0.63(*)	1.89	−0.31(*)	0.73
Residence (1 = rural)	−0.09	0.92	0.18	1.19	0.37*	1.45
Employment (1 = employed)	0.41	1.51	0.04	1.04	0.15	1.16
Home business (1 = yes)	0.95***	2.59	0.88*	2.41	0.01	1.01
Other household earners (1 = yes)	0.20	1.23	0.19	1.21	0.31	1.36
Health insurance through job (1 = yes)	−0.25	0.78	−0.23	0.80	−0.35	0.70
Receives transfer income (1 = yes)	−0.05	0.96	0.35	1.43	−0.22	0.80
Looking for job (1 = yes)	0.69	1.99	0.60	1.82	−0.43	0.65
Constant	0.62		−2.44***		−0.03	
−2 log likelihood	733.45		358.57		829.22	
Model Chi₂ Square	74.48***		16.70		29.89**	
Pseudo R²	0.15		0.06		0.06	

* $p < .05$
** $p < .01$
*** $p < .001$
(*) $p < .10$

employment and income variables were eliminated after preliminary analysis confirmed bivariate results that showed no relationship.[4]

The most conspicuous result of the logistic regressions is what they do not show. Many of the bivariate results disappear. In the model using money as the informal measure, only age and having a home business have significant effects. In the second model, with trade as the dependent variable, only having a home business and (marginally) children in the household show significant effects, in an overall model that is not a particularly good fit. Three household variables influence saving in the multivariate model: both being married and rural residence increase work for savings; having children slightly reduces it. Other employment and income generation variables fail to significantly influence informal work.

This study provides information about the social and economic contexts in which informal work activity takes place. It examines who engages in informal work and under what conditions for a broader sample of population and place than is usually studied. The most noteworthy finding is evidence of widespread participation. Participation in the informal economy is more common than previously thought. Looking at all forms of informal work examined here, more than two-thirds of the sample report at least one activity. The highest levels—as might be expected, given the routine nature of these tasks—are in saving and self-provisioning, but almost a third of the respondents report at least one informal work activity for money. A much lower percentage (8.5 percent) of the sample indicate that they trade goods or services.

The widespread participation may help account for the failure to definitively specify conditions that make informal work more likely. A variety of social, demographic, and economic variables are associated with the different types of informal exchange, but the only clear patterns that emerge are that different social and economic variables are related to different types of informal exchanges. There is some evidence that household factors have a stronger influence on saving and self-provisioning, whereas employment has a more consistent effect on informal work that involves cash exchanges. These results reinforce a view of informal work as a multidimensional phenomena, with different reasons and circumstances contributing to different forms of participation.

Some of the results either run counter to or provide less than definitive support for the findings of past studies. For example, the only gender difference is a slightly higher rate of exchange for money reported by men. This result runs counter to studies that assume greater activity level for women but corresponds to findings reported by Nelson and Smith (1999) that men's informal work is more lucrative. Locational differences only appear on saving, where rural residents are slightly more likely to report engaging in one or more saving and self-provisioning activities. On the surface this provides support for the claim that rural lifestyles lend themselves to informal activity, especially forms of self-provisioning. However, the lack of strong uniform effects across the different indicators of informal work makes it too early to affirm case study results that see informal activity as the outcome of particular locations and economic conditions. The strong relationship with age is not predicted in the literature but, in conjunction with some of the other household factors, suggests that life course may play an important role in determining informal activity. One possible explanation is that as people age they are more often the beneficiaries of services from family and friends rather than active participants themselves. Another possibility is that social networks and contacts diminish with age. These are topics for future research.

The results are mixed with regard to the substitute-versus-supplement hypotheses. The emergence of the effect of running a home business suggests that many of the reported activities conducted in conjunction with this business may well function as a primary source of income. Indeed, some analysts conflate small businesses (very small enterprises) with informal work, an assumption that receives some support in this context. At the same time, the failure to find strong, uniform effects in the multivariate analyses for employment and income variables suggests that those with the least adequate employment or income are no more likely to report informal work than others. This makes it appear that informal work is opportunistic, to be performed when time and circumstances make it convenient and available. This fits with recent research that finds more informal work among families who have at least one member with a well-paying job and whose economic circumstances are relatively stable (Nelson and Smith 1999). In this interpretation, informal work appears more as a supplement to formal labor force participation than as a substitute. Similarly, it supports the idea that informal work is embedded in a larger social and economic context where it represents only one component of complex livelihood strategies that involve multiple sources of income, multiple earners, and multiple activities, regardless of the family's overall economic standing.

To determine more definitively whether informal work serves primarily as a supplement and means to stretch household income requires additional investigation, and the results reported here suggest directions for future study. One key aspect of informal economic activity that was not tapped in this survey is the importance of the activity to the financial well-being of the household. One intriguing clue to this connection emerged in exploratory analysis to see why there was no income variation. Respondents who rated their financial situation as either much better or much worse than in the previous year were more likely to engage in informal economic activities for cash and for saving. This may mean that there are two distinctly different groups of people engaged in informal economic activities. Those who fall on economic hard times (those much worse off than the previous year) may use informal economic activities as a way of getting through those times (i.e., as a substitute). While another distinct sector (those much better off than in the previous year) may engage in informal economic activity as a way of increasing already adequate income levels (i.e., as a supplement). In other words, informal work and exchange is part of a group of livelihood practices that vary less by class or status than by current need and circumstances.

In addition to economic contributions and circumstances, greater scrutiny of different forms of employment will be useful. One direction to examine is the relationship between entrepreneurial activity and self-employment with informal work. The association of having a home business with informal work for money suggests that there is a fine line between formal and informal work. These relationships require more detailed investigation.

This study examines a cross-section of one state, using a relatively limited set of questions in an omnibus survey, one not solely devoted to investigating this topic. It demonstrates the feasibility of the method, the value of broadening the base for studying informal work, and the relative economy of these procedures. Much information can be elicited, even with severe time and space restrictions, suggesting that more routine inclusion of such questions in broad-based survey research would advance understanding of the labor deployment and livelihood practices that individuals and families use under a variety of circumstances. Regular inclusion over time would make it possible to specify the relationship between processes of informalization and changes in the larger economy. The results would be a much better understanding of the social and economic contexts of both informal and formal work and labor market processes as they vary across time and space as well as social group and economic circumstance.

Appendix

Fall 1994 Kentucky Survey/Informal Economy

*** QUESTION # 57 ***
Next I'm going to read a list of extra work some people do to help them get by. You might be doing one or more of these things to save money, earn extra money, or in exchange for something else.

In the past 12 months, have you or any member of your household done any of the following things to save money, earn extra money or in exchange for something else? Please do not include doing something purely for recreation or as a hobby.

Household repair or handiwork (plumbing, roofing, appliance repair, driveway patching)

(IF YES ASK: Did you do this or did someone else in your household do it?)

    GO TO Q. # 58 ====> < 1 > Respondent did it
    GO TO Q. # 58 ====> < 2 > Someone else in household did it
    GO TO Q. # 58 ====> < 3 > Both
    GO TO Q. # 59 ====> < 4 > Did not do
    GO TO Q. # 59 ====> < 8 > DK
    GO TO Q. # 59 ====> < 9 > REF

*** QUESTION # 58 ***

Did you/they do this to save money, earn extra money, or in exchange for something else?

    GO TO Q. # 59 ====> < 1 > Save
    GO TO Q. # 59 ====> < 2 > Earn extra money
    GO TO Q. # 59 ====> < 3 > Exchange for something else
    GO TO Q. # 59 ====> < 4 > (VOLUNTEERED: As a hobby)
    GO TO Q. # 59 ====> < 8 > DK
    GO TO Q. # 59 ====> < 9 > REF

Notes

1. This response rate is lower than usual and may be due to this poll being conducted at the time of a heavily contested state election. While we have no definite support for this hypothesis, we speculate that the very large number of polls and surveys conducted at that time, in and out of state, may have resulted in respondent fatigue or reluctance to participate in one more survey. This does not appear to have any effect on the representativeness of the survey, as respondent characteristics correspond closely both to state demographics and to results from biannual polls before and after this one.

2. The other basic concern was whether it was best to ask about informal work in an open-ended or a closed-ended format. The primary advantage of the open-ended format is that it allows the respondent to mention activities that a researcher might fail to ask about in a closed-ended format. Tightly focused closed-ended questions, on the other hand, have the advantage of giving respondents a fixed issue to respond to and a standardized format for answering the question. In three different administrations of the Kentucky survey we experimented with different question formats. For the initial effort, the fall 1994

survey, we constructed a set of closed-ended questions. We then switched to open-ended questions for the spring and fall 1995 surveys. This procedure allowed us to compare the results of these different methods of question construction. After analysis of all three surveys we concluded that the closed-ended questions provided the most reliable results (for details of this comparison, see Tickamyer and Wood 1998). In the current study, we rely only on the structured questions of the fall 1994 survey to provide the data on the issues of interest.

3. The decision to exclude overtly illegal or illicit activities (as opposed to violations of labor and tax laws and regulations) follows the distinction found in the literature between different dimensions of the "underground economy" (Feige 1990). While it may eliminate livelihood strategies of some individuals or households, it is not the intent of this study to investigate criminal activity.

4. Type of industry and type of occupation were investigated in the preliminary analysis.

References

Campbell, Rex R., John C. Spencer, and Ravindra G. Amonker. 1993. "The Reported and Unreported Missouri Ozarks: Adaptive Strategies of the People Left Behind." In *Forgotten Places: Uneven Development in Rural America,* ed. T. Lyson and W. Falk, 30–52. Lawrence: University Press of Kansas.

Cappechi, Vittorio. 1989. "The Informal Economy and the Development of Flexible Specialization in Emilia-Romagna." In *The Informal Economy: Studies in Advanced and Less Developed Countries,* ed. A. Portes, M. Castells, and L. Benton, 189–215. Baltimore: Johns Hopkins University Press.

Castells, Manuel, and Alejandro Portes. 1989. "World Underneath: The Origins, Dynamics, and Effects of the Informal Economy." In *The Informal Economy: Studies in Advanced and Less Developed Countries,* ed. A. Portes, M. Castells, and L. Benton, 11–37. Baltimore: Johns Hopkins University Press.

Duncan, Cynthia M. 1992. "Persistent Poverty in Appalachia: Scarce Work and Rigid Stratification." In *Rural Poverty in America,* ed. C. Duncan, 111–33. New York: Auburn House.

Edin, Kathryn, and Lein, Laura. 1998. *Making Ends Meet: How Single Mothers Survive Welfare and Low-Wage Work.* New York: Russell Sage Foundation.

Feige, Edgar. 1990. "Defining and Estimating Underground and Informal Economies: The New Institutional Economics Approach." *World Development* 18 (7): 989–1002.

Fitchen, Janet M. 1981. *Poverty in Rural America: A Case Study.* Boulder: Westview.

———. 1991. *Endangered Spaces, Enduring Places: Change, Identity, and Survival in Rural America.* Boulder: Westview.

Gaber, John. 1994. "Manhattan's Fourteenth Street Vendors' Market: Informal Street Peddlers' Complementary Relationship with New York City's Economy." *Urban Anthropology* 23 (4): 373–407.

Gaughan, Joseph, and Ferman, Louis. 1987. "Toward an Understanding of the Informal Economy." *Annals of the American Academy of Political and Social Science* 493 (September): 15–25.

Glazer, Nona Y. 1993. *Women's Paid and Unpaid Labor: The Work Transfer in Health Care and Retailing.* Philadelphia: Temple University Press.

Gringeri, Christina. 1994. *Getting By: Women Homeworkers and Rural Economic Development.* Lawrence: Kansas University Press.

Hoyman, Michele. 1987. "Female Participation in the Informal Economy: A Neglected Issue." *Annals of the American Academy of Political and Social Science* 493 (September): 64–82.

Jensen, Leif, Gretchen T. Cornwell, and Jill L. Findeis. 1995. "Informal Work in Nonmetropolitan Pennsylvania." *Rural Sociology* 60 (1): 67–107.

Jurik, Nancy C. 1998. "Getting Away and Getting By." *Work and Occupations* 25 (1): 7–35

Levitan, Lois, and Shelly Feldman. 1991. "For Love or Money: Nonmonetary Economic Arrangements among Rural Households in Central New York." In *Research in Rural Society and Development* 5, ed. Daniel C. Clay and Harry K. Schwarzweller, 149–72. Greenwich, Conn.: JAI Press.

Lyson, Thomas A., Gilbert W. Gillespie, and Duncan Hilchey. 1995. "Farmer's Markets and Local Communities: Bridging the Formal and Informal Economy." *American Journal of Alternative Agriculture* 10:108–13.

Miller, S. M. 1987. "The Pursuit of Informal Economies." *Annals of the American Academy of Political and Social Science* 493 (September): 26–35.

Mingione, Enzo. 1991. *Fragmented Societies: A Sociology of Economic Life beyond the Market Paradigm.* Cambridge, Mass.: Basil Blackwell.

Nelson, Margaret K. 1999. "Economic Restructuring, Gender, and Informal Work: A Case Study of a Rural County." *Rural Sociology* 64 (1): 18–43.

Pahl, R. E., and Claire Wallace. 1995. "Household Work Strategies in Economic Recession." In *Beyond Employment: Household, Gender, and Subsistence,* ed. Nanneke Redclift and Enzo Mingione, 189–227. London: Basil Blackwell.

Portes, Alejandro. 1994 "The Informal Economy and Its Paradoxes." In *The Handbook of Economic Sociology,* ed. N. J. Smelser and R. Swedberg, 426–49. Princeton: Princeton University Press.

Portes, Alejandro, Manuel Castells, and Lauren A. Benton, eds. 1989. *The Informal Economy: Studies in Advanced and Less Developed Countries.* Baltimore: Johns Hopkins University Press.

Portes, Alejandro, and Saskia Sassen-Koob. 1987. "Making It Underground: Comparative Material on the Informal Sector in Western Market Economies." *American Journal of Sociology* 93 (1): 30–61.

Roberts, Bryan. 1994. "Informal Economy and Family Strategies." *International Journal of Urban and Regional Research* 18 (1): 6–23.

Sassen-Koob, Saskia. 1989. "New York City's Informal Economy." In *The Informal Economy: Studies in Advanced and Less Developed Countries,* ed. A. Portes, M. Castells, and L. Benton, 60–77. Baltimore: Johns Hopkins University Press.

Schuman, Howard, and Stanley Presser. 1981. *Questions and Answers in Attitude Surveys: Experiments on Question Form, Wording, and Context.* Orlando, Fla.: Academic Press.

Smith, James D. 1987. "Measuring the Informal Economy." *Annals of the American Academy of Political and Social Science* 493 (September): 83–99.

Stepick, Alex. 1989. "Miami's Two Informal Sectors." In *The Informal Economy: Studies in Advanced and Less Developed Countries,* ed. A. Portes, M. Castells, and L. Benton, 111–34. Baltimore: Johns Hopkins University Press.

Tickamyer, Ann, and Stephanie Bohon. 2000. "The Informal Economy." In *Encyclopedia of Sociology.* 2d ed. New York: Macmillan.

Tickamyer, Ann R., and Teresa A. Wood. 1998. "Identifying Participation in the Informal Economy Using Survey Research Methods." *Rural Sociology* 63 (2): 323–39.

Tuominen, Mary. 1994. "The Hidden Organization of Labor: Gender, Race/Ethnicity, and Child-Care Work in the Formal and Informal Economy." *Sociological Perspectives* 37:22–45.

Waldinger, Roger. 1996. *Still the Promised City? African-Americans and New Immigrants in Postindustrial New York.* Cambridge, Mass.: Harvard University Press.

Empirical Realities, Theoretical Lessons, and Political Implications

What Have We Learned?

The chapters in this volume represent diverse locales, topics, disciplines, and methods. Overall, we believe they provide a representative account of current trends in rural America and of the social science research that investigates it. They illustrate the richness of the experience of rural communities, the variety of approaches to creating livelihoods, and the fruitfulness of diverse strategies for data collection to tell the story of rural life. What can the reader learn from this collection of case studies?

Rural Realities

The case studies illustrate that no rural area, no matter how remote, has been impervious to the massive social and economic transformations of the post–World War II era. Social and economic restructuring, the reorganization of agriculture and natural resource–based industries, de-industrialization, the shift to a service economy, and major demographic changes in population composition and processes are among the transformations that impact rural communities and residents. There is no single standard response or outcome. The uneven social and economic development of rural communities shows that diverse configurations of geography, economy, population, and history must be respected in analyzing these transformations. In short, place matters.

Work also matters. The viability of local communities depends on the strength of local labor markets and their industrial and occupational composition. Rural America remains a prime site for disproportionate and persistent poverty, a situation that is unlikely to change readily in a time of accelerating globalization guided by free market politics

419

and policies. Residents of remote rural places, bypassed by economic development, struggle to provide livelihoods for themselves and their families. They often rely on forms of public assistance, transfers, and a mix of formal and informal practices, few of which—individually or collectively—provide an adequate living (ch. 11, White et al.).

Even in the face of persistent poverty and diminished opportunities, a sense of community and attachment to place persist and flourish. Several of the case studies demonstrate the lengths that people will go to maintain or recreate cherished forms of family, community, and culture, often pursuing diverse livelihood strategies that transcend definitions of formal employment and stable work (among others, see ch. 6, Deseran and Riden; ch. 7, Brown; ch. 12, Webb; ch. 16, Glasgow and Barton). Yet these diverse forms of work remain a source and force of local culture, reinforcing attachment to place and motivating individuals to seek the means to maintain these connections (ch. 17, Tickamyer and Wood). Americans may be more often "bowling alone" (Putnam 2000), but they continue to find ways to maintain their family and community networks, even in the face of great hardship (ch. 8, Falk). As we state above, place matters (for a wonderful overview of the interdisciplinary literature on place, see Gieryn 2000).

Furthermore, rural areas are the location of substantial social and economic diversity, more than is generally understood or acknowledged, both historically and currently. Rural America has never been the sole bastion of white farmers and shopkeepers of European ancestry, as the popular stereotypes depict. In addition to the large historic presence of African Americans, Latina/os, and Native Americans in particular rural regions, rural America has also been the site of population shifts and movements of different racial and ethnic groups. In these chapters, we catch a glimpse of this diversity and its dynamic nature as it fluctuates with economic changes. Thus African Americans leave and return (ch. 8, Falk; ch. 12, Webb), pushed away by the absence of work and opportunity, lured back by family and community ties and, sometimes, new work. Newer immigrant groups from Latin America, Asia, and Eastern Europe vie for niches in particular industries, creating ethnic enclaves similar to patterns observed among urban immigrants but driven by the unique dynamics of rural regions. Among longtime white rural residents, class differences create huge variations in opportunity, lifestyle, and employment status (ch. 10, McMillan and Schulman).

Class differences permeate social relations and characterize the realities of rural residence (ch. 11, White et al.). Even as new opportunities emerge, old patterns of inequality and deprivation are reinforced or recreated (ch. 2, Anderson, Schulman, and Wood). For many rural regions and communities, economic decline is a long-standing pattern, perhaps best exemplified in the declining agriculture, natural-resource, and manufacturing sectors (ch. 1, Lobao, Brown, and Moore; ch. 4, Latimer and Mencken; ch. 9, Crump). In other rural regions, economic restructuring has created new employment and economic activity, but also new sources of inequality (ch. 3, Henry, Drabenstott, and Mitchell). Innovative survival strategies are often developed to deal with the changed opportunities that restructuring engenders (ch. 13, Struthers and Bokemeier; ch. 15, Carro-Figueroa and Weathers). An influx of wealthy outsiders creates new service sector jobs related to the growth in amenity consumption, tourism, or retirement communities (ch. 5, Goe, Noonan, and Thurston). It also raises prices and the cost of living, pricing low-income residents out of the local housing market (ch. 13, Struthers and Bokemeier; ch. 14, Ziebarth and Tigges). The community as a whole may grow and prosper, but without the participation of large segments of the population, some of whom find it increasingly difficult to hang on to a livelihood.

Despite ongoing problems, rural areas are very much alive. The contributions to this book show the continuities and discontinuities in the traditional social and economic organization of rural America. Economic restructuring has profound impacts on the communities and livelihood practices of rural residents who, in turn, respond as active interpreters, negotiators, and occasional resisters of restructuring.

Theoretical Lessons

The empirical realities are accompanied by important theoretical lessons. These include the primacy of spatial analysis; the importance of recognizing the embedded social relations that link families, households, livelihood practices, and place; the contingent nature of community and social capital; and the need to integrate components of work and community with larger social processes of production and reproduction. The concept of communities of work attempts to embody these connections, emphasizing the links among analytic and spatial categories.

PLACE AND SPACE

Each of these chapters provides a location-based analysis using a case study approach. These strategies put into practice our growing conviction that spatial analysis is an important component of any social analysis and that to understand the social and economic impacts of restructuring requires understanding how processes vary by distinct locales. For example, the social processes that characterize the agriculture and natural resource–based communities of the heavily African American Mississippi Delta and the South Carolina Low Country contrast sharply with industrial-based labor markets of white-dominated North Carolina textiles and South Carolina meat-packing industries. Individually and collectively, the case studies illustrate the issues of scale and measurement, of comparative advantage and disadvantage, and of meaning, control, and construction, which informed analysis of spatial inequalities requires (Tickamyer 2000). We see accounts of how local structures intersect with global processes, how inequalities are transformed or perpetuated in poor rural communities, and how the meaning of place emerges from the lives and livelihoods of local peoples as they intersect with larger economic realities.

EMBEDDED SOCIAL RELATIONS

In contextualizing social processes within spatial parameters and vice versa, our focus on communities of work also represents an effort to move beyond the limits of conceptualizing all social phenomena as products of ahistorical and aspatial interactions among class, race, and gender. This is not to deny the importance of class, race, and gender, as well as age, sexuality, ethnicity, and other sources of categorical inequalities (Tilly 1999). Rather, the failure to contextualize or embed the matrix of domination (Collins 1990) in time and space leads to sociology without society. In this volume we have demonstrated the importance of analyzing these issues, following the prescription to incorporate "spatial context, both as setting and as yet another dynamic component of stratification" (Tickamyer 2000, 810).

The case studies show that, contrary to traditional social science approaches, community is a not a residual category (i.e., what is left after you take account of class, race, and gender) and that work involves more than jobs, markets, and wages. Or perhaps, to phrase this more constructively, work and community are not just separate or equal spheres of social life. Work and community are a series of embedded social relations that are economic and demographic, spatial and temporal, composed of numerous overlapping and nested social forms and processes, linking households, families, industries, and occupations within political and geographic boundaries that maintain and create cultural values. For the individual, decisions to leave or stay, or to pursue one livelihood strategy over another, are partly a rational economic calculus, but they are also the outcome of social forces that impinge and shape economic circumstances. For the community, the outcomes are partly the sum of the individual actions and decisions, equally reflective of the larger structural forces summarized in the weight of history. The chapters in this volume show the profound importance of both structure and action for the analysis of social relations. Social structures are embedded in time and space. They constrain and enable forms of social organization and forms of social action.

COMMUNITIES VERSUS SOCIAL CAPITAL

This collection informs recent debates over the decline of community, the role of social capital, forms of social networks, and sources of civic engagement that have entertained social scientists in recent years (for a good sample of the issues and arguments, see reviews of Putnam by Etzioni, Wilson, and Edwards and Foley in the symposium in the May 2001 issue of *Contemporary Sociology*). Claims about the decline of community, somewhat ironically, have fueled a rebirth in interest in the topic among social scientists, revitalizing the study of community as an analytic concept and as the actual site of social life. Whether one accepts the view that social capital and community are conflated in current usage, that social capital is really just another (weaker) term for community (Etzioni 2001), or that the concept provides one theoretical approach for constructing empirically testable hypotheses about the viability of community (Young 2001), the existence of such arguments speaks to the vitality of community as a sociological subject and the need to understand what makes communities work. They form part of a revived debate over what factors are involved in whether communities decline or prosper or merely survive (Schulman and Anderson 1999).

The studies in this volume and our concept of communities of work are meant to inform these issues. Civic engagement, participation in voluntary organizations, networks of interaction, organizational and physical settings for such interaction—all the elements of social capital—may be necessary for the existence of community, but by themselves they are not sufficient, at least not if community is conceptualized spatially and as actual sites of social action and interaction places—rather than as an ideological abstraction. To have viable communities and community organizations, it is necessary to have discernable livelihoods as well. Work provides the material substance and ideological glue that determines the fortunes of communities as well as those of their individual members. More often than not, it also provides the shared meanings that make communities more than merely the sum of the individuals who reside there (Etzioni 2001). As we have argued previously and as illustrated by these narratives, work and community are embedded concepts that provide the contexts for each other.

INTEGRATING FACTORS OF WORK AND COMMUNITY

Finally, these chapters demonstrate the value of reuniting components of work and community. It has been fashionable among social analysts of different theoretical persuasions to variously emphasize different components of work and livelihood: Marxists focused on production; feminists on reproduction; postmodernists on consumption. These studies demonstrate the value and necessity for considering each of these components individually and combined. The concept of communities of work reunites these concepts, providing a conceptual apparatus for considering the connections between the factors of production and exchange—jobs, enterprises, industries, commodity systems, labor markets; of reproduction—household and family-level social relations and class structures; and consumption—access and availability of resources, goods, and services that determine quality of life. It is through this integrative aspect of the communities of work concept that case studies and narrative approaches can complement more traditional quantitative methods and analyses.

Our emphasis on the embeddedness of work and community in time and space is not meant to substitute for a theory of society and how it changes. The concept of embeddedness cannot replace the theories and worldviews that form the components of one's conceptual and methodological toolbox. While great debate may exist about what worldviews to include in the toolbox, the case studies in this collection all demonstrate the intellectual craftsmanship that characterizes what has been termed the new rural sociology—a logical outgrowth of the larger discipline's introspective sociology of sociology—something that has been ongoing for about thirty years (see *What Is Right/Wrong with Rural Sociology* 1996).

Political Implications

What are the future prospects for the embedded rural communities of work described and analyzed in this volume? Prognostications about the future are both easy and difficult: easy because they are almost always based on projecting past trends and difficult because unanticipated consequences cannot by definition be fully anticipated. Some possible scenarios:

Basically, past trends will continue with little change: preexisting economic and institution infrastructures will constrain future development. Restructuring of rural communities will continue leading to decline for communities dependent on natural-resource extraction and traditional rural manufacturing. A few communities will grow into communities of consumption because of their natural amenities. Some rural industries (e.g., meat processing) will provide jobs for a multicultural immigrant workforce. Devolution will further decrease the capacity of state and local units of government to respond to human and community needs. Households will use a combination of formal and informal work to survive. Generational issues will increase as children of ethnically based rural enterprises find better opportunities in other locations.

HIGH TECH WILL NOT SAVE EVERYONE

The fields will become factories for the latest biotechnology engineered variety that, like its Green Revolution predecessor, promises to revitalize agriculture and the farm family. Such promises appear in cycles and their major impact is to speed up the treadmill of production in agriculture, leading to increased concentration and consolidation of production and processing. The digital divide will grow or bypass rural areas in favor of low-wage international locations. Concurrently, some rural areas will be integrated into urban economies, either by proximity, as the rural-urban interface expands, or by the vagaries of global markets. Others will use their natural amenities to develop new labor market opportunities for their residents.

THE NEW MAGIC BULLET

Social capital will replace human capital as the penicillin for rural social problems. Social scientists will spend a large amount of time and resources identifying and measuring social capital. Radicals will highlight the class, race, and gender inequalities in the distribution of social capital and demand that new forms of taxation be implemented to redistribute social capital. Households and community organizations will utilize local networks to try to maintain viable communities of work in rural locations. While such efforts will result in some success, the human and organizational costs for these efforts make them difficult to reproduce outside their local networks.

The outcomes of these scenarios are contingent on political decisions and public policies that will occur, in all likelihood, without adequate thought about the consequences for rural places and without input from members of these communities. Rural America, with minor exceptions, is the stepchild of public policy. Policies are devised usually for urban populations and national objectives, forgetting the families and communities that subsist in the periphery. The political realities of rural communities reflect this neglect and lack of understanding of the empirical realities of rural life. Our chapters help to document the relationships of rural areas to larger regional, national, and global arenas; and at the same time, embed the problems of poverty and inequities in power and resources into this context. The fortunes of rural jobs and industries—and by extension workers, families, and communities—wax and wane in relationships that are largely beyond local control. Without policy directly addressed to these problems, things are unlikely to change for most rural areas or, alternatively, change will occur as it has in the past—as the outcome of larger structural forces in which rural areas are more often reactors rather than initiators.

If this pattern is to change, social policy needs to revolve around the persistent problems of rural life: lack of jobs, lack of transportation, lack of infrastructure, lack of investment, lack of political representation, lack of human and social capital, problems that cannot necessarily be tackled by local resources alone. This is not to denigrate the strengths and value of local initiatives. Rural areas in all their diversity contain an enormous variety of assets, whether in their people, environment, amenities, organizations, or social relationships. It is important for communities to learn to identify and build on local resources. At the same time, poor, isolated communities cannot prosper without assistance. While it is dangerous to overgeneralize about places as diverse as rural communities, it is safe to say that most rural communities and regions lack the economies of scale, the density of population, the quality of public institutions, and the access to capital and markets to make their voices heard and needs known. These long-standing problems are exacerbated in a political climate that promotes state devolution and local control on the one hand and glorifies market based solutions on the other. The outcome further isolates local jurisdictions unequipped with all forms of capital—financial, human, and social—from state-based relief at the same time that they are not competitive in the marketplace. Part of the purpose of this book is to make these needs known and voices heard.

The contributions to this volume promote knowledge and understanding of the particular circumstances and problems of rural communities of work, illustrating the individual and collective price paid for neglect. The case studies also provide examples of individual resistance and collective action that may be suggestive for directions for future political action. In a popular TV science fiction program, a cyborg culture says, "Resistance is futile." The contributions to this volume show that while resistance to structural changes may be frustrating, unsuccessful, or create unanticipated consequences, it is anything but futile.

References

Collins, P. H. 1990. *Black Feminist Thought: Knowledge, Consciousness, and the Politics of Empowerment.* Boston: Unwin Hyman.

Edwards, B., and M. W. Foley. 2001. "Much Ado about Social Capital." *Contemporary Sociology* 30 (May): 227–30.

Etzioni, A. 2001. "Is Bowling Together Sociologically Lite?" *Contemporary Sociology* 30 (May): 223–24.

Gieryn, Thomas F. 2000. "A Space for Place in Sociology." *Annual Review of Sociology* 26:463–96.

Putnam, R. 2000. *Bowling Alone: The Collapse and Revival of American Community.* New York: Simon and Schuster.

Schulman, M. D., and C. Anderson. 1999. "The Dark Side of the Force: A Case Study of Restructuring and Social Capital." *Rural Sociology* 64:351–72.

Tickamyer, A. R. 2000. "Space Matters! Spatial Inequality in Future Sociology." *Contemporary Sociology* 29:805–13.

Tilly, C. 1999. "Durable Inequality." In *A Nation Divided: Diversity, Inequality, and Community in American Society,* ed. P. Moen, D. Dempster-McClain, and H. Walker, 15–33. New York: Cornell University Press.

What Is Right/Wrong with Rural Sociology? 1996. *Rural Sociology* 61 (special issue).

Wilson, J. 2001. "Dr. Putnam's Social Lubricant." *Contemporary Sociology* 30 (May): 225–27.

Young, F. 2001. "Putnam's Challenge to Community Sociology." Review. *Rural Sociology* 66:469–74.

Contributors

Cynthia D. Anderson is Associate Professor of Sociology at Iowa State University. Her research areas include work, community, and gender/race/class. Currently, Anderson is examining the impact of gender and race concentration on measures of inequality across labor market areas.

Alan Barton is Assistant Professor of Sociology and Community Development at Delta State University in Mississippi. His teaching and research interests include community-based approaches to natural resource management, formal and informal property systems, participatory education, and research methods.

Janet Bokemeier is the Associate Director of the Michigan Agricultural Experiment Station and a Professor of Sociology at Michigan State University. Her research and scholarly work examines rural women's and families' economic and household strategies in changing labor markets.

Lawrence A. Brown is Professor and Chair of Geography at Ohio State University, former president of the Association of American Geographers, and a former Guggenheim Fellow. His studies have focused on Third World development, Latin America, innovation diffusion, regional development processes, and local change as a result of larger-scale forces.

Ralph B. Brown received his Ph.D. in Rural Sociology from the University of Missouri-Columbia. His research focuses on natural resources use and rural community satisfaction and attachment and social impacts in rural communities due to larger economic shifts and large-scale economic developments.

Viviana Carro-Figueroa is a research rural sociologist at the Department of Agricultural Economics and Rural Sociology, University of Puerto Rico Agricultural Experiment Station. Her current research focuses on how global and local forces influence the food system of specific localities, and on the emergence of sustainable community agricultural development alternatives in Puerto Rico.

Jeff Crump is currently an Associate Professor in the Housing Studies Program in the Department of Design, Housing, and Apparel at the University of Minnesota. Dr. Crump's research interests include public housing and urban policy, immigration and housing, and labor geography. He currently serves as co-chair of the Economic Geography Specialty Group of the Association of American Geographers and on the editorial board for *Rural Sociology*.

Forrest A. Deseran is an Adjunct Professor of Sociology at Sonoma State University. Until 2002, he was a Professor of Sociology and Director of the Louisiana Population Data Center at Louisiana State University.

Mark R. Drabenstott is Vice President and Director of the Center for the Study of Rural America at the Federal Reserve Bank of Kansas City. On more than ten occasions, he has testified before Congress on rural and agricultural policy issues, while also advising the World Bank and other international organizations. He has been an ardent observer of the leading issues facing the food and agriculture sector and the rural economy, publishing more than a hundred articles and editing four books. He is chair of the National Policy Association's Food and Agriculture Committee and a director of the National Bureau of Economic Research at Harvard University.

William W. Falk is Professor and Chair of the Department of Sociology at the University of Maryland. Among his books are two with

Thomas A. Lyson, *High Tech, Low Tech, No Tech: Industrial and Occupational Change in the South* (State University of New York Press, 1988) and *Forgotten Places: Uneven Development in Rural America* (University Press of Kansas, 1993), and his own new book, *In the Lion's Mouth: A Story about Race and Place in the American South* (Rutgers University Press, forthcoming).

Nina Glasgow is a Senior Research Associate in the Department of Development Sociology and faculty affiliate of the Bronfenbrenner Life Course Center and the Population and Development Program at Cornell University. Her research focuses on the sociology of aging and the life course, especially in rural environments.

W. Richard Goe is Associate Professor of Sociology at Kansas State University, Manhattan, Kansas. His research interests include regional economic development and the sociology of work and labor markets.

Debra A. Henderson is an Assistant Professor of Sociology at Ohio University. Her research focuses primarily on the impacts of structured inequality on culturally diverse families in rural communities.

Mark S. Henry is Professor and Co-coordinator, Regional Economic Development Research Laboratory, Department of Agricultural and Applied Economics, Clemson University. He has been a visiting scholar at the Federal Reserve Bank of Kansas City and the Economic Research Service, USDA. His work in rural development is published in the *Journal of Regional Science, Land Economics, Regional Science and Urban Economics,* the *American Journal of Agricultural Economics,* and the *Papers in Regional Science.*

Linda M. Lobao is Professor of Rural Sociology, Department of Human and Community Resource Development, and Professor, Department of Sociology and Department of Geography at the Ohio State University. Her research centers on spatial aspects of inequality, political-economic change, and gender. Lobao is president of the Rural Sociological Society for 2002–2003.

Melissa Latimer is an Associate Professor of Sociology at West Virginia University. Her research focuses on the major ways in which sex, race, and class inequality are constructed and reconstructed through labor market processes and welfare policies. More recently, her research has concentrated on the short-term and long-term impacts of welfare reform on individuals in an economically disadvantaged rural state.

MaryBe McMillan is currently Regional Coordinator for the Union Community Fund of North Carolina. She is active in social and economic justice issues.

Carson Mencken is an Associate Professor of Sociology in the Department of Sociology and Anthropology at Baylor University. His research interests include rural sociology and regional economic development.

Kristin Mitchell is a former Research Associate with the Center for the Study of Rural America and the Economic Research Department at the Federal Reserve Bank of Kansas City.

Jon Moore is a doctoral student at the Ohio State University, Department of Geography. His soon to be completed dissertation is titled "Local Economic Development in the Post-industrial Service Economy: Manufacturing Communities in the Ohio River Valley."

Sean Noonan is Assistant Professor of Sociology at Harper College in Chicago, Illinois. His research interests include political economy and social stratification.

Carl Riden recently defended her dissertation in Sociology at Louisiana State University and is currently a Lecturer in the Department of Anthropology, Sociology, and Criminal Justice Studies at Longwood University.

Michael D. Schulman is Alumni Distinguished Graduate Professor and Professor of Sociology at North Carolina State University and Adjunct Professor of Health Behavior and Health Education at the

University of North Carolina–School of Public Health. In addition to research on restructuring and the impact of immigration on rural communities, his current work includes studies of occupation injuries among young workers in collaboration with the University of North Carolina Injury Prevention Research Center.

Cynthia Struthers is an Assistant Professor with the Illinois Institute for Rural Affairs at Western Illinois University. Current research examines the housing conditions of the rural elderly and acceptable housing options. She regularly teaches community and rural social organizations courses for the Department of Sociology and Anthropology and is developing a course on women and poverty for the Women's Studies Department.

Barry Tadlock is Assistant Professor in Ohio University's Department of Political Science. He teaches courses in American national government, legislative processes, and the presidency. One research interest focuses on the impact of welfare reform in Ohio, especially the role played by county commissioners. His other research interest is in the area of identity politics. Along with Ellen Riggle, he co-edited *Gays and Lesbians in the Democratic Process: Public Policy, Public Opinion, and Political Representation* (Columbia University Press, 1999).

Sherry Thurston is ABD in Sociology at Kansas State University and is employed as a Systems Analyst for MCI WorldCom, Tulsa, Oklahoma.

Ann R. Tickamyer is Professor of Sociology, Director of International Development Studies, and Presidential Research Scholar at Ohio University. She is a past president of the Rural Sociological Society and past editor of *Rural Sociology*.

Leann Tigges is Professor of Rural Sociology at the University of Wisconsin. Her research focuses on the social-economic dimensions of local labor markets and economic dimensions of local labor markets and economic restructuring, particularly as they affect women and minorities.

Gwyndolyn J. Weathers is a Ph.D. candidate in Sociology at the University of Maryland with concentrations in comparative sociology and gender. Her dissertation research explores relations between actors in civil society, national governments, and multilateral development banks working to strengthen women's rights in Argentina and Chile.

Susan E. Webb is an Associate Professor of Sociology at Coastal Carolina University. Her research focuses on rural poverty and service employment in tourism.

Julie White is Associate Professor of Political Science at Ohio University. Her work has focused on the ethic of care and the politics of the welfare state.

Philip Wood was educated in Canada and the UK and teaches Comparative and American political economy at Queen's University, Kingston, Ontario. In addition to his work on the southern textile industry, he is also involved in projects on the re-ordering of American politics since the 1970s, the politics of political science research methods, the expansion and radicalization of the prison-industrial complex, and economic development and racial politics in the American South before the Voting Rights Act.

Teresa A. Wood at the time of this research was Director of the University of Kentucky Survey Research Center. She currently serves as the state chronic disease epidemiologist for Kentucky. Dr. Wood's work now focuses on health issues facing rural populations, evaluation of chronic disease intervention programs and grant writing to support population based chronic disease programs.

Ann Ziebarth is an Associate Professor of Housing Studies at the University of Minnesota in the College of Human Ecology's Department of Design, Housing, and Apparel. Her research focuses on economic change and housing issues in rural areas and small towns.

Index